AF669357

FREE
Online Support
See Inside Cover

Concept Map

TOOLKIT

MOST POWERFUL RESOURCE FOR MASTERING CONCEPTS

Physics

A Visual Approach for
Enhanced Learning

Author
Sumit Shukla
B.Tech

arihant
SUCCESS AND NOTHING LESS

arihant
SUCCESS AND NOTHING LESS

ARIHANT PRAKASHAN (Series), MEERUT

Administrative & Production Offices

Regd. Office
'Ramchhaya' 4577/15, Agarwal Road, Darya Ganj, New Delhi -110002
Tele: 011- 47630600, 43518550

Head Office
Kalindi, TP Nagar, Meerut (UP) - 250002
Tel: 0121-7156203, 7156204

Sales & Support Offices
Agra, Ahmedabad, Bengaluru, Bareilly, Chennai, Delhi, Guwahati, Hyderabad, Jaipur, Jhansi, Kolkata, Lucknow, Nagpur & Pune.

PRICE ₹295.00

PO No. : TXT-59-T069368-2-26

Published by Arihant Publications (India) Ltd.

For further information about the books published by Arihant, log on to www.arihantbooks.com or e-mail at info@arihantbooks.com

Follow us on

PRODUCTION TEAM

Project Head
Yojna Sharma

Coordinator
Amit Singh

Inner Designer
Ankit Tyagi

Cover Designer
Rakesh Rawat

Proof Readers
Mansi, Ishan Khan

Map Disigner
Mohit Lakhwan

Contents

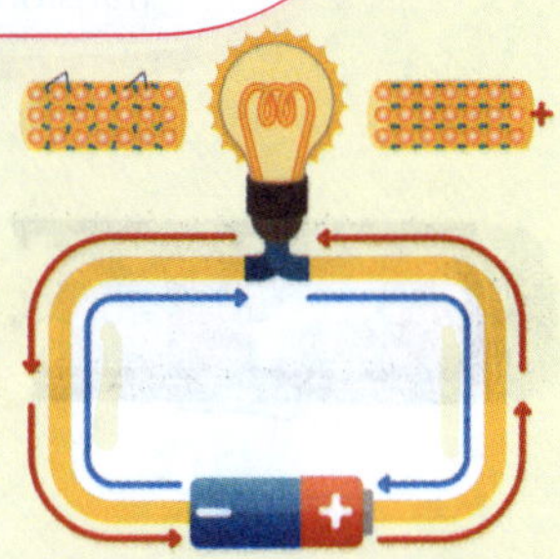

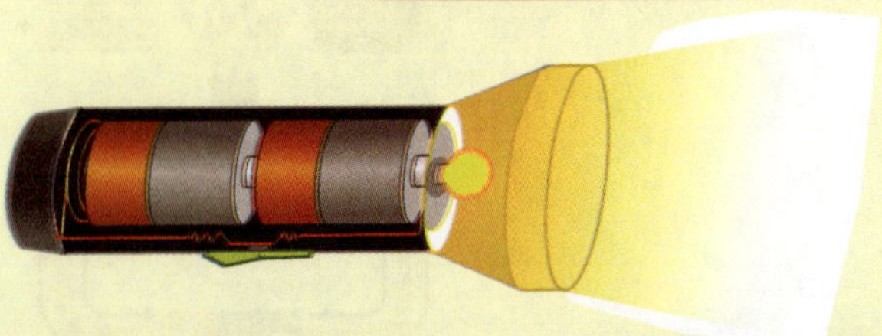

Chapter 01

Units and Measurements

Physical Quantities

Measured directly or indirectly in terms of which, the laws of Physics can be expressed.

Derived Quantities

Based on other physical quantities for defining operations.

Fundamental Quantities

Independent of other physical quantities. There are 7 fundamental quantities.

Fundamental Units

Base Quantity	Name	Symbol
Length	metre	m
Mass	kilogram	kg
Time	second	s
Electric current	ampere	A
Thermodynamic temperature	kelvin	K
Amount of substance	mole	mol
Luminous intensity	candela	cd

Units

A quantity with a constant magnitude, used to measure other quantities of the same type.
Physical quantity $= x$ unit, x = Numerical value

Fundamental Units
The units selected for measurement of the fundamental quantities.

Derived Units
The units derived from the fundamental units.

Supplementary Units
- Units of plane angle and solid angle
- These are dimensionless

Supplementary Units

Quantity	Unit	Symbol
Plane angle	radian	rad
Solid angle	steradian	sr

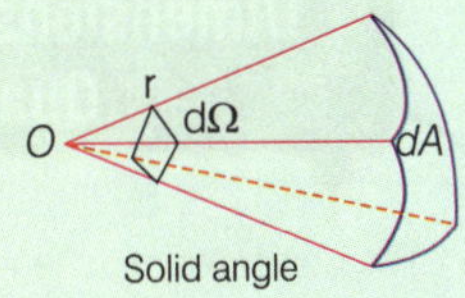

Solid angle

$d\theta = \frac{ds}{r} \rightarrow$ rad

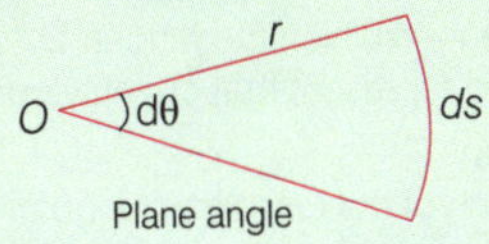

Plane angle

$d\Omega = \frac{dA}{r^2} \longrightarrow$ steradian

System of Units

Used to measure all kinds of fundamental and derived quantities.

CGS System
The units of length, mass and time are centimetre (cm), gram (g) and second (s), respectively.

MKS System
The units of length, mass and time are metre (m), kilogram (kg) and second (s), respectively.

FPS System
The units of length, mass and time are foot (ft), pound (lb) and second (s), respectively.

International System of Units (SI)
SI unit is accepted internationally for measurement and uses decimal system, hence conversations within the system are quite simple and convenient.
In SI system, 7 base units and 2 supplementary units.

	MKS	CGS	FPS
(i)	Length (m)	Length (cm)	Length (ft)
(ii)	Mass (kg)	Mass (g)	Mass (lb)
(iii)	Time (s)	Time (s)	Time (s)

Conventions for Writing SI Units in Symbols

- Small letters are used for symbols of units.
- Symbols are not followed by a full stop.
- The initial letter of a symbol is capital, only if the unit is named after a scientist.
- The full name of a unit is never written with initial capital letter, even if it has been named after a scientist.
- Symbols are never written in plural form.

Common SI Prefixes and Symbols for Multiples and Sub-Multiples

Multiple			Sub-multiple		
Factor	Prefix	Symbol	Factor	Prefix	Symbol
10^{18}	Exa	E	10^{-18}	atto	a
10^{15}	Peta	P	10^{-15}	femto	f
10^{12}	Tera	T	10^{-12}	pico	p
10^{9}	Giga	G	10^{-9}	nano	n
10^{6}	Mega	M	10^{-6}	micro	μ
10^{3}	Kilo	k	10^{-3}	milli	m
10^{2}	Hecto	h	10^{-2}	centi	c
10^{1}	Deca	da	10^{-1}	deci	d

Dimensions of Physical Quantity

The power (or exponent) to which the fundamental quantities are raised to represent that quantity completely.

Dimensional Formula

It shows how and which of the fundamental quantities represent the dimension of physical quantity.

e.g. Acceleration = $[M^0L^1T^{-2}]$

Mass density = $[ML^{-3}T^0]$

Dimensional Equation

Equation obtained by equating a physical quantity with its dimensional formula.

Key Points of Dimensions

- Trigonometric functions sinθ, cosθ, tanθ etc, and their arithmetic operations are dimensionless.
- Dimensions of differential coefficients $\left[\frac{d^ny}{dx^n}\right]=\left[\frac{y}{x^n}\right]$
- Dimensions of integrals $[\int y dx]=[yx]$
- We can't add or subtract two physical quantities of different dimensions.
- Independent quantities may be taken as fundamental quantities in a new system of units.

Limitations of Dimensional Analysis

- Does not give any information about the dimensionless constant *K*.
- It fails, when a physical quantity depends on more than three physical quantities.
- It fails, when a physical quantity is the sum or difference of two or more quantities.
- It fails to derive relationship which involve trigonometric, logarithmic or exponential functions.
- Sometimes, it is difficult to identify the factors on which the physical quantity depends.

USES OF DIMENSIONAL ANALYSIS

- Conversion of units from one system to another
- To check dimensional correctness of a given physical relation
- To derive a relationship between different physical quantities

Say $Q = f(x, y, z)$

Let $Q \propto x^a$, $Q \propto y^b$, $Q \propto z^c$

Thus, $Q \propto x^a y^b z^c$

Homogeneity Principle

A physical equation will be dimensionally correct, if the dimension of all terms occuring on both sides of the equation are same.

Units and Measurements

Significant Figures

Those digits in a measured quantity which are known reliably plus one additional uncertain digits.

Examples

- 0.108 → 3 significant figures
- 40.000 → 5 significant figures
- 1.23×10^{-19} → 3 significant figures
- 0.0018 → 2 significant figures

Logarithmic Operations

In logarithmic operations, the number of significant figures in the mantissa of the result should equal to the number of significant figures in the original number.

Rules for Counting Significant Figures

For a number greater than 1

- All non-zero digits are significant.
- All zeros between two non-zero digits are significant. Location of decimal does not matter.
- If the number is without decimal part, then the terminal or trailing zeros are not significant.
- Trailing zeros in the decimal part are significant.

For a number less than 1

Any zero to the right of a non-zero digit is significant. All zeros between decimal point and first non-zero digit are not significant.

Rules of Arithmetic Operations with Significant Figures

Addition and Subtraction

The result should have the same number of decimal places as the term with the smallest decimal places.

Multiplication and division

The result should have the same number of significant figures as term with the smallest significant figures.

Exact Numbers

Have infinite significant figures and do not affect the precision of the result.

Rounding Off the Uncertain Digits

Rule-1
If the digit to be dropped is less than 5, then the preceding digit is left unchanged.
e.g., 5.24=5.2

Rule-2
If the digit to be dropped is more than 5, then the preceding digit is raised by one.
e.g., 7.356 = 7.36

Rule-3
If the digit to be dropped is 5 followed by non-zero digits, then the preceding digit is raised by one.
e.g.,12.252 = 12.3

Rule-4
If the digit to be dropped is 5 or 5 followed by zero, then preceding digit is left unchanged, if it is even.
e.g., 5.25 = 5.2

Rule-5
If the digit to be dropped is 5 or 5 followed by zero, then the preceding digit is raised by one, if it is odd.
e.g., 7.35 = 7.4

Errors

Difference between the measured value and the true value.

Least Count Error

- This error is due to the limitation imposed by the least count of the measuring instrument.
- It is a uncertainty associated with the resolution of the measuring instrument.

Random Error

Occurs irregularly and at random, in magnitude and direction.

Formula for elimination of random error, $\bar{a} = \dfrac{a_1 + a_2 + a_3 + \dots + a_n}{n} = \dfrac{1}{n}\sum_{i=1}^{n} a_i$

Absolute Error

The magnitude of the difference between the true value and the measured value.

$|\Delta a|$ = Actual value – Measured value

Percentage Error

- Relative error expressed in percent.
- Percentage error $= \dfrac{\Delta\bar{a}}{\bar{a}}\times100$

Mean Absolute Error

Arithmetic mean of the positive magnitudes of all the absolute errors.

$$\Delta\bar{a} = \frac{|\Delta a_1| + |\Delta a_2| + \dots + |\Delta a_n|}{n} = \frac{1}{n}\sum_{i=1}^{n}|\Delta a_i|$$

Relative Error

- Ratio of the mean absolute error to the true value. $\delta a = \dfrac{\Delta\bar{a}}{\bar{a}}$

Accuracy and Precision

Accuracy

The closeness of a measurement to the true value of the physical quantity.

Precision

The resolution or limit to which the quantity is measured.

Propagation of Combination of Errors

It is summarised in the table given below

Operation	Formula Z	Absolute error ΔZ	Relative error $\Delta Z/Z$	Percentage error $100\times\Delta Z/Z$
Sum	$A+B$	$\Delta A+\Delta B$	$\dfrac{\Delta A+\Delta B}{A+B}$	$\dfrac{\Delta A+\Delta B}{A+B}\times100$
Difference	$A-B$	$\Delta A+\Delta B$	$\dfrac{\Delta A+\Delta B}{A-B}$	$\dfrac{\Delta A+\Delta B}{A-B}\times100$
Multiplication	$A\times B$	$A\Delta B+B\Delta A$	$\dfrac{\Delta A}{A}+\dfrac{\Delta B}{B}$	$\left(\dfrac{\Delta A}{A}+\dfrac{\Delta B}{B}\right)\times100$
Division	$\dfrac{A}{B}$	$\dfrac{B\Delta A+A\Delta B}{B^2}$	$\dfrac{\Delta A}{A}+\dfrac{\Delta B}{B}$	$\left(\dfrac{\Delta A}{A}+\dfrac{\Delta B}{B}\right)\times100$
Power	A^n	$nA^{n-1}\Delta A$	$n\dfrac{\Delta A}{A}$	$n\dfrac{\Delta A}{A}\times100$
Root	$A^{1/n}$	$\dfrac{1}{n}A^{1/n-1}\Delta A$	$\dfrac{1}{n}\dfrac{\Delta A}{A}$	$\dfrac{1}{n}\dfrac{\Delta A}{A}\times100$

General Rule for Finding Error

If $Z = \dfrac{A^pB^q}{C^r}$, then maximum fractional or relative error in Z will be

$$\frac{\Delta Z}{Z} = p\frac{\Delta A}{A} + q\frac{\Delta B}{B} + r\frac{\Delta C}{C}$$

$$\%\text{Error in } Z = \frac{\Delta Z}{Z}\times100 = p\frac{\Delta A}{A}\times100 + q\frac{\Delta B}{B}\times100 + r\frac{\Delta C}{C}\times100$$

Chapter **02**

Motion in a Straight Line

Frame of Reference

Coordinate system, which is used to define the position, orientation and motion of objects.

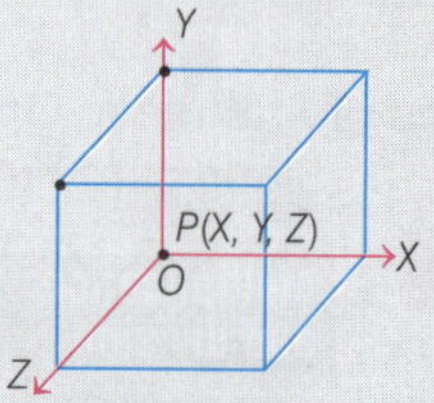

Types of Frame of Reference

Inertial frame of reference
This frame either remains at rest or moving with constant velocity.

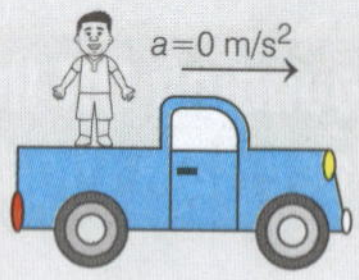

Inertial Frame

Non-inertial frame of reference
An accelerating frame of reference.

Non-inertial Frame

Rest position

Object does not change its position with respect to surrounding over time.

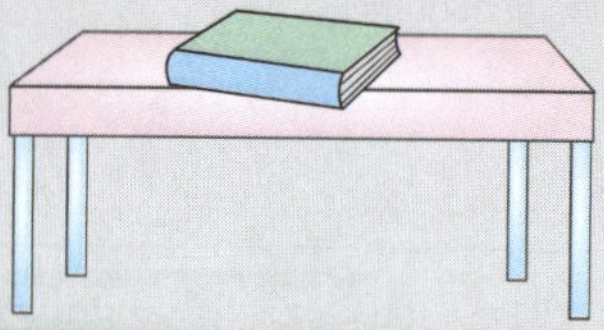

Motion

Object changes its position with respect to its surrounding over time.

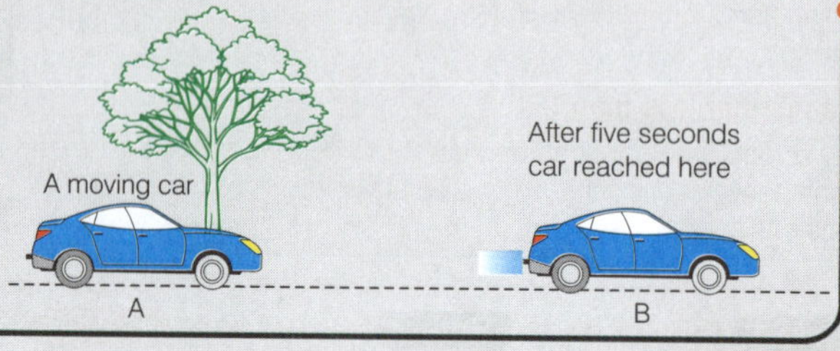

Types of Motion

Translational Motion

All the points of a body moving uniformly in a single direction.

(a) Rectilinear Motion
Motion along a straight line.

(b) Curvilinear Motion
Motion along a curved path.

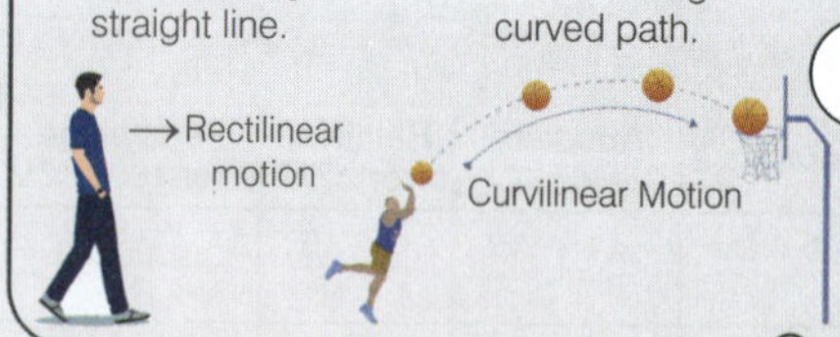

Rotational Motion

When an object rotates about a fixed axis.

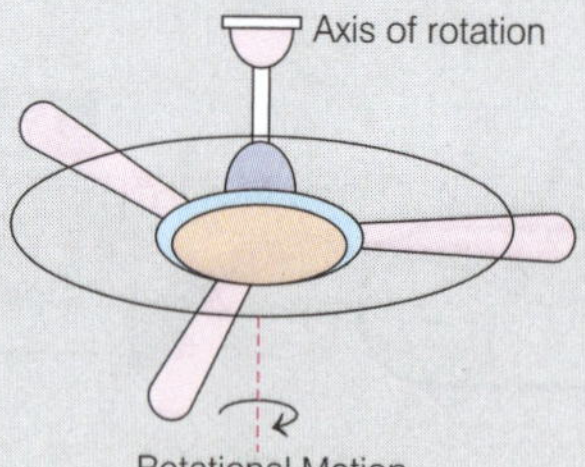

Rotational Motion

Oscillatory Motion

Back and forth motion of an object about a mean position.

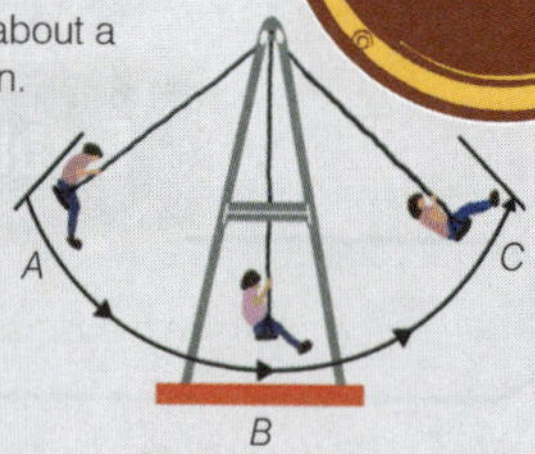

Oscillatory Motion

Terms Related to Motion

01 Position

Position is the location of an object at a given time.

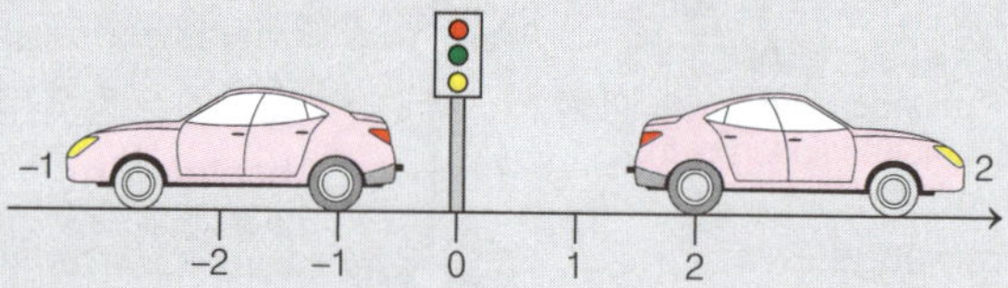

02 Distance

Total length of path travelled by an object irrespective of its direction.
– Scalar quantity
– SI Unit-metre (m)
– Distance > 0 (always)

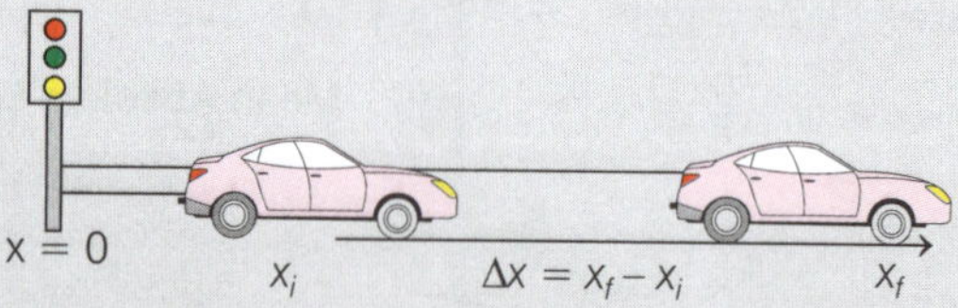

Δx = Distance

03 Displacement

It is the shortest distance between two points.

- Vector quantity.
- Displacement can be greater than zero, less than zero or equal to zero.
- Displacement is always less than or equal to distance.

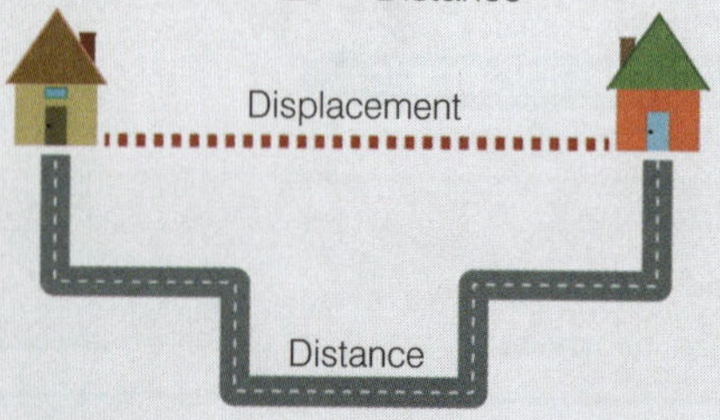

Speed

Speed is simply how fast you are travelling

This car is travelling at a speed of 20 m/s

The rate at which an object's position changes or the distance an object travels per unit of time.

$$\text{Speed} = \frac{\text{Distance}}{\text{Time}}$$

- Scalar quantity
- SI unit—metre per second (m/s)
- Speed > 0 (always)

Average speed

The total distance travelled by the object in a particular time interval.

$$\text{Average speed} = \frac{\text{Total distance travelled}}{\text{Total time taken}}$$

If body covers equal distances with different speeds, then

$$v_{av} = \frac{2v_1v_2}{v_1 + v_2}$$

Instantaneous Speed

The rate of change of distance of an object over a very short time interval.

$$v_{ins} = \lim_{\Delta t \to 0} \frac{\Delta s}{\Delta t} = \frac{ds}{dt}$$

Velocity

Velocity is speed in a given direction

This car is travelling at a velocity of 20 m/s towards east.

The speed at which something moves in a particular direction.

$$\text{Velocity} = \frac{\text{Displacement}}{\text{Time}}$$

- Vector quantity
- SI unit—metre per second (m/s)
- Velocity can be greater than zero, less than zero or equal to zero.

Average Velocity

It is the ratio of the total displacement to the total time interval in which that displacement occurs.

$$\text{Average velocity} = \frac{\text{Total displacement}}{\text{Total time}}$$

Instantaneous Velocity

$$v_{ins} = \lim_{\Delta t \to 0} \frac{\Delta s}{\Delta t} = \frac{ds}{dt}$$

Graph of instantaneous velocity of a particle

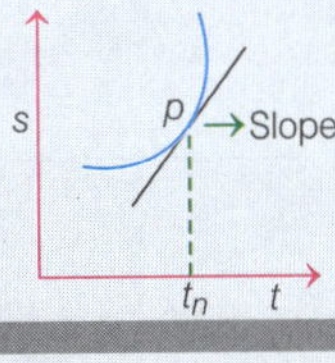

→Slope = Instantaneous velocity of a particle at $t = t_n$

Acceleration

Initial position

Initial velocity = v_i
Initial time = t_i

Final position

Final velocity = v_f
Final time = t_f

$$a = \frac{\Delta v}{\Delta t} = \frac{v_f - v_i}{t_f - t_i}$$

Acceleration is the rate of change of velocity.

$$\text{Acceleration } (a) = \frac{\text{Change in velocity}}{\text{Change in time}}$$

- Vector quantity
- SI unit-metre per second square (m/s^2)

Average Acceleration

$$\text{Average acceleration} = \frac{\text{Total change in velocity}}{\text{Total time taken}} = \frac{\Delta v}{\Delta t}$$

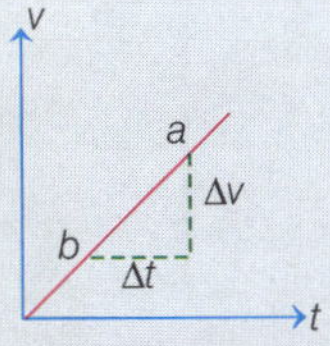

Instantaneous Acceleration

$$a_{ins} = \lim_{\Delta t \to 0} \frac{\Delta v}{\Delta t} = \frac{dv}{dt}$$

Slope = Instantaneous acceleration of particle at time $t = t_n$

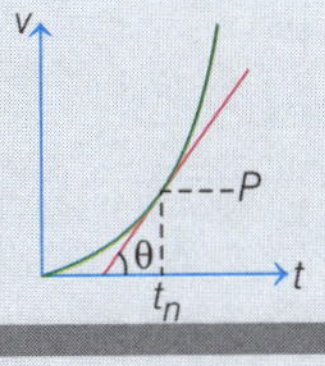

Uniform Motion

Object covers equal distance in equal interval of time. The speed and velocity of the object remains constant. The object's acceleration is zero.

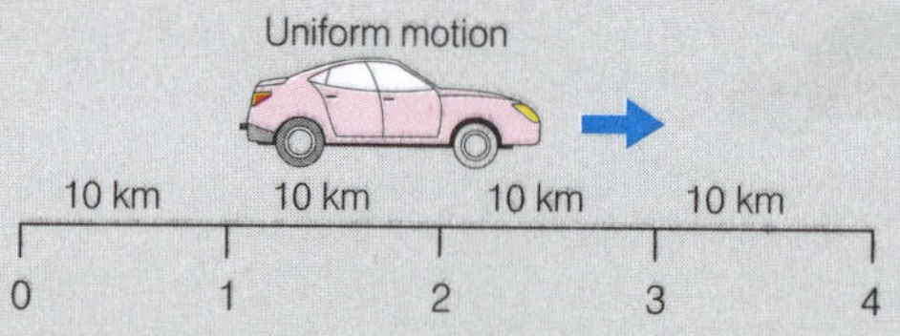

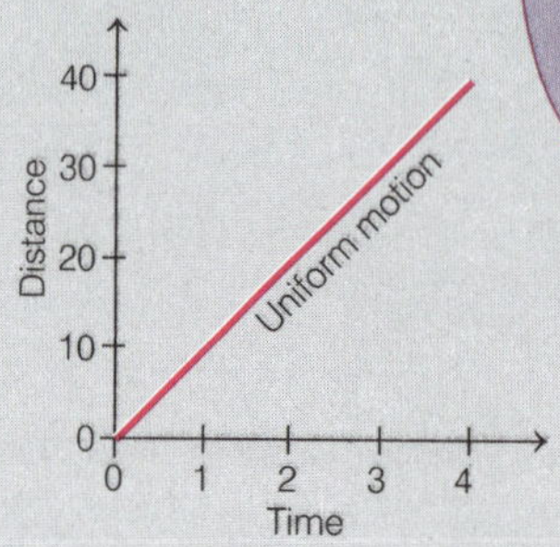

Some Important Features of Uniform Motion

- The velocity in uniform motion does not depend on the choice of origin.
- For uniform motion along a straight line in the same direction, the magnitude of displacement is equal to the actual distance covered by the object.
- The velocity in uniform motion does not depend on the choice of the time interval.

Non-Uniform Motion

Objects speed and direction changes over time, causing it to travel unequal distances in equal time intervals. The object's velocity and acceleration is non-zero

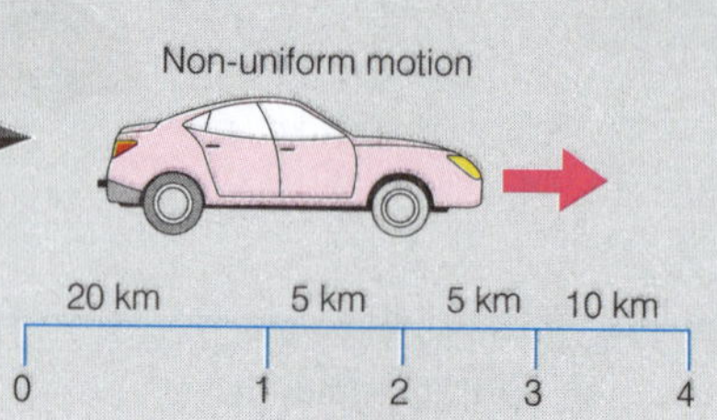

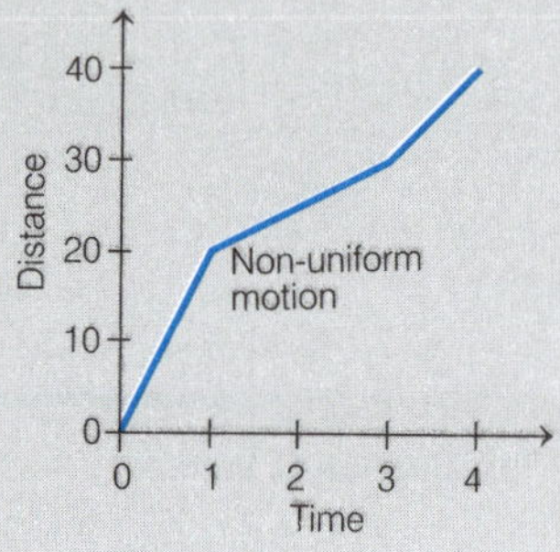

Stopping Distance

The distance covered by moving vehicle before stopping, when brakes are applied to it.

$$s = \frac{u^2}{2a}$$

Kinematic Equations For Uniformly Accelerated Motion

Equations of motion of a particle moving with constant acceleration in a straight line

(I) $v = u + at$

(ii) $s = ut + \frac{1}{2}at^2$

(iii) $v^2 = u^2 + 2as$

(iv) Distance travelled in nth second

$$s_n = u + \frac{a}{2}(2n-1)$$

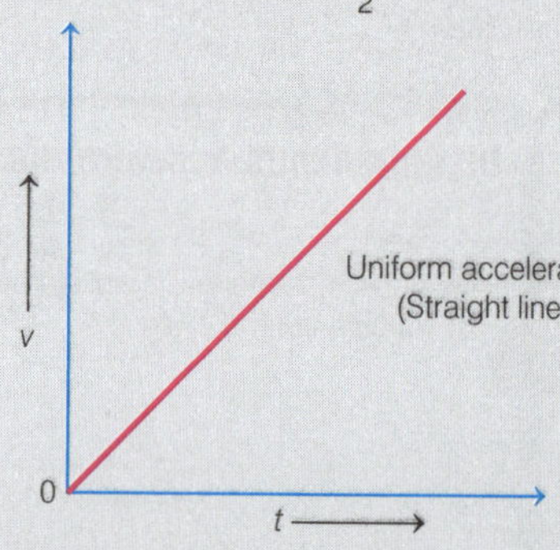

POWER TIPS

- If object starts from rest, then $u = 0$
- If object comes to rest, then $v = 0$
- If velocity increases with time, then acceleration (a) = Positive
- If velocity decreases with time, then a = Negative.
- If both $a, v > 0$ or $a, v < 0$ then particle is speeding up.
- If both a and v have opposite sign, then particle is speeding down.
- Ratio of distance travelled in equal interval of time in uniformly accelerated motion from rest.

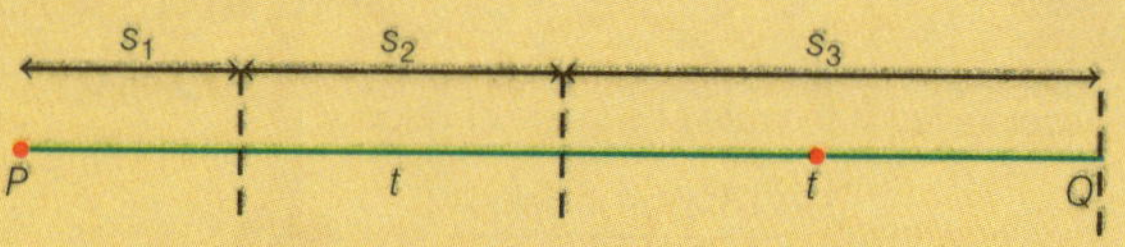

$$s_1 : s_2 : s_3 = 1 : 3 : 5$$

- For uniform accelerated motion

$$\text{Average Velocity} = \frac{\text{Initial velocity} + \text{Final velocity}}{2} = \frac{u+v}{2}$$

Free Fall

01 The object falling towards the earth under the gravitational force alone (air resistance neglected).

02 A falling object have an acceleration due to earth's gravitational pull, is known as acceleration due to gravity.

03 Acceleration due to gravity (g) is independent of the mass of the freely falling object. It is constant and approximately 9.8 m/s^2 near the surface of earth.

Equations of Motion for Object Under Gravity

(i) If particle is projected vertically upwards

$v = u - gt, \; h = ut - \frac{1}{2}gt^2$

$v^2 = u^2 - 2gh$

Total flight time, $T = \frac{2u}{g}$

Time of ascent = Time of descent $= \frac{\text{Total flight time}}{2} = \frac{u}{g}$

Maximum height attained $= \frac{u^2}{2g}$

($g \downarrow$, $u \uparrow$)

(ii) If particle is projected vertically downwards

$v = u + gt$

$h = ut + \frac{1}{2}gt^2$

$v^2 = u^2 + 2gh$

If $u = 0$, then

Velocity of particle on reaching the ground, $v = \sqrt{2gh}$

Time of collision with ground, $t = \sqrt{\frac{2h}{g}}$

($u \downarrow$, $g \downarrow$)

POWER TIPS

- For a freely falling body released from rest, ratio of successive distance covered in equal time interval t.
  $S_1 : S_2 : S_3 = 1 : 3 : 5$
- For a freely falling body released from rest, ratio of total distance covered at the end of time t, $2t$, $3t$ will be in the ratio of $1^2 : 2^2 : 3^2$.

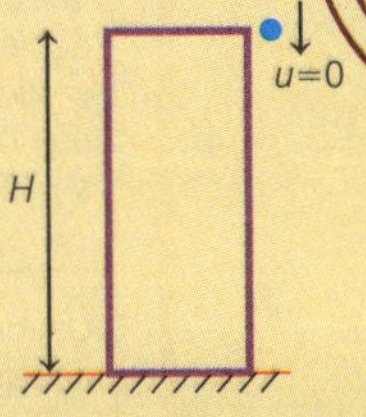

- If a body is thrown vertically up with a velocity u in the uniform gravitational field, then at any point on its path the body will have same speed for upward journey and downward journey.

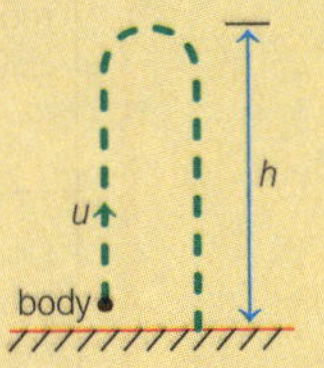

- If a body thrown upwards crosses a point in time t_1 and t_2 respectively, then

Height of point, $h = \frac{1}{2}gt_1t_2$

Maximum height, $H = \frac{1}{8}g(t_1+t_2)^2$

Time of flight, $= t_1+t_2 = \frac{2u}{g}$

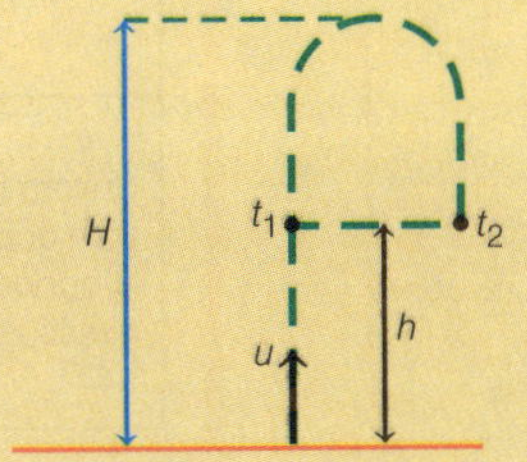

Non-Uniformly Accelerated Motion

Acceleration of a particle is not constant

General equations of motion

(i) $v = \frac{dx}{dt} \Rightarrow dx = vdt \Rightarrow \int dx = \int vdt$

(ii) $a = \frac{dv}{dt} \Rightarrow dv = adt \Rightarrow \int dv = \int adt$

(iii) $a = v\frac{dv}{dx} \Rightarrow vdv = adx \Rightarrow \int vdv = \int adx$

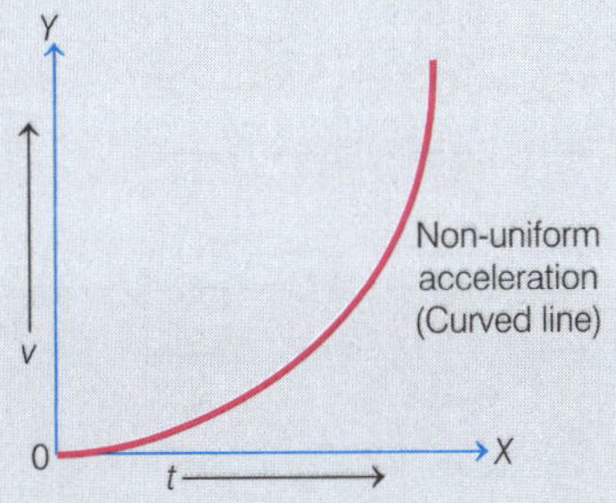

Relative Velocity

Measure of how fast one object is moving with respect to other object.

$$\mathbf{v}_{BA} = \mathbf{v}_B - \mathbf{v}_A$$

v_{BA} = Relative velocity of B with respect to A.

Different Cases of Relative Velocity

Case 1 Objects are moving in the same directions with equal velocity.

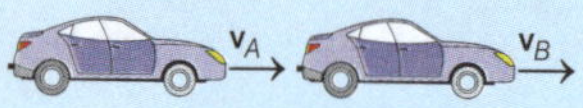

$$\mathbf{v}_A = \mathbf{v}_B$$

$$\mathbf{v}_{BA} = \mathbf{v}_B - \mathbf{v}_A = 0$$

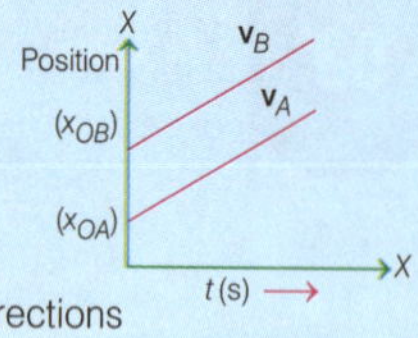

Case 2 Objects are moving in opposite directions

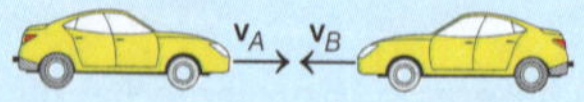

Relative velocity of B w.r.t $A = \mathbf{v}_{BA} = \mathbf{v}_B + \mathbf{v}_A$

Relative velocity of A w.r.t. $B = \mathbf{v}_{AB} = \mathbf{v}_A + \mathbf{v}_B$

Case 3 When objects are moving in same direction and $\mathbf{v}_B > \mathbf{v}_A$ or relative velocity $(\mathbf{v}_B - \mathbf{v}_A)$ is positive.

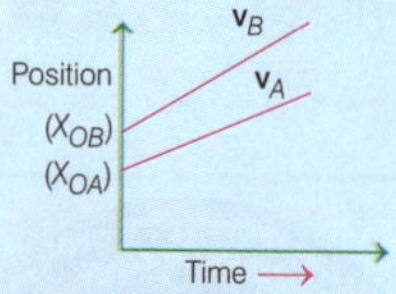

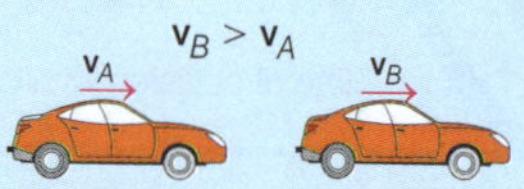

Case 4 When objects are moving in same direction and $\mathbf{v}_A > \mathbf{v}_B$ or relative velocity $(\mathbf{v}_B - \mathbf{v}_A)$ is negative.

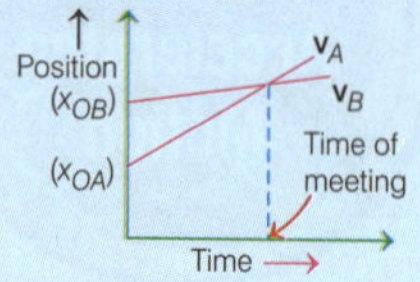

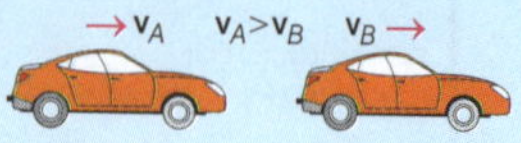

Time to Overtake or Chase a Vehicle

1. 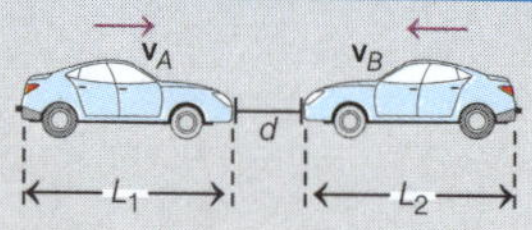

$$t = \frac{d + L_1 + L_2}{v_A + v_B}$$

2. 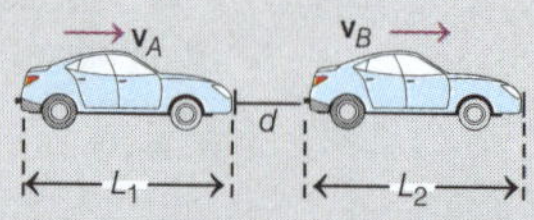

$$t = \frac{d + L_1 + L_2}{v_A - v_B}$$

3. 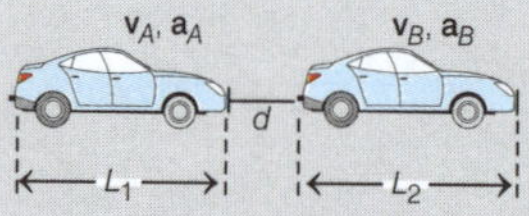

$$d + L_1 + L_2 = (v_A - v_B) + \frac{1}{2}(\mathbf{a}_A - \mathbf{a}_B)t^2$$

Position-Time Graph

Gives instantaneous value of position at any instant.

The slope of tangent drawn to the graph at any instant of time gives the instantaneous velocity at that instant.

Instantaneous velocity, $v = \dfrac{dx}{dt}$

$\dfrac{dx}{dt}$ = Slope of position - time curve

$\Delta x = \int v dt$

$\tan\theta = \dfrac{dx}{dt} = v$

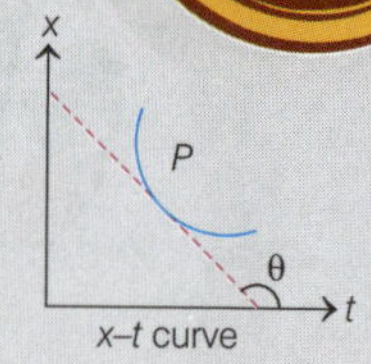

Different Cases of Position-Time Graph

Different Cases	Equation	s–t graph
At rest	$v = 0$	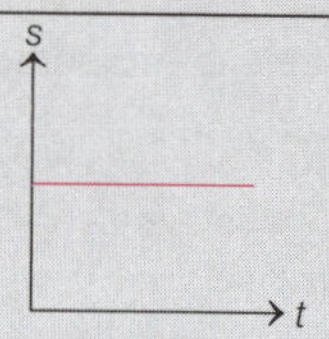
Uniform motion	$s = vt$ v = Constant	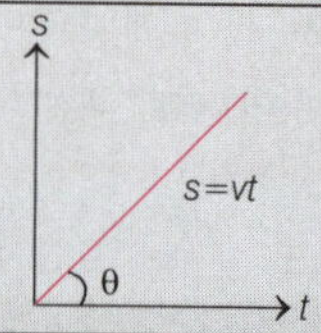
Uniformly accelerated motion with $u = 0$ $s = 0$ at $t = 0$	$s = \frac{1}{2}at^2$	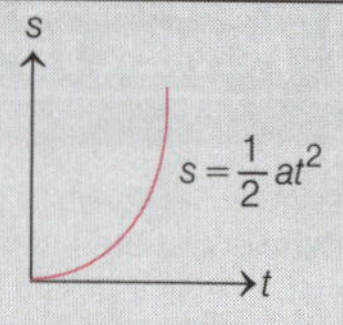
Uniformly accelerated motion with $u \neq 0$ but $s = 0$ at $t=0$	$s = ut + \frac{1}{2}at^2$	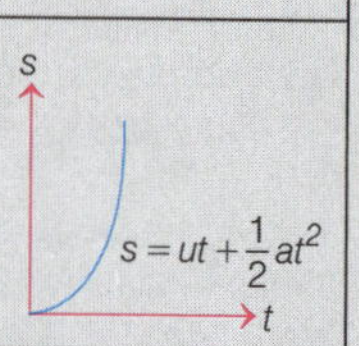
Uniformly retarded motion till velocity becomes zero.	$s = ut - \frac{1}{2}at^2$	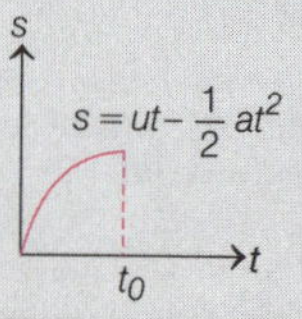
Uniformly retarded then accelerated in opposite direction	$s = ut - \frac{1}{2}at^2$	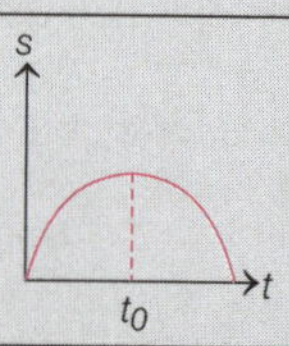

Velocity-Time Graph

- It gives instantaneous value of velocity at any instant.
- Area of *v-t* curve gives displacement $\Delta x = \int v\, dt$
- Slope of velocity - time curve = instantaneous acceleration $= dv/dt$

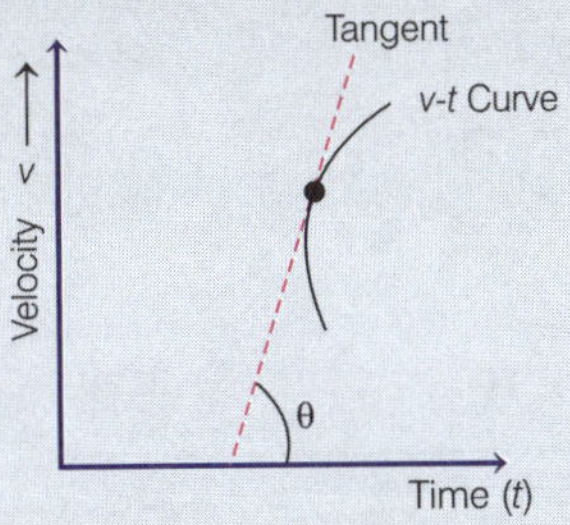

$\tan\theta = \frac{dv}{dt} = a$ = instantaneous acceleration

Different Cases of Velocity–Time Graph

Different Cases	Equation	*v-t* graph
Uniform motion	v = constant	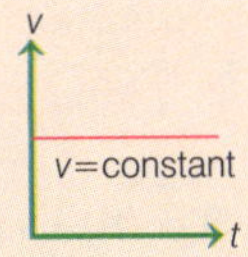
Uniformly accelerated motion with $u=0$ and s= 0 at $t=0$	$v = at$	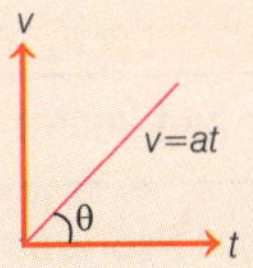
Uniformly accelerated motion with $u \neq 0$ and $s=0$ at $t=0$	$v = u + at$	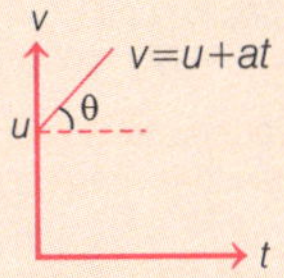
Uniformly retarded motion till velocity becomes zero	$v = u - at$	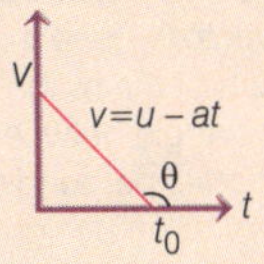
Uniformly retarded then accelerated in opposite direction	$v = u - at$	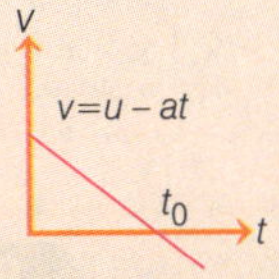

Acceleration-Time Graph

Different Cases	Equation	*a–t* graph
Body moving with constant acceleration	a = constant	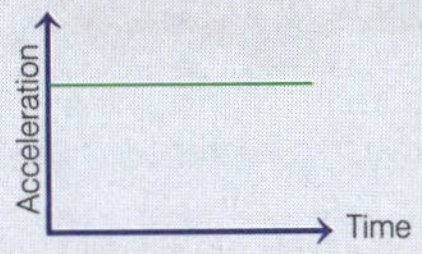
Acceleration of a body increases uniformly with $a=0, u=0, s=0$ at $t=0$	$a = vt$	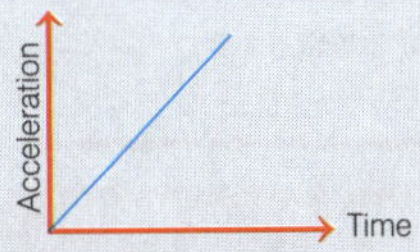
The area of the *a-t* graph between time t_1 to t_2 gives the change in velocity.	$v_2 - v_1 = \int_{t_1}^{t_2} a\,dt$	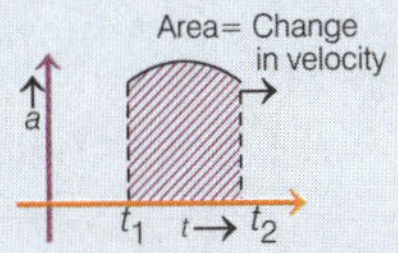
Acceleration of body changes sinusoidally with time.	Change in velocity = Area 1– Area 2 +Area 3	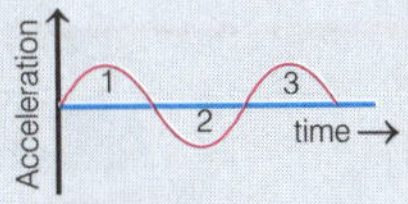

POWER TIPS

A bike accelerates from rest at a constant rate P for some time, after which decelerates at a constant rate Q, to come to rest, if the total time elapsed is t, then

$$v_{max} = \frac{PQ}{P+Q}t$$

$$\text{Total distance} = \frac{1}{2}\left(\frac{PQ}{P+Q}\right)t^2$$

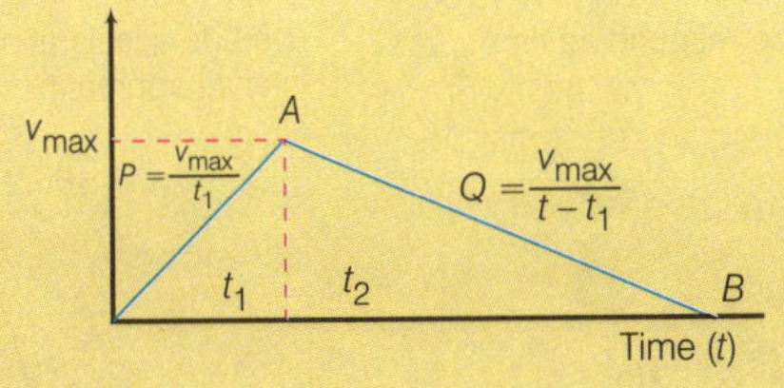

Chapter 03 Motion in a Plane

SCALARS AND VECTORS

Scalar Quantity
The physical quantity which has magnitude only.
e.g. Distance, speed.

Vector Quantity
The physical quantity which have both magnitude and direction. e.g, Weight, displacement.

Position & Displacement Vectors

Position Vector

A vector that denotes the position of a point relative to a reference origin.

$$\mathbf{r} = x\hat{\mathbf{i}} + y\hat{\mathbf{j}} + z\hat{\mathbf{k}}, |\mathbf{r}| = \sqrt{x^2 + y^2 + z^2}$$

$$\text{Unit Vetor, } \hat{\mathbf{r}} = \frac{\mathbf{r}}{|\mathbf{r}|} = \frac{x\hat{\mathbf{i}} + y\hat{\mathbf{j}} + z\hat{\mathbf{k}}}{\sqrt{x^2 + y^2 + z^2}}$$

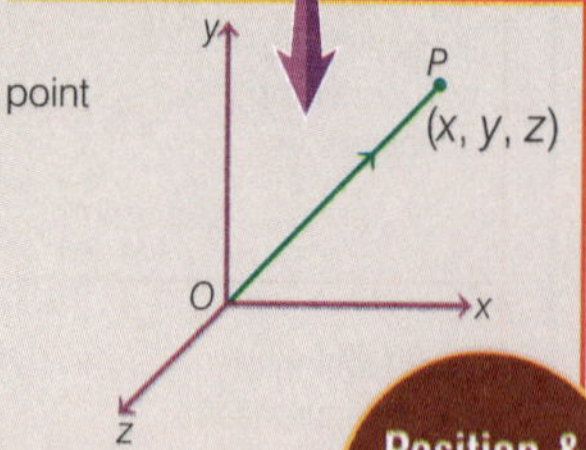

Displacement Vector

A vector representing the change in position of an object.
Displacement vector

$$\Delta\mathbf{r} = (x_2 - x_1)\hat{\mathbf{i}} + (y_2 - y_1)\hat{\mathbf{j}} + (z_2 - z_1)\hat{\mathbf{k}}$$

$$|\Delta\mathbf{r}| = \sqrt{(x_2 - x_1)^2 + (y_2 - y_1)^2 + (z_2 - z_1)^2}$$

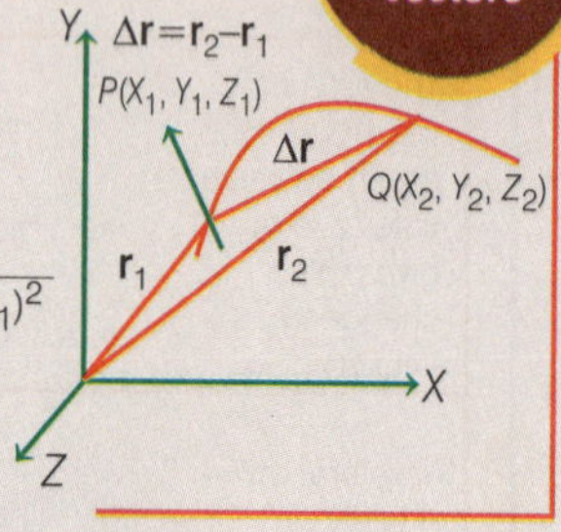

Resolution of Vector

Projections of the vectors present along the axes of a coordinate system.

- **Resolution of vector in two dimensions**

$$\mathbf{R} = R\cos\theta\,\hat{\mathbf{i}} + R\sin\theta\,\hat{\mathbf{j}}$$

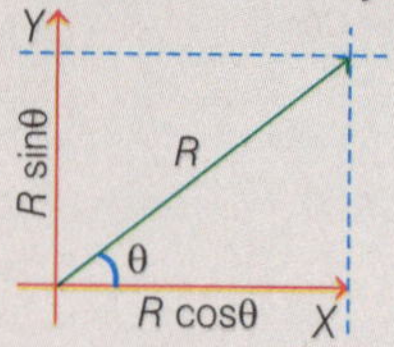

- **Resolution of vector in three dimensions**

$$R = R\cos\alpha\,\hat{\mathbf{i}} + R\cos\beta\,\hat{\mathbf{j}} + R\cos\gamma\,\hat{\mathbf{k}}$$

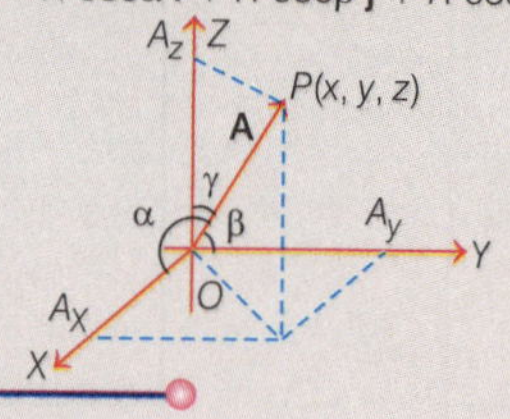

Addition & Products of two Vectors

Addition of two Vectors

- **Triangular Law**
For two vectors **A** and **B**, the resultant is given by

$$\mathbf{R} = \mathbf{A} + \mathbf{B} \Rightarrow |\mathbf{R}| = \sqrt{A^2 + B^2}$$

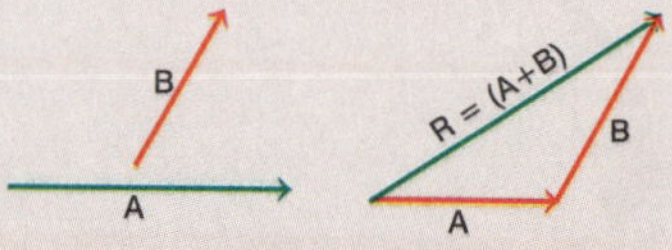

- **Parallelogram Law**
For two vectors **A** and **B** representing two adjacent sides of a parallelogram,

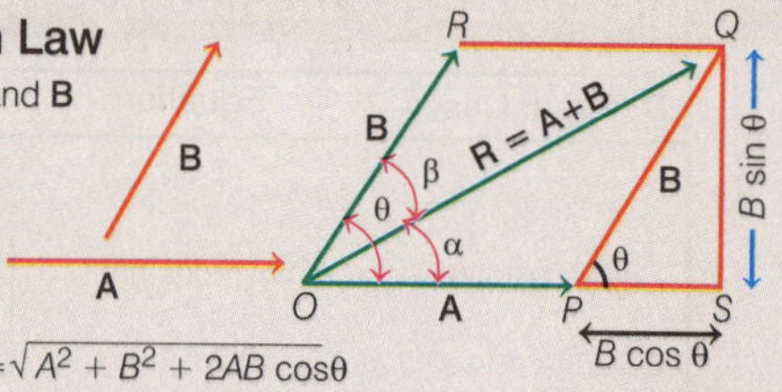

$$\mathbf{R} = \mathbf{A} + \mathbf{B} \Rightarrow |\mathbf{R}| = \sqrt{A^2 + B^2 + 2AB\cos\theta}$$

Direction of Resultant $\alpha = \tan^{-1}\left(\frac{B\sin\theta}{A + B\cos\theta}\right)$

Scalar and Vector Product of two Vectors

- **Scalar Product of two Vectors**
The product of the magnitude of two vectors and cosine of the angles between them.

$$\mathbf{A}\cdot\mathbf{B} = |\mathbf{A}||\mathbf{B}|\cos\theta = AB\cos\theta$$

If **A**·**B** are non-zero vectors, angle between them can be given by

$$\cos\theta = \frac{\mathbf{A}\cdot\mathbf{B}}{|\mathbf{A}||\mathbf{B}|}$$

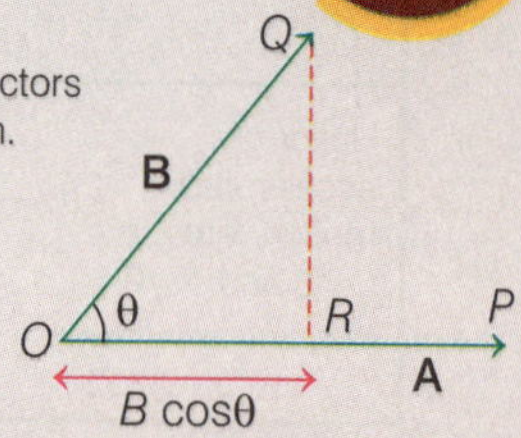

- **Vector Product of two Vectors**
The vector whose magnitude is equal to the product of the magnitudes of two vectors and sine of angle between them and whose direction is perpendicular to the plane of two vectors given by right hand rule.

$$\mathbf{A}\times\mathbf{B} = AB\sin\theta\,\hat{\mathbf{n}}$$

- $\hat{\mathbf{i}}\times\hat{\mathbf{j}} = \hat{\mathbf{k}}, \hat{\mathbf{j}}\times\hat{\mathbf{k}} = \hat{\mathbf{i}}, \hat{\mathbf{k}}\times\hat{\mathbf{i}} = \hat{\mathbf{j}}$
- $\sin\theta = \frac{|\mathbf{A}\times\mathbf{B}|}{|\mathbf{A}||\mathbf{B}|}$ • Unit vector $\hat{\mathbf{n}} = \frac{\mathbf{A}\times\mathbf{B}}{|\mathbf{A}\times\mathbf{B}|}$

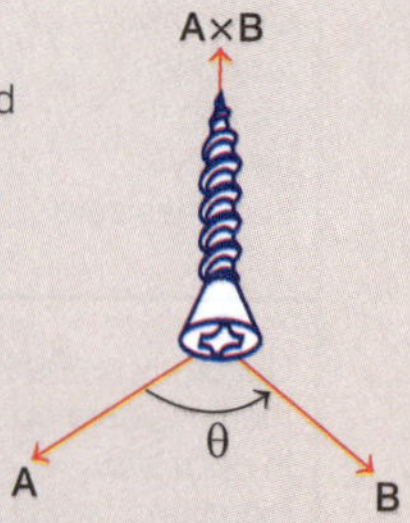

Properties of Vectors

- $\mathbf{a} + \mathbf{b} = \mathbf{b} + \mathbf{a}$
- $\mathbf{a} + (\mathbf{b} + \mathbf{c}) = (\mathbf{a} + \mathbf{b}) + \mathbf{c}$
- $\mathbf{a} + 0 = \mathbf{a}$
- $\mathbf{a} + (-\mathbf{a}) = 0$
- $c(\mathbf{a} + \mathbf{b}) = c\mathbf{a} + c\mathbf{b}$
- $(c + d)\mathbf{a} = c\mathbf{a} + d\mathbf{a}$
- $(cd)\mathbf{a} = c(d\mathbf{a})$

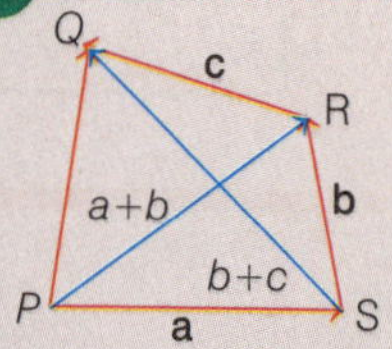

Velocity & Acceleration Vectors

Velocity Vector

Average Velocity
The ratio of the displacement and the corresponding time interval.

$$\mathbf{v}_{av} = \frac{\Delta\mathbf{r}}{\Delta t} = \frac{\Delta x\hat{\mathbf{i}} + \Delta y\hat{\mathbf{j}}}{\Delta t} = \mathbf{v}_x\hat{\mathbf{i}} + \mathbf{v}_y\hat{\mathbf{j}}$$

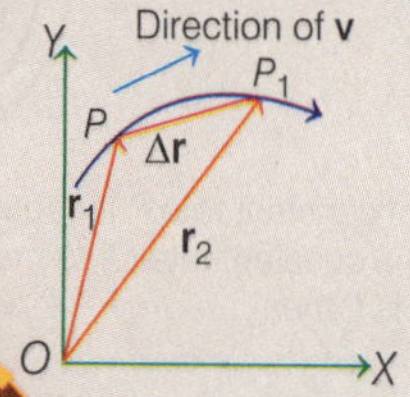

Instantaneous Velocity
Equal to the limiting value of its average velocity when time interval approaches to zero.

$$\mathbf{v} = \lim_{\Delta t\to 0}\frac{\Delta\mathbf{r}}{\Delta t} = \frac{d\mathbf{r}}{dt}$$

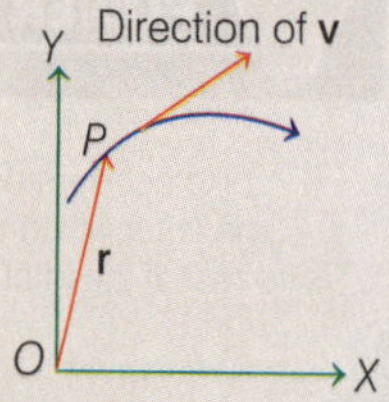

Acceleration Vector

Average Acceleration
The ratio of the change in velocity and the corresponding time interval.

$$\mathbf{a}_{av} = \frac{\Delta v}{\Delta t} = \frac{\Delta v_x\,\hat{\mathbf{i}} + \Delta v_y\,\hat{\mathbf{j}}}{\Delta t}$$

$$|a_{av}| = \sqrt{a_x^2 + a_y^2}$$

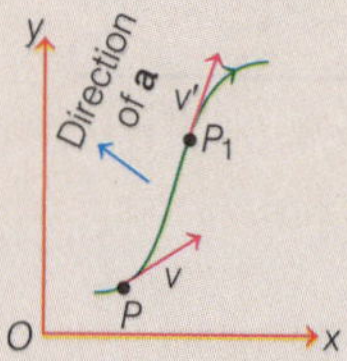

Instantaneous Acceleration
Equal to the limiting value of its average acceleration when the time interval approaches to zero.

$$\mathbf{a} = \frac{d\mathbf{v}}{dt}$$

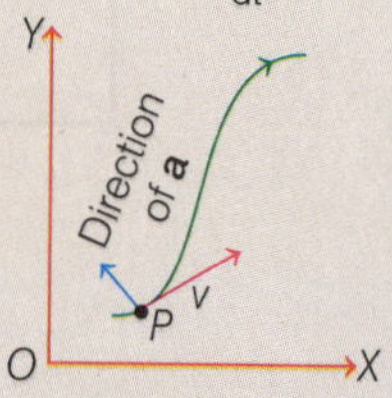

Projectile Motion

It is a form of motion where an object moves in parabolic path.

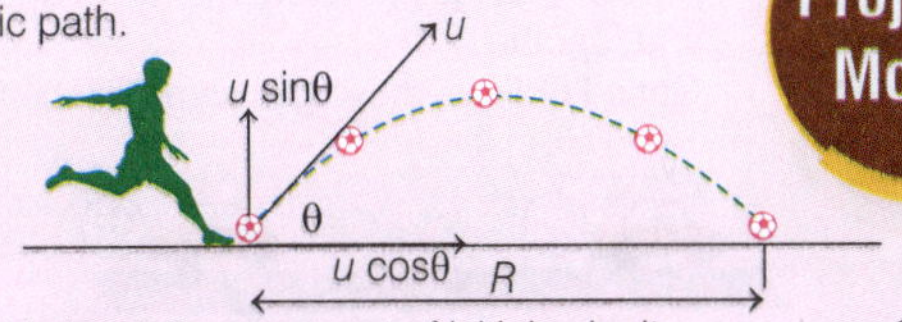

Horizontal component of initial velocity, $u_x = u\cos\theta$
Vertical component of initial velocity, $u_y = u\sin\theta$

Projectile Projected Horizontally from a Tower

Horizontal component	Vertical component
$u_x = u$ $a_x = 0$	$u_y = 0$ $a_y = -g$

Equations of Projectile Motion

(i) Equation of trajectory, $y = \frac{-1}{2}\left(\frac{g}{u^2}\right)x^2$

(ii) Time of flight, $T = \sqrt{\frac{2h}{g}}$

(iii) Horizontal range, $R = u\sqrt{\frac{2h}{g}}$

(iv) Velocity of projectile at any instant, $v = \sqrt{u^2 + g^2t^2}$

Angle of velocity at any instant with horizontal

$$\theta = \tan^{-1}\left(\frac{v_y}{v_x}\right) = \tan^{-1}\left(\frac{-gt}{u}\right)$$

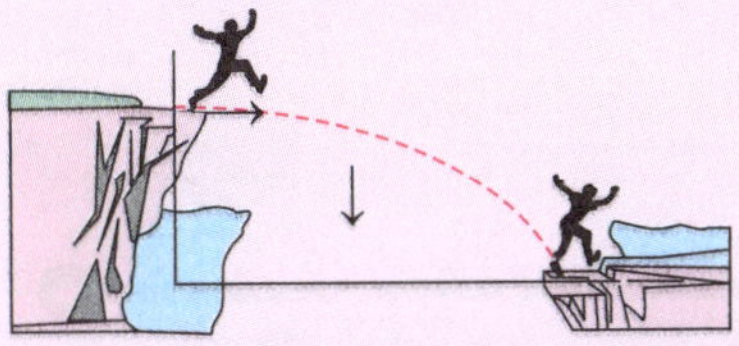

Horizontal Projectile

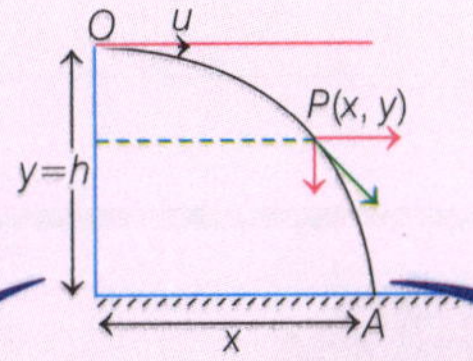

Projectile Projected from the Ground

Particle projected with an initial velocity u from origin O at an angle θ with the horizontal.

Maximum height $H = \frac{u^2\sin^2\theta}{2g}$

Trajectory $y = x\tan\theta - \frac{gx^2}{2u^2\cos^2\theta}$

Horizontal range $R = \frac{u^2\sin 2\theta}{g}$

Time of flight $T = 2t = \frac{2u\sin\theta}{g}$

Position of projectile at time t
$x = (u\cos\theta)t$
$y = u\sin\theta\, t - 1/2gt^2$

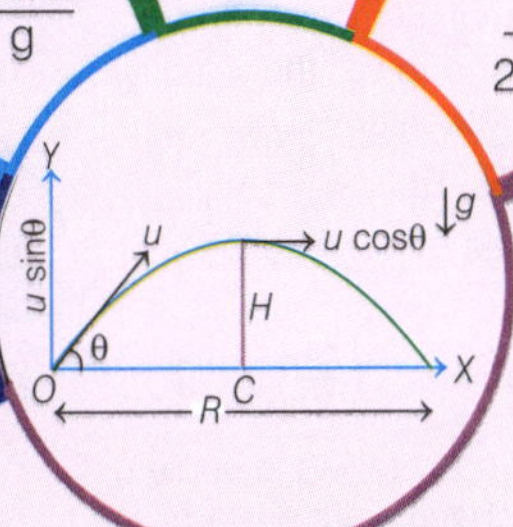

Projectile Projected at an angle θ above Horizontal

Horizontal component	Vertical component
$u_x = u\cos\theta$ $a_x = 0$	$u_y = u\sin\theta$ $a_y = -g$

Equations of Projectile Motion

(i) Equation of horizontal motion $x = u\cos\theta\, t$

(ii) Equation of vertical motion $-h = u\sin\theta t - \frac{1}{2}gt^2$

(iii) Time of flight, $T = \frac{u\sin\theta}{g} \pm \sqrt{\frac{u^2\sin^2\theta}{g^2} \times \frac{2h}{g}}$

(iv) Horizontal distance covered $(OB) = \frac{u^2\sin 2\theta}{g}$

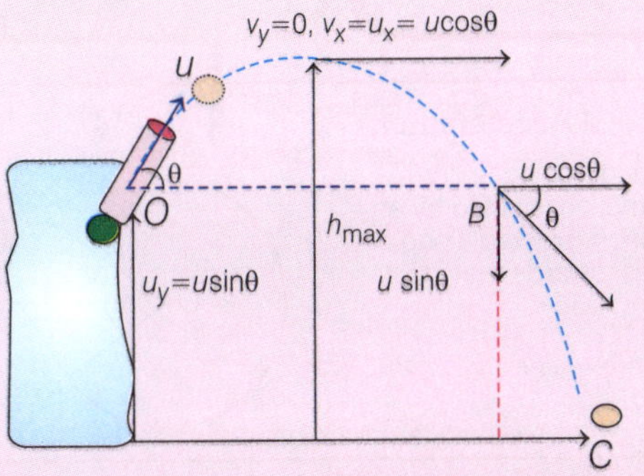

Projectile Projected at an Angle θ below Horizontal

Horizontal component	Vertical component
$u_x = u\cos\theta$ $a_x = 0$	$u_y = -u\sin\theta$ $a_y = -g$

Equations of Projectile Motion

(i) Equation of horizontal motion, $x = u\cos\theta t$

(ii) Equation of vertical motion, $-h = -u\sin\theta\, t - \frac{1}{2}gt^2$

(iii) Time of flight, $T = \frac{-2u\sin\theta \pm \sqrt{4u^2\sin^2\theta + 8gh}}{2g}$

(iv) Horizontal range, $R = (u\cos\theta)t$

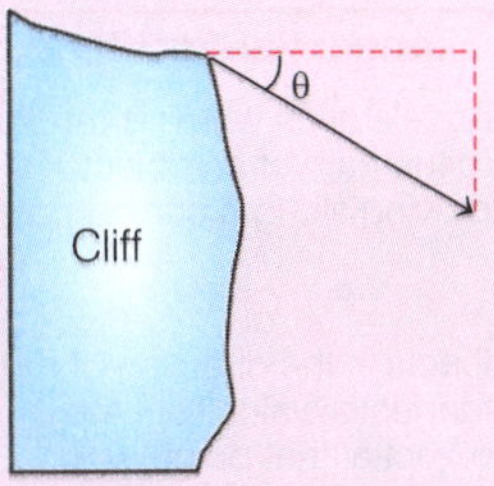

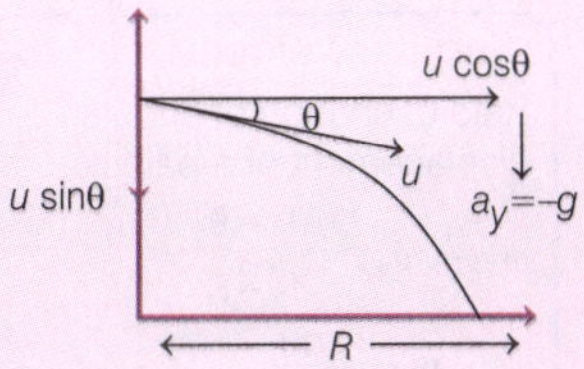

Relative Motion

Rate of change of relative motion of one object w.r.t. another.

Case I Objects moving in same direction.

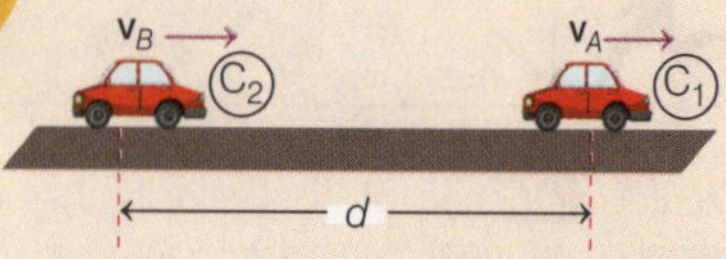

$\mathbf{v}_{AB} = \mathbf{v}_A - \mathbf{v}_B$, $\mathbf{v}_{BA} = \mathbf{v}_B - \mathbf{v}_A$ and $\mathbf{v}_{AB} = -\mathbf{v}_{BA}$

Case II Objects moving in opposite direction.

$\mathbf{v}_{AB} = \mathbf{v}_A - (-\mathbf{v}_B)$

$= \mathbf{v}_A + \mathbf{v}_B$

River-Boat Problem

A boat rows with a velocity v_b w.r.t. water in river. The water in river is flowing with a velocity v_r.

v_r = Velocity of river water

v_b = Velocity of boat in still water

v_{br} = Velocity of boat w.r.t. river.

(i) To cross the river over shortest distance, $t = \frac{d}{v_{br}} = \frac{d}{\sqrt{v_b^2 - v_r^2}}$

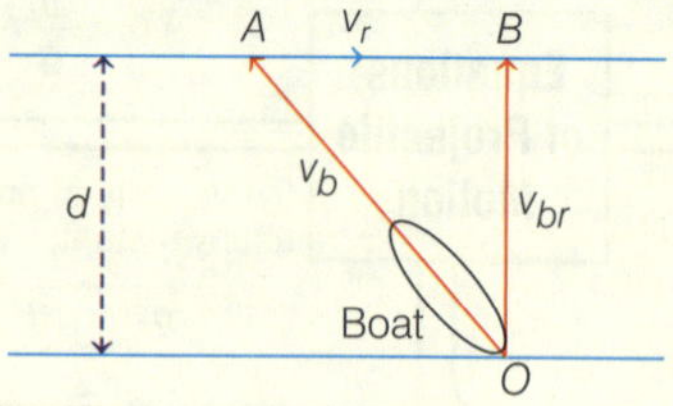

(ii) To cross the river in minimum time

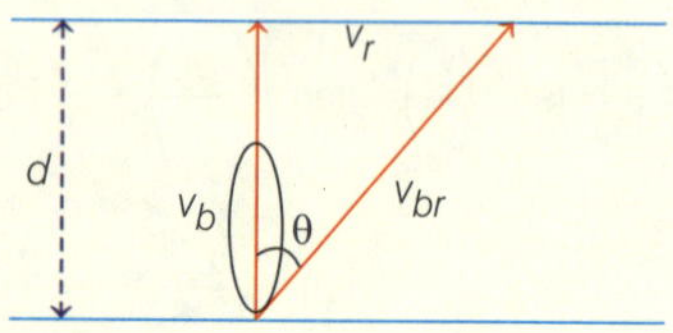

$t_{\min} = \frac{d}{v_b}$

Rain-Man Problem

Case I If rain is falling vertically with a velocity $\mathbf{v}_r$ and a man is moving horizontally with speed $\mathbf{v}_m$, the velocity of rain relative to observer will be

$$\mathbf{v}_{rm} = \mathbf{v}_r - \mathbf{v}_m,\ v_{rm} = \sqrt{v_r^2 + v_m^2}$$

θ is the angle made by $\mathbf{v}_{rm}$ with the vertical direction,

$$\tan\theta = \frac{v_m}{v_r},\ \theta = \tan^{-1}\left(\frac{v_m}{v_r}\right)$$

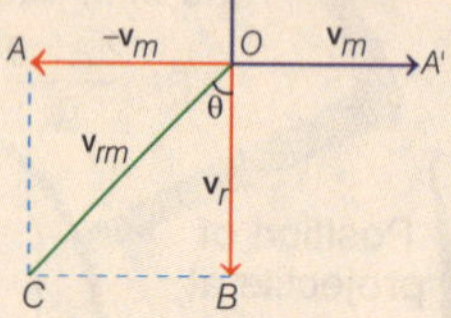

Case II Rain is already falling at angle θ with vertical and observer is moving horizontally.

$$v_{rm} = \sqrt{(v_r \sin\theta - v_m)^2 + (v_r \cos\theta)^2}$$

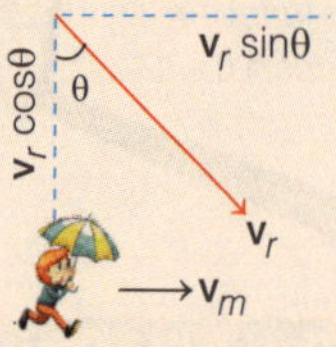

Circular Motion

When a particle moves in a plane such that its distance from a fixed (or moving) point remains constant.

Uniform Circular Motion

Particle moving along a circular path with a constant speed.

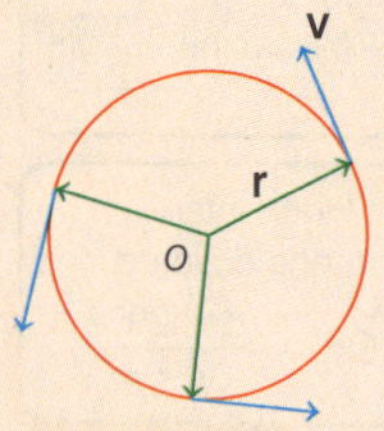

Non-Uniform Circular Motion

Tangential component of acceleration due to change in speed. $a_t = \frac{dv}{dt} = r\alpha$

Radial component of acceleration due to change in direction,

$a_r = \frac{v^2}{r}$

Net acceleration,

$a = \sqrt{a_r^2 + a_t^2}$

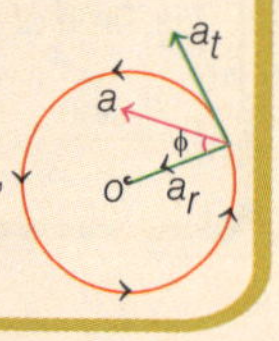

Angular Acceleration

Rate of change of angular velocity of a body moving on a circular path.

$$\alpha = \frac{\Delta\omega}{\Delta t}$$

$$\alpha_{ins} = \lim_{\Delta t \to 0} \frac{\Delta\omega}{\Delta t} = \frac{d\omega}{dt} = \frac{d^2\theta}{dt^2}$$

Its SI unit is rad/s^2.

Relation between various terms of circular motion.

(i) $\omega = \frac{2\pi}{t} = 2\pi\nu$

(ii) $v = \omega r$

(iii) $a = \alpha r$

Angular Displacement

Angle traced out by the radius vector at the centre of the circular path in the given time interval. $\Delta\theta = \theta_2 - \theta_1$

It is a scalar quantity with SI unit radian.

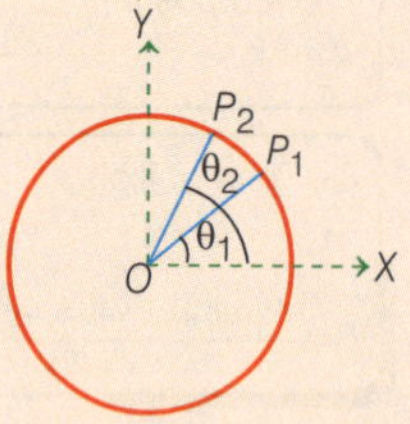

Angular Velocity

Rate of change of angular displacement of a particle.

$$\omega = \frac{\theta}{t},\ \omega_{av} = \frac{\theta_2 - \theta_1}{t_2 - t_1} = \frac{\Delta\theta}{\Delta t},$$

$$\omega_{inst} = \frac{d\theta}{dt}$$

Its unit is rad/s.

Tangential Acceleration

Acceleration which is tangent to the path of an object moving along a curved path.

$$a_t = \frac{dv_t}{dt} = r\alpha$$

It acts in the direction of the tangential velocity of the object at that point.

Centripetal Acceleration

A body undergoing uniform circular motion is acted by an acceleration directed along the radius towards the centre.

$$a_c = \frac{v^2}{r} = \omega^2 r$$

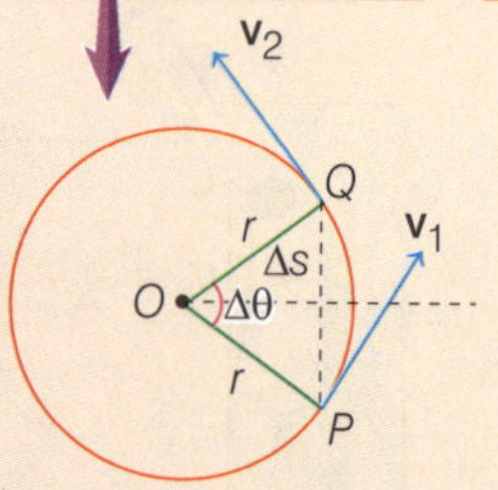

Chapter **04**

Laws of Motion

Force

A push or pull which tends to change the state of rest or uniform motion or direction of motion of a body.

Inertia

A body cannot change its state of rest or uniform motion along a straight line by itself.

Inertia of Rest
Inability to change the state of rest by itself.

Inertia of Motion
Inability to change its state of uniform motion by itself.

Inertia of Direction
Inability to change the direction of motion by itself.

Newton's Laws of Motion

Newton's First Law of Motion

A body continues in its state of rest or uniform motion in a straight line unless it is compelled by some external force.

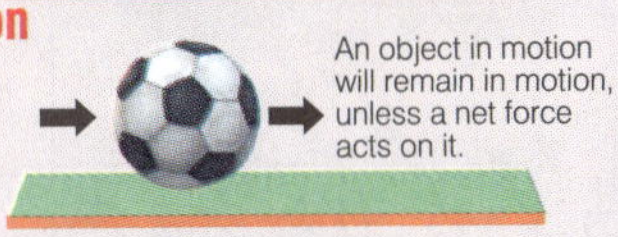

Newton's Second Law of Motion

Rate of change of momentum of a body is directly proportional to the external force applied on the body and changes takes place in the direction of applied force.

$F = \frac{d\mathbf{p}}{dt}$, $F_{av} = \frac{\Delta \mathbf{p}}{\Delta t} = \frac{\mathbf{p}_f - \mathbf{p}_i}{\Delta t}$

$\Rightarrow$ $F = ma$ where, F = force
m = mass of the body
and a = acceleration of the body

Newton's Third Law of Motion

To every action, there is always an equal and opposite reaction.

$\mathbf{F}_1 = -\mathbf{F}_2$

$\mathbf{F}_1$ = Force applied by the man on the wall

$\mathbf{F}_2$ = Force exerted by the wall on the man

Man pushing against a wall

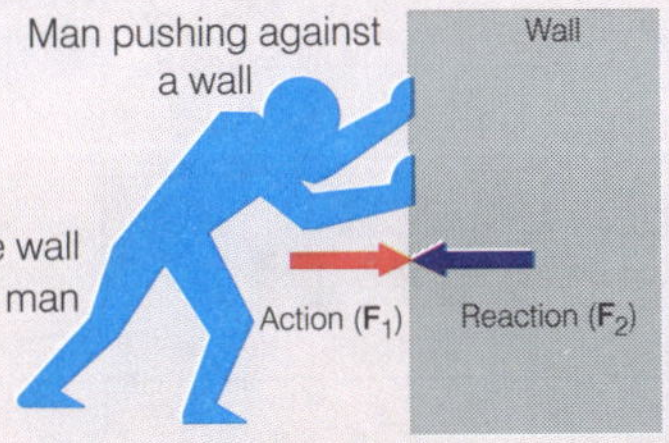

Conservation of Linear Momentum

If no external force is acting on a system, the momentum of the system remains constant.

$$F_{ext} = 0 \Rightarrow \Delta p = 0 \text{ or } p_i = p_f$$

It is the consequence of Newton's second and third laws of motion.

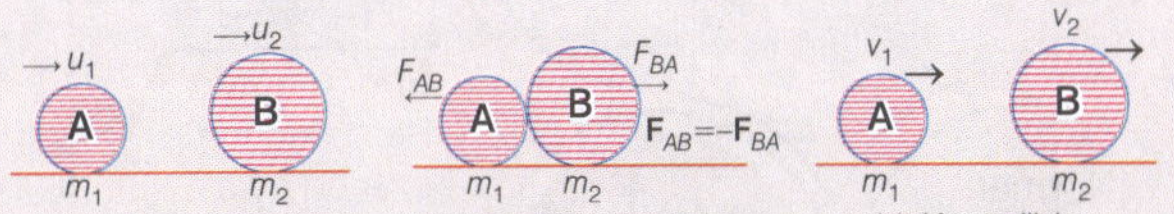

(a) Before collision (b) At the time of collision (c) After collision

$$m_1u_1 + m_2u_2 = m_1v_1 + m_2v_2$$

Total linear momentum before collision = Total linear momentum after collision

Momentum

Quantity of motion possessed by a moving body.

$\mathbf{p} = m\mathbf{v}$

It is a vector quantity.
Its SI unit is kg-ms^{-1}.

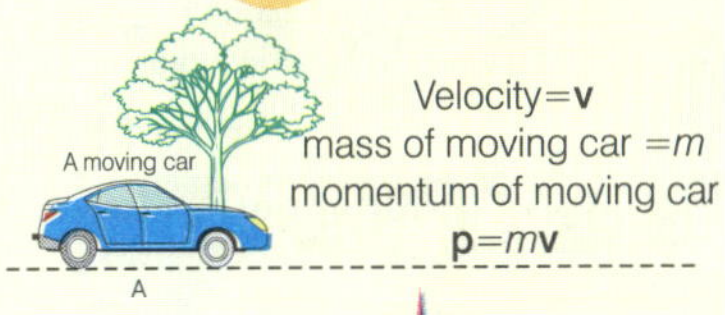

Velocity = $\mathbf{v}$
mass of moving car = m
momentum of moving car
$\mathbf{p} = m\mathbf{v}$

Impulse

A large force acts for a very short duration of time producing a finite change in momentum.

$I = F\Delta t$

Its SI unit is N-s.

POWER TIPS

Measurement of Impulse by Graphical Method

- When a **constant force** acts on a body.

Impulse (I) = Area of rectangle $ABCD$
= Force × Time

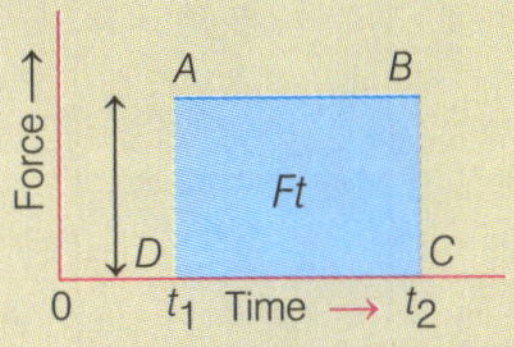

- When a variable force acts on a body.

Impulse (I) = $\int_{t_1}^{t_2} F dt$ = Area under the force-time curve ABC

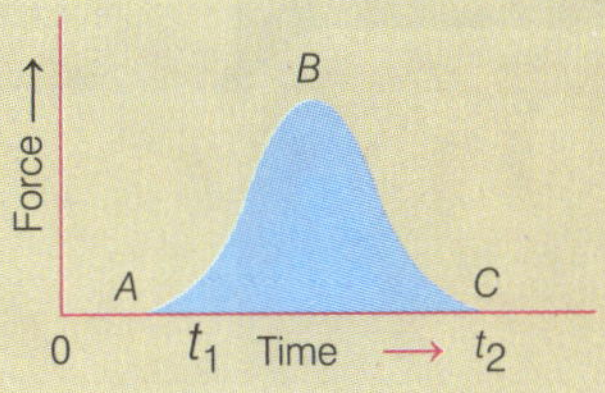

Equilibrium of Concurrent Forces

Forces acting at the same point on a body are said to be concurrent.

$F_1 + F_2 + F_3 = 0$

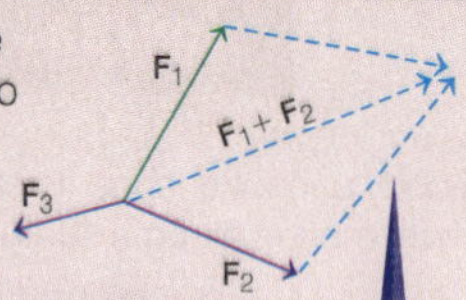

Lami's Theorem

In equilibrium, each force is proportional to the sine of angle between the other two forces.

$$\frac{F_1}{\sin\alpha} = \frac{F_2}{\sin\beta} = \frac{F_3}{\sin\gamma}$$

Motion of Connected Bodies

Case I : Bodies in contact

$$a = \frac{F}{m_1 + m_2 + m_3}$$

$$f_1 = \frac{(m_2 + m_3)F}{m_1 + m_2 + m_3}$$

$$f_2 = \frac{m_3 F}{m_1 + m_2 + m_3}$$

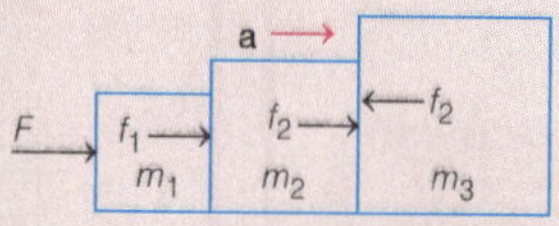

Case II : Bodies connected by massless string

$$a = \frac{F}{m_1 + m_2 + m_3}$$

$$T_1 = \frac{m_1 F}{m_1 + m_2 + m_3}$$

$$T_2 = \frac{(m_1 + m_2)F}{m_1 + m_2 + m_3}$$

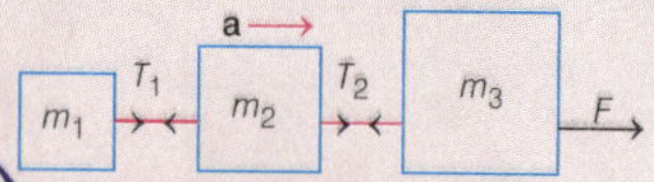

Some Common Forces

Weight
A gravitational pull on a body by earth.
$w = mg$

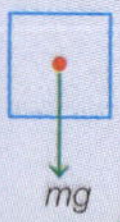

Spring Force
Restoring force exerted by a spring when it is compressed or stretched.
$F = -kx$

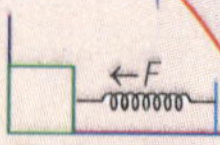

Normal Reaction
Occurs when two surfaces are in contact. It is always perpendicular to the surfaces in contact.

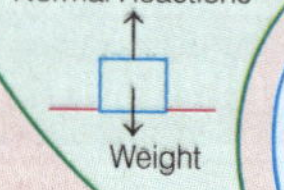

Tension Restoring force transmitted through a string when a longitudinal force is applied on the body.

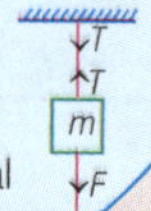

Weight of a Body in Lift

Lift at rest or moving with constant velocity
$R = mg$
$w_{app} = mg$
Apparent weight will be equal to true weight.

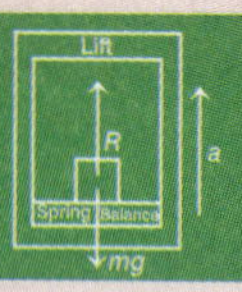

Lift accelerating upward
$R = m(g + a)$
$w_{app} = m(g + a)$
Apparent weight will be more than true weight.

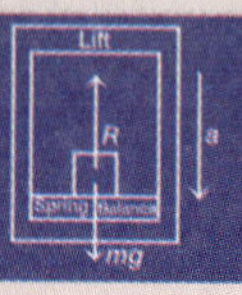

Lift accelerating downward
$mg - R = ma$
$w_{app} = m(g - a)$
Apparent weight will be lesser than true weight.

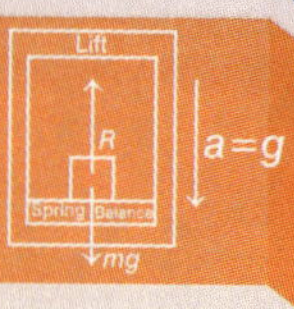

Lift in free fall $a = g$, $mg - R = mg$
$R = 0$
$w_{app} = 0$
Apparent weight of freely falling body is zero.

Pulley-Block System

Cases	Free Body Diagram	Equation of Motion	Acceleration and Tension
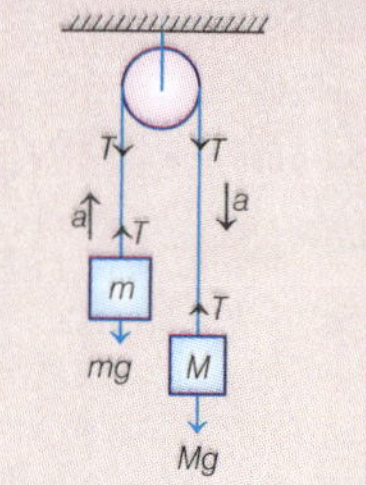	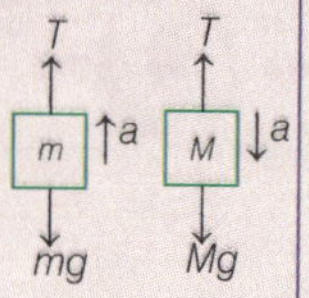	For $M > m$ $a(m + M) = (M - m)g$ $T(m + M) = 2mMg$	$a = \frac{M - m}{M + m}g$ $T = \frac{2mM}{m + M}g$
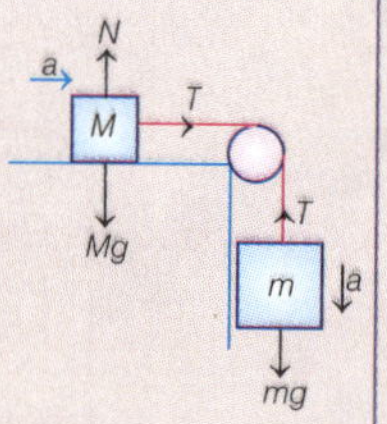	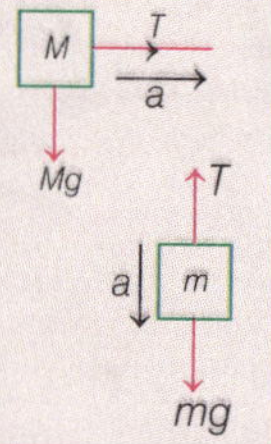	For $m > M$ $T = Ma$ $mg - T = ma$	$a = \frac{mg}{m + M}$ $T = \frac{mM}{m + M}g$
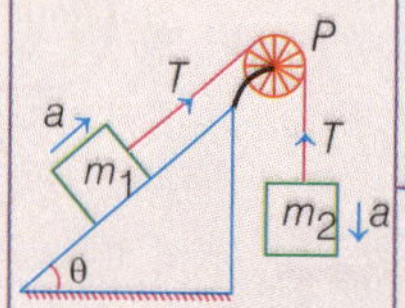	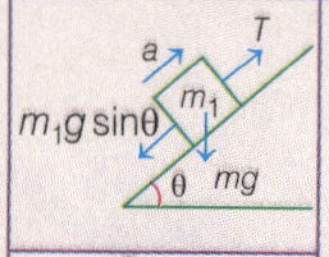 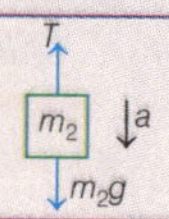	For $m_2 > m_1$ $m_1a = T - m_1g\sin\theta$ $m_2a = m_2g - T$	$a = \left[\frac{m_2 - m_1\sin\theta}{m_1 + m_2}\right]g$ $T = \frac{m_1m_2(1 + \sin\theta)}{m_1 + m_2}g$
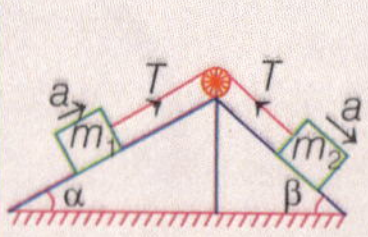	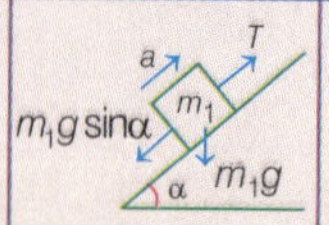 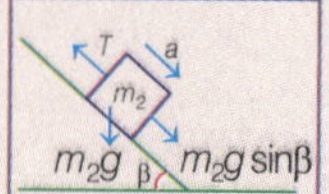	For $m_2 > m_1$ $T - m_1g\sin\alpha = m_1a$ $m_2a = m_2g\sin\beta - T$	$a = \frac{(m_2\sin\beta - m_1\sin\alpha)}{m_1 + m_2}g$ $T = \frac{m_1m_2(\sin\alpha + \sin\beta)}{m_1 + m_2}g$
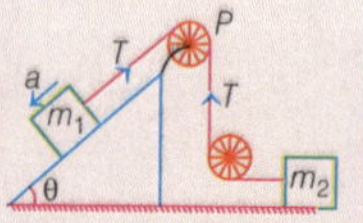	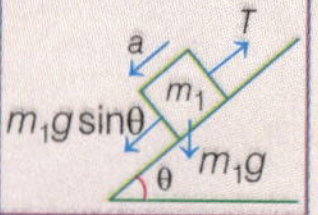 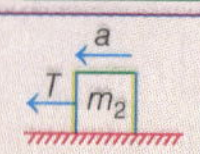	For $m_1 > m_2$ $m_1g\sin\theta - T = m_1a$ $T = m_2a$	$a = \frac{m_1g\sin\theta}{m_1 + m_2}$ $T = \frac{m_1m_2\sin\theta g}{m_1 + m_2}$

Friction

Resistance offered to the relative motion between the surfaces of the two bodies in contact.

1 Static Friction

- It acts when object tends to slip over the surface of other object.
- It is a self adjusting force with upper limit.

$(f_s)_{max} = \mu_s N$

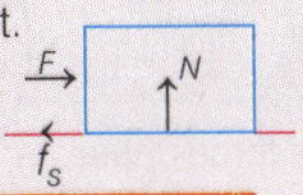

2 Kinetic Friction

- It acts when object starts moving.

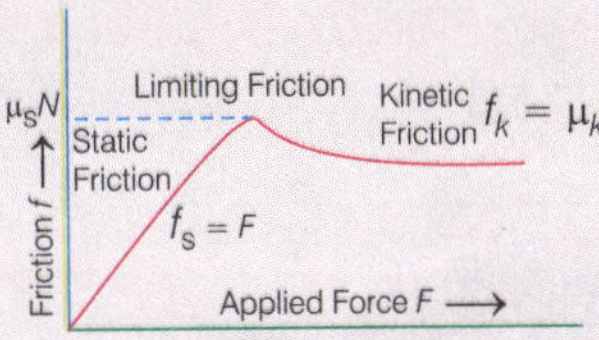

3 Methods of Reducing Friction

- By polishing
- Lubrication
- Streamlining
- By using ball bearings

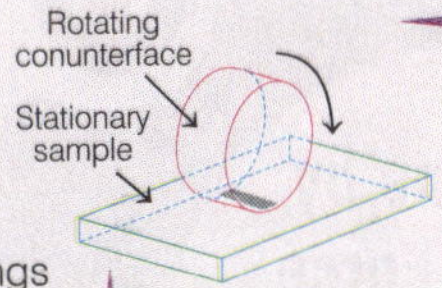

Angle of Friction

Angle made by resultant of normal and limiting frictional force with normal.

$\lambda = \tan^{-1}(\mu_s)$

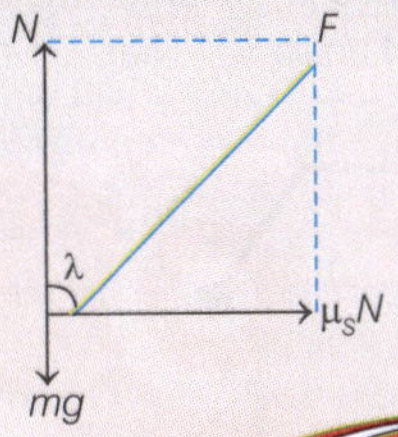

Angle of Repose

Minimum angle of inclination at which a body begins to slide down.

$\alpha = \tan^{-1}(\mu_s)$

$\theta < \alpha, F < f_L$, block at rest

$\theta = \alpha, F = f_L$, block is about to slide

$\theta > \alpha, F > f_L$, block slides down

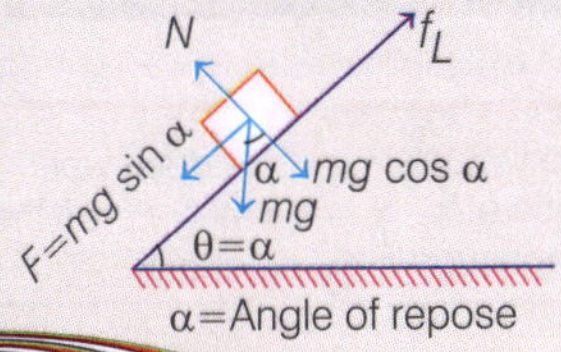

Motion of a Body on Rough Inclined Plane

(i) Body is moving downward

$R = mg\cos\theta$

$a = (\sin\theta - \mu_k \cos\theta)\, g$

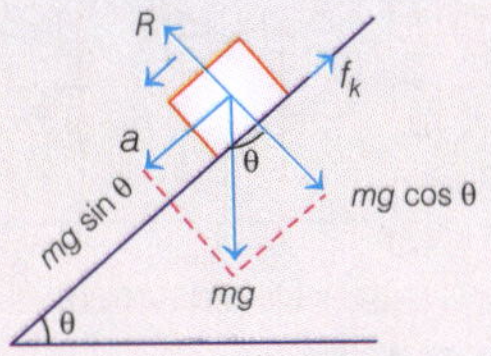

(ii) Body is moving upward

$R = mg\cos\theta$

$$a = \frac{F - mg\sin\theta - \mu_k mg\cos\theta}{m}$$

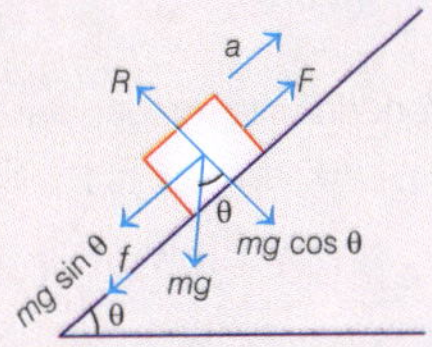

Forces in Circular Motion

Centripetal Force

- Force required to make a body move along a circular path with uniform speed.
- Acts along the radius of circular path.

$a_c = r\omega^2$

$F_c = mr\omega^2$

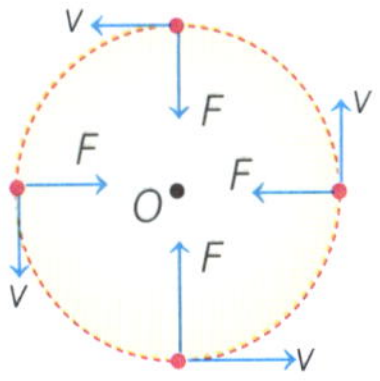

- **Tangential force**

$F_t = Ma_t$

- Net force, $F_{net} = ma = m\sqrt{a_c^2 + a_t^2}$

Motion of Car on Banked Road

- Optimum speed on a smooth banked road

$v_0 = \sqrt{rg\tan\theta}$

- Maximum speed to avoid skidding

$$v_{max} = \sqrt{\frac{rg(\mu_s + \tan\theta)}{1 - \mu_s \tan\theta}}$$

- Minimum speed to avoid skidding

$$v_{min} = \sqrt{\frac{rg(\tan\theta - \mu_s)}{1 + \mu_s \tan\theta}}$$

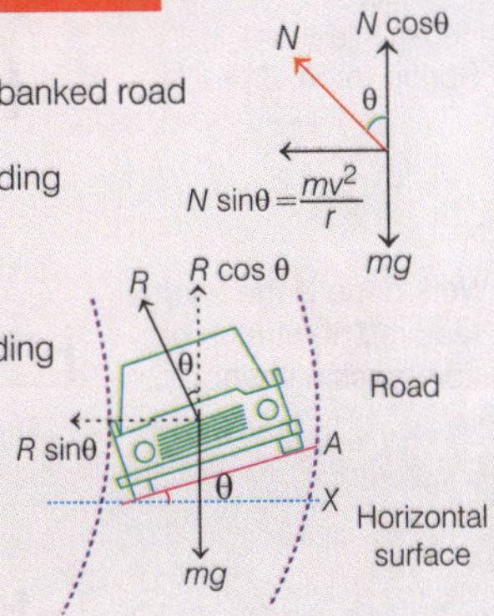

Bending of Cyclist

Angle of bending, $\tan\theta = \frac{v^2}{rg}$

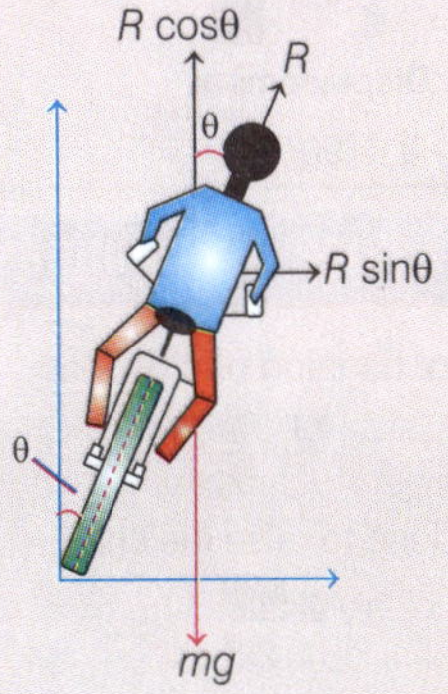

Chapter 05

Work, Energy and Power

Work

- Work is done on an object when a force causes a displacement of the object.
- $W = \mathbf{F} \cdot \mathbf{s} = Fs \cos\theta$

  SI unit = Newton-metre (N-m) = Joule (J)
- 1 Joule = 1 N-m = 1 (kg-m/s^2)$\cdot$ m = 1 kg-m^2/s^2

Work done by Constant Force

A constant force of magnitude F, ... acting in the direction of a displacement of magnitude d ... does work $W = Fd$ on the object.

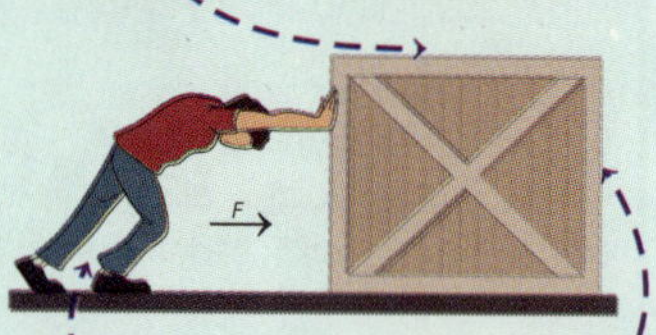

When a constant force (F) applied on a body and it moves through displacement (d) in the direction of force F. $W = Fd$

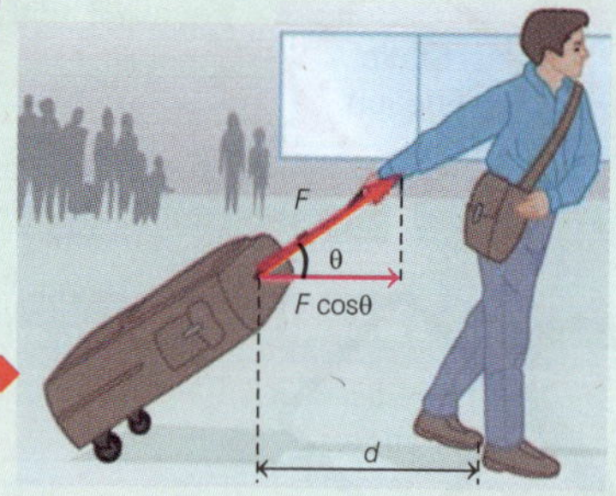

- Force at an angle to the displacement. The component of force in the direction of displacement is $F \cos \theta$. This is the only component of the force that does work. $W = Fd \cos \theta$

Nature of Work

$\theta < 90°$ i.e. $\theta = 0°$

Positive Work

Force acting has a component in the direction of the displacement.

$W = Fs \cos \theta \ (\theta < 90°)$

Negative Work

Force acting has a component opposite to the direction of displacement.

$W = Fs \cos \theta, \theta > 90°$

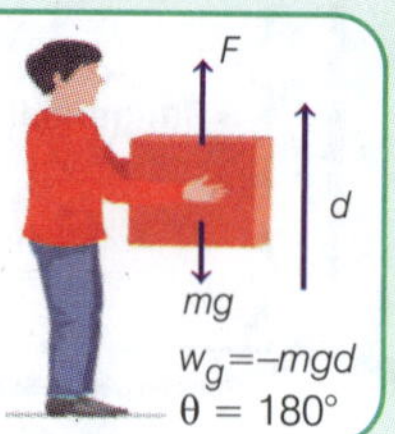

$W_g = -mgd$

$\theta = 180°$

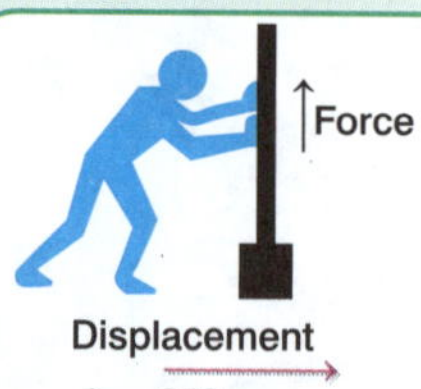

$\theta = 90°$

Zero Work

Force acting has no component in the direction of motion.

$W = Fs \cos \theta = 0 \ (\theta = 90°)$

Work done in Pulling a Chain

- Mass of hanging part of chain

$$= \frac{M}{L} \times \frac{L}{x} = \frac{M}{x}$$

- Work done to raise the chain

$$W = \frac{MgL}{2x^2}$$

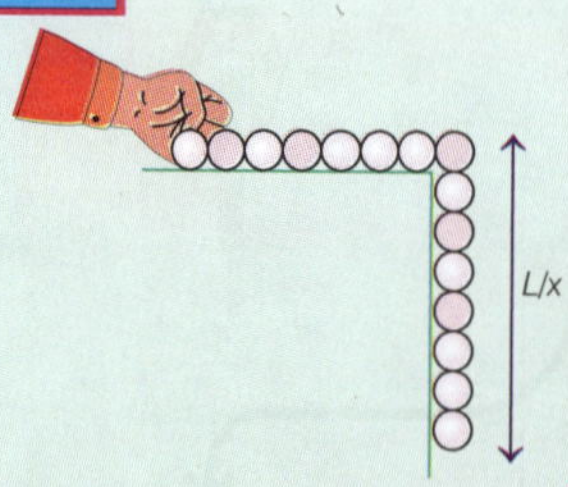

Work Done by a Variable Force

$dW = \mathbf{F} \cdot d\mathbf{s} \Rightarrow W = \int \mathbf{F} \cdot d\mathbf{s} = \int Fds \cos \theta$ W=Area

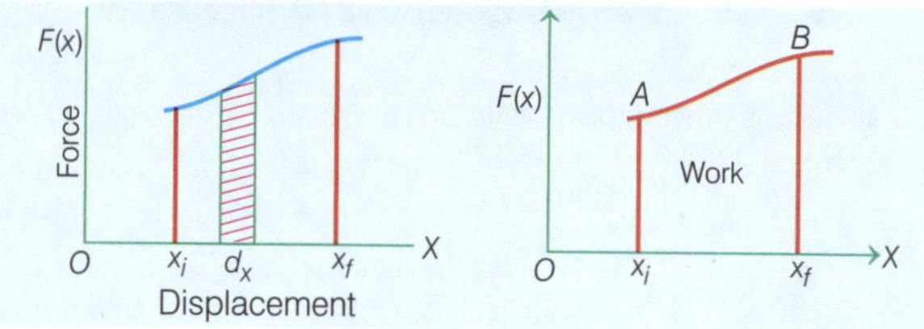

From graph,

$$W = \int_{x_i}^{x_f} \mathbf{F} \cdot d\mathbf{x}$$

- Work done in rectangular component

$$\mathbf{F} = F_x \hat{\mathbf{i}} + F_y \hat{\mathbf{j}} + F_z \hat{\mathbf{k}}, \quad d\mathbf{s} = d_x \hat{\mathbf{i}} + d_y \hat{\mathbf{j}} + d_z \hat{\mathbf{k}}$$

$$W = \int dW = \int_{x_1}^{x_2} \mathbf{F}_x \cdot d\mathbf{x} + \int_{y_1}^{y_2} \mathbf{F}_y \cdot d\mathbf{y} + \int_{z_1}^{z_2} \mathbf{F}_z \cdot d\mathbf{z}$$

W = Area under the force-displacement curve between the initial and final positions of the body.

Work done by a Spring Force

- Hooke's law

  Spring force, $F = -kx$
- Work done is the energy required to stretch or compress a spring.

$$W = \frac{1}{2}kx^2$$

- It acts opposite to the displacement.

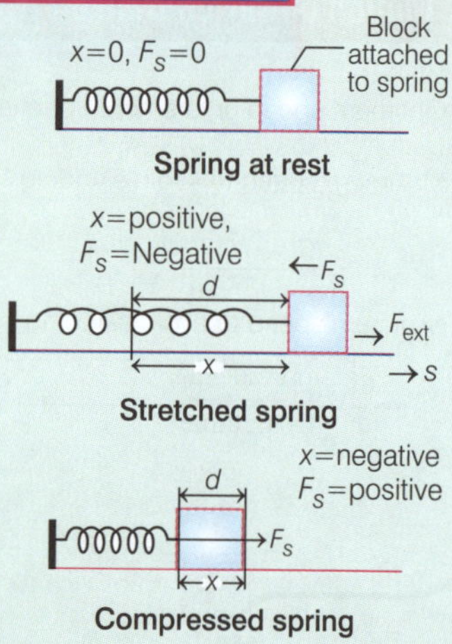

Conservative and Non-conservative Forces

Consrevative Forces

- Path independent in nature and only depends on initial and final positions.
  $W_I = W_{II}$

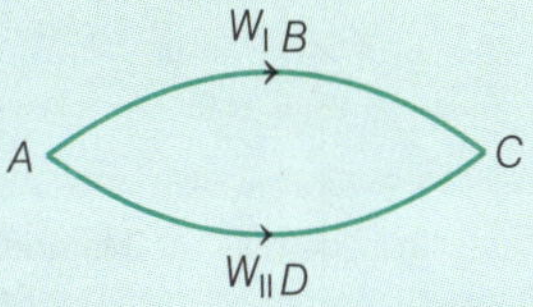

- Work done by the conservative force in moving a particle around any closed path is zero.
  Examples Gravitational force, electrostatic force.

Non-conservative Forces

- Path dependent ,i.e. depends on the path taken. $W_I \neq W_{II}$

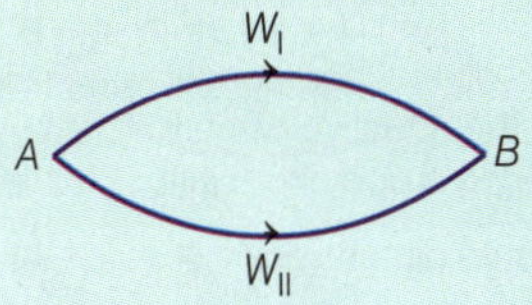

- Work done by the non-conservative force in moving a particle along a closed path is not zero.
  Example - Friction, viscosity.

Energy

- It is the capacity or ability to do work.
- It is a scalar quantity.
- Its SI unit is Joule.
- Its dimensional formula is $[ML^2T^{-2}]$.
- **Forms of Energy** Mechanical energy, sound energy, heat energy, etc.

Kinetic Energy

- Energy possessed by a body by virtue of its motion.
  Kinetic energy $= \frac{1}{2}mv^2$

- For system of n particles
  $$KE = \sum_{i=1}^{n} \frac{1}{2} m_i v_i^2$$
- Relation between kinetic energy (KE) and momentum (p),
  $$KE = \frac{p^2}{2m}$$

Potential Energy

- Its the energy possessed by a body by virtue of its position or configuration.
- Gravitational potential energy is due to the virtue of a body's position above the surface.
  Potential energy $= mgh$
- The change in potential energy
  $(dU) = -F \cdot ds = -dW$
  $F \to$ Conservative Force

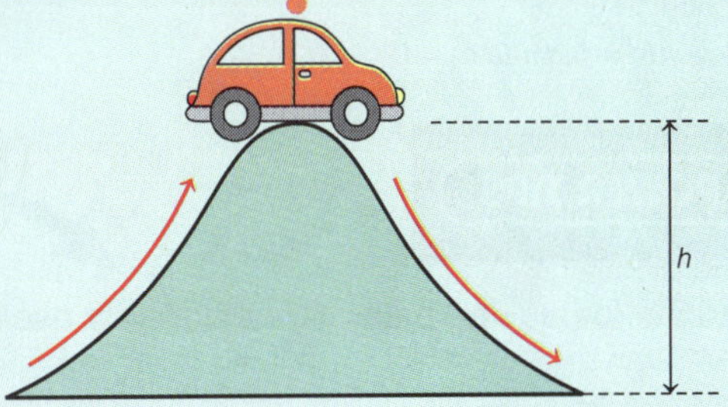

Relation of Kinetic Energy with other Quantities

$\because$ Linear momentum, $p = \sqrt{2mk}$,

Variation of graph of Kinetic Energy

m constant, $K \propto v^2$

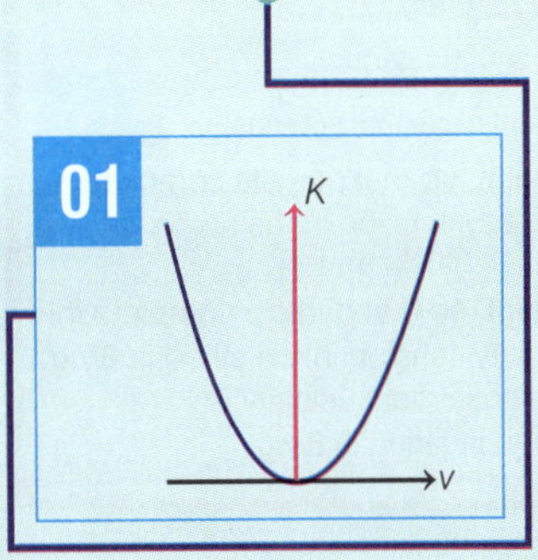

m constant, $K \propto p^2$

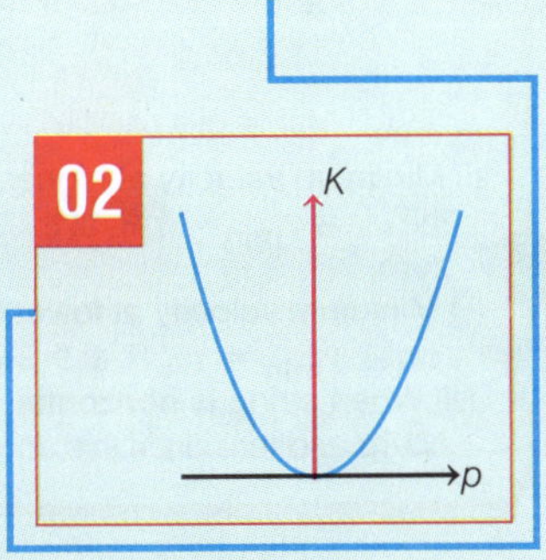

p constant, $K \propto \frac{1}{m}$

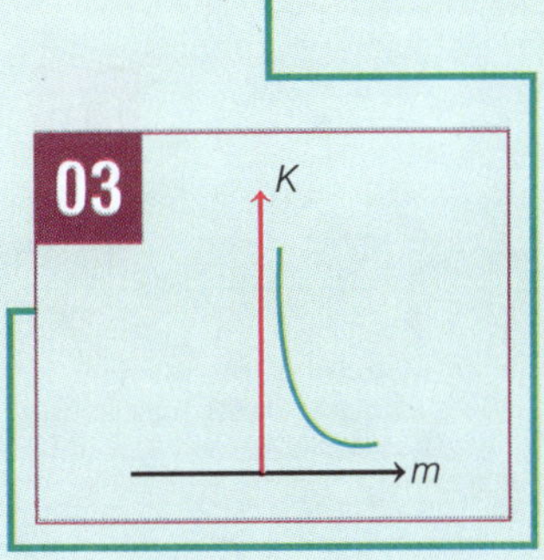

m constant, $K \propto p^2$

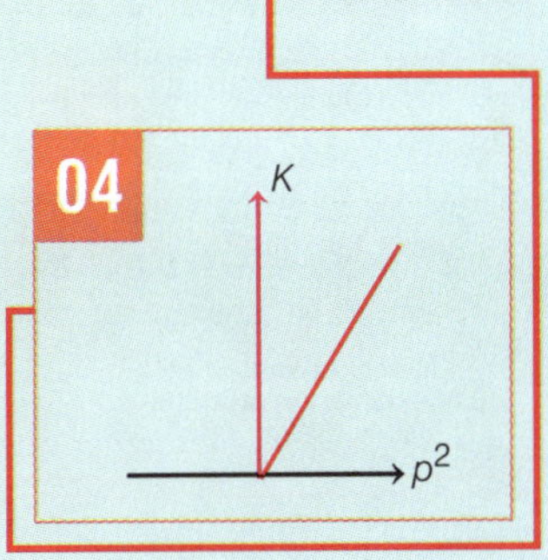

Potential Energy and Force Relation

- Potential energy is defined for conservative force field only.
  $U = -\int_{\infty}^{r} \mathbf{F}\cdot d\mathbf{r} = -W$
- Not valid for non-conservative field.
- It is the negative of work done by the conservative forces in moving a body from infinity to the present position.
- In three dimensions $\mathbf{F} = -\left(\frac{\partial u}{\partial x}\hat{\mathbf{i}} + \frac{\partial u}{\partial y}\hat{\mathbf{j}} + \frac{\partial u}{\partial z}\hat{\mathbf{k}}\right)$

Potential Energy of Spring

The potential energy stored as a result of the deformation of a particular elastic object or a spring.

- Energy at any arbitrary point $U = 1/2\, kx^2$
- Applied force $= F_{app}$

  $F_{app} = \frac{1}{2}kx$

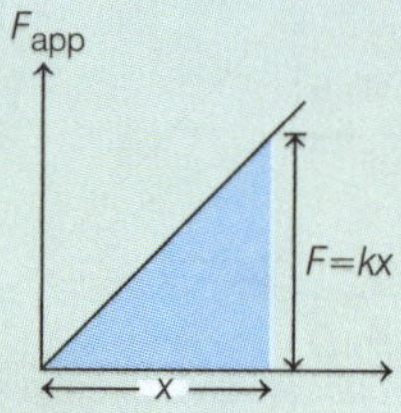

Method A

$W = \frac{1}{2}bh = \frac{1}{2}kxx$

$W = \frac{1}{2}kx^2$

Method B

$W = F\cdot x = \left[\frac{1}{2}kx\right]x$

Equilibrium

- A state where the net force on an object is zero.
- Object is either at rest or moving with constant velocity.

Stable Equilibrium

- Object return to its equilibrium position when slightly displaced.
- Potential energy is minimum at the equilibrium position.
- $F = -du/dx = 0,\ d^2u/dx = +ve$

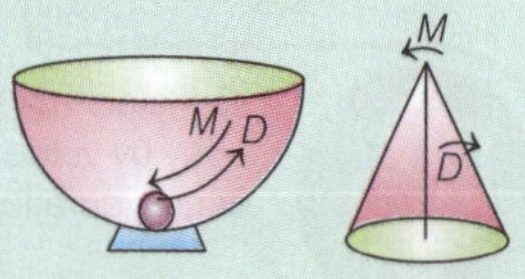

Unstable Equilibrium

- Object will move further away from the equilibrium position when slightly displaced.
- Potential energy is maximum at unstable equilibrium position.
- $F = -du/dx = 0, d^2u/dx^2 = -ve$

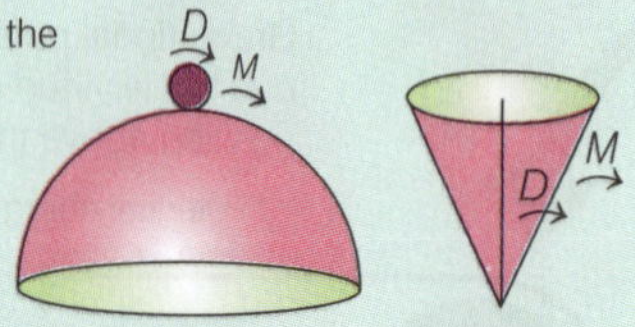

Neutral Equilibrium

- Object remains in its position after displacement position from the previous position.
- Potential energy is constant throughout.
- $F = -du/dx = 0, d^2u/dx^2 = 0$

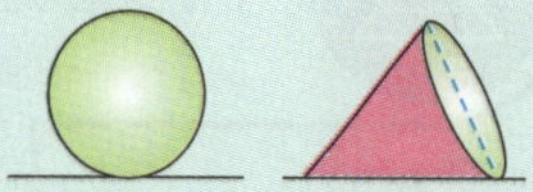

Work-Energy Theorem

- The work done by all the forces (conservative or non-conservative, external or internal) acting on a particle or an object is equal to the change in its kinetic energy.
  $W_{net} = \Delta KE = K_f - K_i = 1/2\, m\,(v_f^2 - v_i^2)$
- Work done by the resultant force is equal to the sum of the work done by individual forces. $W = \int \mathbf{F}_1\cdot d\mathbf{r} + \int \mathbf{F}_2\cdot d\mathbf{r} + \int \mathbf{F}_3\cdot d\mathbf{r}$

Conservation of Mechanical Energy

- For an isolated system or body in the presence of conservative forces the sum of kinetic and potential energy remains constant.

KE+PE = Constant, $K_f + U_f = U_i + K_i$

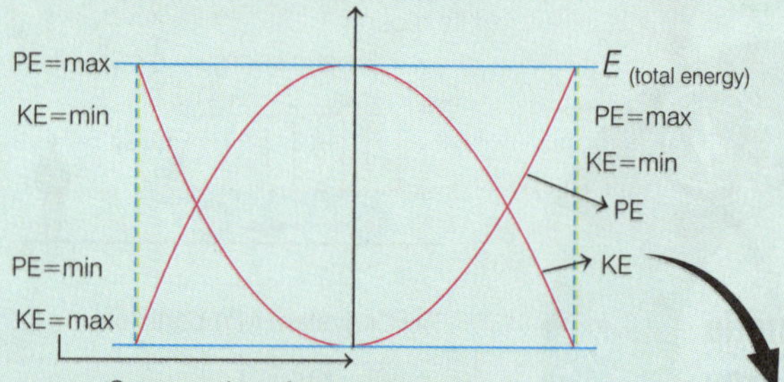

Conservation of energy in an elastic spring

POWER TIPS

Conditions for leaving path

(i) If velocity at lowest point is $\sqrt{2gR} < v < \sqrt{5gR}$, then tension in the string becomes zero but velocity is not zero, the particle will leave circle at $90^\circ < \theta < 180^\circ$ or $h > R$.

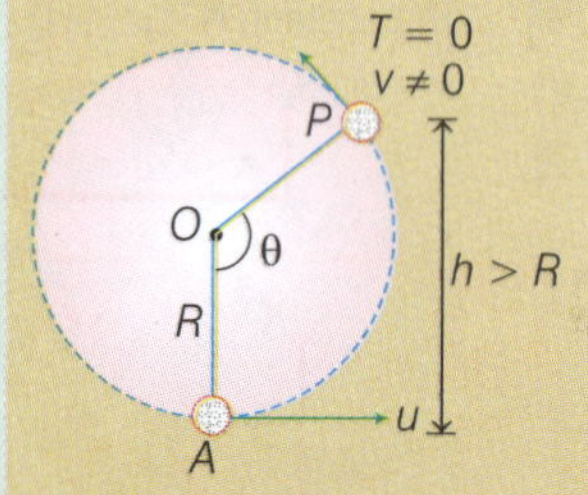

Motion of particle when velocity at lowest point is less than $\sqrt{5Rg}$

Conditions for oscillation

(ii) If velocity at lowest point is, $0 < v \le \sqrt{2gR}$ the particle will oscillate. In this condition, velocity becomes zero but tension is not zero. The particle will oscillate in lower half of circle, i.e. $0^\circ < \theta < 90^\circ$.

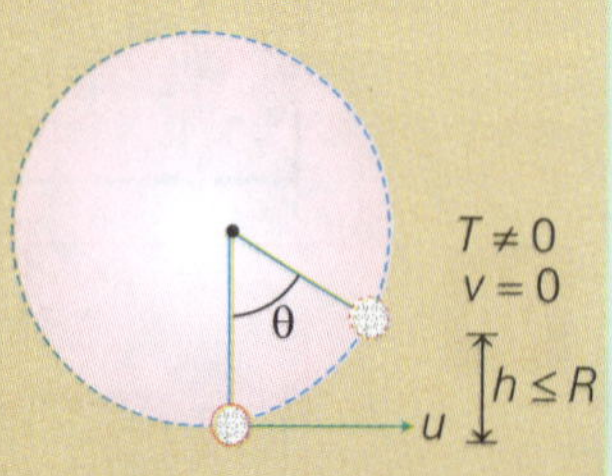

Motion of particle when velocity at lowest point is less than $\sqrt{2gR}$

Motion of a Particle in Vertical Circle

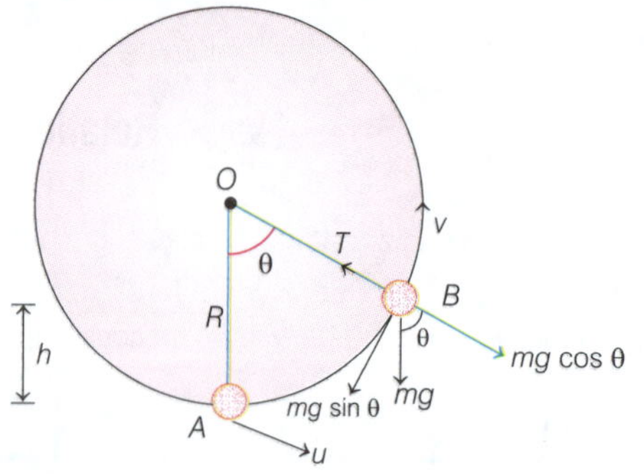

Motion of a particle in vertical circle, $h = R(1-\cos\theta)$

(I) **Minimum velocity at highest point**, so that particle complete the circle $\mathbf{v_{min}} = \sqrt{gR}$, at this velocity, tension in the string is **zero**.

(ii) **Minimum velocity at lowest point**, so that particle complete the circle. $\mathbf{v_{min}} = \sqrt{5gR}$, at this velocity, tension in the string is ***6mg***.

(iii) **When string is horizontal**, then minimum velocity is $\sqrt{3Rg}$ and tension in this condition in string is ***3mg***.

Power

Rate of doing work or the rate of using energy

$$P = \frac{\text{Work}}{\text{Time}} = \frac{\text{Energy}}{\text{Time}}$$

- Power is a scalar quantity.
- The SI unit of power is watt (W).
- 1 horse power = 746 W
- Power dimensions = $[M^1L^2T^{-3}]$

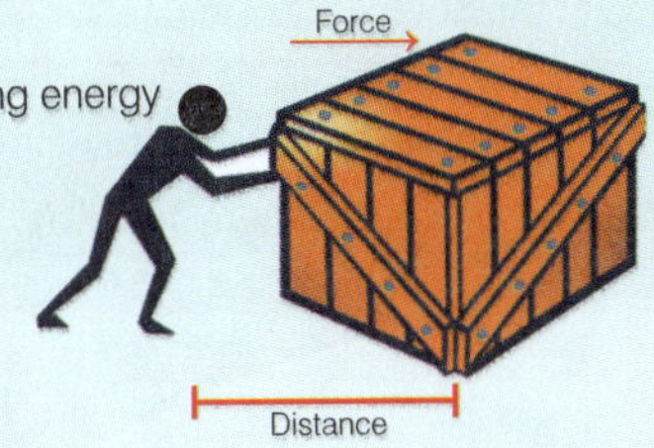

01 Average Power

$$P_{av} = \frac{\Delta W}{\Delta t}$$

$$P_{av} = \frac{W_2 - W_1}{t_2 - t_1} = \frac{\Delta W}{\Delta t}$$

02 Instantaneous Power

$$P_{ins} = \frac{dW}{dt} = \frac{\mathbf{F}.d\mathbf{r}}{dt}$$

$$= \mathbf{F}.\mathbf{v} = Fv\cos\theta$$

$$\Rightarrow P_{ins} = \frac{dw}{dt} = \tan\theta$$

Head-On Elastic Collision

Before collision

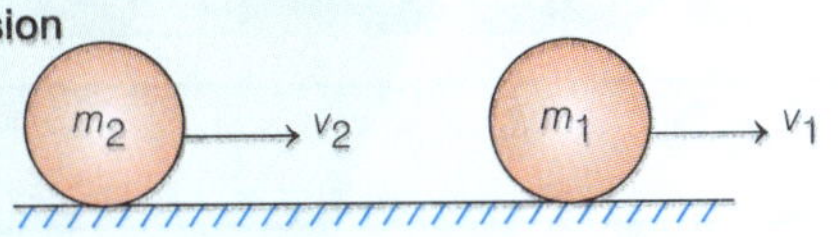

$$v_1' = \left(\frac{m_1 - m_2}{m_1 + m_2}\right)v_1 + \left(\frac{2m_2}{m_1 + m_2}\right)v_2$$

After collision

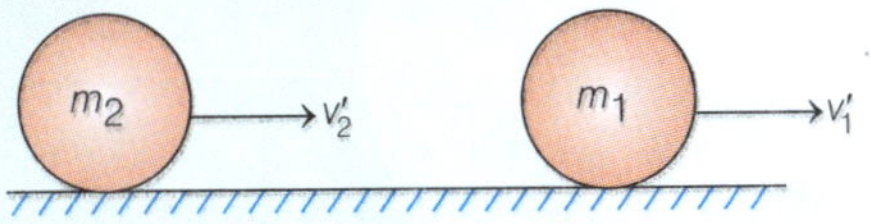

$$v_2' = \left(\frac{m_2 - m_1}{m_1 + m_2}\right)v_2 + \left(\frac{2m_1}{m_1 + m_2}\right)v_1$$

Head-On Inelastic Collision

$$m_1v_1 + m_2v_2 = m_1v_1' + m_2v_2'$$

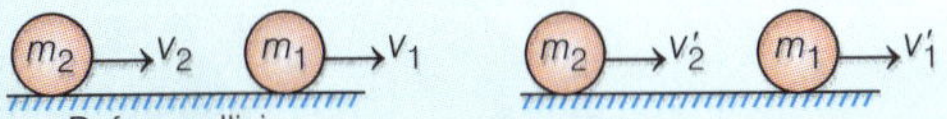

Before collision	After collision

Perfectly Inelastic Collision

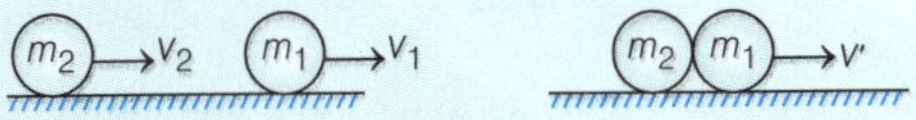

Before collision	After collision

$$m_1v_1 + m_2v_2 = (m_1 + m_2)\,v'$$

$$v' = \frac{m_1v_1 + m_2v_2}{m_1 + m_2}$$

Loss in kinetic energy in inelastic collision

$$\Delta K = \frac{m_1m_2}{2(m_1 + m_2)}(1 - e^2)\,(v_1 - v_2)^2$$

Loss in kinetic energy in perfectly inelastic collision

$$\Delta K = \frac{m_1m_2}{2(m_1 + m_2)}\,(v_1 - v_2)^2$$

Collision

- When two colliding bodies exert strong force on each other for a very short interval of time.
- Actual physical contact is not necessary for a collision.

Elastic Collision

- Linear momentum is conserved before and after the collision.
- Kinetic energy is conserved before and after the collision.

Inelastic Collision

- Linear momentum is conserved before and after the collision.
- Kinetic energy is not conserved before and after the collision.

Perfectly inelastic collision

- If colliding particles stick to each other and move with common velocity.

Oblique Collision

- Velocity vectors are not directed along the line of impact.

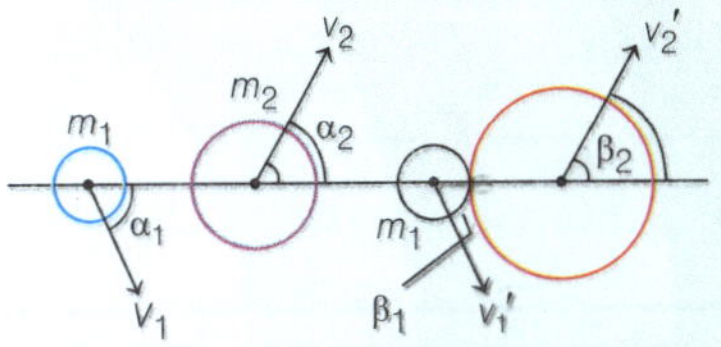

- $m_1v_1\cos\alpha_1 + m_2v_2\cos\alpha_2 = m_1v_1'\cos\beta_1 + m_2v_2'\cos\beta_2$
- $m_2v_2\sin\alpha_2 + m_1v_1\sin\alpha_1 = m_2v_2'\sin\beta_2 + m_1v_1'\sin\beta_1$

Head-On Collision

- Velocity vectors are directed along the line of impact.

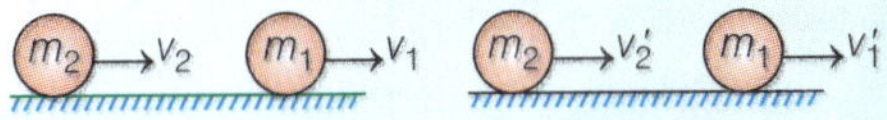

Before collision	After collision

Coefficient of Restitution

$$e = \frac{v_2 - v_1}{u_1 - u_2}$$

e = 1 (elastic collision)
e = 1 (perfectly inelastic collision)
0 < e < 1 (inelastic collision)

Velocities after Collision in Terms of Coefficient of Restitution (e) for Inelastic Collision

$$v_1' = \left[\frac{m_1 - em_2}{m_1 + m_2}\right]v_1 + \left[\frac{(1 + e)\,m_2}{m_1 + m_2}\right]v_2$$

$$v_2' = \left[\frac{m_2 - em_1}{m_1 + m_2}\right]v_2 + \left[\frac{(1 + e)\,m_1}{m_1 + m_2}\right]v_1$$

Chapter **06**

Rotational Motion

Centre of Mass

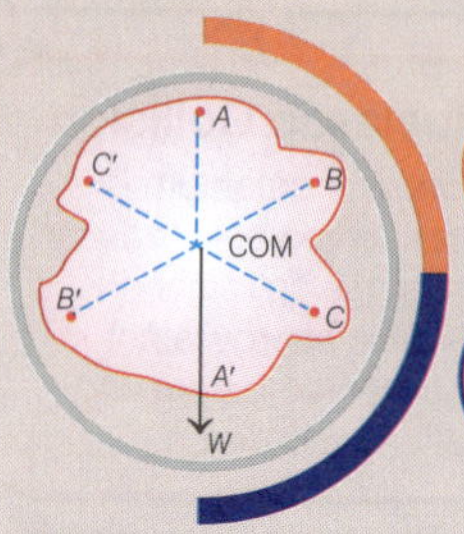

- A point where the whole mass of the body is supposed to be concentrated for describing its translatory motion.
- It represents the average position of all the mass in the system.

Centre of Mass of Two Particles System

- Position of centre of mass of two particles system

$$r_{CM} = \frac{M_1 r_1 + M_2 r_2}{M_1 + M_2}$$

- It is closer to the particle with the larger mass.
- If $M_1 = M_2$ the centre of mass lies exactly mid-way between them.

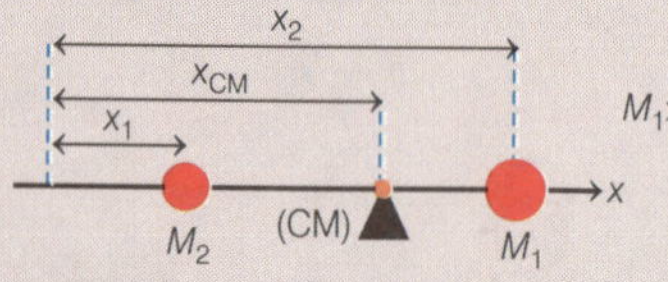

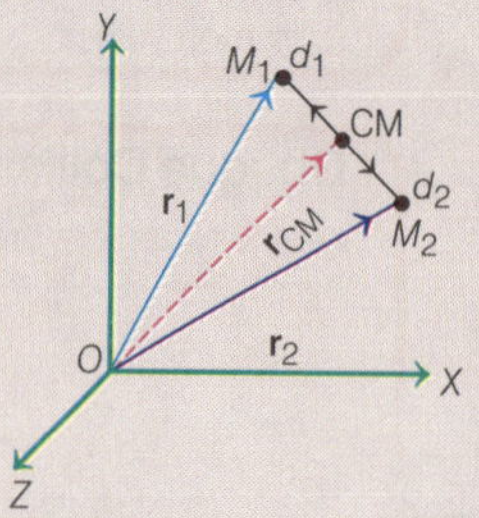

Centre of Mass of *n*-Particles System

$$\mathbf{r}_{CM} = \frac{m_1\mathbf{r}_1 + m_2\mathbf{r}_2 + \dots + m_n\mathbf{r}_n}{m_1 + m_2 + \dots + m_n} = \frac{\sum_{i=1}^{n} m_i r_i}{\sum_{i=1}^{n} m_i}$$

- In cartesian coordinate

$$x_{CM} = \sum_{i=1}^{n} \frac{m_i x_i}{m_i}$$

$$y_{CM} = \sum_{i=1}^{n} \frac{m_i y_i}{m_i}$$

$$z_{CM} = \sum_{i=1}^{n} \frac{m_i z_i}{m_i}$$

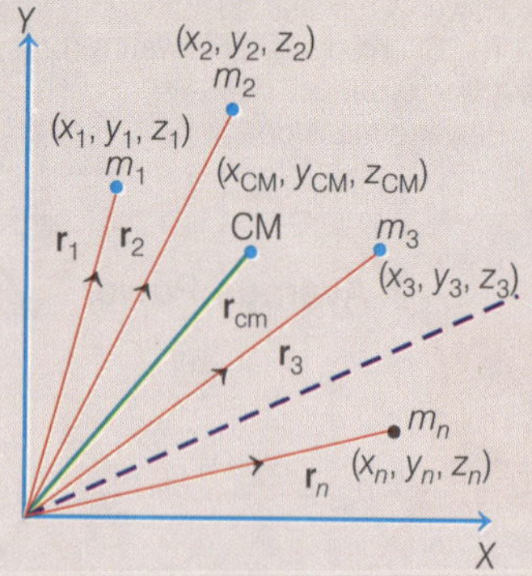

Centre of Mass in Case of a Body with Continuous Mass Distribution

- A body is said to be a rigid body when it has perfectly definite shape and volume
- A real rigid body can be treated as continuous distribution of matter.

$$r_{CM} = \frac{\int r dm}{\int dm}$$

- In cartesian coordinate

$$x_{CM} = \frac{\int x dm}{\int dm}$$

$$y_{CM} = \frac{\int y dm}{\int dm}, \quad z_{CM} = \frac{\int z dm}{\int dm}$$

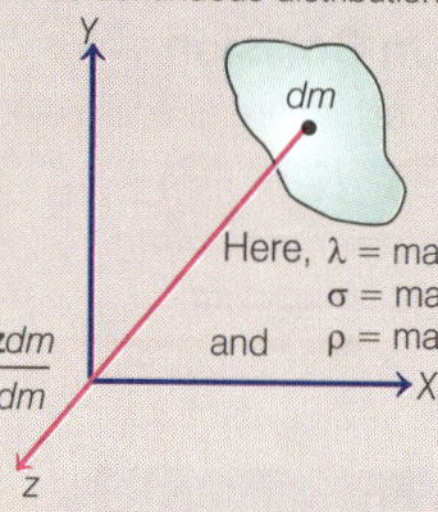

Here, λ = mass per unit length
σ = mass per unit area
and ρ = mass per unit volume

(i) Mass distributed over length $\Rightarrow dm = \lambda\, dl$
(ii) Mass distributed over area $\Rightarrow dm = \sigma\, dA$
(iii) Mass distributed over volume $\Rightarrow dm = \rho dV$

Centre of Mass of Some Regular Bodies

Regular Body	Geometrical Shape	Position of centre of mass
• Rod	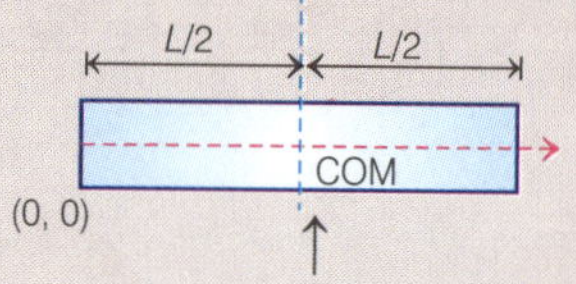	$\left(\frac{L}{2}, 0\right)$
• Plane Square Lamina	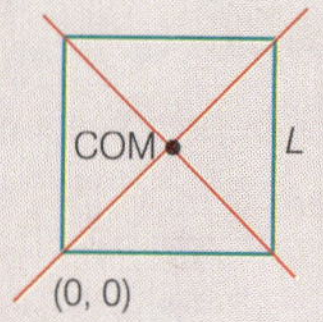	$\left(\frac{L}{2}, \frac{L}{2}\right)$
• Uniform Sphere, Ring	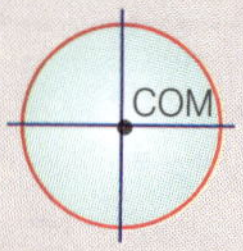	(0, 0)
• Semicircular Ring	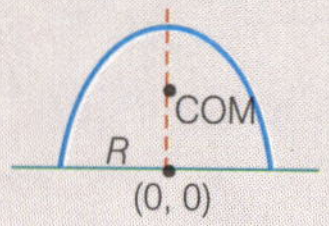	$\left(0, \frac{2R}{\pi}\right)$
• Hemispherical Shell	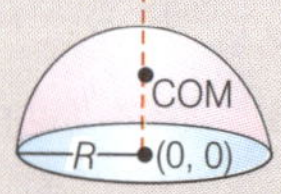	$\left(0, \frac{R}{2}\right)$
• Solid Circular Cone	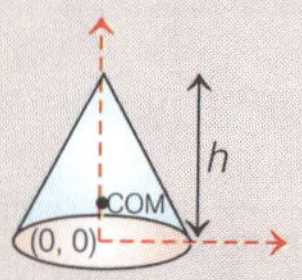	$\left(0, \frac{h}{4}\right)$
• Solid Hemisphere	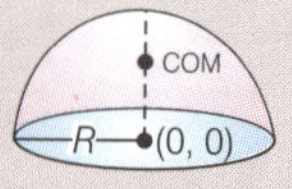	$\left(0, \frac{3R}{8}\right)$

Linear Momentum of Particles

- The total momentum of a system of particles is equal to the product of the total mass of the system and velocity of its centre of mass.

$$\mathbf{p} = m_1\mathbf{v}_1 + m_2\mathbf{v}_2 + \dots + m_n\mathbf{v}_n$$

$$\mathbf{p} = \mathbf{p}_1 + \mathbf{p}_2 + \dots + \mathbf{p}_n$$

$$\mathbf{p} = M\mathbf{v}_{CM}$$

Conservation of Linear Momentum

- If net external force on the system is zero, then the total linear momentum of the system is constant. Hence, centre of mass will move with constant velocity.

$$\mathbf{p}_{\text{inital}} = \mathbf{p}_{\text{final}},$$

$$v_{CM} = \text{constant}$$

Torque

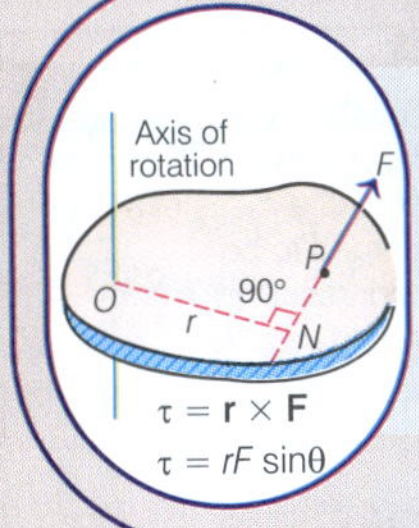

$\tau = \mathbf{r} \times \mathbf{F}$

$\tau = rF \sin\theta$

- It is the turning effect of the force about the axis of rotation.
- Measured as the product of the force and the perpendicular distance between the line of action of the force and the axis of rotation.
- SI unit is newton-metre (N-m).
- Positive when anti-clockwise, negative when clockwise.

Work done by Torque

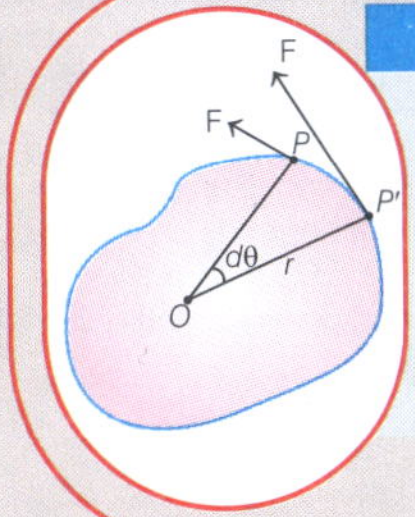

- Work done = Torque × Angular displacement $= \tau d\theta$
- Power associated with the work done by the torque on rotating body,
  $\frac{dW}{dt} = \tau \frac{d\theta}{dt} = \tau\omega$
- $\tau\omega$ is also called instantaneous rotational power.

Principle of Moment

- In rotational equilibrium, the sum of the clockwise moments about any point is equal to the sum of anti-clockwise moments about that point.

$F_1 \times d_1 = F_2 \times d_2$

Load × Load arm = Effort × Effort arm

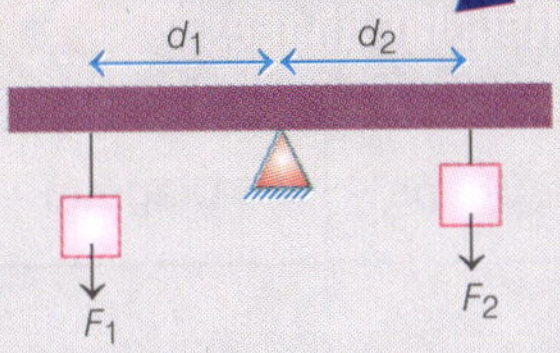

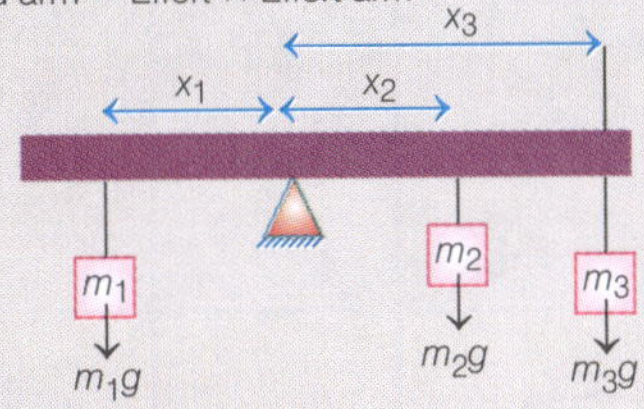

$m_1gx_1 = m_2gx_2 + m_3gx_3$

Angular Momentum

- Measure of rotational motion of an object around a point or axis.
- It represents the rotational equivalent of linear momentum.
- $\mathbf{L} = \mathbf{r} \times \mathbf{p} \Rightarrow L = mvr\sin\theta$
- In rectangular component,
  $L_x = m(y v_z - z v_y)$, $L_y = m(zv_x - x v_z)$,
  $L_z = m(x v_y - y v_x)$

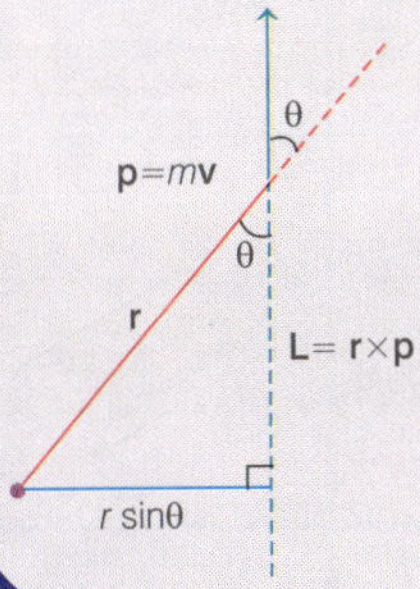

Angular Momentum for a Rigid Body

- $L = I\omega$
- Rate of change of angular momentum is equal to the torque due to an external force. $\frac{dL}{dt} = \tau_{ext}$
- Angular impulse $= \int \tau dt = \int d\mathbf{L} = L_f - L_i$
- $\mathbf{L} = 2m\frac{\Delta \mathbf{A}}{\Delta t}$

Conservation of Angular Momentum

- If no external torques act on a system, the angular momentum of the rigid body is conserved.

i.e $\Delta L = 0$

Rigid Body

- A system of particles in which distance between any two particle does not change.

Equilibrium of Rigid Bodies

- When both the linear and angular momenta of the rigid body remains constant with time.

Translational Equilibrium

- Sum of all forces acting must be zero.
  $\Sigma F = 0$
- Ensures no linear acceleration.

Rotational Equilibrium

- Sum of all torques about any axis must be zero. $\Sigma\tau = 0$
- Ensures no angular acceleration.

Rigid body rotation

- Angular velocity, $\omega = d\theta/dt$
- Angular acceleration, $\alpha = d\omega/dt$
- Euations of rotational motion
  (i) $\theta = \omega_0 t + \frac{1}{2}\alpha t^2$
  (ii) $\omega = \omega_0 + \alpha t$
  (iii) $\omega^2 = \omega_0^2 + 2\alpha\theta$
- Torque, $\tau = I\alpha$
- Angular momentum, $L = I\omega$

Rotational Kinetic Energy of Particles

- Energy due to rotational motion of a body,
  $KE_{rot} = \frac{1}{2}I\omega^2$
- Rotational Work : $W_r = \tau\theta$ (If torque is constant)
- $W_r = \int_{\theta_1}^{\theta_2} \tau d\theta$ (if torque is variable)
- Work done by torque $= \frac{1}{2}I(\omega_2^2 - \omega_1^2)$
- Instantaneous power, $P = \tau\omega$, Average power, $P_{av} = \frac{\Delta W}{\Delta t}$

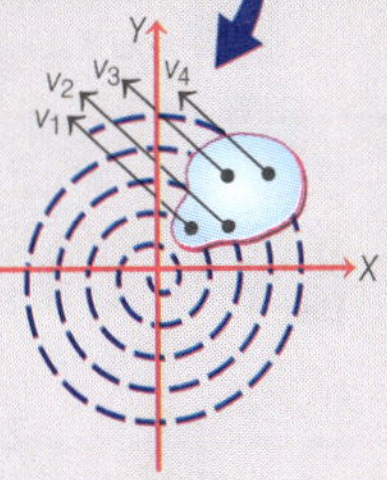

Rotation of a rigid body

POWER TIPS

Rolling Motion

- Body performing translatory motion as well as rotational motion

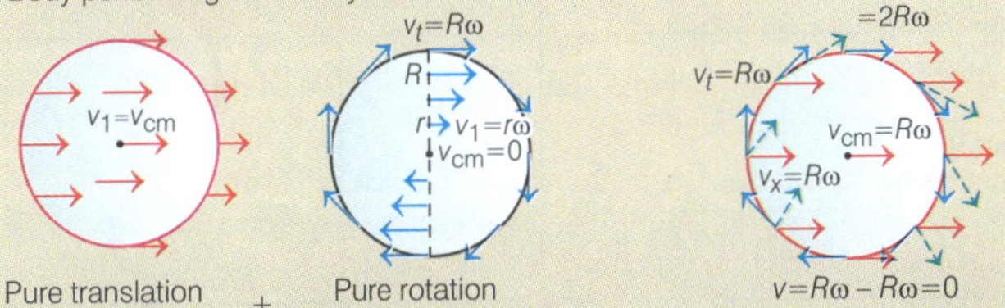

Pure translation without rotation + Pure rotation without translation = Combined translation plus rotation

$v = R\omega - R\omega = 0$

Pure rolling without slipping condition;

- Kinetic energy of a rolling body $= \frac{1}{2}I\omega^2 + \frac{1}{2}mv_{CM}^2$
- Angular momentum, $L = I_{CM}\omega + mvR$

$E_{trans} : E_{rot} : E_{total} = 1 : \frac{K^2}{R^2} : 1 + \frac{K^2}{R^2}$

Moment of Inertia

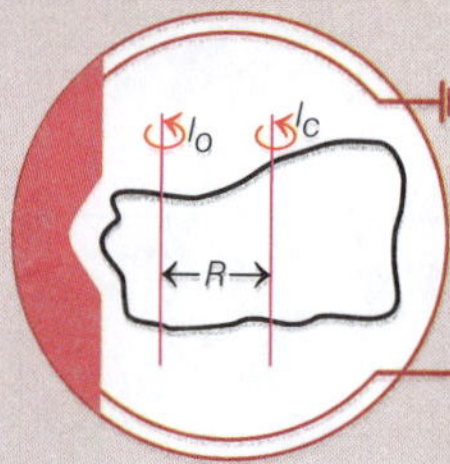

Theorem of Parallel Axis

- $I_{parallel} = I_{CM} + MR^2$
- Applicable for any type of rigid body (two dimensional or three dimensional)

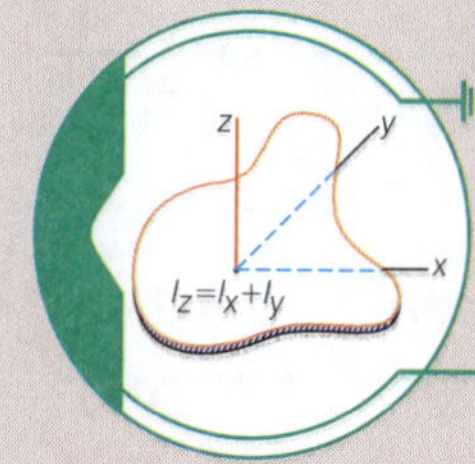

Theorem of Perpendicular Axis

- For any plane object $I_Z = I_X + I_Y$
- X and Y axes must lie in the plane of the body and Z-axis must be perpendicular to this plane.

- Property of a rotating body due to which it opposes any change in its state of uniform rotation.
- For a point mass, $I = mR^2$

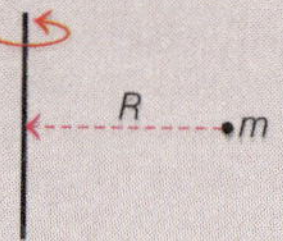

- For two point masses,

$$I_{CM} = m_1R_1^2 + m_2R_2^2$$

$$R_1 = \frac{m_2R}{m_1 + m_2}, R_2 = \frac{m_1R}{m_1+m_2}$$

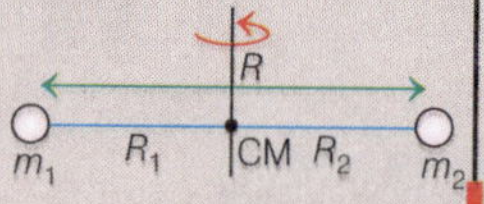

- For continuous mass distribution in rigid body, $I = \int R^2 dm$

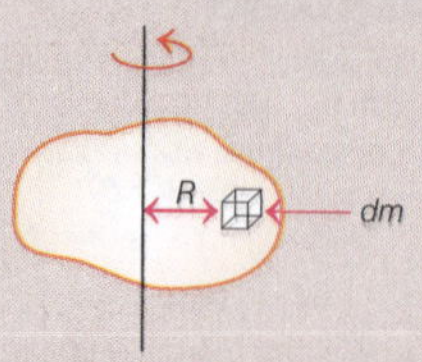

Radius of Gyration

- Distance from the axis of rotation at which the entire mass of a body can be assumed to be concentrated, resulting in same moment of inertia.

$$K = \sqrt{\frac{I}{M}} \Rightarrow I = MK^2$$

- Root mean square value of distance of all particles about the axis of rotation.

$$K = \sqrt{\frac{R_1^2 + R_2^2 + R_3^2 + ... + R_n^2}{n}}$$

- Radius of Gyration is a scalar quantity and it depends on
(i) shape and size of the body
(ii) position and configuration of the axis of rotation.

Factors Affecting Moment of Inertia

(i) Mass of body
(ii) Size and shape of body
(iii) Distribution of mass about the axis of rotation
(iv) Position and orientation of the axis of rotation w.r.t. the body.

Moment of Inertia of Regular Shapes

Shape	Diagram	Axis of Rotation	I, K
Thin Ring	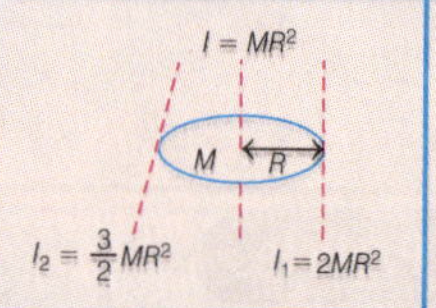	Through centre, perpendicular to plane	$I = MR^2$ Radius of Gyration $K = R$
Solid Disc	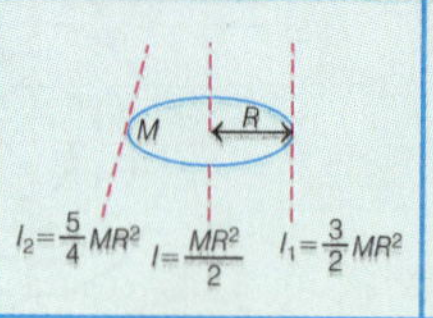	Through centre, perpendicular to surface	$I = \frac{1}{2}MR^2$ Radius of Gyration $K = \frac{R}{\sqrt{2}}$
Solid Sphere	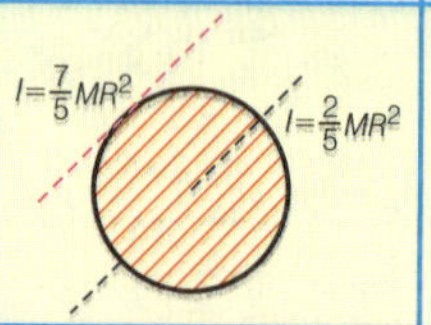	Through centre	$I = \frac{2}{5}MR^2$ Radius of Gyration $K = \sqrt{\frac{2}{5}}R$
Thin Rod (about centre)	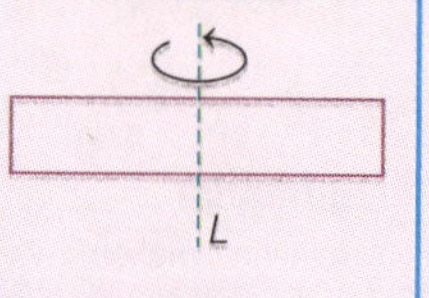	Through centre, perpendicular to length	$I = \frac{1}{12}ML^2$ Radius of Gyration $K = \frac{L}{\sqrt{12}}$
Thin Rod (about end)	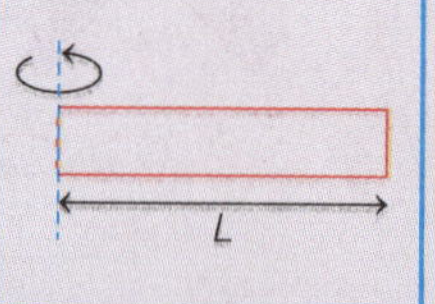	About one end, perpendicular to length	$I = \frac{1}{3}ML^2$ Radius of Gyration $K = \frac{L}{\sqrt{3}}$
Rectangular Plate	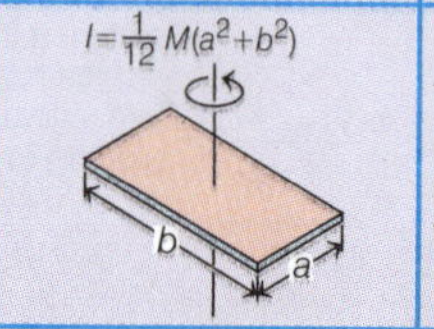	Through centre, perpendicular to plane	$I = \frac{1}{12}M(a^2 + b^2)$ Radius of Gyration $K = \sqrt{\frac{a^2 + b^2}{12}}$

Shape	Diagram	Axis of Rotation	I, K
Hollow Cylinder	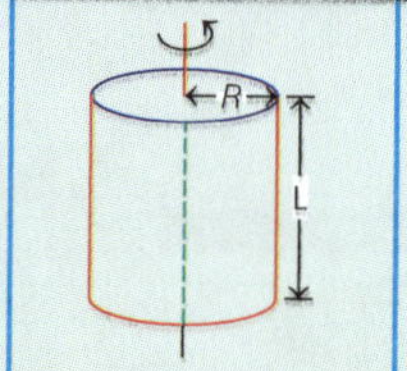	Through centre, along central axis	$I = MR^2$ $(R_{outer}^2 + R_{max})$ Radius of Gyration $K=R$
Solid Cylinder	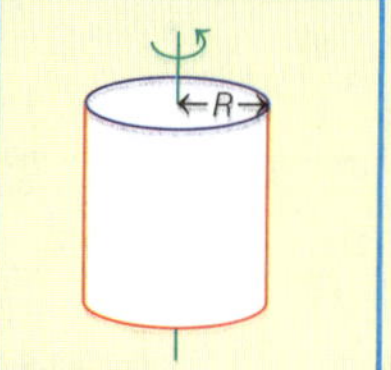	Through centre, along central axis	$I = \frac{1}{2}MR^2$ Radius of Gyration $K = \frac{R}{\sqrt{2}}$
Rectangular Plate (about edge)	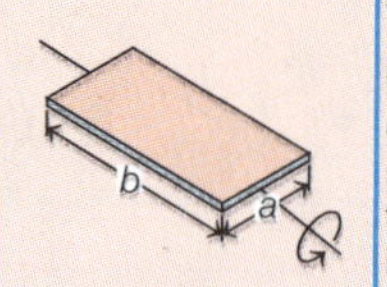	About an axis passing through centre of mass and perpendicular to side a in its plane	$I = \frac{Ma^2}{12}$ Radius of Gyration $K = \frac{a}{2\sqrt{3}}$
Hollow Sphere	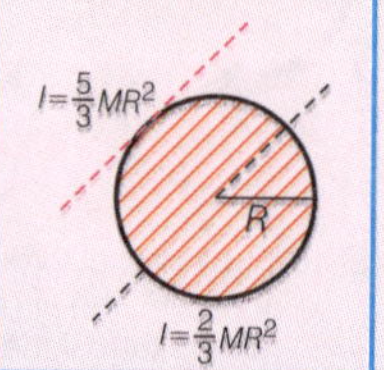	Through centre	$I = \frac{2}{3}MR^2$ Radius of Gyration $K = \sqrt{\frac{2}{3}}R$
Solid Cone	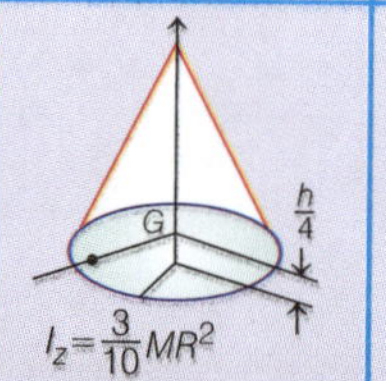	Along vertical axis through centre	$I = \frac{3}{10}MR^2$ Radius of Gyration $K = \sqrt{\frac{3}{10}}R$

Chapter **07**

Gravitation

Universal Law of Gravitation

Gravitational force of attraction between any two bodies is directly proportional to the product of their masses and inversely proportional to square of the distance between them.

$$F_g = G\frac{M_1 M_2}{d^2}$$

G = Universal gravitational constant
Value of $G = 6.67 \times 10^{-11}\ \text{N-m}^2/\text{kg}^2$
Dimensions of $[G] = [M^{-1}L^3T^{-2}]$

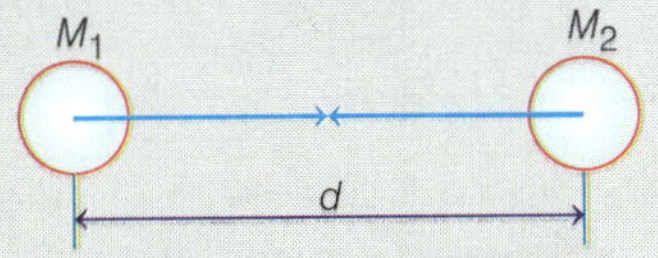

Vector Form of Gravitation Law

$$\mathbf{F}_{21} = -\frac{GM_1M_2\mathbf{r}_{21}}{|\mathbf{r}_{21}|^2}$$

$$\mathbf{F}_{12} = \frac{GM_1M_2\mathbf{r}_{12}}{|\mathbf{r}_{12}|^2}$$

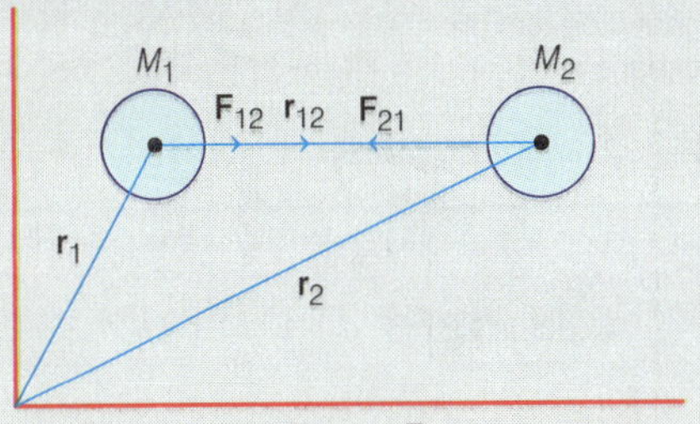

$$\mathbf{F}_{21} = -\mathbf{F}_{12}$$

Acceleration due to Gravity (g)

Acceleration of an object during its free fall towards earth.

$$g = \frac{GM}{R^2}$$

$M = 6 \times 10^{24}$ kg (Mass of the earth)
$R = 6.4 \times 10^6$ m (Radius of the earth)

$g \propto \rho R_e$, ρ = density of the earth
R_e = radius of the earth

POWER TIPS

Important Points about Gravitational Force

- Always attractive in nature.
- Independent of the nature of the medium.
- Conservative force.
- Independent of presence of other bodies.
- Follow Newton's third law.

Variation of g with Altitude

$$g' = g\left(1 - \frac{2h}{R}\right)\ h << R$$

$$\text{Percentage decrease} = \frac{\Delta g}{g} \times 100 = \frac{g - g'}{g} \times 100 = \frac{2h}{R} \times 100$$

- Value of g decreases, if we move above the surface of the earth.

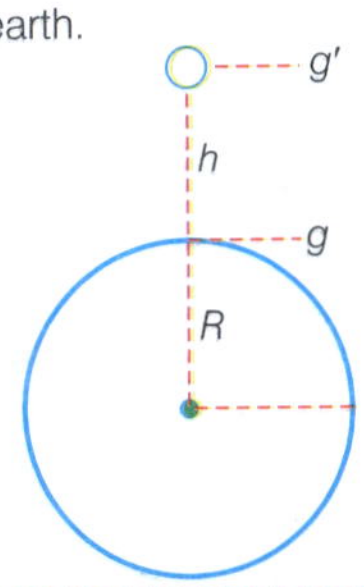

Variation of g with Depth

$$g' = g\left(1 - \frac{d}{R}\right)$$

$$\text{Percentage decrease} = \frac{\Delta g}{g} \times 100 = \frac{g - g'}{g} \times 100 = \frac{d}{R} \times 100$$

- At the centre of the earth, $d = R$ and hence $g' = 0$.
- Value of g decreases, if we move below the surface of the earth.

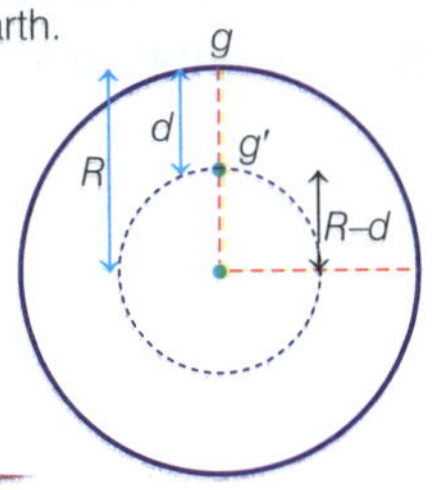

Variation of g with Shape of the Earth

- g is minimum → at equator
- g is maximum → at poles
- The weight of the body increases when it is taken from the equator to the pole.

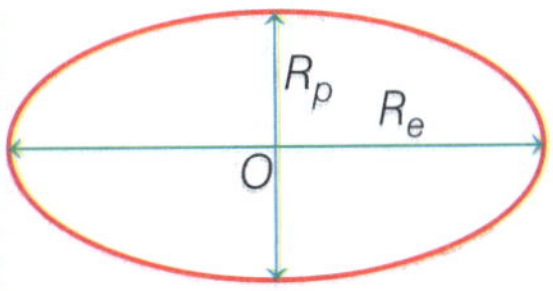

$R_e > R_p$
$g_p > g_e$

Variation of g due to Rotation of the Earth

- Due to rotation of the earth, the value of g decreases
$g' = g - R\omega^2\cos^2\lambda$
- At the equator,
$\lambda = 0° \rightarrow g' = g - R\omega^2$
- At the poles,
$\lambda = 90° \rightarrow g' = g$

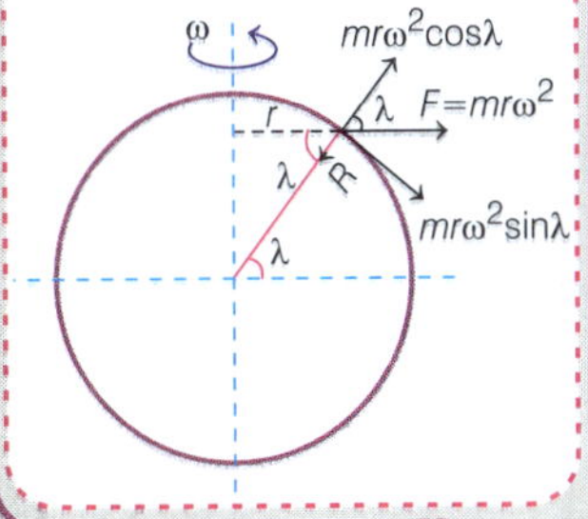

Graphical Representation of Variation of g due to Depth and Altitude from the Earth's Surface.

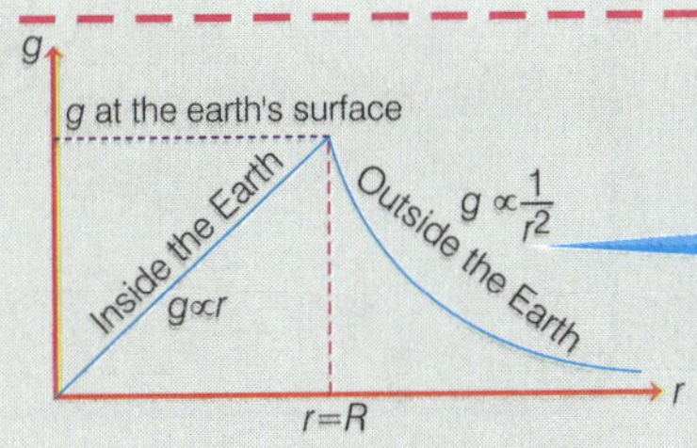

Relation between height h and depth d for the same change in g

$$g_h = g\left(1 - \frac{2h}{R}\right),\ g_d = g\left(1 - \frac{d}{R}\right)$$

$h << R$

$g_h = g_d \Rightarrow d = 2h$

Gravitational Field and Intensity

Gravitational Field

The space surrounding a material body within which its gravitational force of attraction can be experienced.

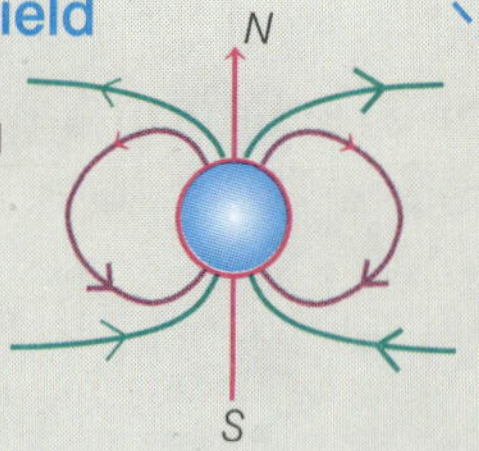

Gravitational Field Intensity (I)

$I = \frac{F}{m}$

- Vector quantity
- Direction same as gravitational force
- SI unit - N/kg.

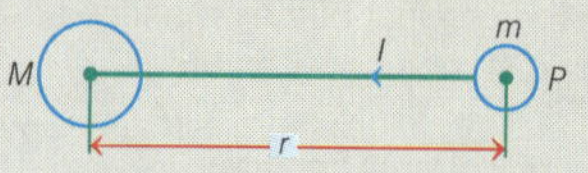

$\mathbf{I} = \frac{GM}{r^3}\mathbf{r}$

Magnitude, $I = \frac{GM}{r^2}$

Gravitational Field Intensity due to Uniform Solid Sphere

Case 1 $r > R$: $\mathbf{I}_{outside} = \frac{GM}{r^2}(-\hat{\mathbf{r}})$

Case 2 $r = R$: $\mathbf{I}_{surface} = \frac{GM}{R^2}(-\hat{\mathbf{r}})$

Case 3 $r < R$: $\mathbf{I}_{inside} = \frac{GMr}{R^3}(-\hat{\mathbf{r}})$

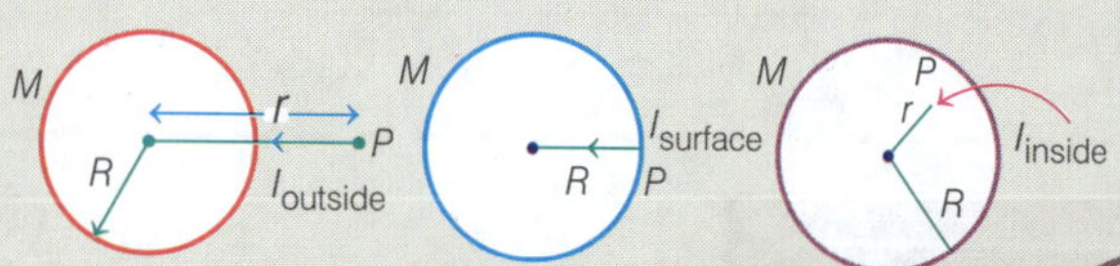

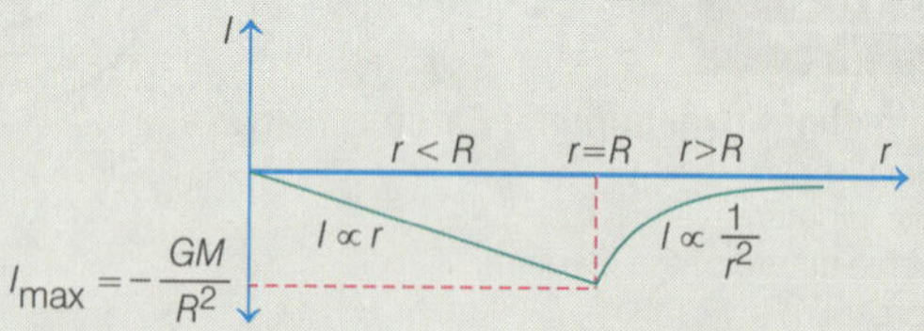

Gravitational Field Intensity due to a Spherical Shell

Case 1 $r > R$: $\mathbf{I}_{outside} = \frac{GM}{r^2}(-\hat{\mathbf{r}})$

Case 2 $r = R$: $\mathbf{I}_{surface} = \frac{GM}{R^2}(-\hat{\mathbf{r}})$

Case 3 $r < R$: $\mathbf{I}_{inside} = 0$

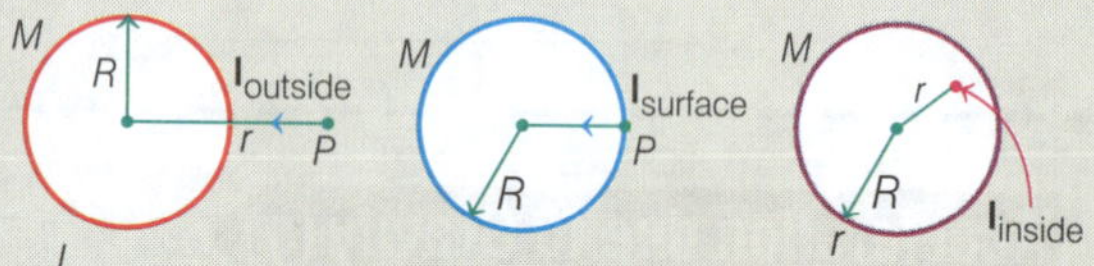

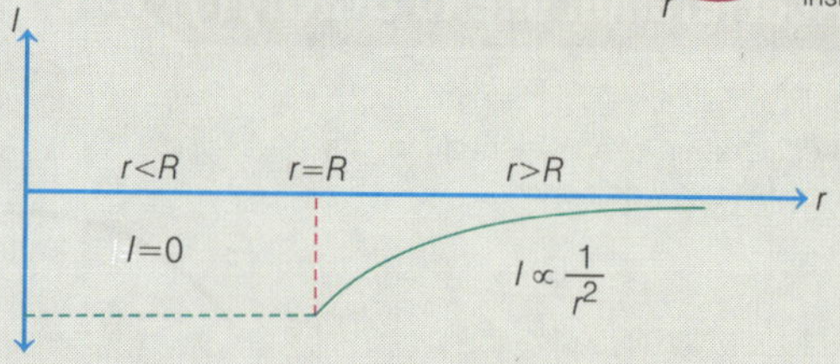

Gravitational Potential

- Work done in bringing unit mass from reference point (infinity) to a given point.

$V = \frac{W_{net}}{m}$

- SI unit is J/kg

Gravitational Potential for point mass

$V_p = -\frac{GM}{r}$

at $r = \infty$, $V_p = 0$ (maximum)

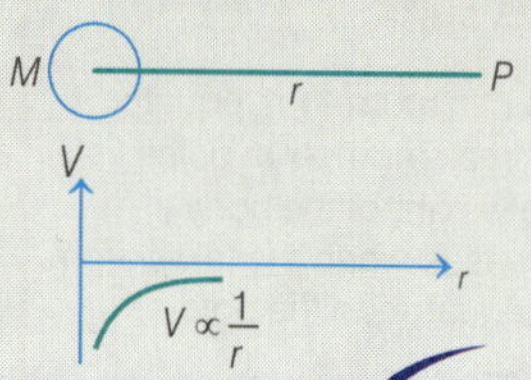

Relation between Gravitational Field and Potential

$I = -\frac{dV}{dr}$, $\Delta V = -\int I dr$, $I = -\left(\frac{\partial V}{\partial x}\hat{\mathbf{i}} + \frac{\partial V}{\partial y}\hat{\mathbf{j}} + \frac{\partial V}{\partial z}\hat{\mathbf{k}}\right)$

Gravitational Potential Energy (U)

U = Gravitational potential × Mass $= -\frac{GMm}{r}$

The amount of work done in bringing a body from infinity to a given point in the gravitational field of other.

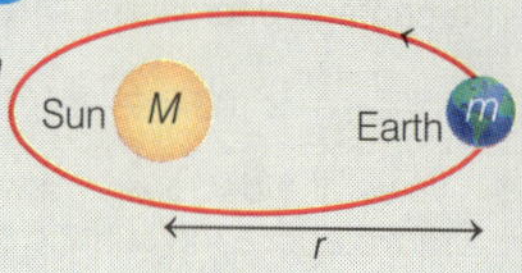

Gravitational Potential due to Solid Sphere

Case 1 $r > R$: $V_{outside} = -\frac{GM}{r}$

Case 2 $r = R$: $V_{surface} = -\frac{GM}{R}$

Case 3 $r < R$: $V_{inside} = -\frac{GM}{2R^3}(3R^2 - r^2)$

$V_{centre} = -\frac{3}{2}\frac{GM}{R} = \frac{3}{2}V_{surface}$

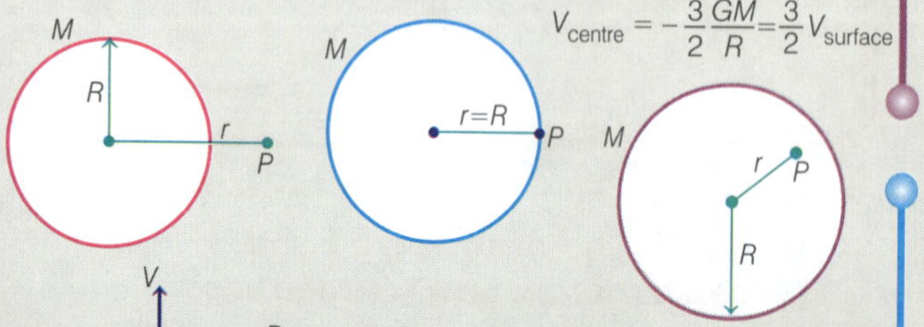

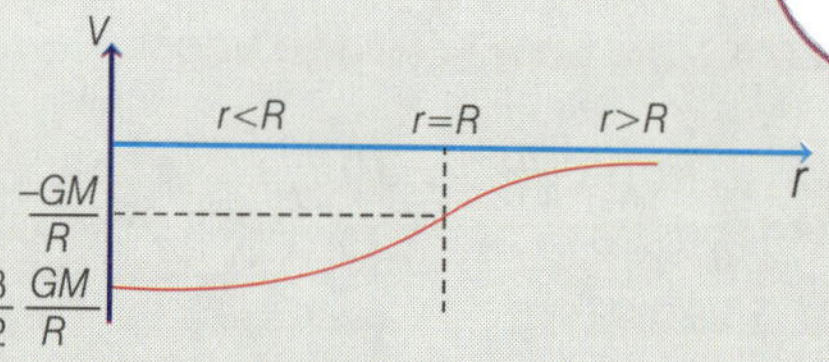

Gravitational Potential due to Hollow Sphere

Case 1 $r > R$: $V_{outside} = -\frac{GM}{r}$

Case 2 $r = R$: $V_{surface} = -\frac{GM}{R}$

Case 3 $r < R$: $V_{inside} = V_{surface} = -\frac{GM}{R}$

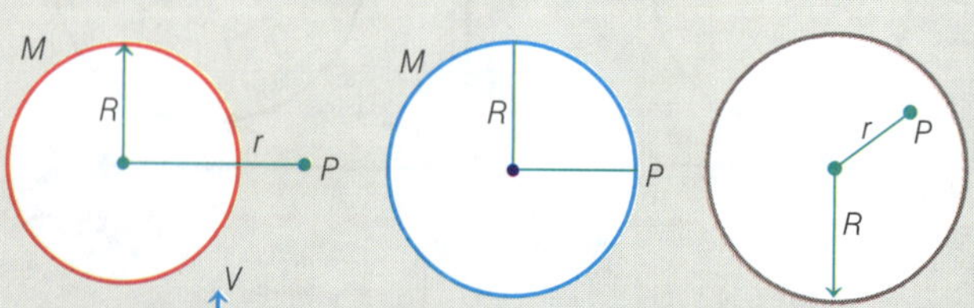

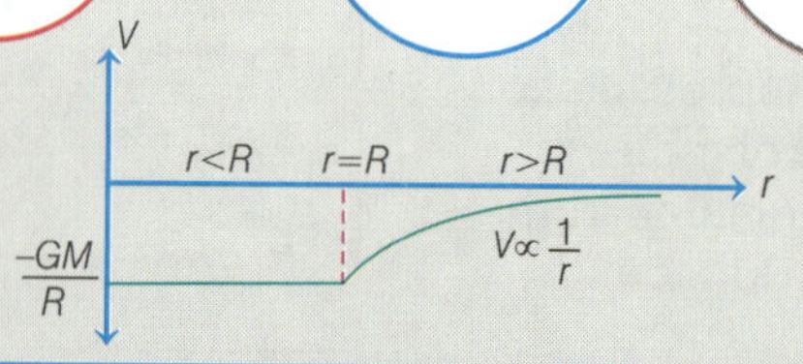

Kepler's Law

01 Law of Orbits

- Every planet revolves in an elliptical orbit, with the sun at one of the two foci of the ellipse.
- The point at which the planet is closer to the sun is known as **perihelion** and the point at which the planet is farthest from the sun is known as **aphelion**.

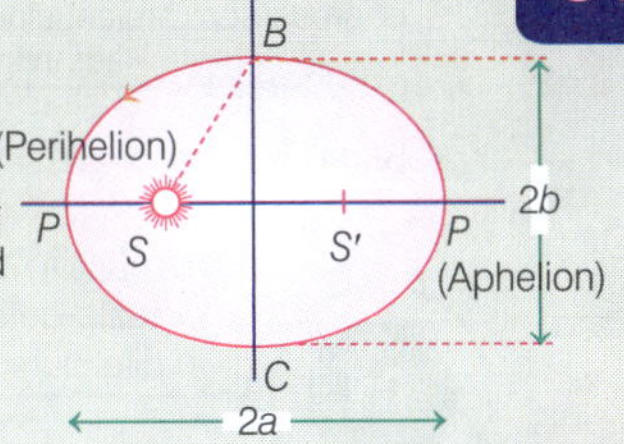

02 Law of Areas

- The line segment joining a planet and sun sweeps out equal areas in equal interval of time.

$$\frac{dA}{dt} = \text{constant}$$

- Planets move faster when closer to the sun (perihelion) and slower when farther from the sun (aphelion).

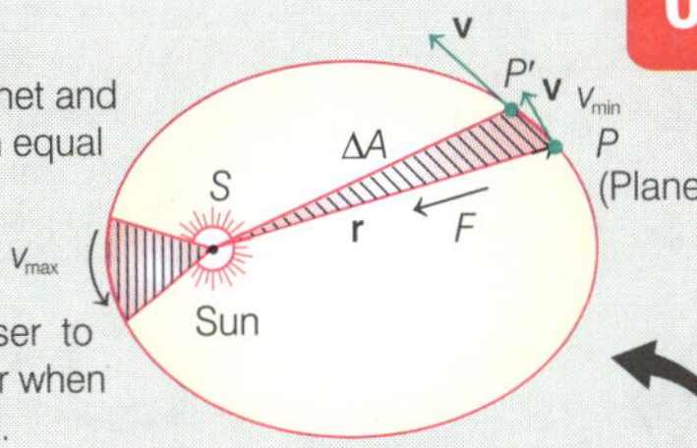

03 Law of Periods

- The square of the orbital period T of a planet is directly proportional to the cube of the semi-major axis of its orbit. $T^2 \propto r^3$
- Planet farther from the sun takes longer to complete an orbit.

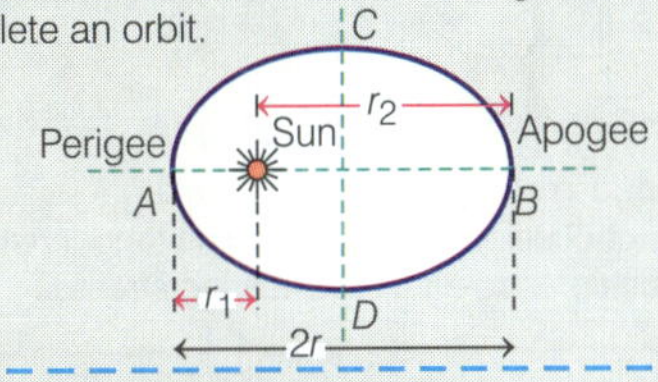

Satellites

- It revolves around planet.
- **Two types of satellites**
  - **(i) Natural Satellite**
    e.g. Moon, Phobos
  - **(ii) Artificial Satellite**
    e.g. INSAT, IRS, SPUTNIK-1

Time period

- Time taken by a satellite to complete one revolution around the planet.

$$T = \frac{2\pi r}{v_0} \qquad v_0 = \text{orbital speed}$$

$$T = 2\pi\sqrt{\frac{r^3}{GM}} \Rightarrow T = 2\pi\sqrt{\frac{(R_e + h)^3}{gR_e^2}}$$

If $h << R_e$

$$T_{min} = 84.6 \text{ min}$$

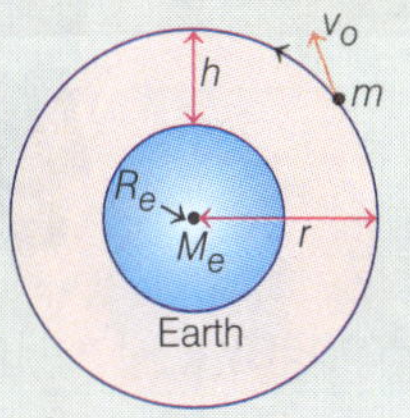

- Variation of time period with radius of orbit.

$$T^2 \propto r^3$$

- Satellite obeys Kepler's third law of planetary motion.

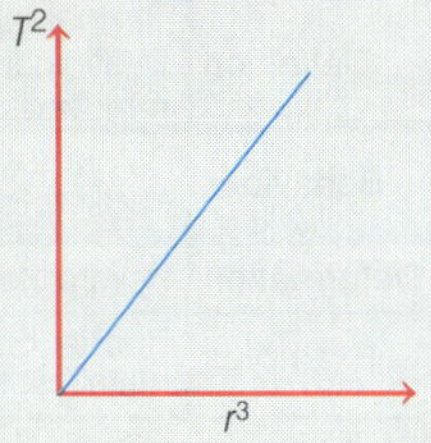

Energy

- For an orbiting satellite, potential energy $(U) = -\frac{GMm}{r}$
- For an orbiting satellite, kinetic energy $(KE) = \frac{GMm}{2r}$
- Total energy $(TE) = -\frac{GMm}{2r}$

$$|TE| = |KE| = \frac{1}{2}|U|$$

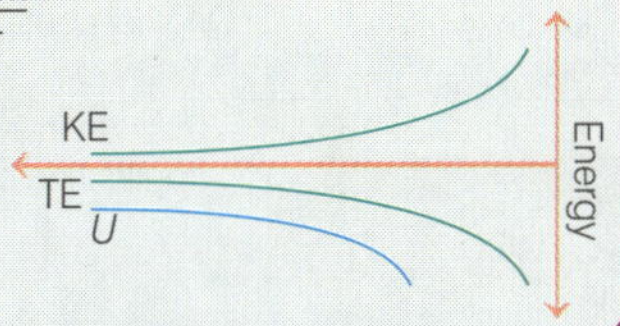

Binding Energy of Satellite (BE)

$$BE = -TE = +\frac{1}{2}\frac{GMm}{r}$$

The minimum energy required by a satellite to escape from the gravitational pull of the planet.

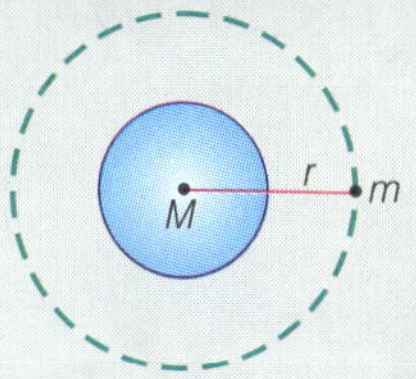

Orbital Velocity

- Minimum velocity required by a satellite to revolve around a planet.

Orbital velocity, $v_0 = \sqrt{\frac{GM}{(R + h)}}$

If $h << R_e$

$$v_o = \sqrt{\frac{GM}{R_e}} = \sqrt{gR_e}$$

- Variation of orbital speed with radius of orbit, $v_o = \sqrt{\frac{GM}{r}}$

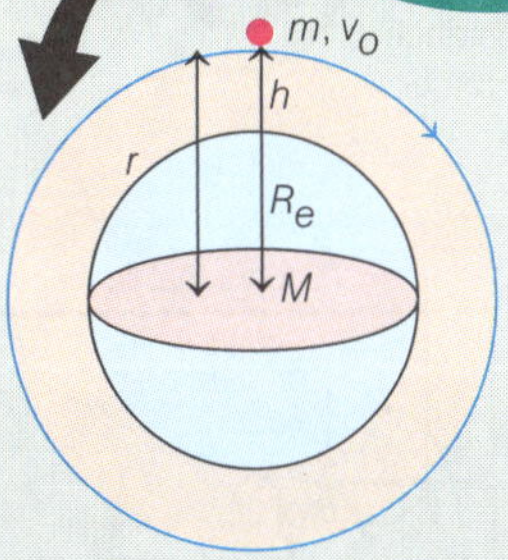

Escape Velocity

Minimum velocity required for an object to escape out from earth's gravitational field.

$$v_e = \sqrt{\frac{2GM_e}{R_e}} = \sqrt{2gR_e}$$

$$v_e = 11.2 \text{ km/s}$$

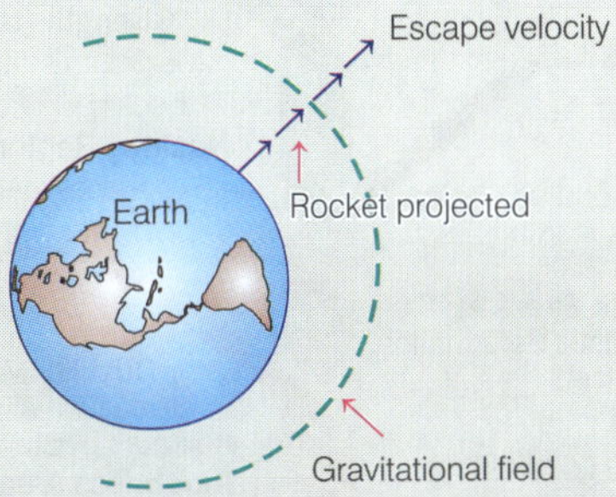

Relation between Orbital Velocity and Escape Velocity

If satellite is revolving close to the earth's surface,
then, escape velocity $= \sqrt{2}$ (orbital velocity)

$$v_e = \sqrt{2}v_o$$

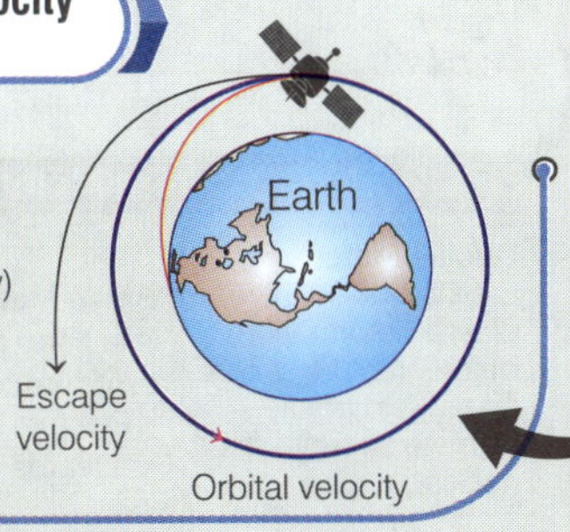

Chapter **08**

Mechanical Properties of Solids

Property	Elasticity	Plasticity
Definition	Temporary deformation; returns to original shape when stress is removed.	Permanent deformation; does not return to original shape when stress is removed.
Behaviour	Deforms under stress within the elastic limit, following Hooke's law	Deforms permanently after reaching the yield point.
Deformation	Reversible	Irreversible
Examples	Rubber bands, springs,most metals at low stress	Clay, plasticine, metals under high stress
Applications	Springs, shock absorbers, structural resilience	Metal forming, forging, plastic moulding

Stress

- Internal restoring force acting per unit area of cross-section, causing deformation.

$$\text{Stress} = \frac{\text{Restoring force}}{\text{Area}} = \frac{F_{res}}{A}$$

- SI unit is Nm^{-2} or pascal (Pa).

01 Longitudinal Stress

- Stress produced when the length of the body increases in direction of the deforming force.

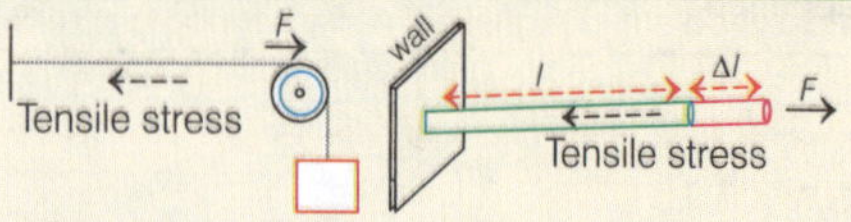

02 Compressive Stress

- Stress produced when the length of the body decreases under a deforming force.

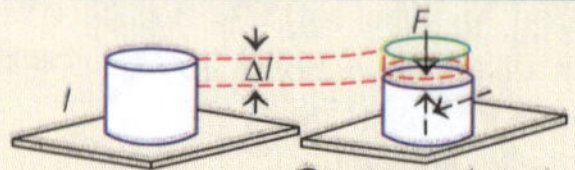

03 Volumetric Stress

- Stress that causes an object to deform in all directions when loaded uniformly in all directions.

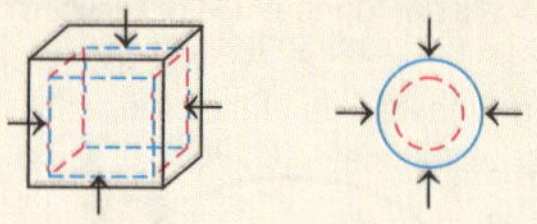

04 Shearing or Tangential Stress

- Change in shape produced by a tangential force without changing its volume. The tangential force per unit area is equal to shearing stress.

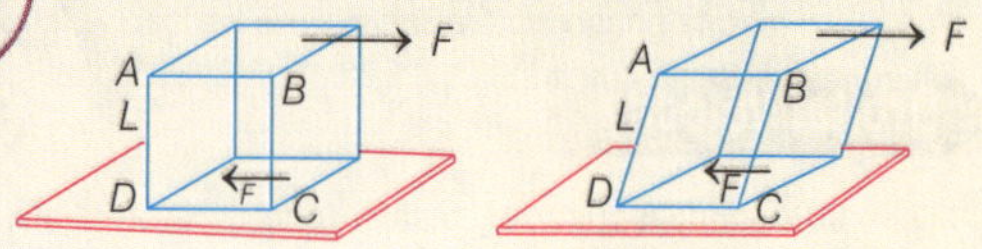

Strain

Measure of deformation, representing, the change in dimensions relative to the original size.

$$\text{Strain} = \frac{\text{Change in configuration of object}}{\text{Original configuration of object}}$$

Longitudinal Strain

Change in length per unit length of the object on the application of deforming force.

$$\text{Longitudinal strain} = \frac{\text{Change in length } (\Delta l)}{\text{Original length } (l)}$$

Volumetric Strain

Change in volume per unit volume of the object on the application of deforming force.

$$\text{Volumetric strain} = \frac{\text{Change in Volume } (\Delta V)}{\text{Original Volume } (V)}$$

Shearing or Tangential Strain

Ratio of displacement (x) of the upper surface to the distance (L) between two faces on the application of deforming force.

$$\text{Shearing strain} = \frac{\text{Displacement } (x)}{\text{Distance } (L)}$$

Stress-Strain Curve

Features

Elastic Region

- **Proportional Limit** Linear portion, obeys Hooke's Law, reversible deformation
- **Elastic Modulus (Young's Modulus)** Slope of the curve,

Yield Point/Yield Strength

- **Elastic Limit** End of elastic region, start of plastic deformation
- **Yield Strength** Stress at noticeable plastic deformation (e.g., 0.2% offset)

Fracture Point

- Final breaking point of material

Plastic Region

- **Ultimate Tensile Strength (UTS)** Maximum stress before necking.
- **Necking Region** Cross-sectional area reduces, material weakens.

Material Properties Derived from Curve

- **Ductility** Measured by elongation at fracture, indicates plastic deformability.
- **Toughness** Area under the curve, represents energy absorbed before fracture.

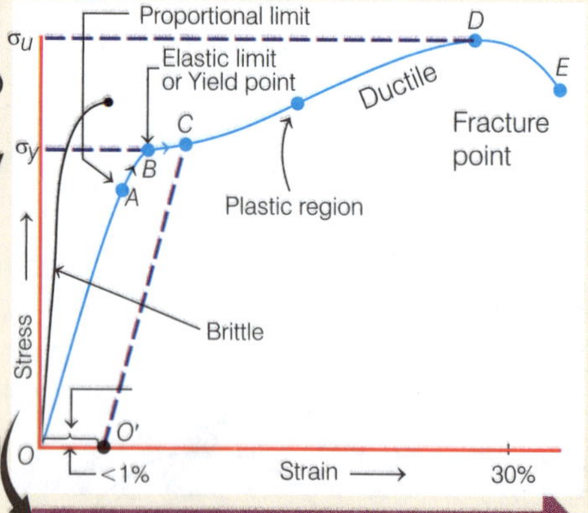

Behaviour of Different Materials

Ductile Material Exhibit significant plastic deformation before fracture, with a clean yield point, ultimate strength and necking region.

Brittle Materials Show little or no plastic deformation.

- Fracture occurs soon after the elastic limit.

Hooke's Law

Within the elastic limit, stress applied to the material is directly proportional to the resulting strain.

Stress = $k \times$ strain

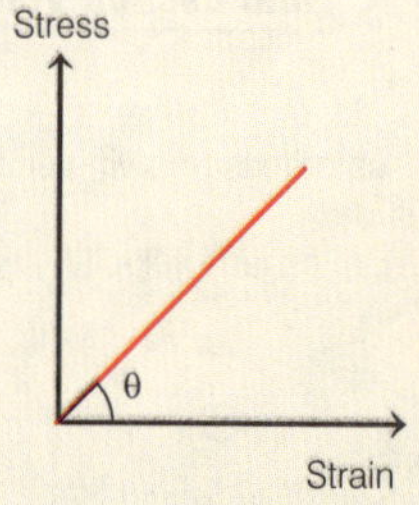

Elastic Moduli

These are the constants that quantify the stiffness of a material in response to various types of stress.

Young's Modulus

- It is the measure of material's stiffness or resistance to elastic deformation under tensile or compressive stress.
- Describes the ability of material to return its original length.

$$Y = \frac{F/A}{\Delta l/l} = \frac{Fl}{A\Delta l}$$

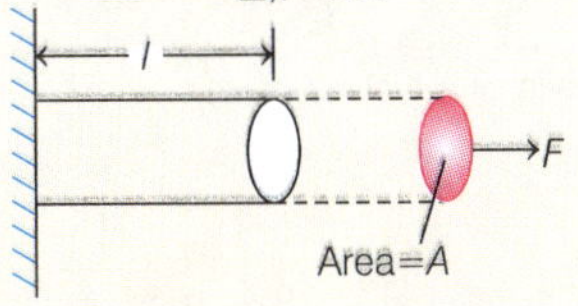

- High Young's modulus indicates a stiff material that resists deformation (e.g. steel).
- Low Young's modulus indicates flexibility in material (e.g. rubber)

Force Constant of a Wire

- Force required to produce unit elongation in a wire. $k = \frac{F}{\Delta l} = \frac{YA}{l}$
- Higher the force constant, stiffer is the wire.
- Lower the force constant, more flexible is the wire.

Bulk Modulus

- Measure of a material's resistance to Bulk compression.
- Describes how much a material compresses under applied pressure.

$$B = \frac{F/A}{-\Delta V/V} = \frac{-p}{\Delta V/V}$$

- –ve sign implies that as pressure increases, volume decreases.

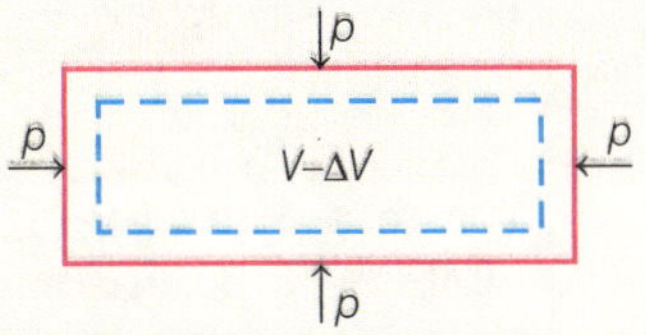

- High Bulk modulus shows the incompressibility of material or highly resistant to volume change.
- Low Bulk modulus shows the material compresses easily.

Compressibility Reciprocal of the Bulk modulus.

$$\text{Compressibility} = \frac{1}{|B|} = \frac{\Delta V}{pV} = k$$

Shear Modulus or Modulus of Rigidity

- Measures a material's resistance to deformation under shear stress.
- If quantifies how a material deforms when force acts parallel to its surface.

$$\eta = \frac{F/A}{\theta} = \frac{F}{A\theta}$$

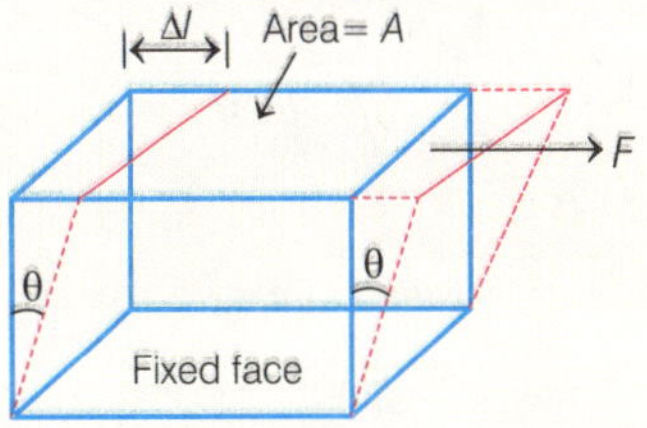

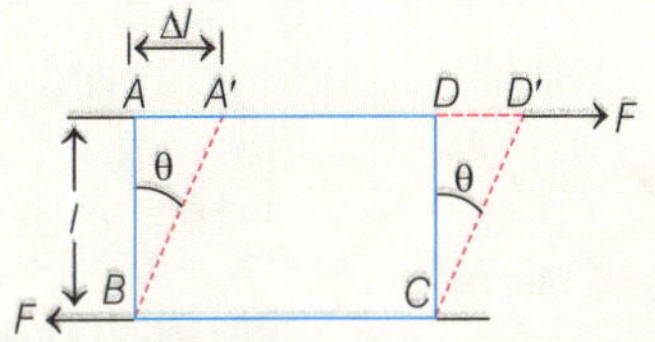

- High shear modulus means rigid material, low shear modulus means more flexible.

Elastic Potential Energy of a Stretched Wire

- When a wire is stretched, an external work is done against internal restoring force produced in the wire. This work is stored in the form of elastic potential energy in the wire.
- **Elastic potential energy,**

$$U = W = \frac{1}{2} \times \text{Weight} \times \text{Extension in length}$$

$$U = W = \frac{1}{2} F \times \Delta L$$

- **Energy stored in the wire per unit volume or Energy density is given by** $U' = \frac{U}{V} = \frac{1}{2} \times \text{Stress} \times \text{Strain}$

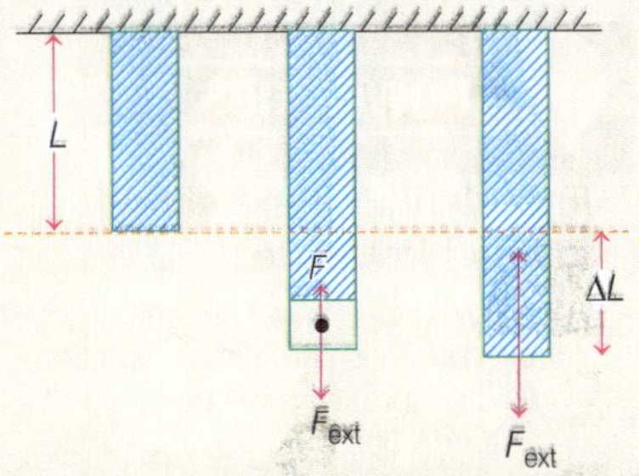

- Elastic potential energy per unit volume in terms of longitudinal strain X and Young's modulus Y is

$$\frac{1}{2} YX^2$$

- If a pressure p is applied to a wire, Young's modulus Y, the elastic potential energy stored per unit volume is

$$\frac{1}{2} \frac{p^2}{Y}$$

POWER TIPS

Thermal Stress and Strain

- Expansion or contraction occurs with temperature change.
- If expansion or contraction is unrestricted, no stress develops.
- Restriction of expansion or contraction induces thermal stress.
- Resulting deformation is thermal strain.

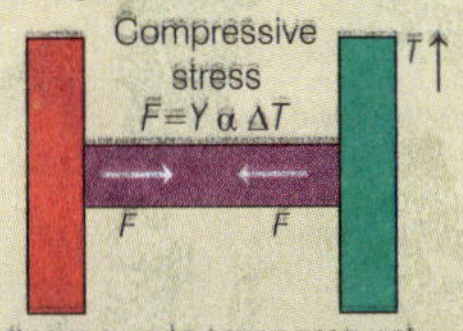

(Increase in temperature) → Compressive stress

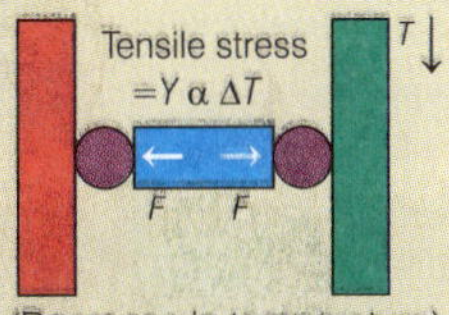

(Decrease in temperature) → Tensile stress

Applications of Elasticity

- A mild steel has a yield strength (σ_y) and has a lifting capacity M kg, then area of cross-section of the rope should atleast be

$$A \geq \frac{Mg}{\sigma_y}$$

- A bar of length l, breadth b, and depth d when loaded at the centre by a load w sags by

$$\delta = \frac{wl^3}{4bd^3Y}$$

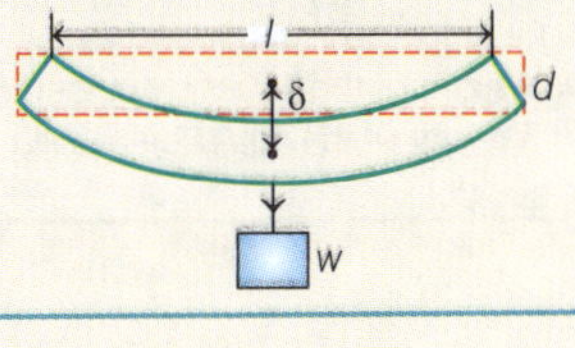

Chapter 09

Mechanical Properties of Fluid

Density

Density (ρ) = $\dfrac{\text{Mass } (m)}{\text{Volume } (V)}$

Unit = kg/m^3, Dimension = $[ML^{-3}]$

CGS Unit = g/cm^3, 1 m^3 = 1000 L

Relative Density

Relative Density = $\dfrac{\text{Density of given liquid}}{\text{Density of pure water at 4°C}}$

- It is dimensionless quantity.

Specific Gravity

Specific Gravity = $\dfrac{\text{Specific weight of given liquid}}{\text{Specific weight of pure water at 4°C}} = \dfrac{\rho_l \times g}{\rho_w \times g} = \dfrac{\rho_l}{\rho_w}$

- It is a dimensionless quantity.

Pressure

It is the force acting on a surface per unit area.

- $p = F/A$
- It is a scalar quantity.
- SI unit—N/m^2 or Pascal (Pa)
- Dimension—$[ML^{-1}T^{-2}]$

Variation of Pressure with Depth

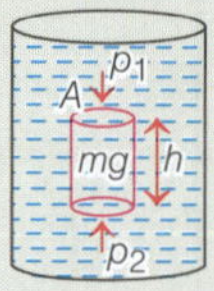

- Pressure difference $p_2 - p_1 = h\rho g$

Absolute Pressure and Gauge Pressure

Gauge pressure = Absolute pressure − Atmospheric pressure

- Absolute pressure always greater than or equal to zero.
- Gauge pressure can be negative also.

Pascal's Law

The increase in pressure at any point of the enclosed liquid in equilibrium is transmitted equally to all other points of the liquid and also to the walls of the container.

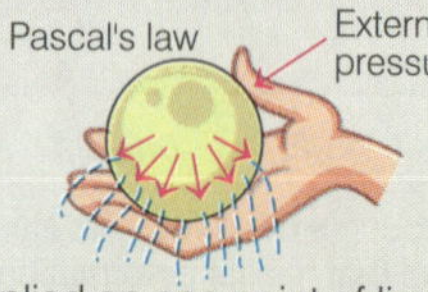

Pressure applied on one point of liquid transmits equally in all directions

Hydrostatic Paradox

- Pressure at particular depth is same irrespective of shape or width of vessel.

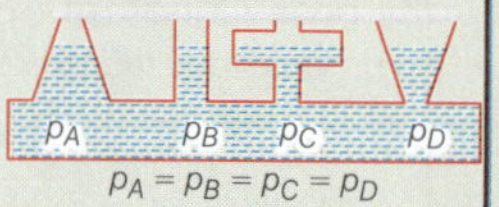

Pressure measuring Instrument

1 Manometer

- It is a device used to measure the pressure of a fluid.

$p_x = p_{atm} + h\rho_m g$

$h\rho_m g = p_x - p_{atm}$

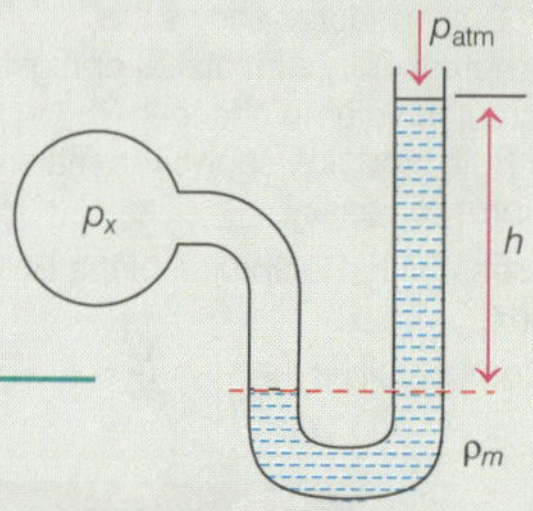

2 Barometer

- It is a device used to measure atmospheric pressure.

$p_1 = p_2$

$p_2 = \rho g h$

ρ = density of mercury

$p_a = \rho g h$

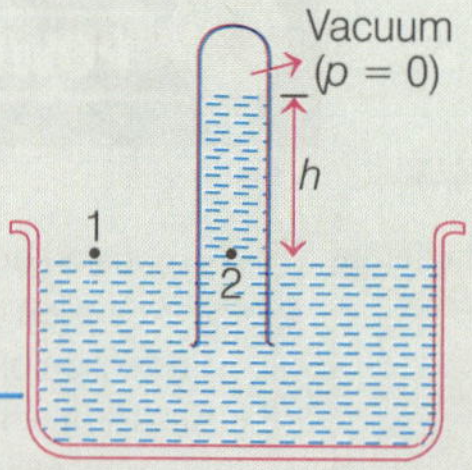

Application of Pascal's Law

Hydraulic Lift It is an arrangement to lift heavy objects by applying a small force.

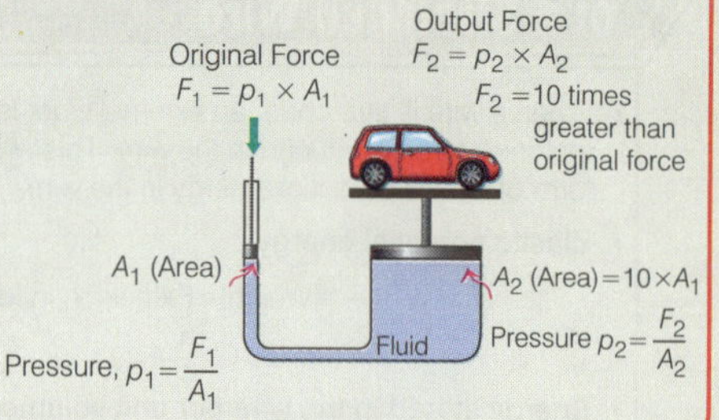

Buoyant Force

The buoyant force is the upward force exerted on an object wholly or partly immersed in a fluid.

$p_2 - p_1 = h\rho g$

$F_2 - F_1 = h\rho g A$

$F_{Buoyant} = V\rho g$ = loss of weight

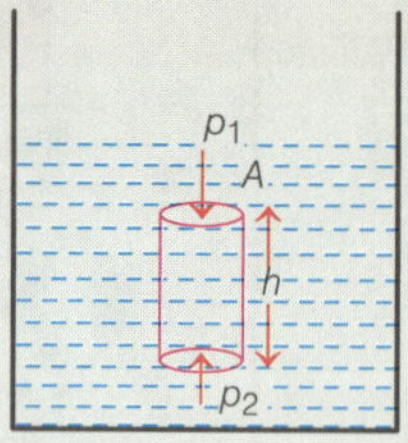

Archimedes' Principle

- The upward thrust experienced by a body partially or fully immersed in a fluid is equal to the weight of the fluid displaced by it.
- Buoyant force = Weight of the liquid displaced = $V\rho g$
- Loss of weight = Weight of the liquid displaced

POWER TIPS

Important Points Related to Fluid Pressure

- At a point in the liquid column, the pressure applied on it, is same in all directions.
- In a liquid, pressure will be same at all points at the same level.

Pressure at the base of the vessel is

$$p = p_0 + \rho g h + \frac{mg}{A}$$

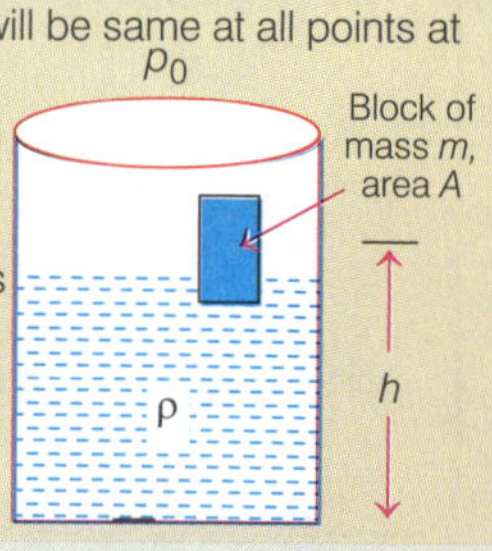

Fluid Flow

Laminar Flow

- Steady flow
- Layers of different velocities which do not mix with each other.

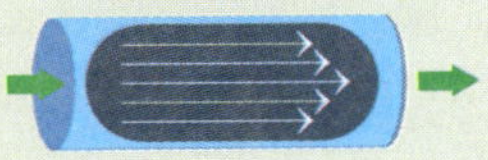

Streamline Flow

- In steady flow, the line of flow is known as streamline.
- No two streamlines can cross each other.
- The greater is the crowding of streamlines at a place greater velocity at that place.
- The tangent at a streamline indicates the direction of motion of a fluid.

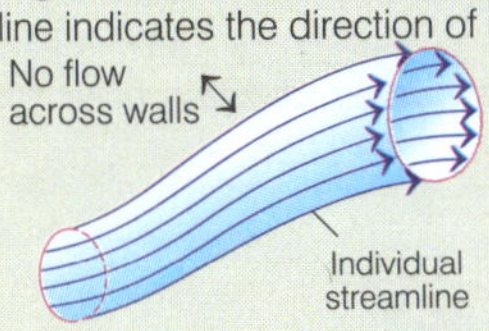

Turbulent Flow

Liquid moves with velocity greater than its critical velocity

- It is disordered and irregular flow.

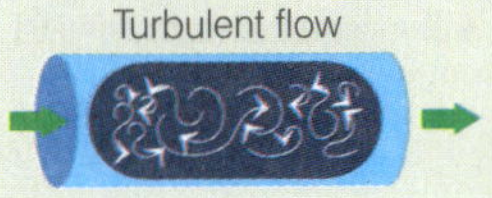

Critical Velocity: The velocity upto which its flow remains streamlined and beyond which its flow becomes turbulent.

Equation of Continuity

For the incompressible and non-viscous fluid,

$A_1v_1 = A_2v_2 = \text{Constant}$

$Av = \text{constant} = Q = \frac{dV}{dt}$ → Volume rate of flow

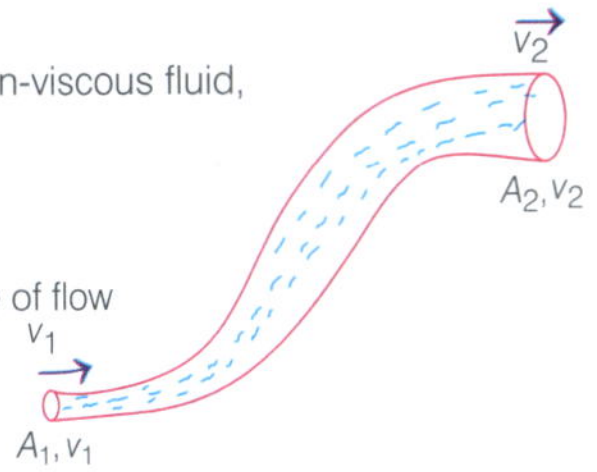

- Equation of continuity is a special case of the law of conservation of mass.
- Equation of continuity is valid for streamlined flow of the non-viscous and incompressible fluids.

Bernoulli's Principle

- It is based on the law of conservation of energy.
- At each point of flow

Pressure energy per unit volume + Kinetic energy per unit volume + Potential energy per unit volume = Constant

- $p_1 + \frac{1}{2}\rho v_1^2 + \rho g h_1 = p_2 + \frac{1}{2}\rho v_2^2 + \rho g h_2$

Pressure head + Velocity head + Gravitational head = Constant

Conditions

- It is applicable for incompressible, non-viscous fluid.
- It is applicable for streamlined, irrotational flow.

Venturimeter

- Device used to measure the rate of flow through a pipe.
- $v_1 = \sqrt{\dfrac{2gh}{\dfrac{A_1^2}{A_2^2} - 1}}$
- The discharge or volume flow rate $Q = A_1v_1 = A_1A_2\sqrt{\dfrac{2gh}{(A_1^2 - A_2^2)}}$

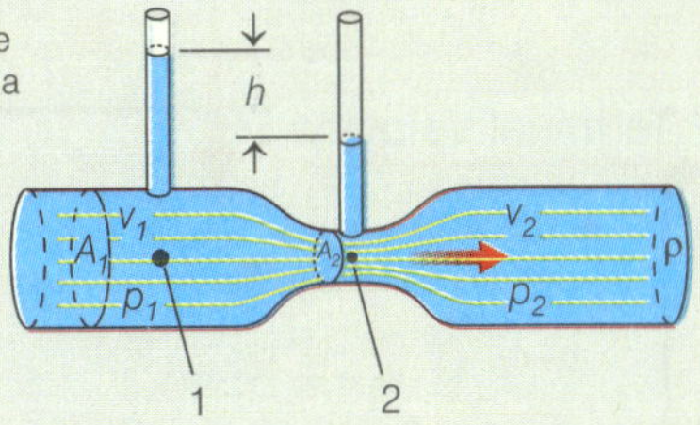

Applications of Bernoulli's Theorem

SPEED OF EFFLUX

The velocity with which the liquid comes out of a small hole is called velocity of efflux.

Here, $v = \sqrt{2gh}$

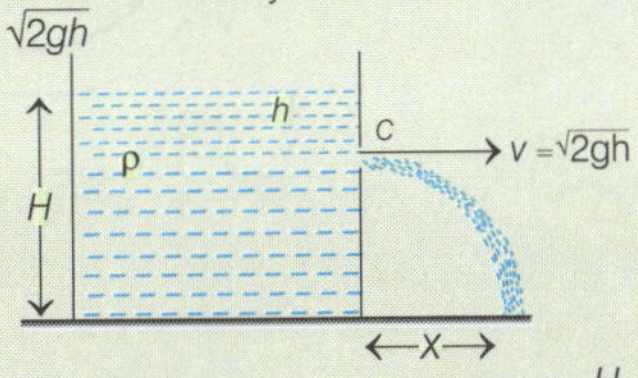

Range $(R) = 2\sqrt{h(H-h)}$, R is max, when $h = \frac{H}{2}$

Time taken to empty a tank when orifice is at the bottom,

$t = \frac{A}{A_o}\sqrt{\frac{2H}{g}}$ [A = area of the container, A_o = area of the orifice]

MAGNUS EFFECT

It is a force that occurs when a spinning object moves through a fluid causing it to deviate from its path.

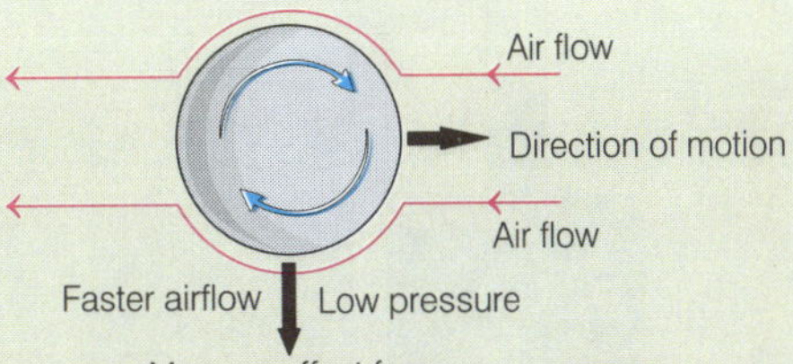

AEROFOIL OR LIFT ON AIRCRAFT WING

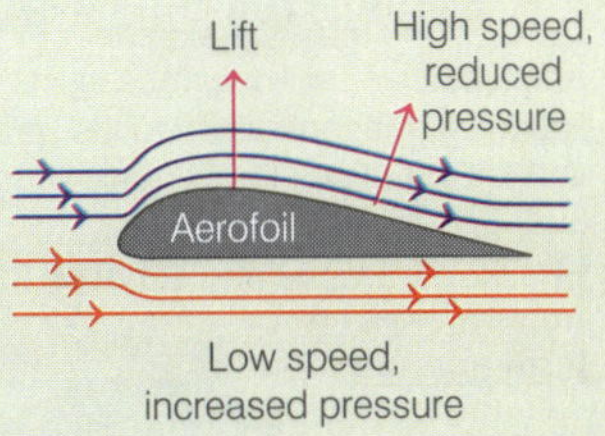

Viscosity

- The property of liquid by virtue of which it opposes the relative motion between its adjacent layers.
- Viscous force, $F = -\eta A \frac{dv}{dy}$
  where, η = coefficient of viscosity
- SI unit—Nsm^{-2} or decapoise or Pa-s.
- CGS unit—dyne s cm^{-2} or poise (1 decapoise = 10 poise)
- Dimensional formula - $[ML^{-1}T^{-1}]$

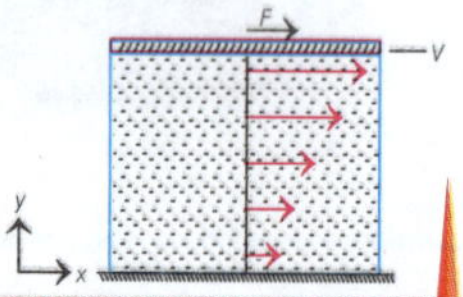

Flow of Liquid through a Cylindrical Pipe

- The flow speed v at a distance r from the axis of a pipe of radius R is
  $v = \frac{p_1 - p_2}{4\eta L}(R^2 - r^2)$
- The velocity of viscous fluid flowing along a pipe is maximum along its axis.
  $v_{max} = \frac{p_1 - p_2}{4\eta L}R^2$

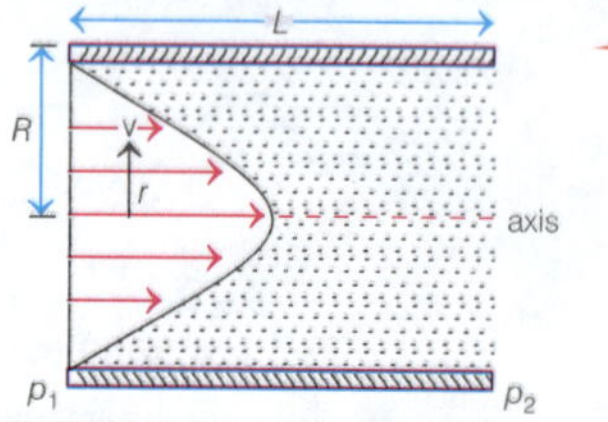

Poiseuille Equation Volume Flow Rate

- Volume flow rate across a tube with pressure difference between its ends,
  $Q = \frac{dV}{dt} = \frac{\pi}{8}\frac{r^4 p}{\eta L}$
  where, $p = p_1 - p_2$ = Pressure difference
- The electrical resistance $R\left(= \rho\frac{L}{A}\right)$ is replaced by flow resistance $X = \left(\frac{8\eta L}{\pi r^4}\right)$
- The electrical current i is replaced by volume flow rate Q or $\frac{dV}{dt}$

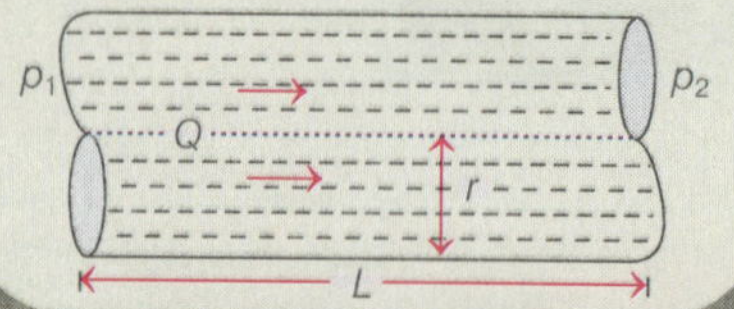

Stokes' Law

Retarding viscous force experienced by a small spherical body moving through a perfectly homogeneous medium.

$F = 6\pi\eta r v$

F_{net} = Apparent weight – Retarding viscous force

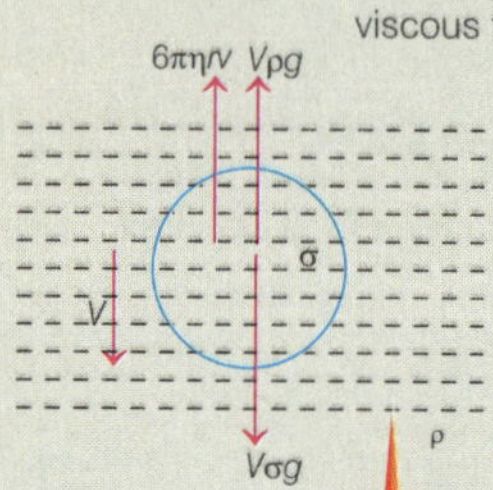

Terminal Velocity

- Maximum constant velocity attainable by an object as it falls through a liquid.

$$v_T = \frac{2}{9}\frac{r^2 g}{\eta}(\sigma - \rho)$$

Here, σ = density of body and ρ = density of liquid or fluid.

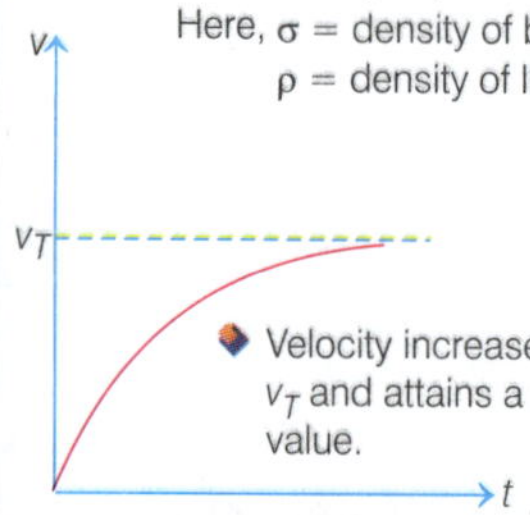

- Velocity increases from 0 to v_T and attains a maximum value.

Surface Tension

It is the property of liquid due to which it behaves like a stretched membrane to acquire minimum surface area.

Surface tension, $T = \frac{\text{Force}}{\text{Length}} = \frac{F}{L}$

SI unit - Nm^{-1} Dimension - $[M T^{-2}]$

Cohesive force - Force of attraction between similar molecules.

Adhesive force - Force of attraction between dissimilar molecules.

Surface Energy

Surface energy = $\frac{\text{Work done in increasing the surface area}}{\text{Increase in surface area}}$

Surface energy = $T \times$ Surface area

- Surface energy of a liquid drop of radius R, $S = T \times 4\pi R^2$
- Surface energy of a soap bubble of radius R, $S = 2 \times T \times 4\pi R^2$

Applications of Surface Tension

- Work done to blow a soap bubble of radius (r) $W = 2 \times T \times 4\pi r^2$
- When a drop of radius R breaks up into n identical drops, work done $W = 4\pi R^2 T\,[n^{1/3} - 1]$
- Temperature increases → Surface tension decreases
- Adding sparingly soluble impurities like detergents → Surface tension decreases
- Adding soluble impurities like NaCl, sugar → Surface tension increases
- A needle floats on the surface of a liquid due to surface tension.

Excess Pressure

Excess pressure = $p_i - p_a$ p_a = Atmospheric pressure
p_i = Pressure inside soap bubble

- Excess pressure for a liquid drop,
  $p_i = p_a + \frac{2T}{R}$

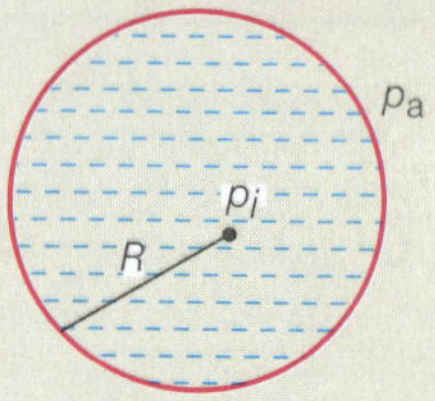

- Excess pressure for a soap bubble,
  $p_i = p_a + \frac{4T}{R}$

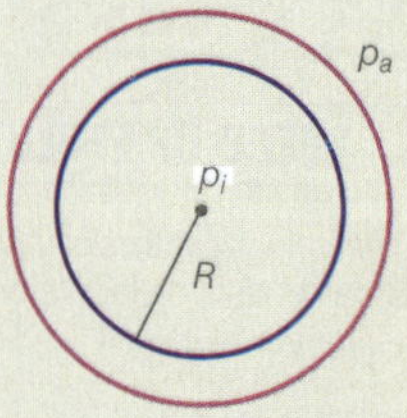

- Excess pressure for air bubble,
  $p_i = p_a + \frac{2T}{R}$

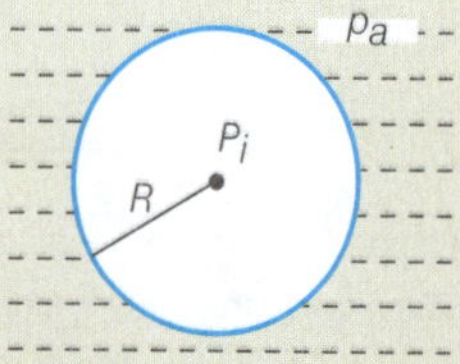

Capillarity

- Rise or fall of liquid in a narrow diameter tube.
- Angle of contact = Acute → Liquid rises
- Angle of contact = Obtuse → Liquid falls
- Rise of liquid (h) = $\frac{2T\cos\theta}{r\rho g}$

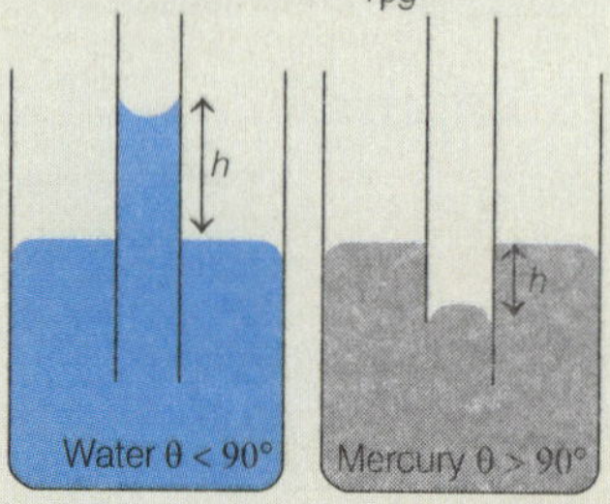

Angle of Contact

Angle between solid surface inside the liquid and tangent drawn to the liquid surface at the point of contact.

It depends on
- Relative cohesive and adhesive force of solid-liquid pair
- Temperature

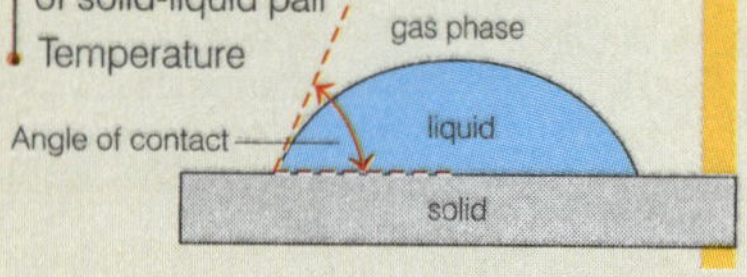

Chapter 10

Thermal Properties of Matter

Heat and Temperature

Heat Form of energy which flows from higher temperature body to a lower temperature body when in contact. It's SI unit is joule (J)

Temperature Measurement of hotness or coldness of a body in specified scale.

Conversion of Temperature

$$\frac{C}{100}=\frac{F-32}{180}=\frac{K-273}{100}=\frac{R}{80}$$

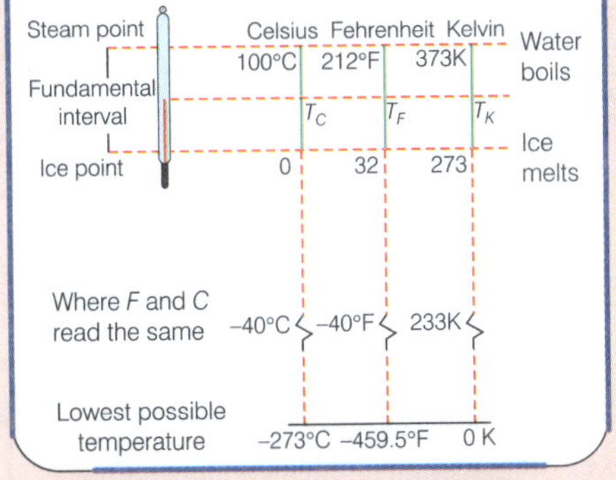

For any Temperature Scale

$$\frac{\text{Scale reading} - \text{lower fixed point}}{\text{Upper fixed point} - \text{lower fixed point}} = \text{constant}$$

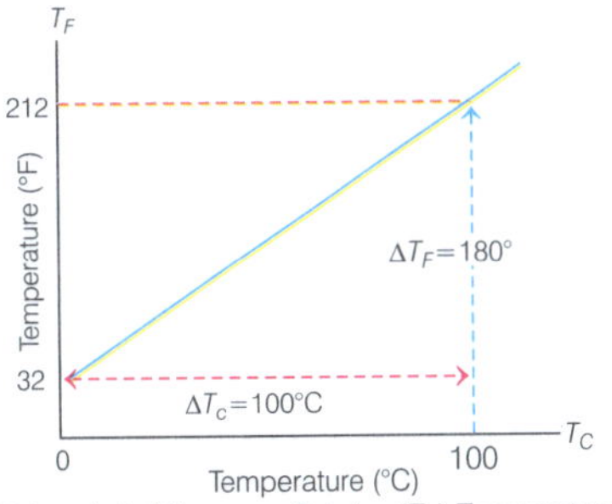

Fahrenheit (T_f) *versus* Celsius (T_C) Temperature

Absolute Temperature

Theoretically, there is no limit for maximum temperature but there is a sharp point for minimum temperature called absolute temperature.

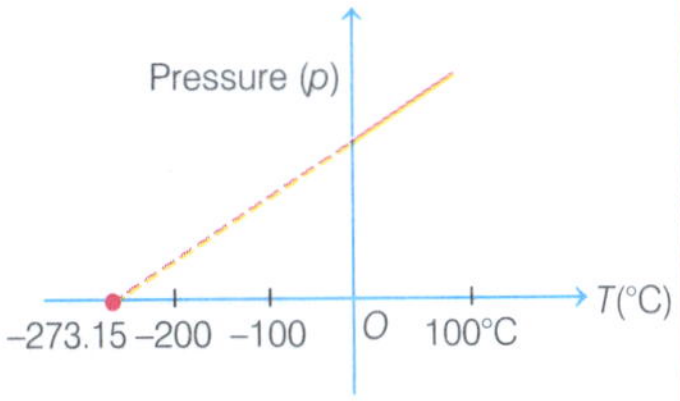

Anomalous Expansion of water

- Water contracts on heating between 0°C to 4°C
- Water has maxmimum density at 4°C (minimum volume)

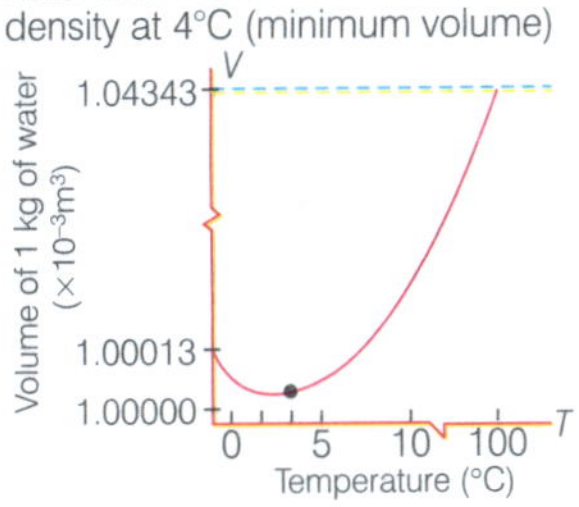

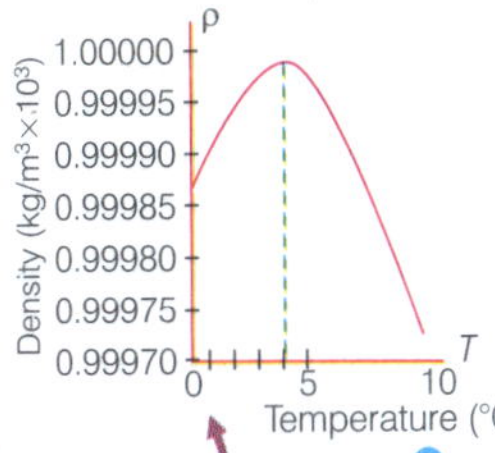

Ideal Gas Equation

The ideal gas equation

$pV = nRT \Rightarrow \frac{pV}{T} = nR$ (constant), $R = 8.314$ J/mol K^{-1}

Boyle's Law

This law is a gas law which states that the pressure exerted by a gas is inversely proportional to the volume occupied by it.

$\Rightarrow p \propto \frac{1}{V}$ [Temperature constant]

$\Rightarrow pV =$ constant

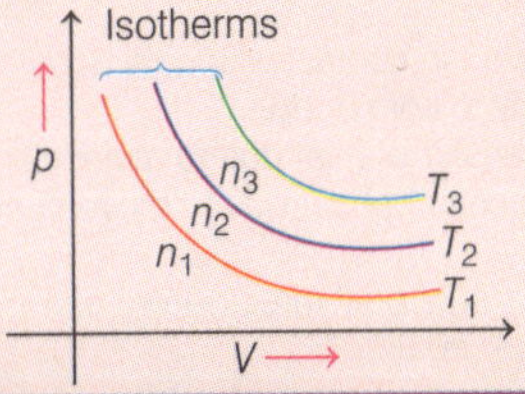

Charle's Law

This law states that the volume of an ideal gas is directly proportional to the absolute temperature at constant pressure.

$V \propto T$ [Pressure constant]

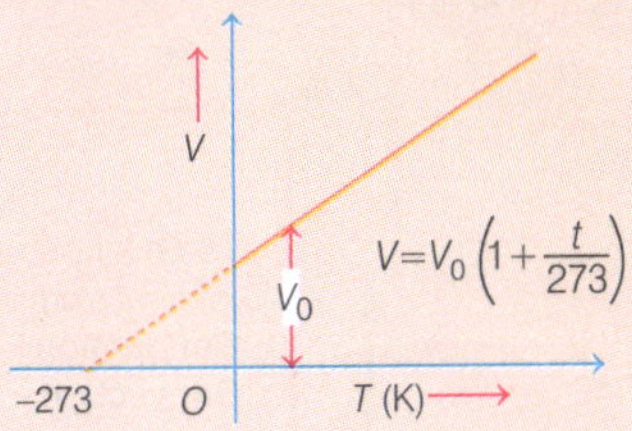

Variation of Density with Temperature

Most of the substances expand when they are heated

Density ∝ 1/Volume

$V = V_0(1+\gamma\Delta T)$

Then, $\rho = \rho_0(1-\gamma\Delta T)$

Thermal Expansion

It is the increase in the size of the body due to heating.

(i) Linear Expansion

Increase in length of a metal rod.

$l_2 = l_1(1+\alpha\Delta t)$

Coefficient of linear expansion

The increase in length per unit original length per degree rise in temperature.

$$\alpha = \frac{\Delta l}{l \times \Delta t}$$

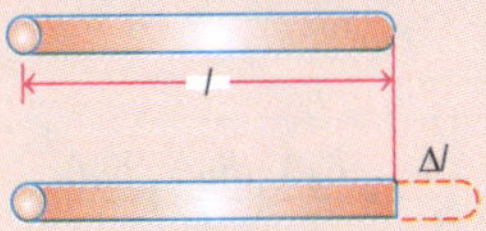

(ii) Superficial (Areal) Expansion

Increase in the area of a body due to heating. $A = A_0[1+\beta\Delta T]$

Coefficient of area expansion

The increase in surface area per unit original area per degree rise in temperature.

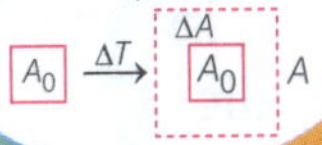

(iii) Volume Expansion

Increase in the volume of a body due to heating $V = V_0(1+\gamma\Delta T)$

Coefficient of volume expansion

The increase in volume per unit original volume per degree rise in temperature.

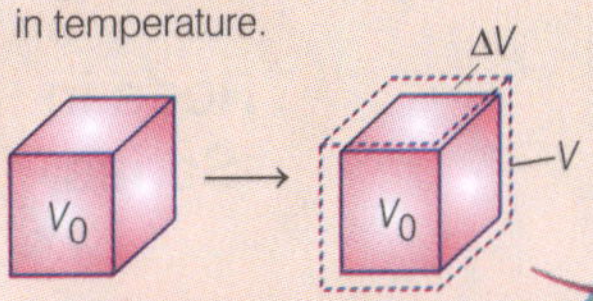

Relation among coefficients of expansion

$\alpha : \beta : \gamma = 1 : 2 : 3$

Heat Supplied to a Body (ΔQ)

Change in Temperature of Body

$\Delta Q = ms\Delta T$

s=specific heat capacity

SI unit $\rightarrow$ J $kg^{-1}K^{-1}$

$S_{water} = 1\frac{cal}{g°C} = 4.2\frac{J}{g°C}$

$= 4200\frac{J}{kg°C}$

$S_{ice} = \frac{1}{2}\frac{cal}{g°C} = 2.1\frac{J}{g°C} = 2100\frac{J}{kg°C}$

Change of state of body

Melting $\Delta Q = mL_f$, L_f = Latent heat of fusion	Boiling $\Delta Q = mL_v$, L_v = Latent heat of vaporization

$L_f = L_{ice} = 80\frac{cal}{g} = 80\times4.2\frac{J}{g}$

$= 80 \times 4200\frac{J}{kg}$

$L_v = L_{steam} = 540\frac{cal}{g} = 540 \times 4.2\frac{J}{g}$

$= 540 \times 4200\frac{J}{kg}$

Heat Capacity

Thermal Capacity
Amount of heat required to raise the temperature of a given body by 1°C (or 1 K). Thermal capacity of a body $=Q/\Delta T$

Specific Heat Capacity
Amount of heat required to raise the temperature of unit mass of a body through 1°C (or 1 K). Specific heat capacity $=Q/m\Delta T$ (m = mass)

Molar Heat Capacity
The amount of heat required to raise 1 mole of a substance by 1 kelvin.
Molar heat capacity $= Q/n\Delta T$ (n = number of moles)

Water Equivalent

Quantity of water, whose heat capacity is the same as the heat capacity of the body.

Water equivalent of the body = Mass of body $\times \frac{\text{Specific heat of body}}{\text{Specific heat of water}}$

Calorimetry

Measurement of heat [1 cal = 4.186 J = 4.2 J]

Principle of Calorimetry

Heat lost = Heat gained

For temperature change, $Q = ms\Delta T$

For phase change $Q = mL$

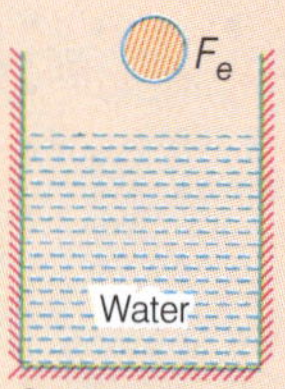

Cu glass vessel

Cu glass vessel	Liquid	Hot iron sphere
m_1	m_2	m_3
s_1	s_2	s_3
T_1	T_2	T_3

Heat lost by the hotter bodies = Heat gained by colder bodies, $Q_3=Q_1+Q_2$

Final equilibrium temperature

$$T_{eq} = \frac{m_1s_1T_1+m_2s_2T_2+m_3s_3T_3}{m_1s_1+m_2s_2+m_3s_3} = \frac{\Sigma msT}{\Sigma ms}$$

Equivalent Thermal Resistance of Rods in Series and Parallel

Rods in Series

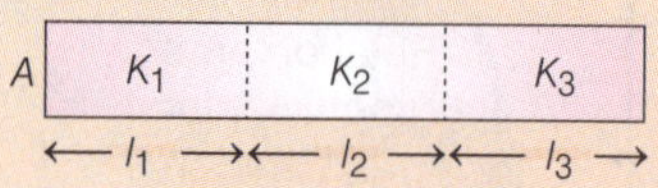

$R_{eq} = R_1 + R_2 + R_3$

$$R_{eq} = \frac{l_1}{K_1A} + \frac{l_2}{K_2A} + \frac{l_3}{K_3A}$$

Rods in Parallel

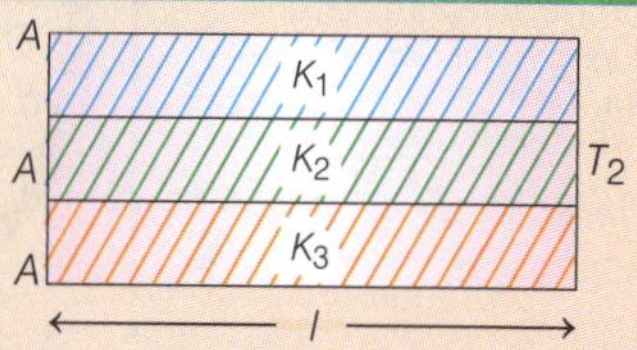

$$\frac{1}{R_{eq}} = \frac{K_1A}{l} + \frac{K_2A}{l} + \frac{K_3A}{l}$$

Phase Diagram and Triple Point

- **Fusion** – Change of state from solid to liquid.
- **Freezing** – Change of state from liquid to solid.
- **Vaporisation** – Change of state from liquid to vapour.
- **Sublimation** – Change of state directly from solid to vapour.
- **Triple Point** – All three phases of a substance co-exist simultaneously.

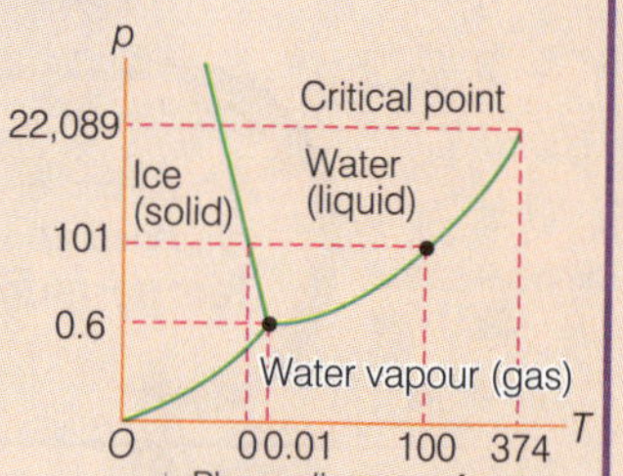

Phase diagram of water

Latent Heat

- Amount of heat that has to supplied to (or removed from) a body for its complete change of state.
- Phase transformation is an isothermal change.

Heat is supplied at constant rate graph and equations

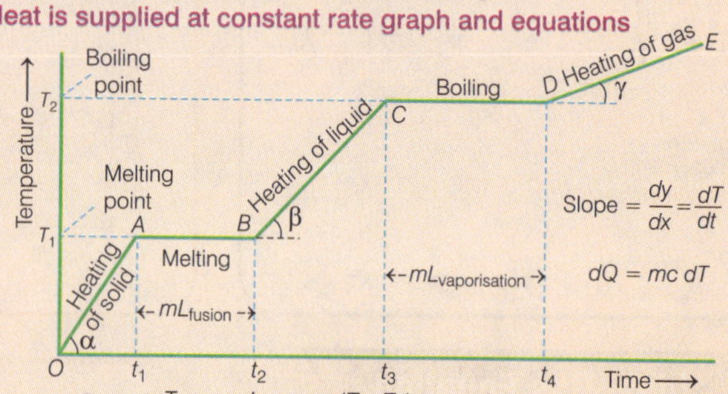

$$\frac{Q}{t} = \frac{msT_1}{t_1} = \frac{mL_f}{t_2-t_1} = \frac{ms(T_2-T_1)}{t_3-t_2} = \frac{mL_v}{t_4-t_3}$$

If specific heat is variable

$$S=f(T)\ T_1 \rightarrow T_2,\ \Delta Q=\int_{T_1}^{T_2} msdT$$

Heat Transfer

- When a hot body is kept in contact with cold body, there is a transfer of heat from hot body to cold body.
- **Conduction** – The transfer of heat due to molecular vibration.
- **Convection** – The transfer of heat due to movement of fluid from one place to another.
- **Radiation** – The transfer of heat directly from one place to other without requiring any medium.

Conduction

Rate of heat flow $= \frac{dQ}{dt} = -KA\frac{dT}{dx}$

$$\frac{Q}{t} = \frac{KA(T_1-T_2)}{l}$$

Thermal resistance $R_H = \frac{L}{KA}$

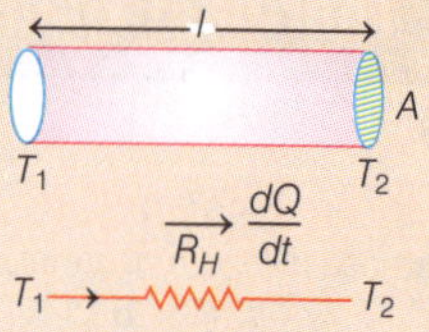

Electrical Equivalent

Chapter 11

Thermodynamics

Thermodynamic System

It is part of the physical world that can be studied using the laws of thermodynamics.

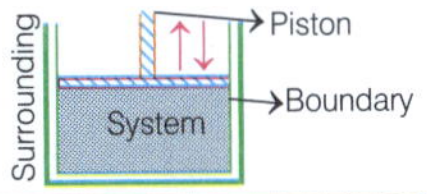

Heat

Energy transferred from an object at a higher temperature to an object at a lower temperature.
It's SI unit is Joule.
Heat is a path function.

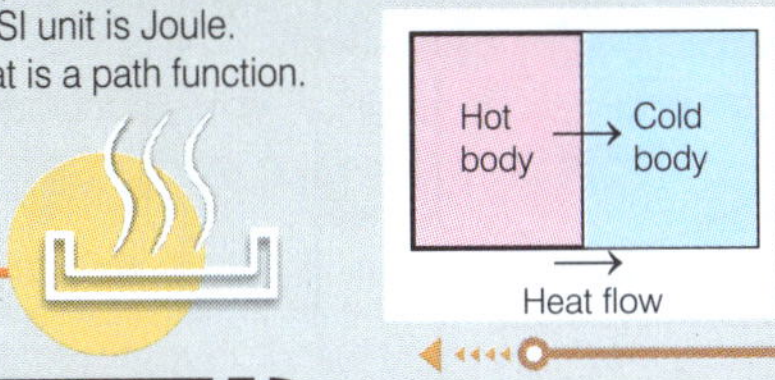

Work

Work done by a thermodynamic system is given by $W = p \times \Delta V$

Work done in process $A \to B = p\int_{V_i}^{V_f} dV$

Work done in process $A \to B$ = curve area $ABCDA$

Work done by thermodynamic system depends upon the path followed in the process.

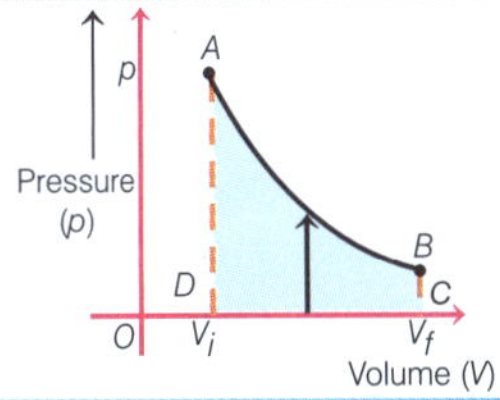

Types of Thermodynamic Systems

Open System

It exchanges both heat and matter with its surrounding.

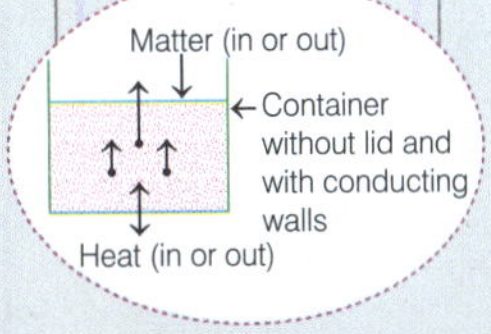

Closed System

It exchanges only heat but no matter with its surrounding.

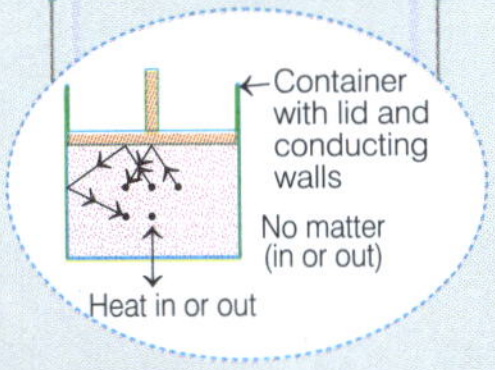

Isolated System

It exchanges neither heat nor matter with surroundings.

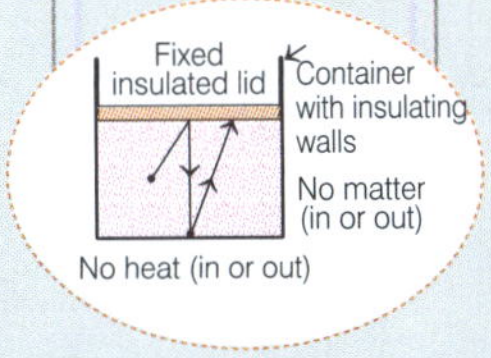

First Law of Thermodynamics

The increment in internal energy (ΔU) of a system equals to the heat added to the system minus the work done. $\Delta U = Q - W$

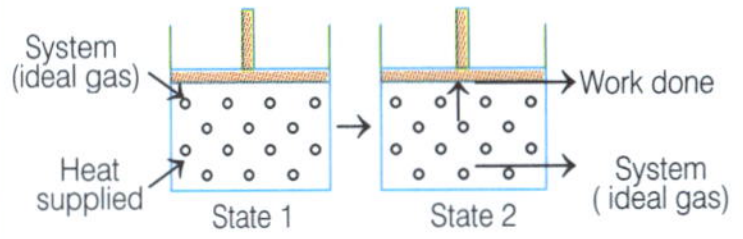

Heat supplied $(Q) = \Delta U + W$

- The first law of thermodynamics is based on the law of conservation of energy.
- **Limitation of first law of thermodynamics**
  It does not indicate direction of heat.

State Variables

Extensive State Variables

It depends on the size of the system. e.g. volume, total mass, internal energy

Intensive State Variables

It does not depend on the size of the system. e.g. pressure, temperature, density

Zeroth Law of Thermodynamics

If two bodies A and B are in thermal equilibrium with third body C, then bodies A and B are also in thermal equilibrium with each other.

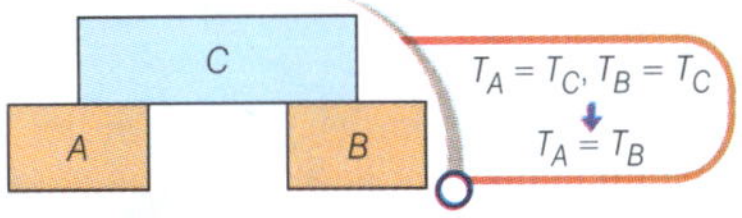

Zeroth law of thermodynamics is the basis for defining temperature.

Temperature It is the measure of hotness or coldness of the body.

INTERNAL ENERGY

Total energy contained within the system.

$$\Delta U = nC_V\Delta T = n\frac{f}{2}R\Delta T$$

Internal energy is only the function of the temperature of the gas.

Thermodynamic Terms

01 Thermal Equilibrium

There is no flow of heat between two systems when they are in thermal equilibrium.

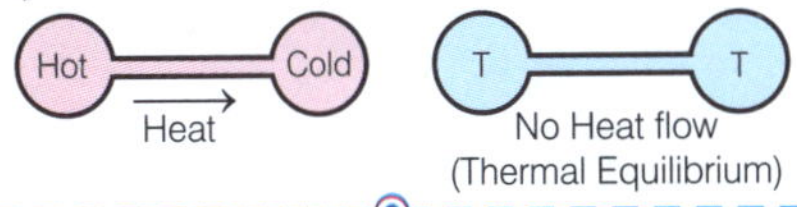

02 Adiabatic Wall

Insulating Wall It does not allow flow of heat.

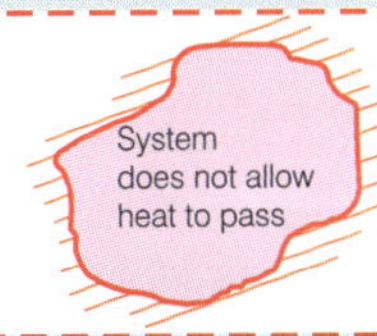

03 Diathermic Wall

Conducting Wall
It allows flow of heat.

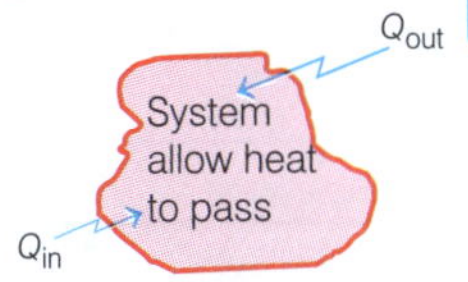

POWER TIPS

THERMODYNAMICS SIGN CONVENTIONS

Condition		Convention
Heat added to the system	+ve Q → System	$Q > 0$, i.e + ve
Heat removed from the system	System → Q (-ve)	$Q < 0$, i.e. – ve
Work done by the system (Volume increases)	System → W(+ve)	$W > 0$, i.e. + ve
Work done on the system (Volume decreases)	W(-ve) → System	$W < 0$, i.e. –ve
Temperature of the system rises	System, $\Delta T > 0$	$\Delta U > 0$, i.e. + ve
Temperature of the system falls	System, $\Delta T < 0$	$\Delta U < 0$, i.e. –ve

Thermodynamic Process

When some changes occur in the state of a thermodynamic system.

Isothermal Process

- The process in which temperature remains constant.

Example — melting of ice

p-V graph of isothermal process

$pV = \text{constant} \Rightarrow p_iV_i = p_fV_f$

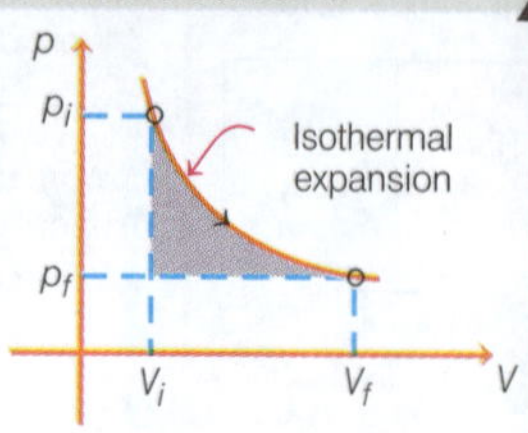

Work done = Area under p-V graph

$W = 2.303\, nRT \log\left(\frac{V_f}{V_i}\right)$

$W = 2.303\, nRT \log\left(\frac{p_i}{p_f}\right)$

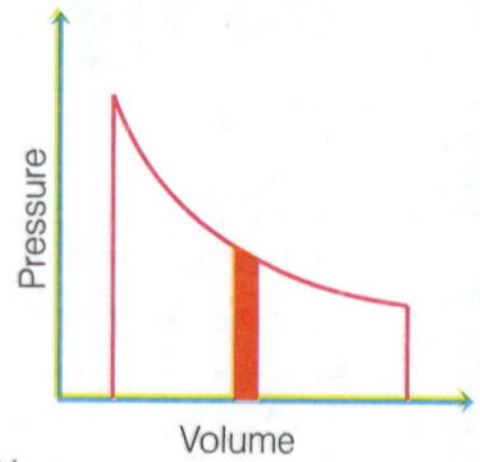

V-T graph of isothermal process

Slope $= \frac{dV}{dT} = \infty$

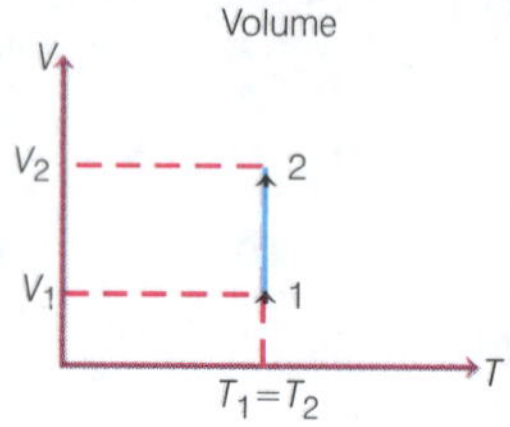

p-T graph of isothermal process

Slope $= \frac{dp}{dT} = \infty$

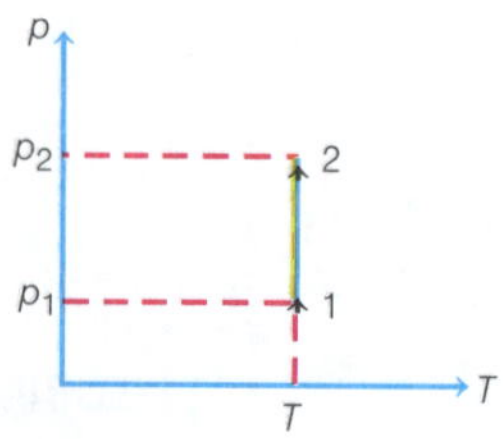

Slope of p-V graph

slope $= -\tan\phi$

$= \frac{dp}{dV} = -\frac{p}{V}$

Specific and Molar Heat Capacity

For isothermal process $\Delta T = 0$

$\therefore$ Specific heat capacity, $s = \frac{\Delta Q}{m\Delta T} = \infty$

$\therefore$ Molar heat capacity $C = \frac{\Delta Q}{n\Delta T} = \infty$

Adiabatic Process

- $Q = 0$ [No exchange of heat]
- Very fast process

$TV^{\gamma-1} = \text{constant}$, $p^{1-\gamma}T^{\gamma} = \text{constant}$

- $pV^{\gamma} = \text{constant}$

$p_1V_1^{\gamma} = p_2V_2^{\gamma}$

$T_1V_1^{\gamma-1} = T_2V_2^{\gamma-1}$

$p_1^{1-\gamma}T_1^{\gamma} = p_2^{1-\gamma}T_2^{\gamma}$

- p-V graph of adiabatic process

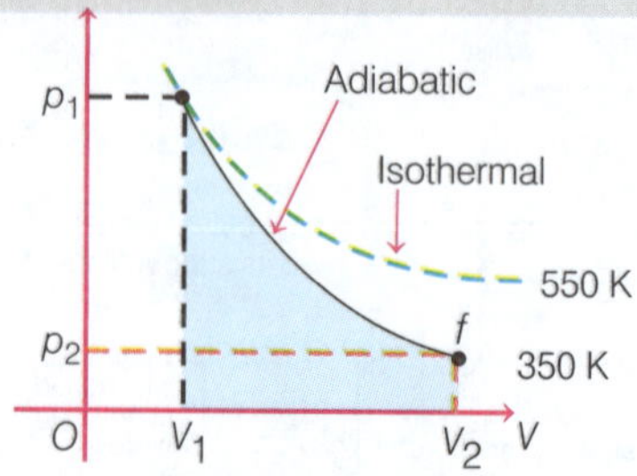

- Work done in adiabatic process, $W = \int_{V_1}^{V_2} p\,dv$

$W = \frac{nR(T_1 - T_2)}{\gamma - 1} = \frac{p_1V_1 - p_2V_2}{\gamma - 1}$

- Slope of adiabatic process = $\gamma \times$ (Slope of isothermal process)

Isochoric Process

- $\Delta V = 0$ or $V = \text{constant}$

Equation of state $\Rightarrow p \propto T \Rightarrow \frac{p_1}{p_2} = \frac{T_1}{T_2}$

- From first law of thermodynamics,

$\Delta Q = \Delta U + W$

$W = 0$ (Isochoric process)

$\therefore \quad Q = \Delta U = nC_V\Delta T$

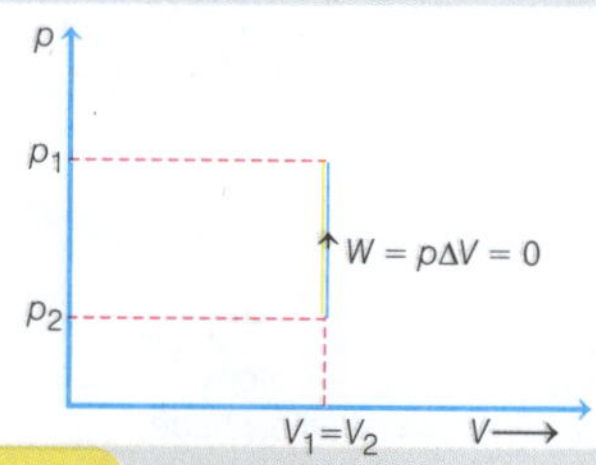

Relation between C_p and C_V

$C_p - C_V = R$ [Mayer's formula]

$\gamma = \frac{C_p}{C_V}$, $C_p = \left(\frac{\Delta Q}{\Delta T}\right)_p$, $C_V = \left(\frac{\Delta Q}{\Delta T}\right)_V$

Isobaric Process

$\Delta p = 0$, Pressure = Constant

$W = p(V_2 - V_1)$

Equation of state

$\Rightarrow V \propto T$ or $\frac{V}{T}$ = Constant

$$\frac{V_1}{T_1} = \frac{V_2}{T_2}$$

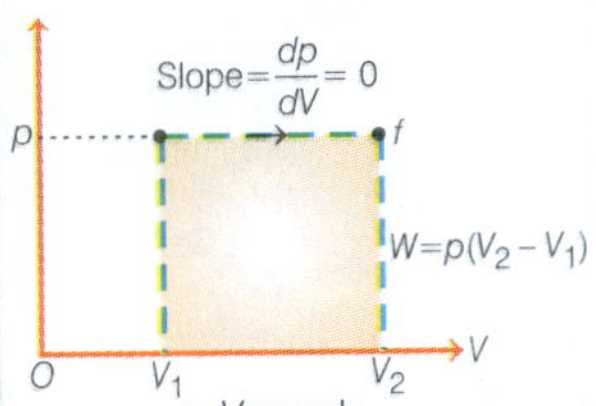

p-V graph

From first law of thermodynamics

$$Q = \Delta U + W$$

$$Q = C_V \Delta T + p(\Delta V)$$

$$Q = C_V (T_2 - T_1) + p(V_2 - V_1)$$

Cyclic Process

- **For cyclic process**, Initial state = Final state

  $\Delta U = 0$ (For cyclic process) or $\Delta Q = \Delta W$

  Work done (W) = Area enclosed by cycle on p-V curve
- **For clockwise process**, $W = +$ ve
- **For anti-clockwise process**, $W = -$ ve

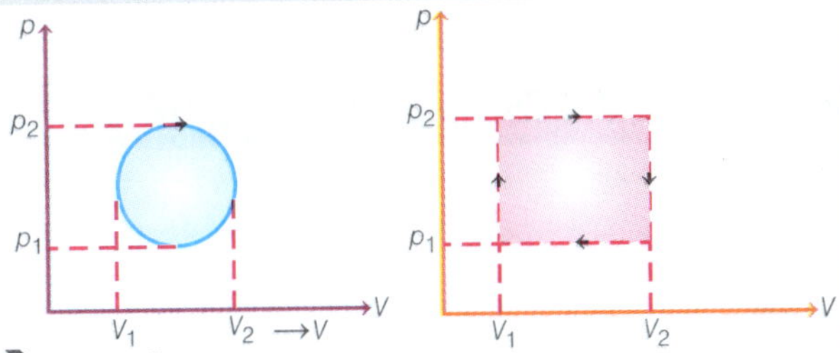

$W = \frac{\pi}{4}(p_2 - p_1)(V_2 - V_1)$ $\qquad$ $W = (p_2 - p_1)(V_2 - V_1)$

POWER TIPS

p-V diagram for different thermodynamic processes

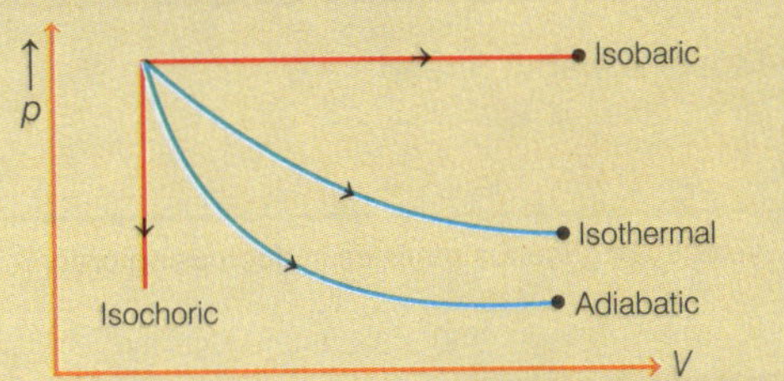

$$W_{isobaric} > W_{isothermal} > W_{adiabatic} > W_{isochoric}$$

Conditions For a Reversible Process

- The process must be quasi-static (Very slow process).
- The dissipative force should be absent.

Second Law of Thermodynamics

- **Kelvin-Planck Statement** No process is possible which can completely convert heat absorbed from reservoir into work.

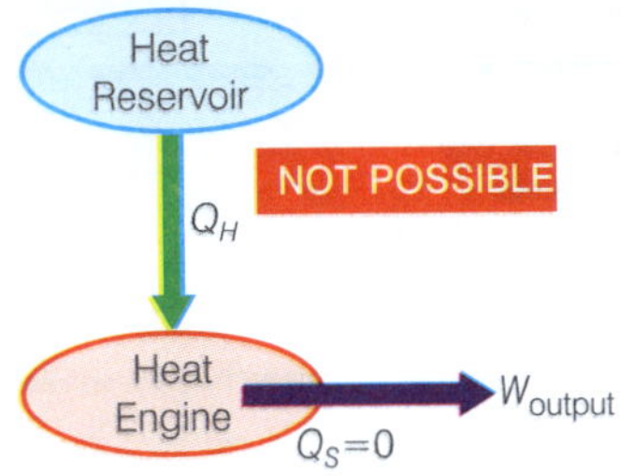

- **Clausius Statement** – No process is possible which can transfer heat from a cold body to hot body without doing any external work.

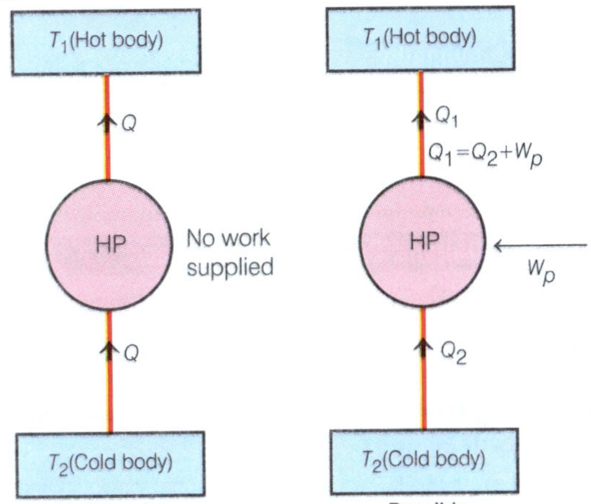

Not Possible $\qquad$ **Possible**

- Entropy measures the randomness of a system
- Entropy of an isolated system always increases. $\Delta S_{universe} > 0$
- **Application** Design of heat engines and refrigerator.

Reversible and Irreversible Processes

Reversible Process

The system and its surroundings can return to their original state by following the reverse path with no other changes anywhere else in the universe.
- It is ideal process.
- System remains in equilibrium at all times

Irreversible Process

The system and its surroundings do not return to their original state by following the reverse path.
- This process is fast.
- It is real process.
- Occurs due to frictions viscosity and other dissipative effects.
- Entropy increases ($\Delta S > 0$)

Chapter 12

Kinetic Theory of Gases

Gas Laws

Boyle's Law

$V \propto \frac{1}{p}$, if M and T = constant

pV = constant $\Rightarrow p_1V_1 = p_2V_2$

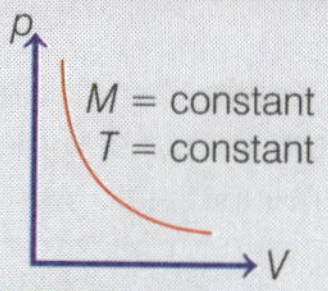

Charle's Law

$V \propto T$, if M and p = constant

$\frac{V}{T}$ = constant $\Rightarrow \frac{V_1}{T_1} = \frac{V_2}{T_2}$

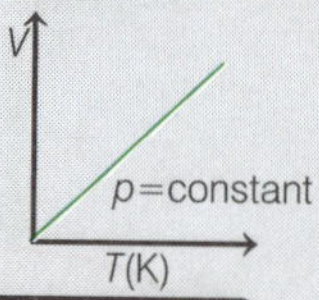

Gay-Lussac's Law

$p \propto T$, if M and V = constant

$\frac{p}{T}$ = constant $\Rightarrow \frac{p_1}{T_1} = \frac{p_2}{T_2}$

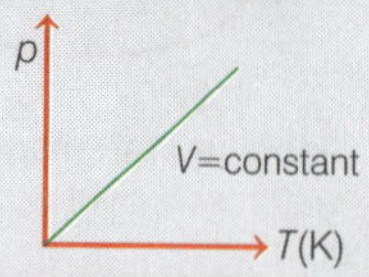

Avogadro's Law

At same temperature and pressure, equal volume of all gases contain equal number of molecules.

i.e., $N_1 = N_2$ [if p, V, T = constant]

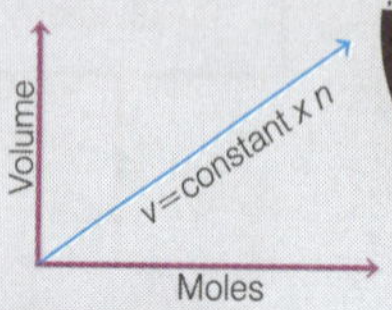

Dalton's Partial Pressure Law

p_{total} = Sum of partial pressure of each component of gases present in mixture.

$p_{total} = p_1 + p_2 + p_3 + ... p_n$

Graham's Law of Diffusion

The rate of diffusion is inversely proportional to square root of density of gas, if gases at the same temperature and pressure.

$$r \propto \frac{1}{\sqrt{\rho}} \Rightarrow \frac{r_2}{r_1} = \sqrt{\frac{\rho_1}{\rho_2}}$$

Work Done on Compressing a Gas

The work done on compressing a gas can be shown under three processes.

Isothermal Compression

$$W = \mu RT \ln \frac{V_2}{V_1}$$

$V_2 < V_1$, the value of work done is negative.

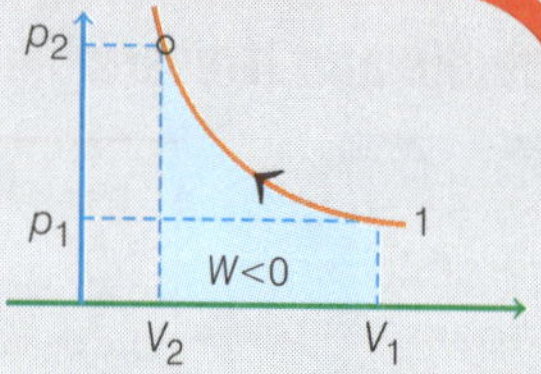

Adiabatic Compression

$$W = \frac{p_1V_1 - p_2V_2}{\gamma - 1} = \frac{R(T_1 - T_2)}{\gamma - 1}$$

$T_2 > T_1$ hence, the value of work done is negative.

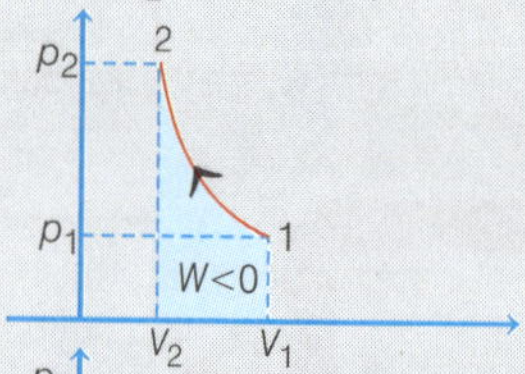

Polytropic Compression

$$W = \frac{p_1V_1 - p_2V_2}{n-1} = \frac{\mu R(T_1 - T_2)}{n-1}$$

as $T_2 > T_1$, the value of work done is negative.

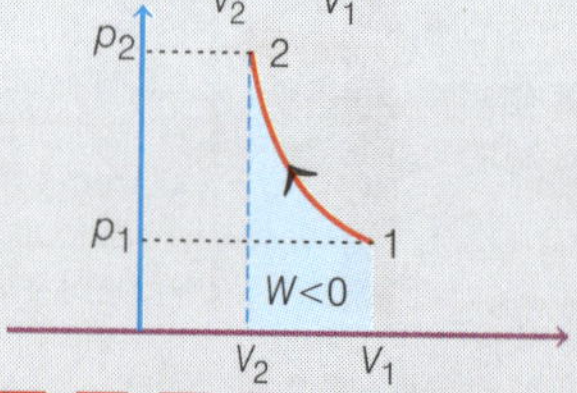

Gas

A state of matter with no fixed shape or volume but with a definite mass

Ideal Or Perfect Gas Equation

- **Perfect Gas** It obeys all gas laws in all conditions of pressure and temperature. Equation of perfect gas, $pV = nRT$ [R=8.31 $Jmol^{-1}K^{-1}$]
- **Real Gases** Real gases deviate from ideal gas because
  (i) Real gas molecules attract one another.
  (ii) Real gas molecules occupy a finite volume.
- **Real or Van der Waal's Gas Equation**

$$\left(p + \frac{a}{V^2}\right)(V - b) = RT \text{ [For 1 mole of gas]}$$

Dimension [a] = $[ML^5T^{-2}]$, Unit [a] = $N\text{-}m^4$

Dimension [b] = $[L^3]$, Unit $b = m^3$

Assumptions of Kinetic Theory of Gas

(i) Molecular size is negligible in comparison to intermolecular distance.
(ii) No attractive or repulsive force acts between gas molecules.
(iii) The force due to gravity on the molecules is neglected.
(iv) All collisions between the molecules and a wall are considered to be perfectly elastic.
(v) Inspite of the molecular collisions, the density remains uniform throughout the gas.
(vi) All gases are at high temperature and low pressure behave like an ideal gas.

Kinetic Interpretation of Temperature

Kinetic energy per molecule $(E) \propto T$

$v_{rms} \propto \sqrt{T}$, at, $T = 0$ K, $v_{rms} = 0$

At absolute zero, all molecular motion stops.

Velocity of Gaseous Particles

Root Mean Square Speed

$$v_{rms} = \sqrt{\frac{v_1^2 + v_2^2 + ... + v_n^2}{n}}, \; v_{rms} = \sqrt{\frac{3RT}{M}} = \sqrt{\frac{3p}{\rho}} = \sqrt{\frac{3kT}{m}}$$

Average Speed

$$v_{avg} = \frac{v_1 + v_2 + ... + v_n}{n}, \; v_{avg} = \sqrt{\frac{8RT}{\pi M}} = \sqrt{\frac{8p}{\pi\rho}}$$

Most Probable Speed

$$v_{mp} = \sqrt{\frac{2RT}{M}} = \sqrt{\frac{2p}{\rho}} = \sqrt{\frac{2kT}{m}}$$

Velocity of gaseous particles in decreasing order

$v_{rms} > v_{avg} > v_{mp}$, $\quad v_{rms} : v_{avg} : v_{mp} = \sqrt{3} : \sqrt{\frac{8}{\pi}} : \sqrt{2}$

POWER TIPS

Pressure Exerted by the Gas

$$p = \frac{1}{3}\frac{M}{V}v_{rms}^2 = \frac{1}{3}\frac{mN}{V}v_{rms}^2 = \frac{1}{3}\rho v_{rms}^2$$

Relation between Pressure and Kinetic Energy

$$p = \frac{2}{3}E$$

Here, E = Kinetic energy per unit volume

Degrees of Freedom

Number of minimum co-ordinates required to specify the dynamical state of system.

For Monoatomic Gas

$f = 3$

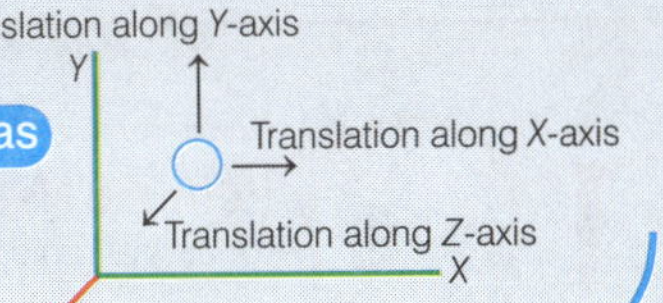

For Diatomic Gas

(a) At room temperature $f = 5$

(b) At high temperature $f = 7$

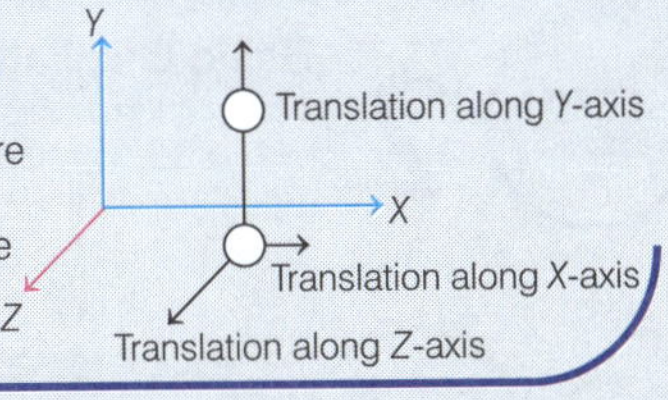

For Triatomic Gas

(a) Linear $f = 5$

(b) Non-linear $f = 6$

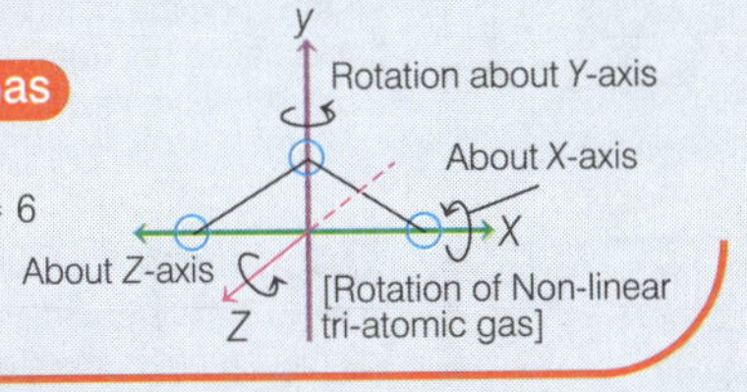

For Polyatomic Gas

$f = 6$

For each vibrational mode, $f = 2$

Maxwell's Law of Equipartition of Energy

For a dynamic system in thermal equilibrium

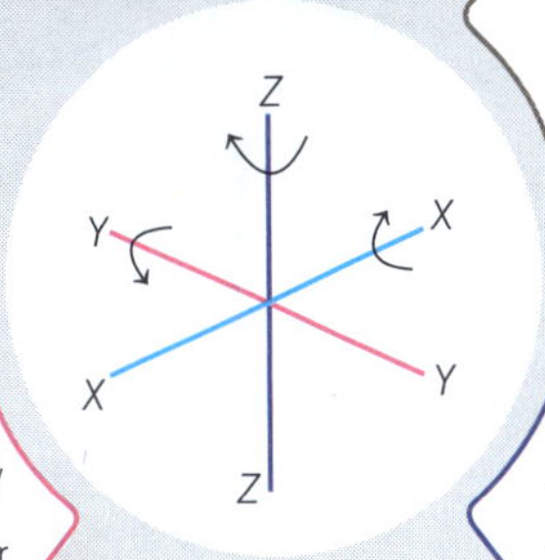

- Total energy is distributed equally amongst all the degree of freedom.
- The energy associated with each molecule per degree of freedom $= \frac{1}{2}k_BT$
- Average KE of a particle having f-degree of freedom $= \frac{f}{2}k_BT$
- Translation KE of a molecule (Monoatomic) $= \frac{3}{2}k_BT$
- Translation KE of a mole (Monoatomic) $= \frac{3}{2}RT$
- Internal energy of an ideal gas (μ moles) $= \frac{f}{2}\mu RT$
- Translation KE (1 mole, Diatomic) $= \frac{3}{2}RT$

Specific Heat Capacity

$C_V = \frac{1}{n}\left(\frac{dQ}{T}\right)$, $V =$ constant

$C_p = \frac{1}{n}\left(\frac{dQ}{T}\right)$, $p =$ constant

$C_p = C_V + R$ Mayer's equation

Atomicity	Transla-tional	Rotati-onal	Total (f)	$\gamma = \frac{C_p}{C_V} = 1+\frac{2}{f}$	$C_V = \frac{f}{2}R = \frac{R}{\gamma-1}$	$C_p = \left(1+\frac{f}{2}\right)R = \frac{\gamma R}{\gamma-1}$
Monotomic (He, Ar, Ne)	3	0	3	$\frac{5}{3} = 1.67$	$\frac{3}{2}R$	$\frac{5}{2}R$
Diatomic (H_2, N_2)	3	2	5	$\frac{7}{5} = 1.4$	$\frac{5}{2}R$	$\frac{7}{2}R$
Triatomic (Linear) CO_2	3	2	5	$\frac{7}{5} = 1.4$	$\frac{5}{2}R$	$\frac{7}{2}R$
Triatomic Non-Linear –NH_3 & Polyatomic	3	3	6	$\frac{4}{3} = 1.33$	$3R$	$4R$

Mixing of Gases

1 Molecular weight

$$M_{W_{mix}} = \frac{n_1 M_{W_1} + n_2 M_{W_2} + \ldots}{n_1 + n_2}$$

2 Specific heat at constant volume

$$C_{V_{mix}} = \frac{n_1 C_{V_1} + n_2 C_{V_2} + \ldots}{n_1 + n_2}$$

3 Specific heat at constant pressure

$$C_{p_{mix}} = \frac{n_1 C_{p_1} + n_2 C_{p_2} + \ldots}{n_1 + n_2}$$

4 Heat capacity ratio

$$\gamma_{mix} = \frac{C_{p_{mix}}}{C_{V_{min}}} = \frac{n_1 C_{p_1} + n_2 C_{p_2} + \ldots}{n_1 C_{V_1} + n_2 C_{p_2} + \ldots}$$

MEAN FREE PATH

The mean free path is the average distance a moving particle travels between two successive collisions

Mean free path $\longrightarrow \lambda_m = \frac{1}{\sqrt{2}\pi d^2 n} \longleftarrow$ Number density $= \frac{\text{Number of molecules}}{\text{Volume}}$

d: Diameter of molecule

Volume $= \pi d^2 vt$

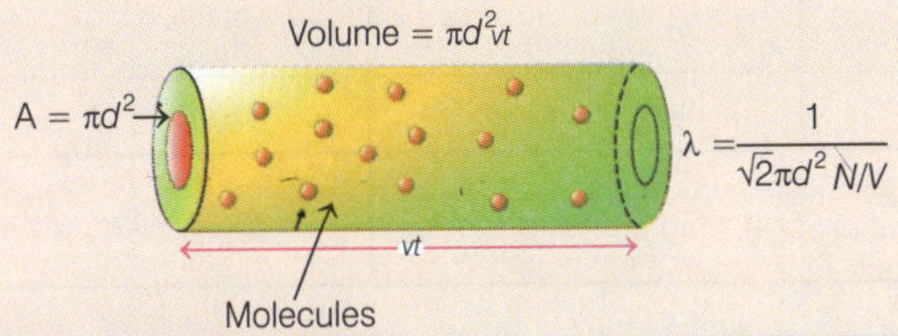

$$\lambda = \frac{1}{\sqrt{2}\pi d^2 N/V}$$

Chapter 13

Oscillation

Periodic Motion

- Any motion that repeats itself over and over again at a regular intervals of time. e.g. motion of planets around sun, motion of hands of a clock.

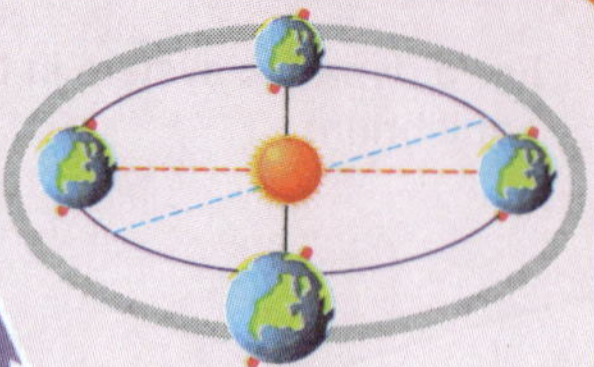

Restoring Force

A force acting on a system to bring back the system in its original position when it is displaced from its equilibrium position.
It is directed opposite to the displacement.

$F = -Kx$

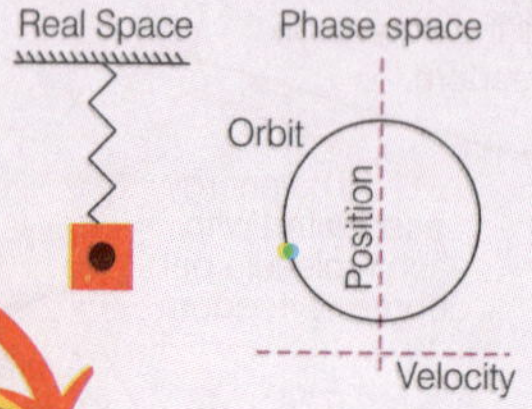

Simple Harmonic Motion

It is the simplest form of oscillatory motion.
e.g. Simple pendulum, mass spring system.

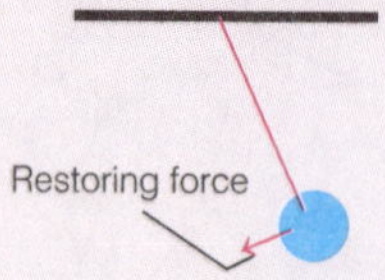

Important Features of Simple Harmonic Motion (SHM)

1 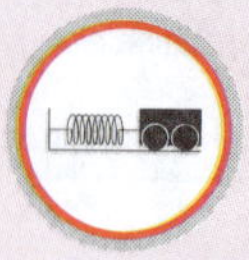 **Periodic Nature** The motion of the particle repeats at regular intervals, making it periodic.

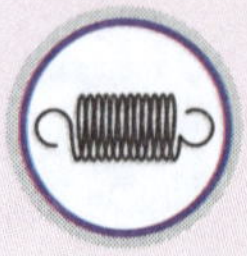 2 **Basic Oscillatory Motion** SHM is the simplest form of oscillation, where the particle moves back and forth around a central position with a constant amplitude and fixed frequency.

3  **Proportional Restoring Force** The force acting on the particle is directly proportional to its displacement from the mean position, pulling it back toward equilibrium.

 4 **Opposition to Displacement** The force always acts to counter any increase in the particle's displacement from its mean position.

5  **Representation by Harmonic Function** SHM can be described using a single sine or cosine function, capturing its regular, wave-like motion.

Types of SHM

Linear SHM To and fro motion about a fixed axis along a straight line. e.g., motion of block connected to spring.

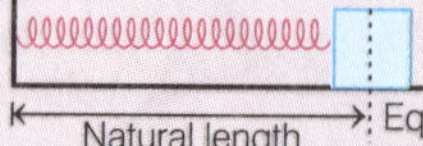

Angular SHM A system oscillating angularly with respect to a fixed position.
e.g. motion of bob

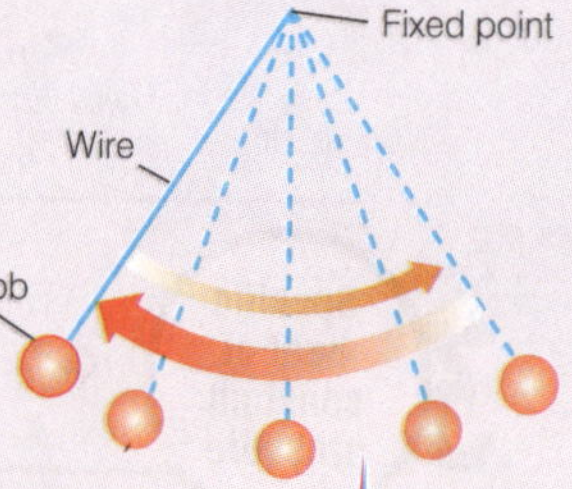

Comparision of Linear and Angular SHM

S.No	Linear SHM	Angular SHM
(i)	$F \propto (-x)$ $F = -kx$ where k restoring force, constant.	$\tau \propto (-\theta)$ $\tau = -C\theta$ where C is restoring torque, constant.
(ii)	$a = -\frac{k}{m}x$	$\alpha = -\frac{C}{I}\theta$
(iii)	$\frac{d^2x}{dr^2} + \frac{k}{m}x = 0$	$\frac{d^2\theta}{dr^2} + \frac{C}{I}\theta = 0$
(iv)	$a = -\omega^2 x$	$\alpha = -\omega^2\theta$
(v)	$\omega^2 = \frac{k}{m}; \omega = \sqrt{\frac{k}{m}} = \frac{2\pi}{T}$	$\omega = \sqrt{\frac{C}{I}} = 2\pi\nu = \frac{2\pi}{T}$

Oscillatory Motion

- A repeated back and forth motion about a mean position.
- It is also called **vibratory** or **harmonic motion**
  e.g. motion of pendulum or a motion of spring.

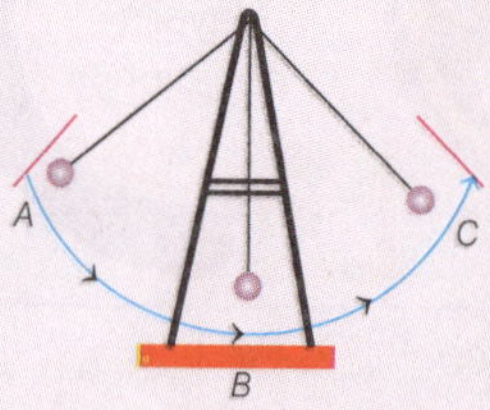

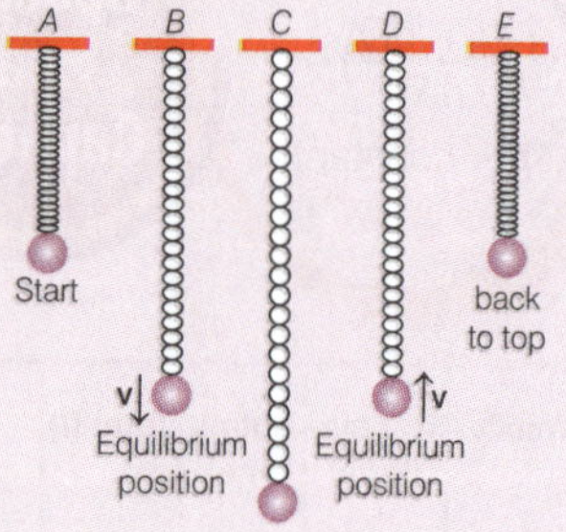

Characteristics of Oscillatory Motion

- **Stable Equilibrium and Tendency to Return** When a particle is slightly displaced from a stable equilibrium position, it naturally moves back towards this position.
- **Restoring Force Towards Mean Position** A force acts on the particle, always directed towards the equilibrium position, opposing its displacement.
- **Conservation of Energy** The total energy in an ideal oscillatory motion is conserved.
- **Periodicity of Oscillatory Motion** All oscillatory motions are periodic. However, not all periodic motions are oscillatory.

Some Important Terms Connected with SHM

1 Phase

It represents the state of motion of particle.
It is the argument of sine or cosine function.
$x(t) = A \sin(\omega t + \phi_0)$, phase $(\phi) = \omega t + \phi_0$

Phase constant

The phase of a vibrating particle corresponding to time $t = 0$.
$x(t) = A \sin(\omega t + \phi_0)$, phase constant $= \phi_0$

2 Displacement

Distance from the mean position at any given time instant.
It is given by $x(t) = A \sin(\omega t + \phi_0)$

3 Amplitude

Maximum displacement of the particle from the equilibrium position.

4 Frequency

Number of oscillations completed in unit time interval $f = 1/T = \omega/2\pi$
Angular frequency, $\omega = 2\pi f$

5 Time Period

Smallest interval after which the oscillator motion gets repeated.

$$T = 2\pi/\omega = 2\pi\sqrt{(m/k)}$$

Equations of SHM

Curves In SHM

- **Time-displacement equation**

$$y = A \sin \omega t$$

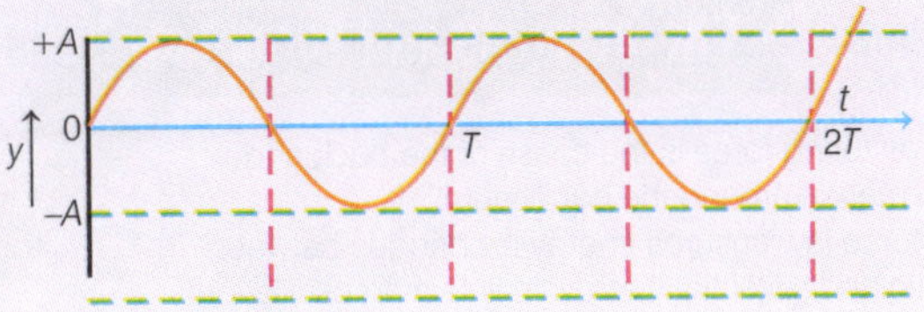

- **Time-velocity equation**

$$v = \frac{dy}{dt} = A\omega \cos \omega t$$

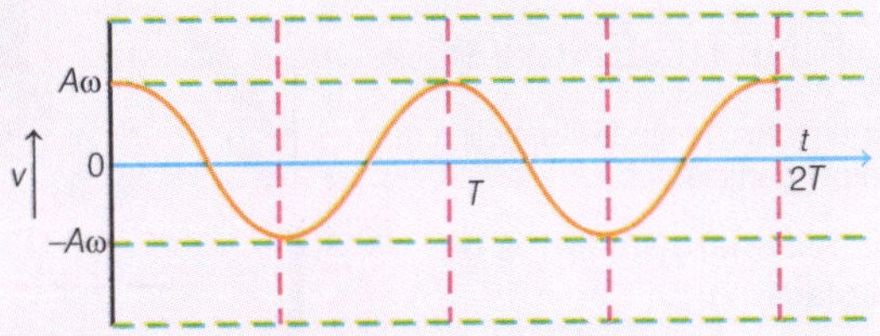

- **Time-acceleration equation**

$$a = \frac{dv}{dt} = -A\omega^2 \sin\omega t$$

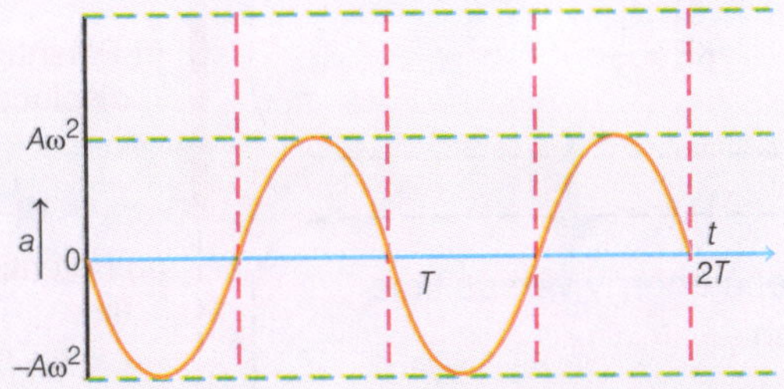

Velocity of particle in SHM

Velocity of particle at any instant t

$$v(t) = \omega\sqrt{(A^2 - x^2)}$$

- Velocity will be maximum when the displacement from mean position is zero i.e. at mean position $v_{max} = \omega A$
- Velocity will be minimum when $x = \pm A$ i.e. at the position of maximum displacement, $v_{min} = 0$.
- Velocity is always ahead of displacement by phase angle $\pi/2$.
- The graph between displacement and velocity is an ellipse.

$$\Rightarrow \frac{v^2}{\omega^2 A^2} + \frac{x^2}{A^2} = 1$$

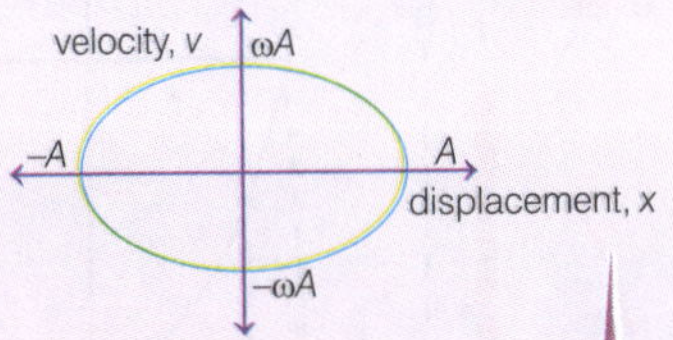

Acceleration of Particle in SHM

- Acceleration of particle at any instant t, $a = -\omega^2 x$.
- Acceleration will be maximum when $x = \pm A$. i.e. $a_{max} = \pm\omega^2 A$
- It will be minimum when $x = 0$ i.e. $a_{min} = 0$.
- It is ahead of displacement by angle π
- Lead the velocity by an angle $\pi/2$.
- The graph between acceleration and displacement is a straight line
- The graph between velocity and acceleration is an ellipse and if $\omega = 1$, then the graph is in the form of circle.

The following table gives the different values of displacement, velocity and acceleration for various values of t for one complete cycle.

Time, (t)	0	$T/4$	$T/2$	$3T/4$	T
Phase angle (ωt)	0	$\pi/2$	π	$3\pi/2$	2π
Displacement $x(t)$	0 (min)	$+A$ (max)	0 (min)	$-A$ (max)	0 (min)
Velocity $v(t)$	$+\omega A$ (max)	0 (min)	$-\omega A$ (max)	0 (min)	$+\omega A$ (max)
Acceleration $a(t)$	0 (min)	$-\omega^2 A$ (max)	0 (min)	$+\omega^2 A$ (max)	0 (min)

Force Law in Simple Harmonic Motion

- Restoring force acts on a particle to bring it back to the equilibrium position whenever it is displaced.
- This force is always directed opposite to the displacement from the mean position.

Characteristics of Force Law

- The restoring force is the cause of the back and forth motion around the equilibrium.
- The force law ensures energy exchanges between kinetic and potential energy, maintaining oscillation.
- This force law is foundational in understanding other oscillatory systems and waves.

Hooke's Law

- The magnitude of the restoring force is directly proportional to the displacement from the mean position.

$$F \propto -x$$

- Negative sign indicates the force is acting in opposite direction.

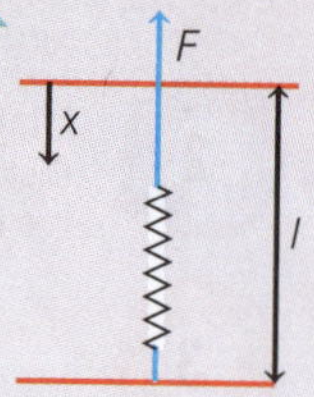

Energy in SHM

KINETIC ENERGY

The Energy associated with motion of an oscillatory particle.

(i) Kinetic energy in terms of displacement

$$KE = \frac{1}{2} m\omega^2 (A^2 - x^2)$$

(ii) Kinetic energy in terms of time

$$KE = \frac{1}{2} m\omega^2 A^2 \cos^2 \omega t$$

Kinetic energy *versus* time graph

$$KE_{max} = \frac{1}{2} m\omega^2 A^2$$

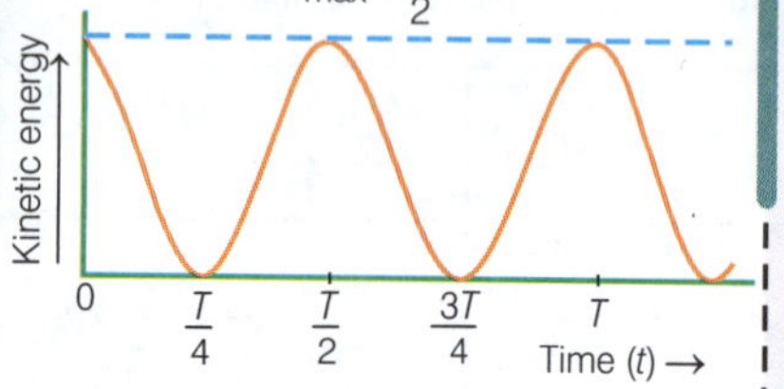

Special cases related to kinetic energy

- Kinetic energy is maximum at mean position, i.e. at $x = 0$,

$$KE_{max} = \frac{1}{2} m\omega^2 A^2$$

- Kinetic energy is minimum or zero at extreme position, i.e. at $x = \pm A$, KE_{min} = zero

POTENTIAL ENERGY

The energy stored due to displacement from the equilibrium position whenever a restoring force acts on the particle.

(i) Potential energy in terms of displacement

$$U = \frac{1}{2} m\omega^2 x^2 = \frac{1}{2} kx^2$$

(ii) Potential energy in terms of time

$$U = \frac{1}{2} m\omega^2 A^2 \sin^2 \omega t$$

Potential energy *versus* time graph

$$U_{max} = \frac{1}{2} kA^2$$

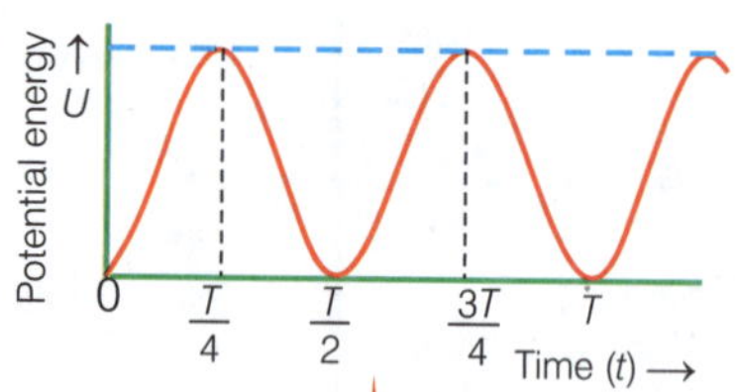

Special cases related to potential energy

- Potential energy is maximum at extreme position, i.e. at $x = \pm A$

$$U_{max} = \frac{1}{2} m\omega^2 A^2$$

- Potential energy is minimum (zero) at mean position, i.e.at $x = 0$, $U_{min} = 0$

TOTAL MECHANICAL ENERGY

Sum of kinetic and potential energies, which remain constant in ideal SHM.

Total Mechanical Energy,

$$E = K + U$$

$$E = \frac{1}{2} m\omega^2 A^2 \text{ or } E = \frac{1}{2} kA^2$$

Total energy *versus* time graph

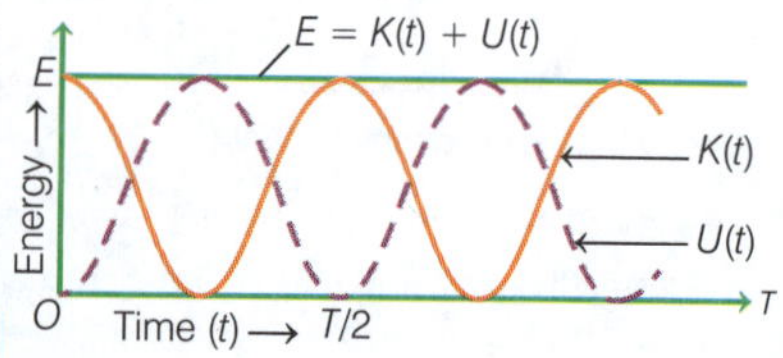

Total energy *versus* displacement graph

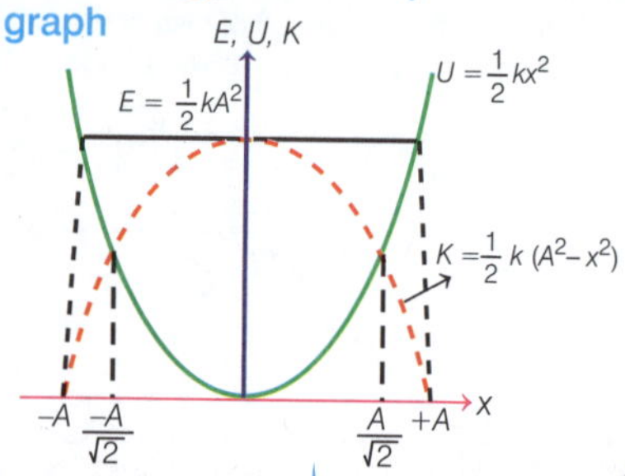

Observations from the graph

- The total mechanical energy remains constant.
- The graphs of U and K *versus* x are parabolic.
- Both kinetic energy and potential energy reach maximum value twice during each period of SHM.

Simple Pendulum

- **Restoring force acting on pendulum**

  $F = -mg\sin\theta$

  $F = -mg(x/L)$

  $ma = -mg(x/L)$
- **Acceleration**, $a = -\omega^2 x$
- **Time period,**

  $T = 2\pi\sqrt{(L/g)}$
- **Frequency** $\nu = 1/T = (1/2\pi)\sqrt{g/L}$

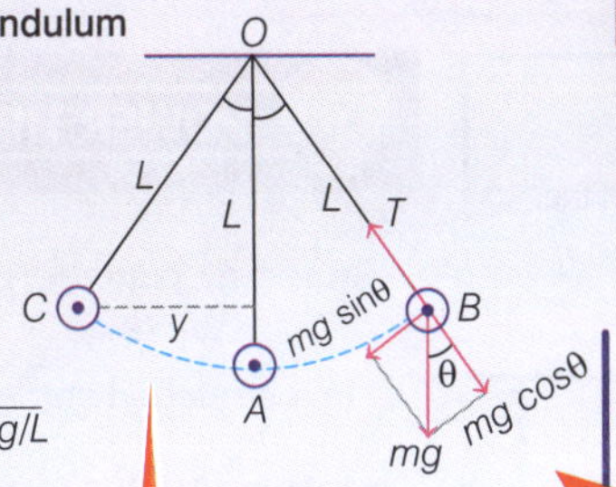

POWER TIPS

(i) If the length of the spring is made n times, then the effective force constant becomes $1/n$ times and the time period becomes $\sqrt{n}$ times.

(ii) If a spring of spring constant k is divided into n equal parts, the spring constant of each part becomes nk and time period becomes $1/\sqrt{n}$ times.

(iii) The force constant of a stiffer spring is more than that of a soft spring.

(iv) Spring constant $\propto \dfrac{1}{\text{Extension}} \propto \dfrac{1}{\text{Length of spring}}$

(v) If a spring is cut into two parts of lengths l_1 and l_2 such that $l_1 = nl_2$, then $\dfrac{k_1}{k_2} = \dfrac{1}{n}$

Simple Pendulum in Lift

Lift at constant velocity

v = constant

$\Rightarrow a = 0 \qquad \therefore T = 2\pi\sqrt{(L/g)}$

- **Lift is moving upward with acceleration a,**

  $g_{eff} = g + a$

  $\therefore \quad T = 2\pi\sqrt{(L/g_{eff})}$
- **Lift is moving downward with acceleration a,**

  $g_{eff} = g - a$

  $\therefore \quad T = 2\pi\sqrt{(L/g_{eff})}$
- **Lift falls freely,** $g_{eff} = 0$
- **Simple pendulum in moving vehicle**

  Reference system moving horizontally with acceleration a,

  $g_{eff} = \sqrt{g^2 + a^2} \quad \therefore T = 2\pi\sqrt{L/(g^2 + a^2)}$

  Reference system is moving on an inclined plane

  $g_{eff} = g\cos\theta \quad \therefore T = 2\pi\sqrt{L/g\cos\theta}$

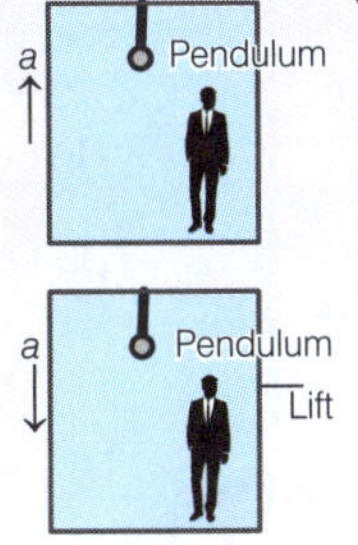

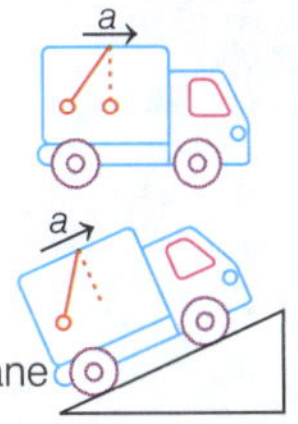

Systems Executing SHM

Vertical Spring System

$mg = kd$

$F = mg - k(d + x)$

$F = -kx$

$a = \dfrac{-k}{m}x$

$a = -\omega^2 x$

$\omega = \sqrt{\dfrac{k}{m}}$

$T = 2\pi\sqrt{\dfrac{m}{k}}$

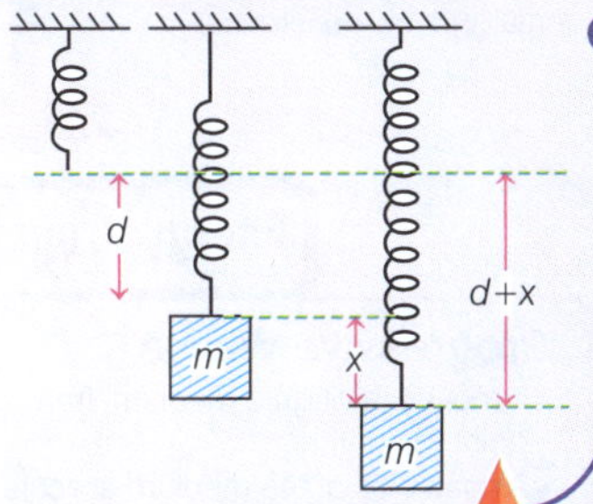

Spring Mass System

- Restoring force,

  $F = -kx$
- Acceleration,

  $a = -(k/m)x, \ a = -\omega^2 x$
- $\omega = \sqrt{(k/m)} = 2\pi/T$

  $\dfrac{1}{T} = \dfrac{1}{2\pi}\sqrt{\dfrac{k}{m}}$ or $T = 2\pi\sqrt{\dfrac{m}{k}}$

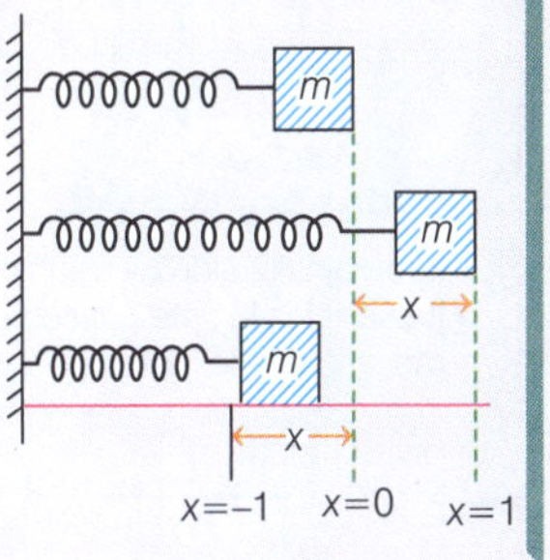

Two Masses Connected by a Spring

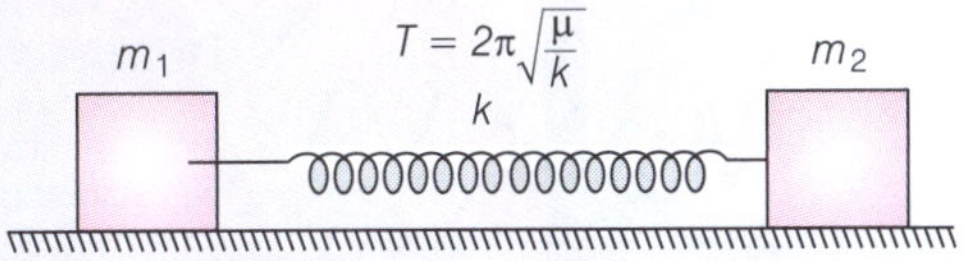

Two blocks connected by a spring

Here, μ = reduced mass $= \dfrac{m_1 m_2}{m_1 + m_2}$

Series Combination of Springs

Total extension $= x_1 + x_2$,

Force on both springs

$F = -k_1x_1 = -k_2x_2, \ x = -F(1/k_1 + 1/k_2)$

$1/k = 1/k_1 + 1/k_2$

Two springs of spring constants k_1 and k_2 are joined in series as shown in figure.

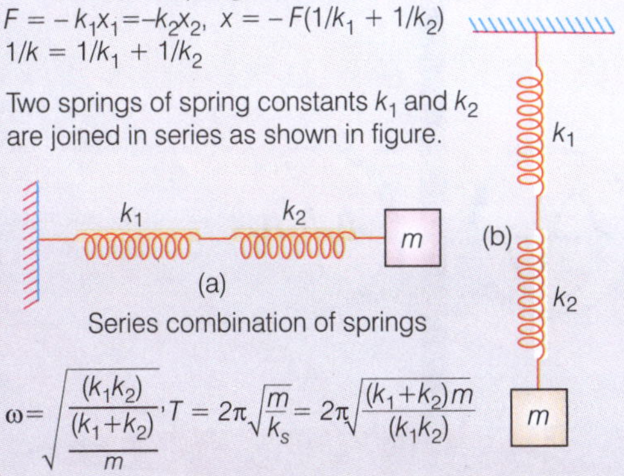

Series combination of springs

$\omega = \sqrt{\dfrac{\frac{(k_1k_2)}{(k_1+k_2)}}{m}}, \ T = 2\pi\sqrt{\dfrac{m}{k_s}} = 2\pi\sqrt{\dfrac{(k_1+k_2)m}{(k_1k_2)}}$

Combination of Springs

Parallel Combination of Springs

- Two springs of spring constants k_1 and k_2 are joined in parallel as shown in figure.

  Then, spring constant $k_p = (k_1 + k_2)$

  Time period,

  $T = 2\pi\sqrt{\dfrac{m}{k_p}} = 2\pi\sqrt{\dfrac{m}{k_1+k_2}}, \ \omega\sqrt{\dfrac{k_1+k_2}{m}}$

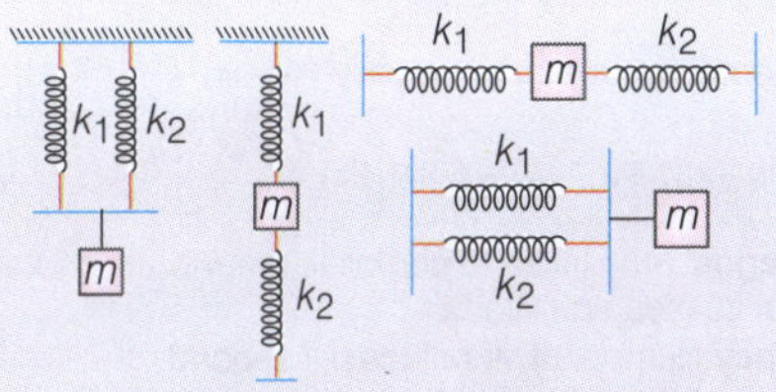

Parallel combination of springs

Chapter **14**

Waves

Characteristics

- The particles of the medium are executing SHM.
- The energy is transferred from one place to another without any actual transfer of the particles of the medium.
- The phase of vibration of the particles keeps on changing.
- The velocity of the particle is not equal to velocity of wave.

POWER TIPS

Speed of Transverse Wave

- **In a stretched string** $v=\sqrt{\frac{T}{\mu}}=\sqrt{\frac{T}{\rho\pi r^2}}$

  where μ is linear mass density and T is tension

  $\frac{v_1}{v_2}=\sqrt{\frac{T_1}{T_2}}\times\frac{r_2}{r_1}$
- **In solid** $v=\sqrt{\frac{\eta}{\rho}}$
- **In liquid** $T=Mg\left(1-\frac{\rho}{\sigma}\right)$

  $v=\sqrt{\frac{Mg\left(1-\frac{\rho}{\sigma}\right)}{\mu}}$

Speed of Longitudinal Wave

- **In liquid or gas** $v=\sqrt{\frac{\beta}{\rho}}$
- **In solid** $v=\sqrt{\frac{\beta+\frac{4}{3}\eta}{\rho}}$
- Where, $\beta+\frac{4}{3}\eta$ is elongational elasticity.
- **In solid Rod** $v=\sqrt{\frac{Y}{\rho}}$
- where, Y is Young's modulus.

WAVES

A disturbance of field in which a physical attribute oscillates repeatedly at each point to neighbouring point.

Medium

Mechanical Waves

- Requires material medium for propagation.

  e.g. Sound waves, waves on string and spring.
- Medium should posses elasticity, inertia and low resistance.

Non-mechanical Waves

- Do not require any medium for their propagation.
- Can transfer energy even in vaccum.
- Propagates due to variation of electric and magnetic fields.
- Electromagnetic waves are the only type of non-mechanical waves.

Dimension

(i) One dimensional

(ii) Two dimensional

(iii) Three dimensional

Energy Propagation

Progressive Waves

- It moves through a medium, transferring energy from one point to another.
- All particles of the medium execute SHM with same amplitude and frequency.
- Average energy over one time period is equal to the sum of KE and PE.

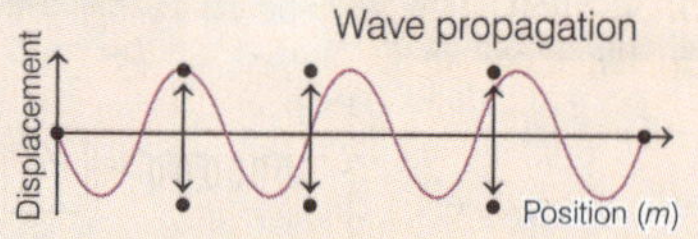

Stationary Waves

- It remains stationary with no net transfer of energy.
- It oscillates in time but its peak amplitude profile does not move in space.

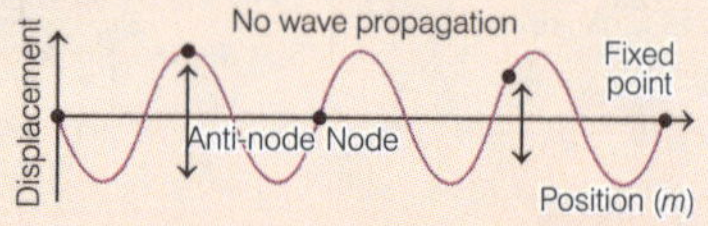

Equation of Progressive Wave

- $y(x,t)=A\sin(\omega t\pm kx+\phi)$
- **Amplitude** Maximum displacement of a particle about their mean position.
- **Wave number** Number of waves accomodated in unit distance. It is equal to $1/\lambda$
- **Phase constant (k)** Change in phase per unit advancement. $k=\frac{2\pi}{\lambda}=\frac{\omega}{v}$
- **Representation of sound wave** $y=A\sin\left[k\left(\frac{\omega}{k}t\mp x\right)\right]$

  $y=A\sin\{k(vt\mp x)\}$, $y=A\sin\left[2\pi\left(\frac{t}{T}\mp\frac{x}{\lambda}\right)\right]$
- **Time period** Time taken to complete one vibration to and fro about its mean position.
- **Frequency** Number of vibrations per second.
- **Wave velocity or phase velocity** Distance covered by a wave per unit time in its direction of propagation.

Vibration

Transverse Waves

- Particles of the medium oscillate in the direction perpendicular to the direction of wave propagation.

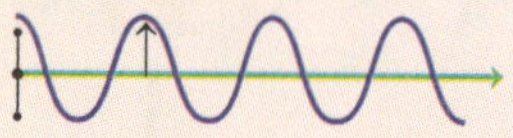

- Travels in the form of crests and trough

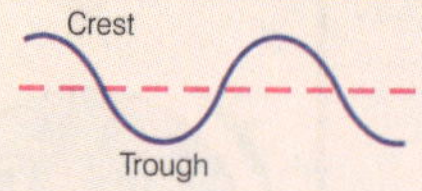

- Can be polarised. e.g. Movement of strings of guitar

Longitudinal Waves

- Particles of the medium oscillates along the direction of wave propagation.

- Travels in the form of compression and rarefaction.
- Cannot be polarised e.g. Sound waves

Beats

- Phenomenon of periodic change in the intensity of sound when two waves of slightly different frequency superpose with each other.
- One beat is the variation in the intensity of sound between successive maxima or minima.
- Number of beats per second is beat frequency.
  Beat frequency $= n_1 - n_2$ $(n \rightarrow \text{frequency})$
- **Time period**
  $$T = \frac{1}{n_1 - n_2}$$
- Frequency of variation of amplitude $= \frac{n_1 - n_2}{2}$
- Frequency of resultant wave $= \frac{n_1 + n_2}{2}$
- Amplitude is function of time.

Interference

- If $y_1 = A_1 \sin \omega t$
  $y_2 = A_2 \sin(\omega t + \phi)$

  Resultant displacement,
  $$y = A \sin(\omega t + \theta)$$
  θ is resultant phase constant
- **Resultant Amplitude**
  $$A = \sqrt{A_1^2 + A_2^2 + 2A_1 A_2 \cos\phi}$$
  $$\tan\theta = \frac{A_1 \sin\phi}{A_1 + A_2 \cos\phi}$$
- **Intensity**
  $$I \propto A^2$$
  $$A^2 = A_1^2 + A_2^2 + 2A_1 A_2 \cos\phi$$
  $$I = I_1 + I_2 + 2\sqrt{I_1 I_2} \cos\phi$$
  $$\left(\frac{I_1}{I_2}\right) = \left(\frac{A_1}{A_2}\right)^2$$
  $$\frac{I_{max}}{I_{min}} = \frac{(a_1 + a_2)^2}{(a_1 - a_2)^2} = \frac{(\sqrt{I_1} + \sqrt{I_2})^2}{(\sqrt{I_1} - \sqrt{I_2})^2}$$

Types of Interference

Constructive Interference

For maximum intensity
Phase difference $\phi = 0, 2\pi, 4\pi$ ......
or $\phi = 2n\pi$, where $(n = 0, 1, 2, 3, ...)$
Path difference $\Delta x = 0, \lambda, 2\lambda$ ...
or $\Delta x = n\lambda$, where $n = 0, 1, 2, ...$
$$I_{max} = I_2 + I_2 + 2\sqrt{I_1 I_2}$$

Destructive Interference

For minimum intensity
Phase difference $\phi = \pi, 3\pi, 5\pi$ ....
or $\phi = (2n - 1)\pi$, (where $n = 1, 2, 3$ ...)
Path difference
$$\Delta x = \frac{\lambda}{2}, \frac{3\lambda}{2}, ... \text{ or } \Delta x = (2n - 1)\frac{\lambda}{2}, \text{ where } n = 1, 2, 3$$
$$I_{min} = I_1 + I_2 - 2\sqrt{I_1 I_2}$$

Superposition of Waves

- When two or more waves overlap, the resulting wave at any point is the sum of the displacement of the individual wave at that point.
  $$y = y_1 + y_2 + y_3 + ... + y_n$$
  Resultant amplitude,
  $$a = a_1 + a_2 + a_3 ... + a_n$$
- Possible only in waves of similar nature.
- Phenomena arising are
  (i) Interference
  (ii) Stationary waves
  (iii) Beats

Stationary or Standing Waves

1. Formed when two identical progressive waves moving in opposite direction superimpose.
2. There is no transfer of energy.
3. Displacement and velocity are zero at nodes and pressure change is zero.
4. Displacement and velocity are maximum at anti nodes and pressure change are zero.
5. Distance between two successive nodes or anti-nodes is $\lambda/2$. Distance between node and the next anti-node is $\lambda/4$.
6. Phase difference between any two particles in successive loop is 180°.

Equation of Standing Waves

- Wave reflected at free boundary.
  $y = 2A \cos kx \sin\omega t$
- Wave reflected at fixed boundary
  $y = 2A \sin kx \cos \omega t$

POWER TIPS

Reflection of waves

- Reflection from rigid end/denser medium changes the phase by angle π.
- Reflection from free end / rarer medium does not change phase.

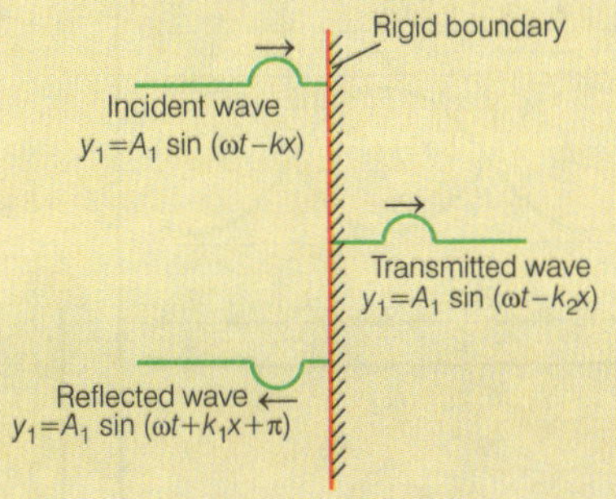

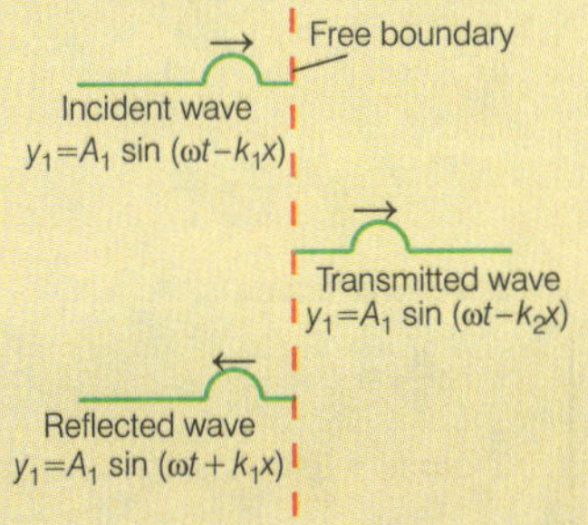

Vibration in String with One Fixed End

First mode of vibration

$f_1 = \frac{v}{2\lambda}$

Second mode of vibration

$f_2 = 2f_1$

Third mode of vibration

$f_3 = 3f_1$

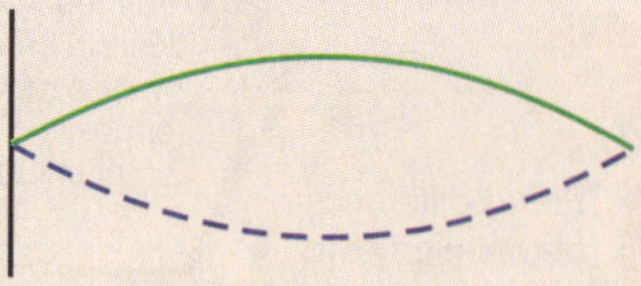

Vibration Of Strings Fixed At Both Ends

- $y = 2A \sin kx \cos \omega t$
- Boundary condition $L = \frac{n\lambda}{2}, n = 1, 2, 3, ...$
- Possible wavelength $\lambda = \frac{2L}{n}, n = 1, 2, 3, ...$ $\quad f = \frac{nl}{2L}, n = 1, 2, 3$

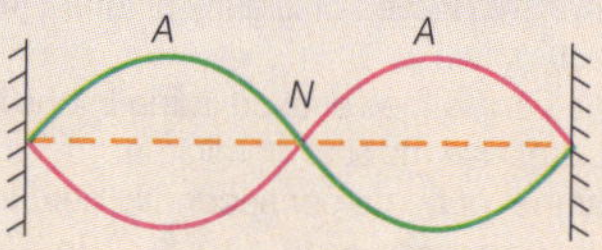

Vibrations of Stretched String

Law of Tension

$f \propto \sqrt{T} \Rightarrow \frac{f}{\sqrt{T}} = \text{Constant}$

$\frac{f_1}{f_2} = \sqrt{\frac{T_1}{T_2}}$

Law of length

$f \propto \frac{1}{L} \Rightarrow fL = \text{Constant}$

$f_1 L_1 = f_2 L_2$

Law of mass

$f \propto \frac{1}{\sqrt{\mu}} = f\sqrt{\mu} = \text{Constant}$

$\frac{f_1}{f_2} = \sqrt{\frac{\mu_2}{\mu_1}}$

Law of diameter

$f \propto \frac{1}{D}$

$FD = \text{Constant}$

Law of density

$f = \frac{l}{\sqrt{\mu}}$

$f\sqrt{\mu} = \text{Constant}$

Modes Of Vibration

- Speed of transverse wave on string is $v = \sqrt{\frac{T}{m}}$
- **First mode of vibration (Fundamental note)**

  $L = \frac{\lambda}{2} \Rightarrow \lambda = 2L$

  $\therefore$ Frequency $f_1 = \frac{v}{\lambda} = \frac{1}{2L}\sqrt{\frac{T}{m}} = f$

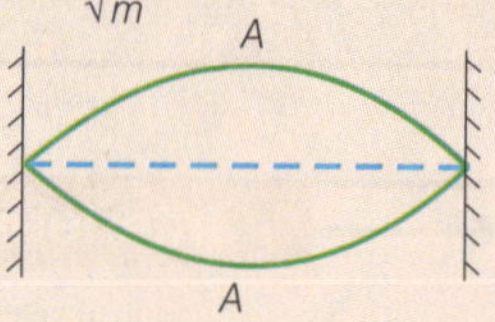

- **Second mode of vibration (First Overtone)**

  $L = 2.\frac{\lambda}{2} \Rightarrow \lambda = L$

  $\therefore$ frequency of vibration

  $f_2 = \frac{v}{\lambda} = \frac{1}{L}\sqrt{\frac{T}{m}} = 2f$

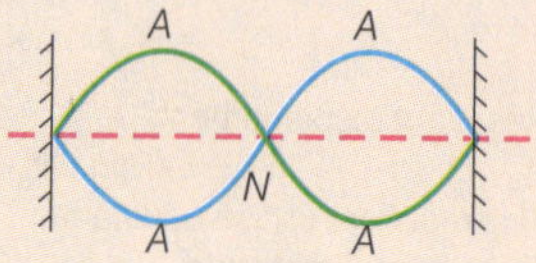

- **Third mode of vibration (Second Overtone)**

  $L = 3\frac{\lambda}{2} \Rightarrow \lambda = \frac{2L}{3}$

  $\therefore$ Frequency of vibration

  $f_3 = \frac{v}{\lambda} = \frac{3}{2L}\sqrt{\frac{T}{m}} = 3f$

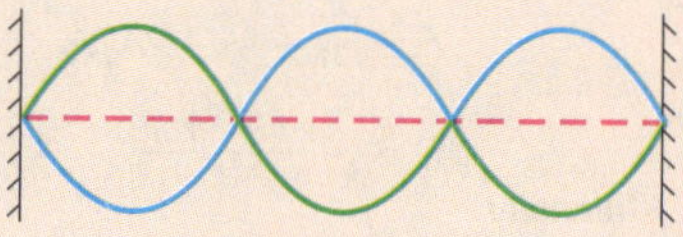

- In general, for p segment vibration $f_p = \frac{p}{2L}\sqrt{\frac{T}{m}} = pf$

Standing Waves

Organ Pipe

It is the simplest musical instrument in which sound is produced by setting an air column into vibrations

Open Organ Pipe

- For a pipe opened at both ends, each end is an anti-node.
- Frequency, $f = n.\frac{v}{2L}$
- **Fundamental tone**

  $L = \frac{\lambda}{2}$ or $\lambda = 2L$,

  $f_1 = \frac{v}{\lambda} = \frac{v}{2L}$

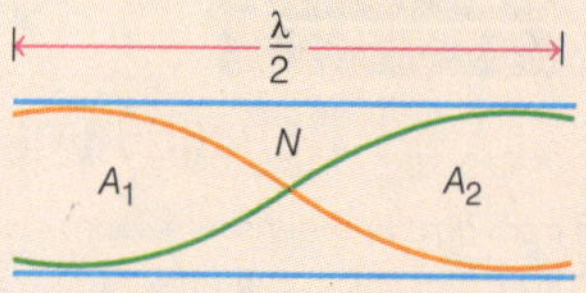

- **First overtone** $L = 2\frac{\lambda}{2}$ or $\lambda = L$

  $f_2 = \frac{v}{\lambda} = \frac{v}{L}$

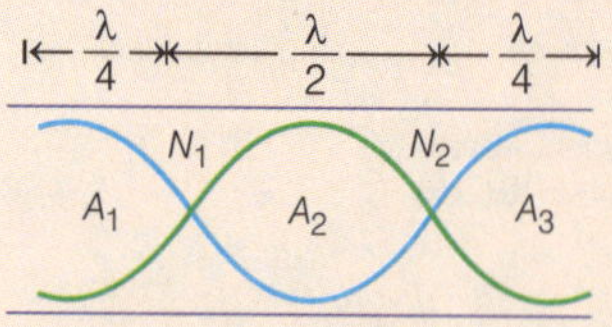

- **Second overtone**

  $\lambda = \frac{2L}{3} \Rightarrow L = \frac{3\lambda}{2}$

  $\Rightarrow f_3 = \frac{3v}{2L}$ or $f_3 = 3f_1$

  This mode is called **3rd harmonic** or **2nd overtone.**

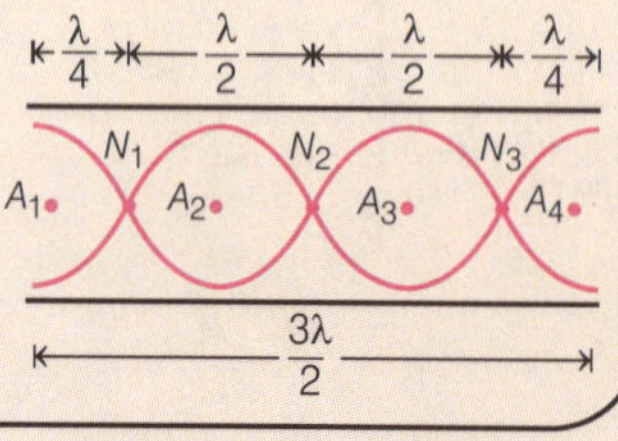

Closed Organ Pipe

- Frequency, $f = (2n + 1)\frac{v}{4L}$ $\quad n = 0, 1, 2, 3 ...$
- **Fundamental tone**

  $L = \frac{\lambda}{4}$ or $\lambda = 4L$

  or $\quad f \propto \frac{1}{L}$

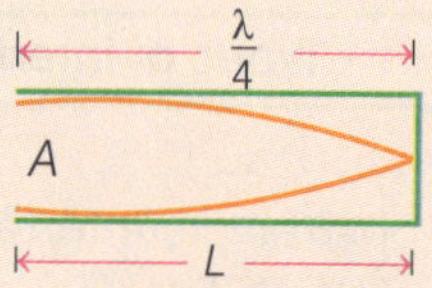

- **First over tone** $L = \frac{3\lambda}{4}$ or $\lambda = \frac{4L}{3}$

  $\therefore$ Frequency of the node produced

  $f = \frac{3v}{4L}$

  It is also called **third harmonics**

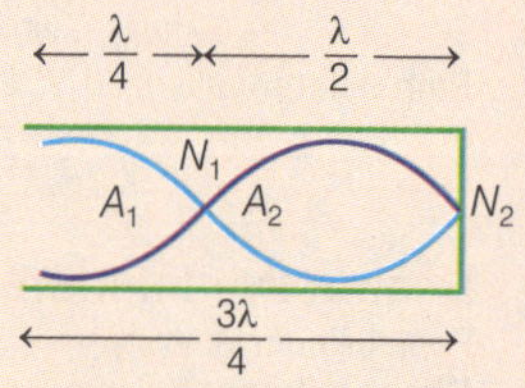

- **Second overtone**

  $L = \frac{5\lambda}{4}, f_5 = \frac{5v}{4L}$

  $\Rightarrow \quad f_3 = 5f_1$

  This mode is called **5th harmonic** or **2nd overtone.**

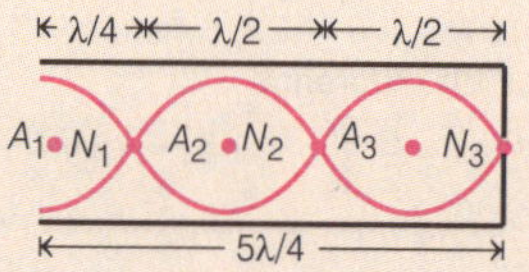

Chapter 15

Electric Charges and Fields

Properties of Electric Charge

Charge

Charge of proton is taken as +ve and that of electron is taken as –ve

Charge of proton
$+e = 1.6 \times 10^{-19}$C

Charge of electron
$-e = -1.6 \times 10^{-19}$ C

1. Like charges repel each other, unlike charges attract each other.
2. Charge can neither be created nor be destroyed, it can only be transferred from one body to another.
3. Charge is quantised, Charge on the body is always an integral multiple of charge of an electron.
   $Q = \pm ne$
   Here, Q = Total charge
   $n = 1, 2, 3 \ldots$
   and $e = 1.6 \times 10^{-19}$ C
4. Charge on a body can never be fractional, i.e. $\pm\frac{1}{2}e, \pm\frac{3}{2}e, \pm 5.2e$
5. Additivity of charge
   $Q' = Q_1 + Q_2$
6. Redistribution of charge
   $Q' = (Q_1 + Q_2)/2$
   Q' = charge on each shell after redistribution.

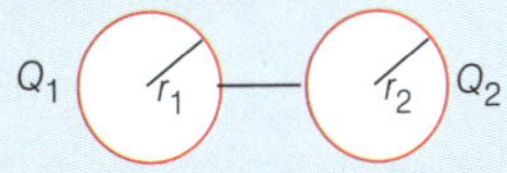

POWER TIPS

Charge on Pendulum

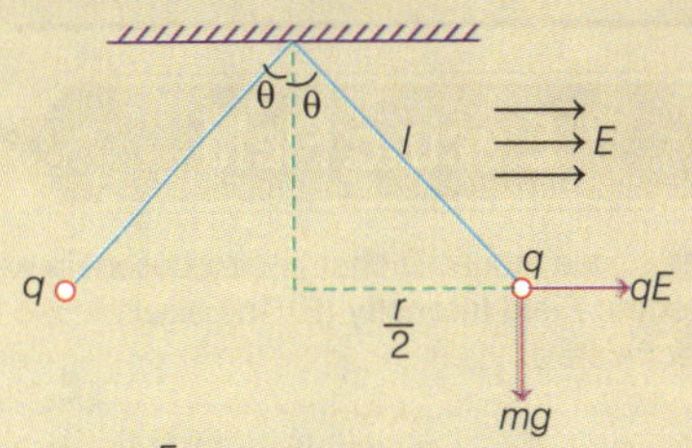

$\tan\theta = \frac{qE}{mg}, \quad \sin\theta = \frac{r}{2l}$

If θ is very small, then sin θ ≈ tanθ

$\frac{r}{2l} = \frac{kq^2/r^2}{mg}$

$r^3 \propto q^2$

Coulomb's Law

- Two point charges q_1 and q_2 are separated in vacuum by a distance r, then force between charges,

$F = \frac{k|q_1 q_2|}{r^2}, k = \frac{1}{4\pi\varepsilon_0} \approx 9 \times 10^9 \ \frac{\text{N-m}^2}{\text{C}^2}$

ε_0 = permittivity of free space
$= 8.85 \times 10^{-12}$ C^2/N-m^2

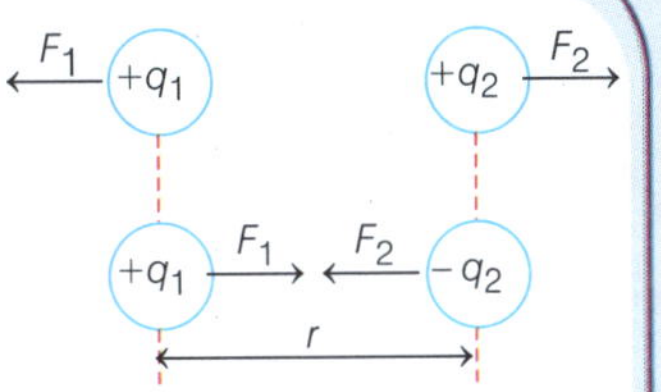

- If the charges are placed in another medium except air or vaccum. k = dielectric constant of the medium

$F_{medium} = \frac{F_{air}}{k}$

For air or vaccum, $k = 1$
For water, $k = 81$
For metals, $k = \infty$

Continuous Charge Distribution

Linear Charge Density (λ)
Charge per unit length
$\lambda dx = dQ$

Linear charge density

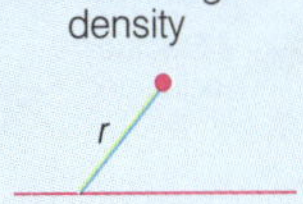

Surface Charge Density (σ)
Charge per unit surface area
$\sigma dA = dQ$

Area charge density

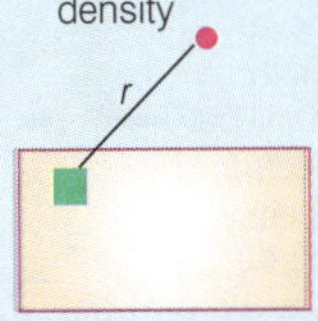

Volume Charge Density (ρ)
Charge per unit volume

Volume charge density

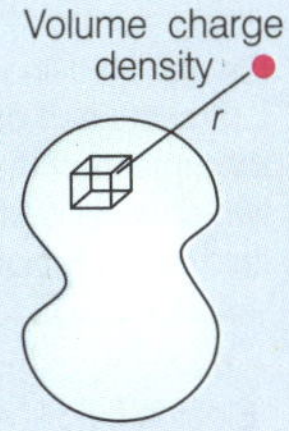

Coulomb's Law in Vector Form

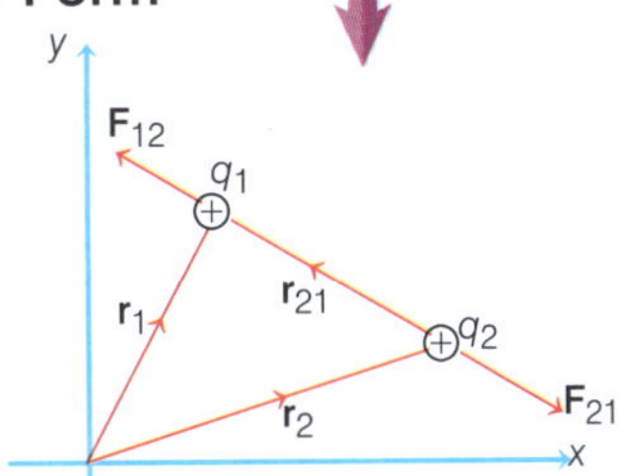

$\mathbf{F}_{12} = \frac{Kq_1q_2}{r^2}\,\hat{\mathbf{r}}_{21}$

$\hat{\mathbf{r}}_{21} \rightarrow$ Unit vector pointing from q_2 to q_1

$\hat{\mathbf{r}}_{12} \rightarrow$ Unit vector pointing from q_1 to q_2

$\mathbf{F}_{21} = \frac{Kq_1q_2}{r^2}\,\mathbf{r}_{12}$

Force on q_1 due to q_2 = – Force on q_2 due to q_1

$\mathbf{F}_{12} = -\mathbf{F}_{21}$

Superposition Principle : Forces between Multiple Charges

The force on any charge due to a number of other charges is the vector sum of all the forces on that charge due to the other charges.

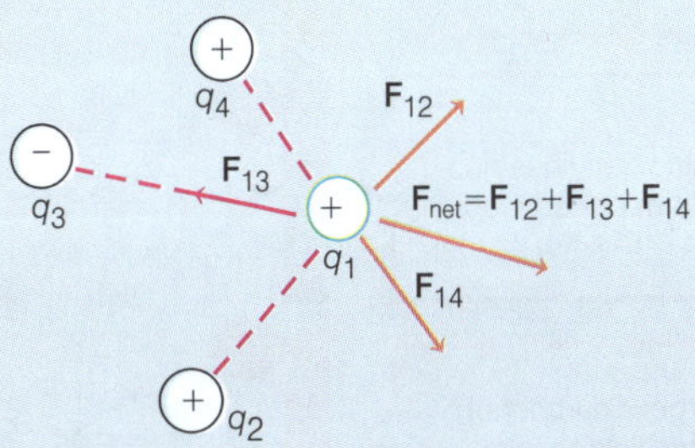

Electric Field Intensity Due to a Point Charge

$$\mathbf{F} = \frac{1}{4\pi\varepsilon_0}\frac{Q(q)}{r^2}\hat{\imath}, \qquad \mathbf{E} = \frac{\mathbf{F}}{q} = \frac{1}{4\pi\varepsilon_0}\frac{Q}{r^2}\hat{\imath}$$

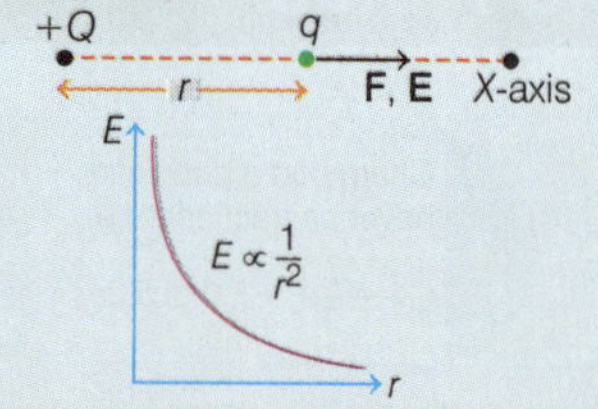

Electric field at a point, due to point charge,

$$E = \frac{kQ}{r^2}$$

Electric Field

The space around a charge distribution, in which the charge can exert force on other charges.

Electric Field Intensity (E) The electrostatic force acting per unit positive charge at a point in electric field.

$$\mathbf{E} = \lim_{\delta q \to 0} \frac{\mathbf{F}}{\delta q}$$

- SI unit → NC^{-1} or V/m, $[E] = [MLT^{-3}A^{-1}]$
- It is a vector quantity.
- Direction - It is in the direction of electrostatic force acting on positive charge.

Torque on Dipole in Uniform Electric Field

$$\tau = \mathbf{p} \times \mathbf{E} = pE \sin\theta$$
$$\theta = 90°, \tau_{max} = pE$$

- **Stable equilibrium** When electric dipole is parallel to electric field.
- **Unstable equilibrium** When electric dipole is anti-parallel to electric field.

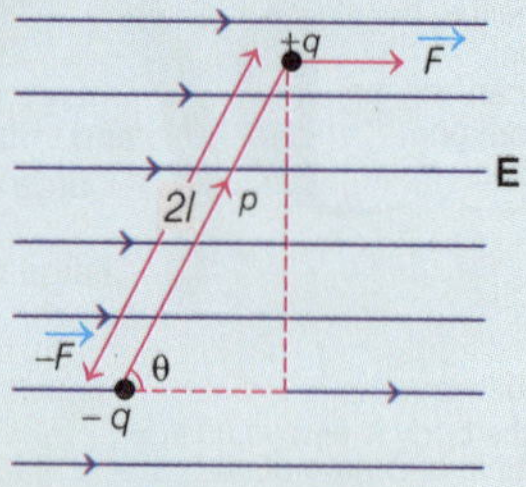

Electric Field Lines

- It is an imaginary line.
- Tangent at any point gives the direction of the electric field vector at that point.

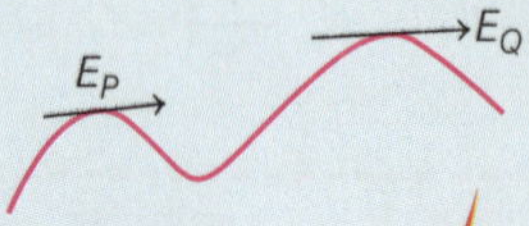

Electric Dipole

Electric Dipole Moment $p = q \times 2l$

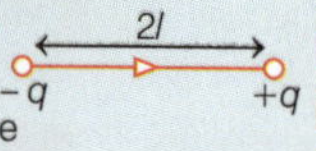

It is a vector quantity.

Direction –*ve* charge to + *ve* charge

SI unit Coulomb-metre. Dimension [LTA]

Properties of Electric Field Lines

1. Electric field lines start from positive charge and terminate on negative charge.

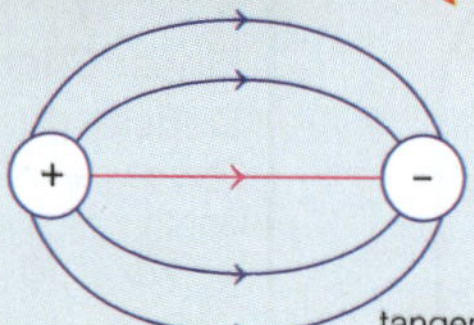

2. Electric field lines never intersect each other. If they intersect there will be two directions of electric field which is not possible.

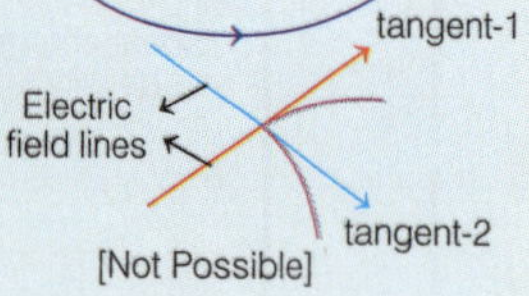

3. Electric field lines are always perpendicular to conducting surface.

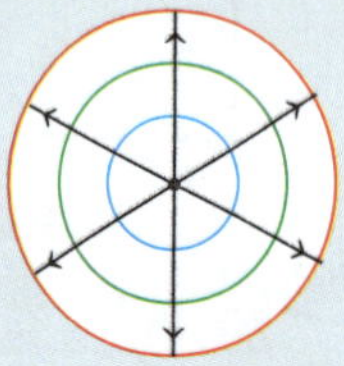

4. Electric field intensity ∝ Electric field lines density

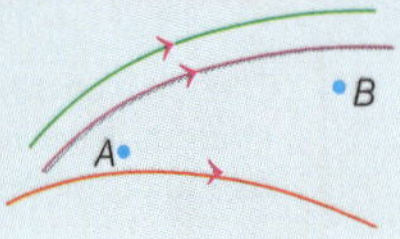

5. Electric field lines do not form closed loops.

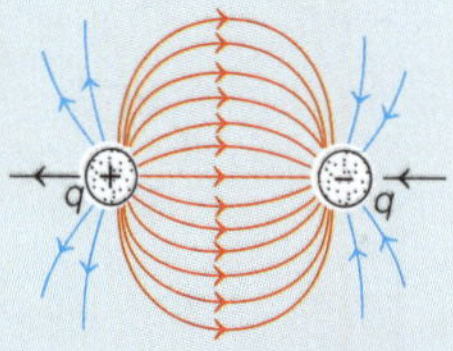

6. Charge ∝ number of electric field lines

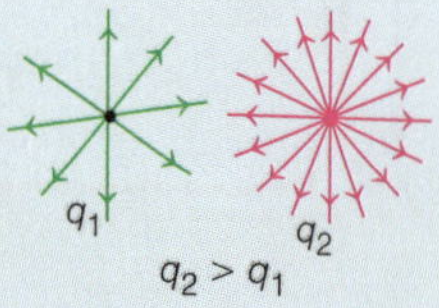

Electric Field Intensity Due to an Electric Dipole

On axial line	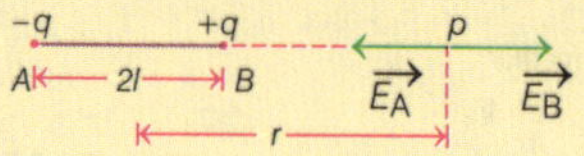	$E = \frac{1}{4\pi\varepsilon_0}\frac{2pr}{(r^2 - l^2)^2}$ If r >> 2l, then $E = \frac{1}{4\pi\varepsilon_0}\frac{2p}{r^3}$
On equatorial line	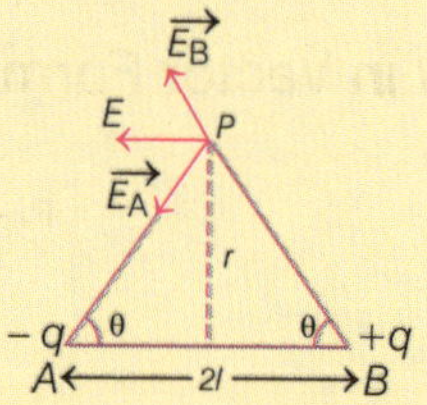	$E = \frac{1}{4\pi\varepsilon_0}\frac{p}{(r^2+l^2)^{3/2}}$ If r >> 2l, then $E = \frac{1}{4\pi\varepsilon_0}\frac{p}{r^3}$
At any general position	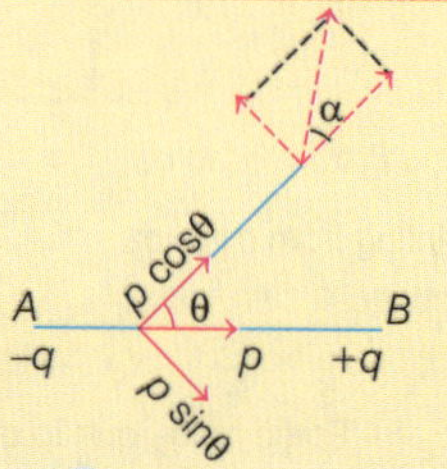	$E = \frac{1}{4\pi\varepsilon_0}\frac{p\sqrt{1 + 3\cos^2\theta}}{r^3}$

Electric Flux

Total number of electric field lines passing through a surface in a direction normal to the surface.

$\phi = \mathbf{E}\cdot\mathbf{A}$ or $\phi = \int \mathbf{E}\cdot d\mathbf{A}$

Unit $\Rightarrow \frac{Nm^2}{C}$, Dimension $\Rightarrow [ML^3T^{-3}A^{-1}]$

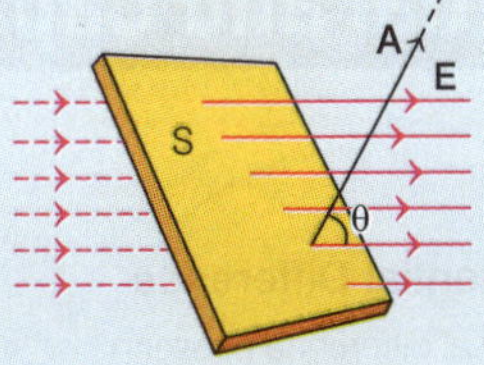

(i) When $\mathbf{E} \parallel \mathbf{A}$, $\phi = EA$

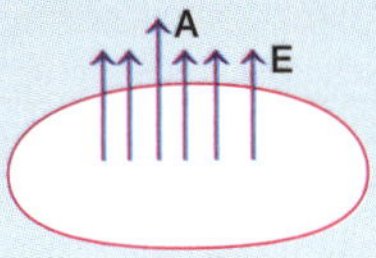

$\phi = EA$

(ii) When $\mathbf{E} \perp \mathbf{A}$, $\phi = 0$

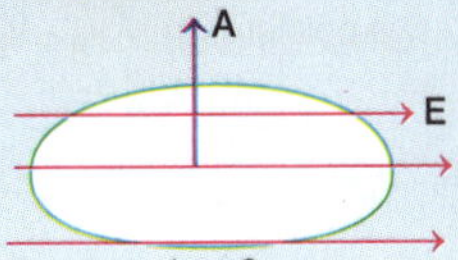

$\phi = 0$

(iii) When $\mathbf{E}$ and $\mathbf{A}$, make angle θ

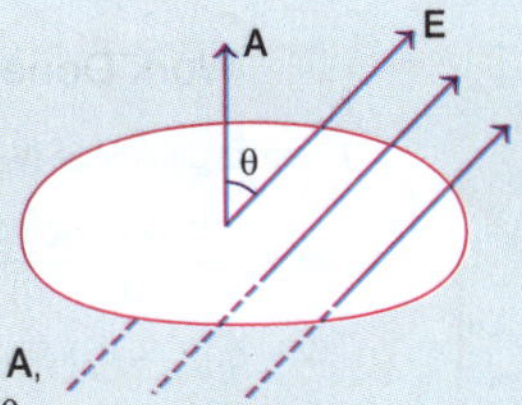

$\phi = EA\cos\theta$

Gauss's Law

The electric flux over any closed surface is $1/\varepsilon_0$ times the total charge enclosed by that surface. $\phi = \oint \mathbf{E}\cdot d\mathbf{A} = \frac{1}{\varepsilon_0}\Sigma q$

Applications

Point Charge

$E = \frac{kq}{r^2}$

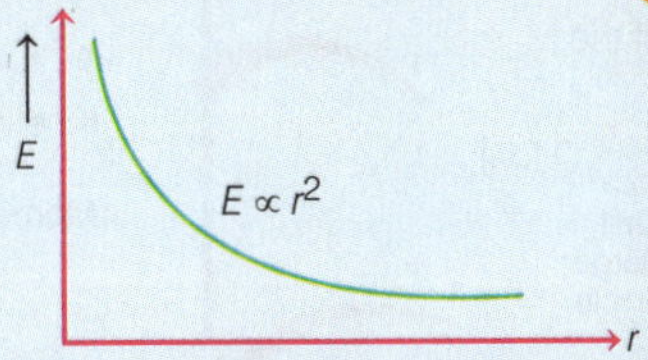

Metal Sphere/ Hollow Sphere

$E_{surface} = \frac{KQ}{R^2}, r = R$

$E_{outside} = \frac{KQ}{r^2}, r > R$

$E_{inside} = 0, r < R$

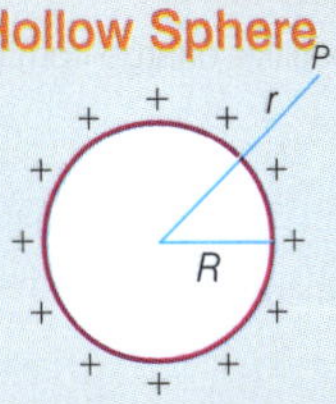

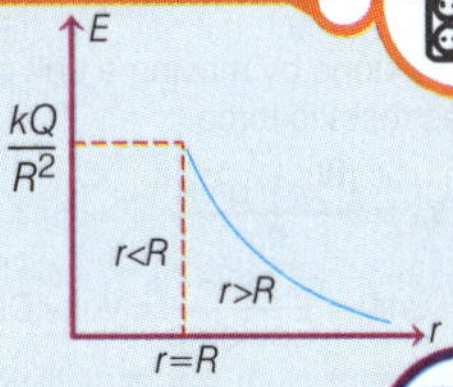

Uniformly Charged Non-Conducting Sphere

$E_{inside} = \frac{KQr}{R^3}, r < R$

$E_{surface} = \frac{KQ}{R^2}, r = R$

$E_{outside} = \frac{KQ}{r^2}, r > R$

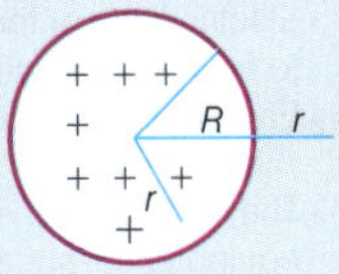

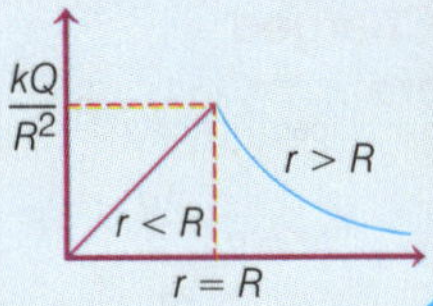

Infinite Charged Conducting Sheet

$E = \frac{\sigma}{\varepsilon_0}$

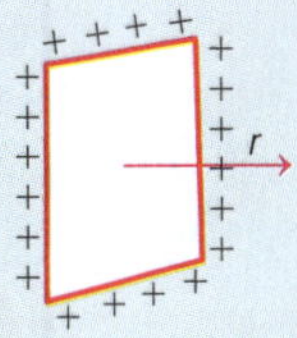

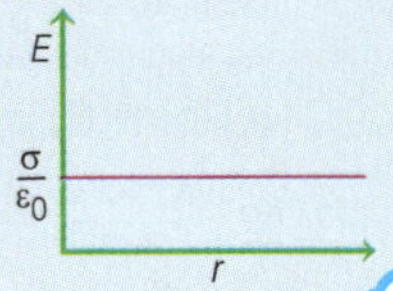

Infinite Charged Non-Conducting Sheet

$E = \frac{\sigma}{2\varepsilon_0}$

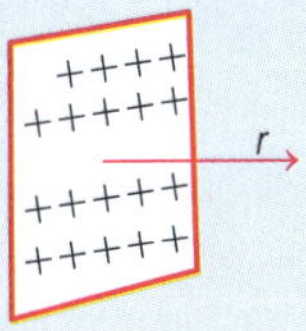

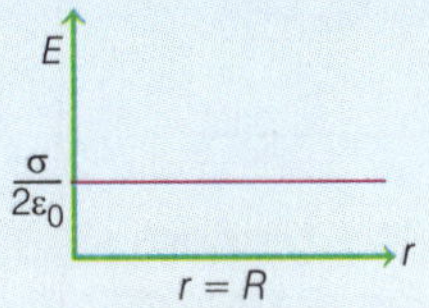

Finite Linear Charge Distribution

$E = \frac{2k\lambda}{r}\sin(\theta/2)$

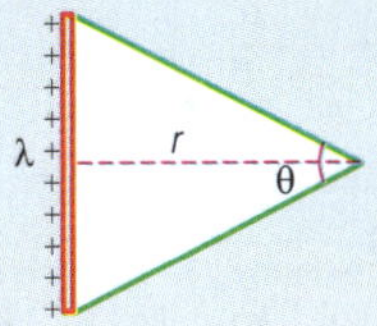

Infinite Linear Charge Distribution

$E = \frac{2k\lambda}{r}$

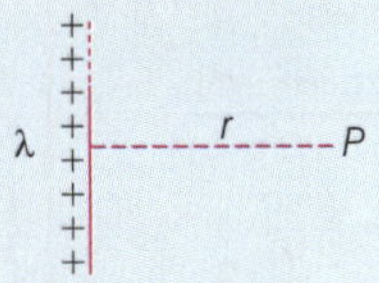

Charged Circular Ring at an Axial Point

$E_p = \frac{kQx}{(R^2 + x^2)}$

Electric field will be maximum at $x = \pm\frac{R}{\sqrt{2}}$

At centre of ring, electric field $(E_O) = 0$

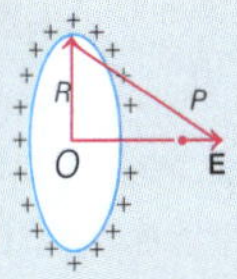

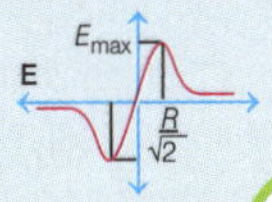

Segment of Ring

$E_p = \frac{2k\lambda}{r}\sin\left(\frac{\alpha}{2}\right)$

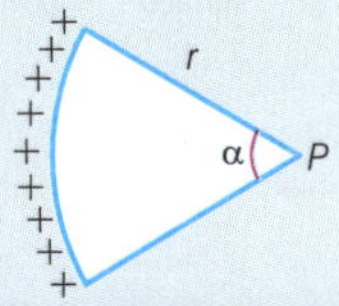

Centre of Circular Ring

$E_O = 0$

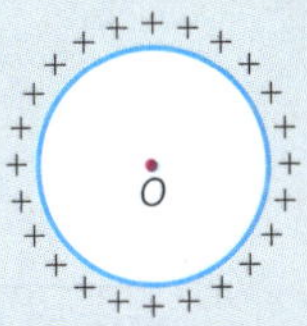

When Charge is Placed at the Face of a Cube

$\phi_{each\ face} = \frac{q}{2\varepsilon_0}$

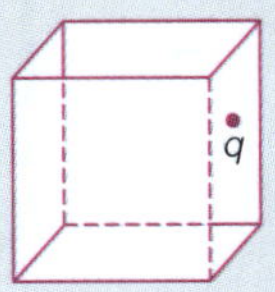

When Charge is Placed at Vertex of a Cube

$\phi_{cube} = \frac{q}{8\varepsilon_0}$

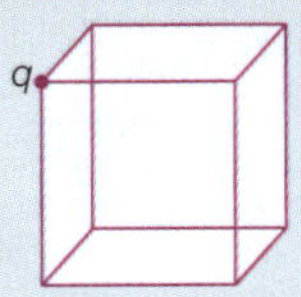

Chapter 16 Electrostatic Potential and Capacitance

1 Work Done

Potential difference $(V_B - V_A)$

$= \frac{\text{Work done } (W)}{\text{Charge } (q)}$

$W = q\,[V_B - V_A]$ or $V = W/q$

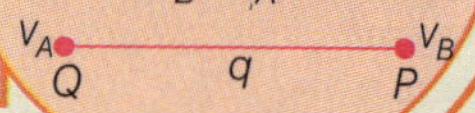

2 Potential Difference

Potential difference between two points $(A, B) = V_A - V_B$

$= \frac{(W_{BA})_{ext}}{q}$

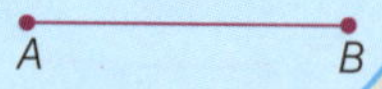

Motion of Charged Particle in Electric Field

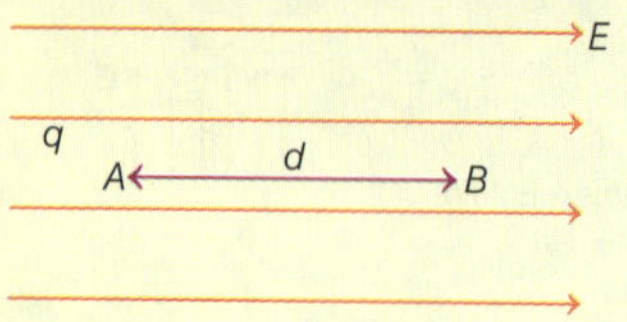

Force, $F = qE$

Acceleration, $a = \frac{qE}{m}$

Velocity, $v = \frac{qEt}{m} = \sqrt{\frac{2q\Delta V}{m}}$

Kinetic energy, $KE = \frac{q^2E^2t^2}{2m} = q\Delta V$

Momentum $= qEt = \sqrt{2mq\Delta V}$

Electrostatic Potential

Work done by moving a unit positive charge from infinity to other point against the electrostatic force.

$V_P = \frac{(W_{\infty - P})_{ext}}{q_0}$

SI unit $= \frac{\text{Joule}}{\text{Coulomb}}$ = Volt, Dimensions $= [ML^2T^{-3}A^{-1}]$

Potential due to Different Charge Bodies

Potential Due to Point Charge

$V_P = \frac{Kq}{r}$

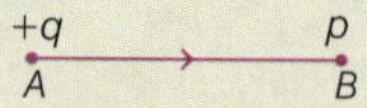

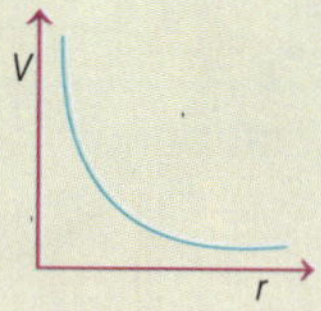

Potential Due to Charged Conducting Sphere

$V_{out} = \frac{kq}{r}, r > R$

$V_{surface} = \frac{kq}{R}, r = R$

$V_{inside} = \frac{kq}{R}, r < R$

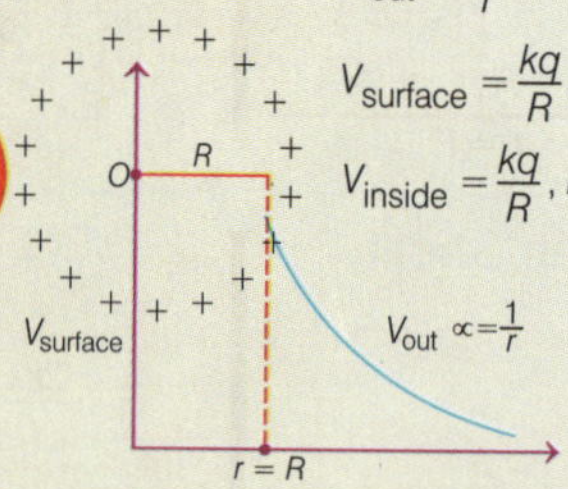

Potential due to System of Charges

$V_0 = \frac{kq_1}{r_1} + \frac{kq_2}{r_2} + \frac{kq_3}{r_3} + \ldots \frac{kq_n}{r_n}$

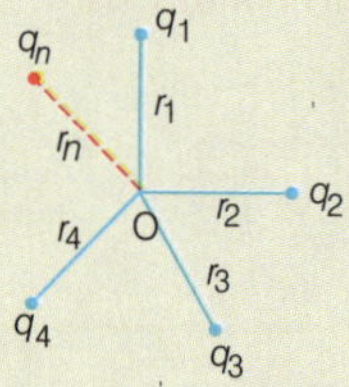

Potential Due to Charged Non-Conducting sphere

$V_{out} = \frac{kq}{r}, r > R, V_{surface} = \frac{kq}{R}, r = R$

$V_{inside} = \frac{kq[3R^2 - r^2]}{2R^3}, r < R$

$V_{centre} = \frac{3}{2}\frac{kq}{R}$

$V_{centre} > V_{surface} > V_{out}$

$V_{out} \propto \frac{1}{r}$

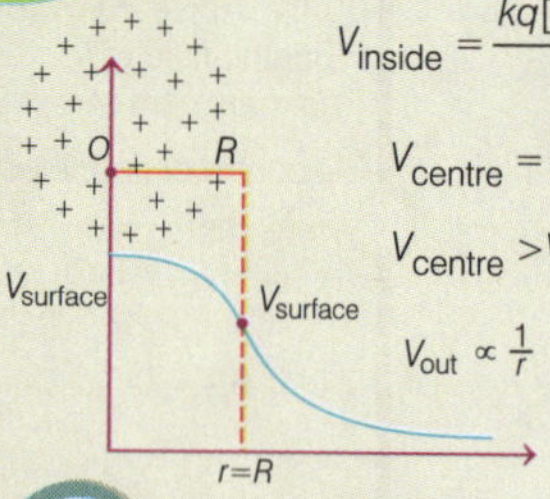

Potential Due to Charged Circular Ring

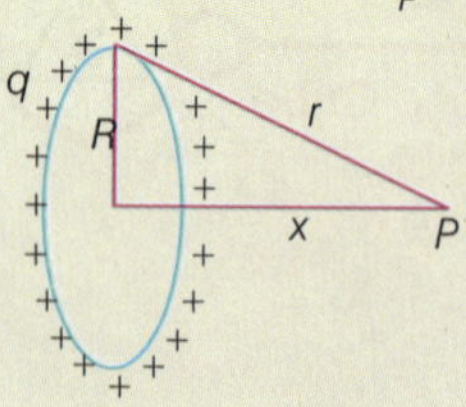

$V_P = \frac{q}{4\pi\varepsilon_0 (R^2 + x^2)^{1/2}}$

At $x = 0$

$V_P = \frac{1}{4\pi\varepsilon_0}\frac{q}{R}$

If $x >> R$, then

$V_P = \frac{1}{4\pi\varepsilon_0}\frac{q}{x}$

Potential Due to Dipole

$V_{axial} = \frac{kp}{r^2}, V_{equatorial} = 0, V_P = \frac{kp\cos\theta}{r^2}$

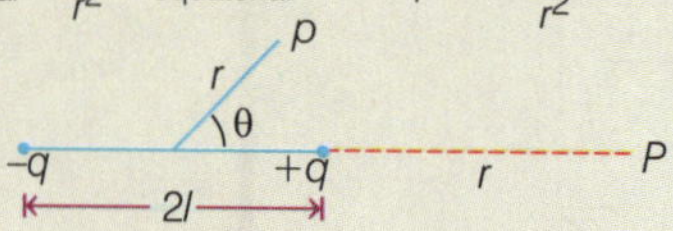

Equipotential Surface

- Electric lines of force are always perpendicular to equipotential surface.
- Equipotential surfaces can never cross each other.
- The work done in moving a charge along an equipotential surface is always zero.

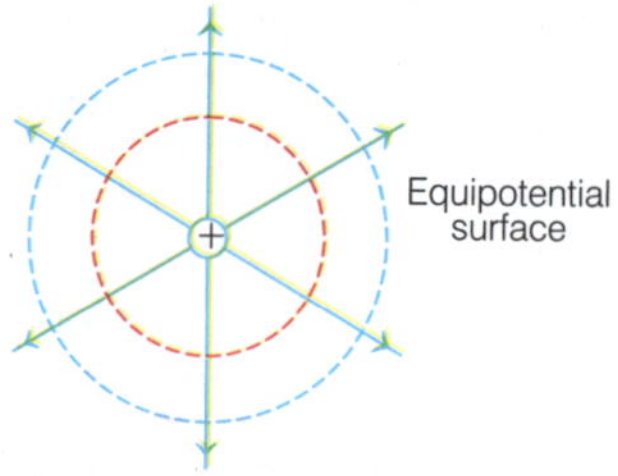

Shape of Equipotential surface

Point Charge	Concentric spheres
Line charge	Co-axial cylinders
Uniform field	Plane parallel to each other

Relation between Electric Field and Potential

$E = -\frac{dV}{dr}$

$V_2 - V_1 = -\int_{r_1}^{r_2} \mathbf{E} \cdot d\mathbf{r}$

$E = -\frac{\partial V}{\partial x}\hat{\mathbf{i}} - \frac{\partial V}{\partial y}\hat{\mathbf{j}} - \frac{\partial V}{\partial z}\hat{\mathbf{k}}$

Electric Potential Energy

It is the total amount of work done in bringing the different charges to their respective positions from infinitely mutual separations. It is represented by U.

$$V = \frac{W}{q} = \frac{U}{q}$$

Electric potential energy is defined only in conservative field.

Potential Energy of a System of two Charges in an Electric Field

- Two point charges q_1 and q_2 separated by distance r in an electric field **E**. U = Potential energy due to interaction between q_1 and q_2 potential energy due to interaction between q_1 and **E** + potential energy due to interaction between q_2 and **E**

$$U = \frac{1}{4\pi\varepsilon_0}\frac{q_1q_2}{r} + q_1V_1 + q_2V_2$$

Potential Energy of a System of *n* Charges in an Electric Field

The potential energy of a system of n charge

$$U = \frac{k}{2}\sum_{\substack{i,j \\ i\neq j}}^{n}\frac{q_iq_j}{r_{ij}}\left[k = \frac{1}{4\pi\varepsilon_0}\right]$$

$U_{system} = U_{pair}$ Number of pairs $= \frac{n(n-1)}{2}$

Electric Potential Energy for two Point Charge System

$$U = \frac{1}{4\pi\varepsilon_0}\frac{q_1q_2}{r}$$

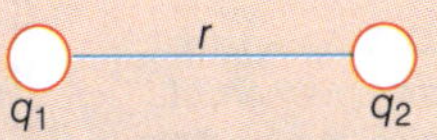

Electric Potential Energy for three Point Charge System

$$U = \frac{1}{4\pi\varepsilon_0}\left[\frac{q_1q_2}{r_1} + \frac{q_2q_3}{r_2} + \frac{q_1q_3}{r_3}\right]$$

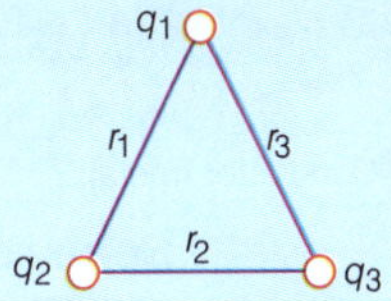

Electron Volt (eV)

It is the potential energy gained or lost by an electron moving through a potential difference of 1 V.

$$\Delta U = q\Delta V = 1.6 \times 10^{-19}\,C \times 1V = 1.6 \times 10^{-19}\,J$$

$$1eV = 1.6 \times 10^{-19}J$$

Potential Energy of a Dipole in a Uniform Electric Field

The total work done in rotating the dipole from an angle θ_1 with the direction of the field to θ_2

$$W = \int dW = \int_{\theta_1}^{\theta_2} pE\sin\theta\, d\theta$$

$$W = pE(\cos\theta_1 - \cos\theta_2)$$

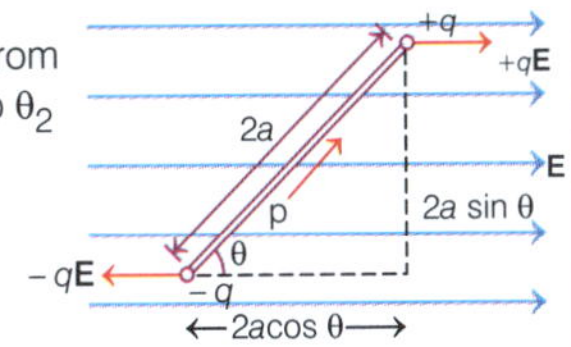

The work done will store as the potential energy,

$$U = pE(\cos\theta_1 - \cos\theta_2)$$

If $\theta_1 = 90°$, $\theta_2 = \theta$

$$U = pE(0 - \cos\theta) = -pE\cos\theta$$

$$U = -\mathbf{p}\cdot\mathbf{E}$$

Special Cases

(Related to potential Energy)

Position of stable equilibrium

$\rightarrow U_{minimum}$

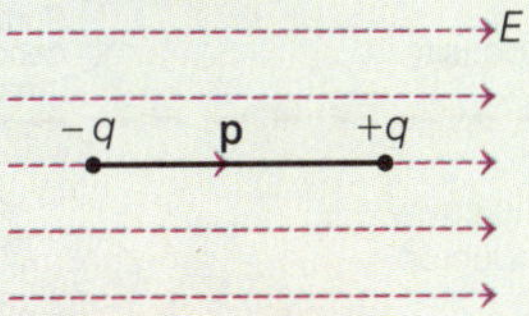

$\theta = 0°$

$U = -pE\cos 0° = -pE$

Position of Zero Energy

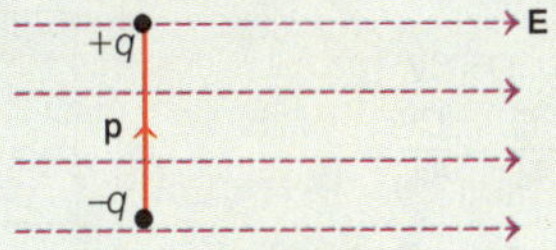

$\theta = 90°$

$U = -PE\cos 90° = 0$

Position of unstable equilibrium

$\rightarrow U_{maximum}$

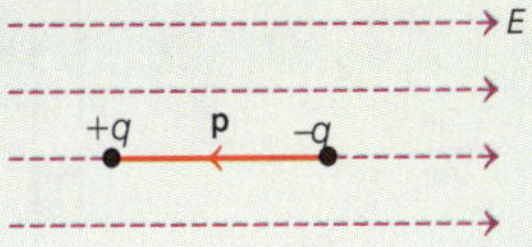

$\theta = 180°$

$\cos 180° = -1$

$U = -pE\cos 180° = +pE$

POWER TIPS

$$U_{system} = \frac{kq_1q_2}{r} + \frac{kq_2q_3}{r} + \frac{kq_3q_4}{r} + \frac{kq_1q_4}{r} + \frac{kq_1q_3}{r\sqrt{2}} + \frac{kq_2q_4}{r\sqrt{2}}$$

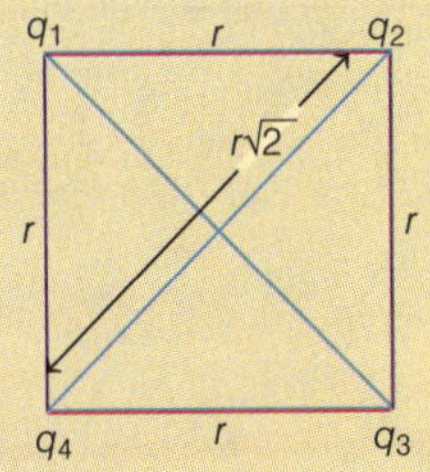

- **Work done in rearrangement of the system**

$$U_i = \frac{3kq^2}{r} \qquad U_f = \frac{kq^2}{r}$$

$$W = U_f - U_i = \frac{kq^2}{r} - \frac{3kq^2}{r} = \frac{-2kq^2}{r}$$

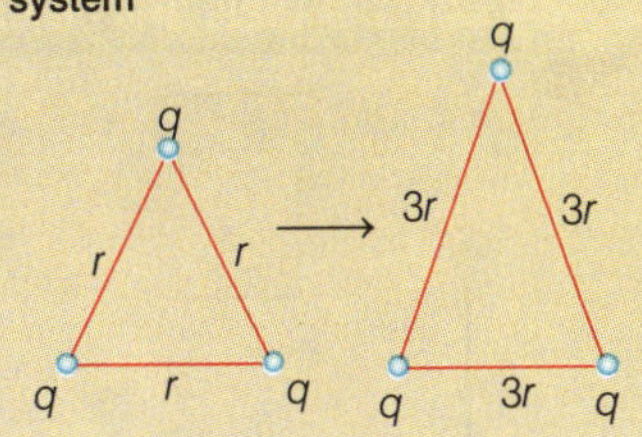

Conductors and Insulators

Conductors Allow large scale physical movement of electric charges through them when an external field is applied. e.g. Silver, copper, aluminium.

Conductor (metal)

Insulators Do not allow physical movement of electric charges through them when an external field is applied. e.g. Wood, rubber etc.

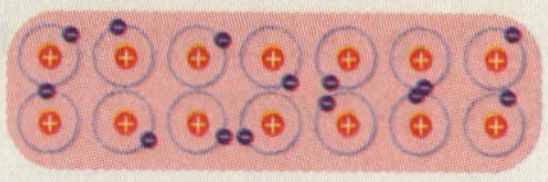

Insulator

Behaviour of Conductors in Electrostatic Fields

- Net electrostatic field is zero in the interior of a conductor.
- Just outside the surface of a charged conductor, electric field is normal to the surface.

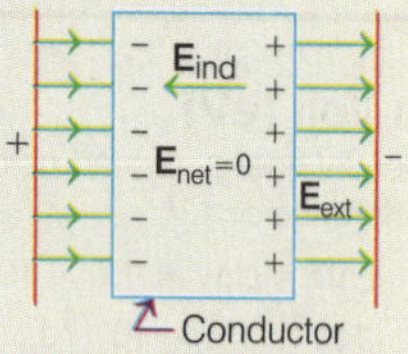

- The net charge in the interior of a conductor is zero and any excess charge resides at its surface.
- Potential (V) = constant → inside the conductor and on the surface of the conductor.

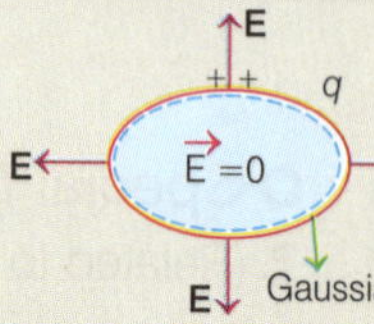

- Electric field at surface of charged conductor is proportional to the surface charge density.

$$E=\frac{\sigma}{\varepsilon_0}$$

σ = surface charge density

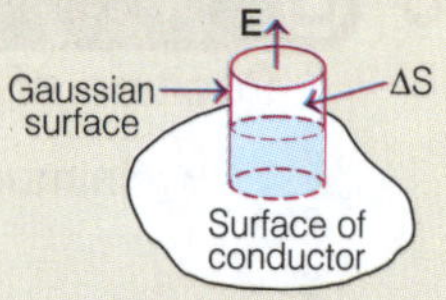

- Electric field is zero in the cavity of a hollow charged conductor.

$E=0$
$V=$ constant

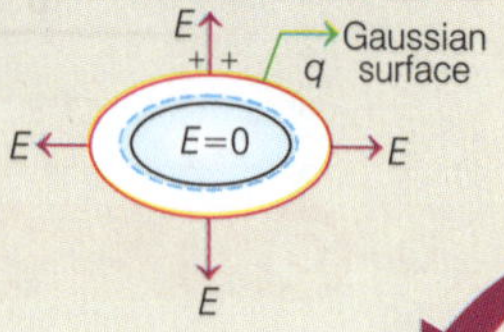

ELECTROSTATIC SHIELDING

- The phenomenon of making a region free from any electric field.
  or
  Electrostatic shielding is a phenomenon seen when a Faraday cage is used to block the effects of an electric field.

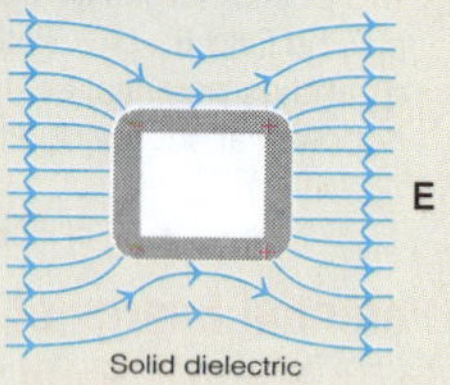

Dielectric

Dielectric are insulating materials which transmit electric effect without conducting.

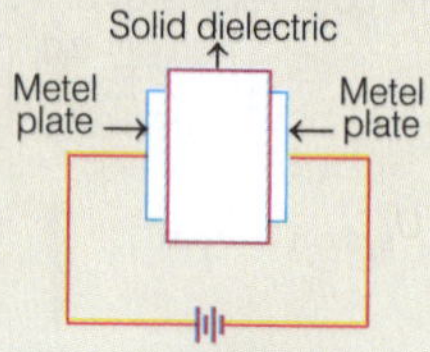

01 Polarisation Process of inducing equal and opposite charges on the two faces of the dielectric on the application of electric field.

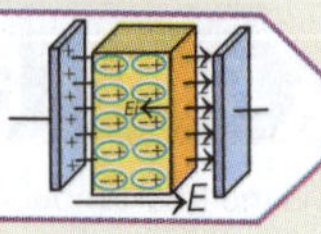

02 Polar dielectric It has net dipole moment zero in the absence of electric field.

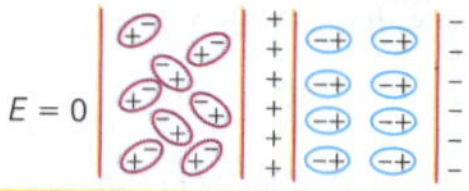

03 Non-polar dielectric each molecule has zero dipole moment in its normal state.

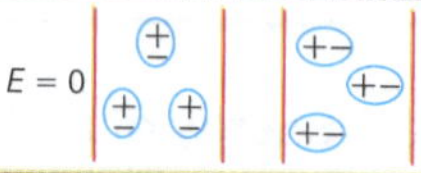

04 Dielectric breakdown When dielectric start behaving as conductor.
Dielectric Strength Maximum value of electric field that a dielectric material can tolerate without its electrical breakdown.

05 Dielectric constant

$$k=\frac{E}{E'}=\frac{\text{Electric field without a dielectric medium}}{\text{Electric field with dielectric}}$$

Capacitor

Parallel Plate Capacitor

Capacitance $C=\frac{\varepsilon_0 A}{d}$ $\quad Q=CV$

$$E=\frac{\sigma}{\varepsilon_0}=\frac{Q}{A\varepsilon_0}=\frac{CV}{A\varepsilon_0}$$

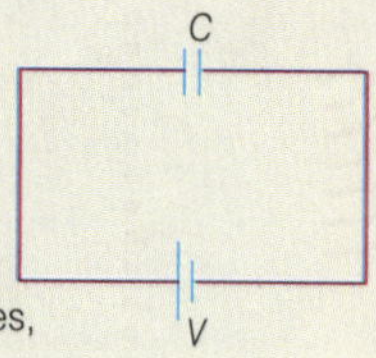

- Capacitance depends on distance between plates, area of plates, medium between plates.
- Capacitance does not depend on charge and potential difference.

Spherical Capacitor

$$C=\frac{4\pi\varepsilon_0 ab}{b-a}$$

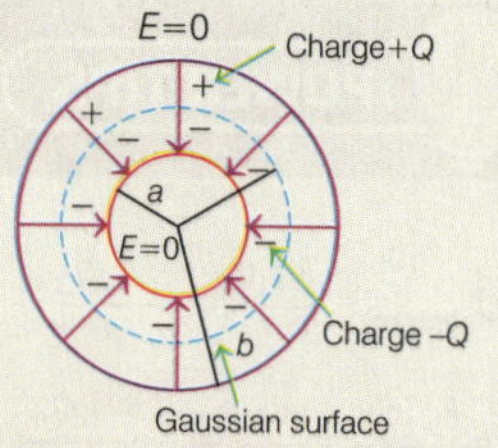

Force of Attraction between the Plates of Capacitor

$$F=\frac{Q^2}{2A\varepsilon_0}$$

Effect of Dielectric on Capacitance

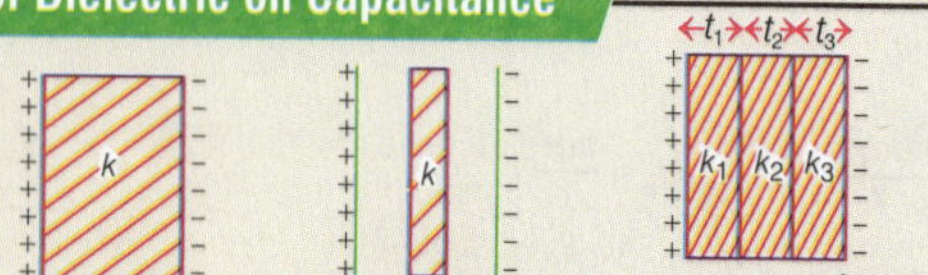

$$C'=\frac{k\varepsilon_0 A}{d}$$

$$C'=kC$$

$$C'=\frac{\varepsilon_0 A}{d-t+\frac{t}{k}}$$

$$C'=\frac{\varepsilon_0 A}{\frac{t_1}{k_1}+\frac{t_2}{k_2}+\frac{t_3}{k_3}}$$

Combinations of Capacitors

Series Combination

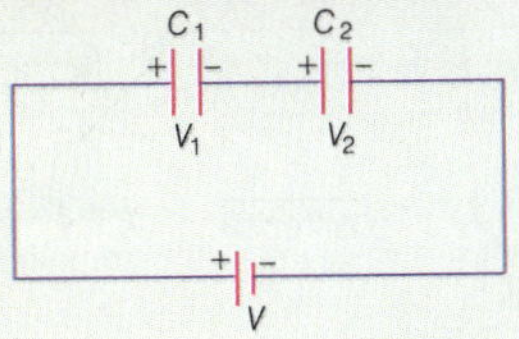

$$\frac{1}{C_{eq}}=\frac{1}{C_1}+\frac{1}{C_2} \qquad C_{eq}=\frac{C_1C_2}{C_1+C_2}$$

$\because V \propto 1/C$

$$\therefore V_1=\left(\frac{C_2}{C_1+C_2}\right)V, V_2=\left(\frac{C_1}{C_1+C_2}\right)V$$

Parallel Combination

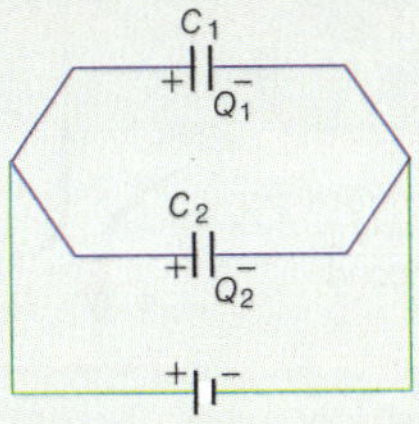

$$C_{eq}=C_1+C_2$$

$$Q_1=\left(\frac{C_1}{C_1+C_2}\right)Q, Q_2=\left(\frac{C_2}{C_1+C_2}\right)Q$$

Sharing of Charges

Case 1 When the positive plate of one capacitor connected to positive plate of other capacitor.

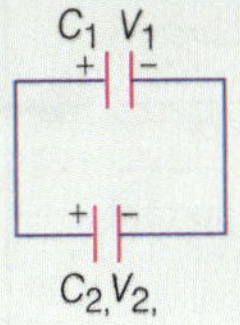

$$V_{common}=\frac{\text{net charge}}{\text{net capacitance}}=\frac{q_1+q_2}{C_1+C_2}=\frac{C_1V_1+C_2V_2}{C_1+C_2}$$

Initial Energy → Heat Loss → Final Energy

$$U_i=\frac{1}{2}C_1V_1^2+\frac{1}{2}C_2V_2^2 \qquad U_f=\frac{1}{2}(C_1+C_2)\left(\frac{C_1V_1+C_2V_2}{C_1+C_2}\right)^2$$

$$\text{Energy Loss}=U_i-U_f=\frac{C_1\cdot C_2}{2(C_1+C_2)}(V_1-V_2)^2$$

Case 2 When the positive plate of one capacitor connected to negative plate of other capacitor.

$$V_{common}=\frac{C_1V_1-C_2V_2}{C_1+C_2}$$

$$\text{Energy Loss } U_i-U_f=\frac{C_1C_2}{2(C_1+C_2)}(V_1+V_2)^2$$

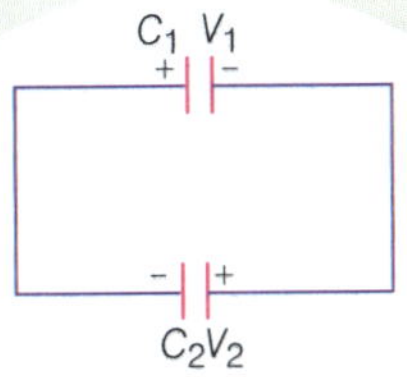

Energy Stored in a Capacitor

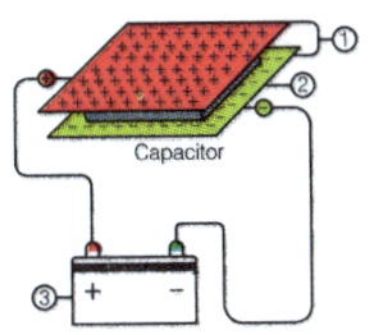

The work done in charging the capacitor is stored as its electrical potential energy.

$$U=\frac{1}{2}CV^2=\frac{1}{2}\frac{Q^2}{C}=\frac{1}{2}QV$$

Energy stored in series combination of capacitors

$$U=\frac{Q^2}{2C_1}+\frac{Q^2}{2C_2}+\frac{Q^2}{2C_3}+\ldots$$

Energy stored in parallel combination of capacitors

$$U=\frac{1}{2}C_1V^2+\frac{1}{2}C_2V^2+\frac{1}{2}C_3V^2$$

Capacitance of a Parallel Plate Capacitor with Compound Dielectric

Series type arrangement

$$C_{eq}=\frac{\varepsilon_0 A}{\frac{t_1}{k_1}+\frac{t_2}{k_2}+\ldots+\frac{t_n}{k_n}}$$

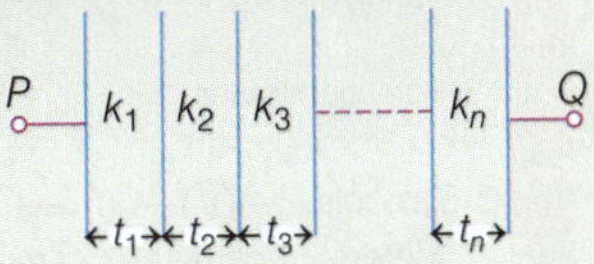

Parallel type arrangement

$$C_{eq}=\frac{\varepsilon_0}{d}\frac{A}{n}(k_1+k_2+\ldots k_n)$$

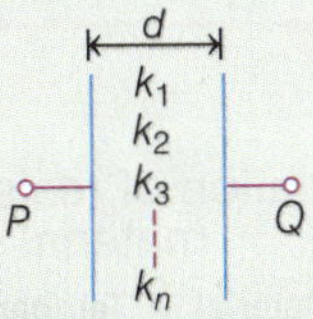

Energy Density of an Electric Field

Energy stored per unit volume,

$$u=\frac{U}{Ad}=\frac{1}{2}\varepsilon_0E^2$$

where, Ad = Volume of capacitor between its two plates.

POWER TIPS

Wheatstone Bridge in Capacitors

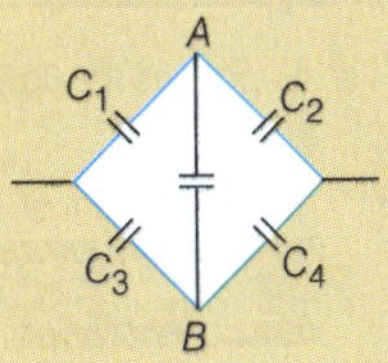

$$\frac{C_1}{C_2}=\frac{C_3}{C_4}, V_A=V_B,$$

$$C=\frac{3\varepsilon_0 A}{d}$$

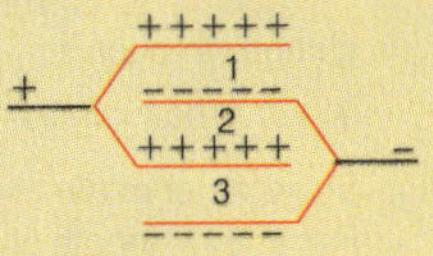

- Energy of big drop of radius R formed by combining n drops of radii r, charge q, capacitance C and potential V is

n drops (V, q, C, r)

$Q'=nq$

$C'=n^{1/3}C$

$V'=n^{2/3}V$

$$U'=\frac{1}{2}CV^2=\frac{1}{2}(n^{1/3}C)(n^{2/3}V)^2$$

$$=n^{5/3}U$$

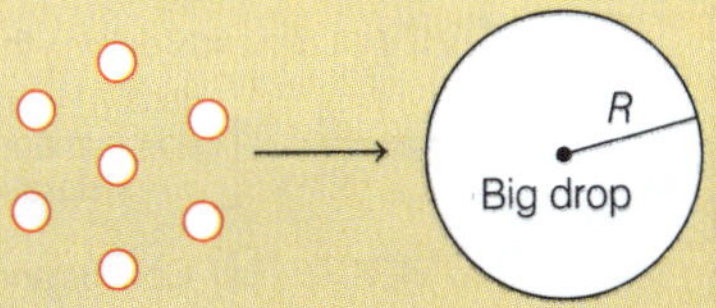

Chapter 17

Current Electricity

Direction of Current

Conventional Current

Electronic Current

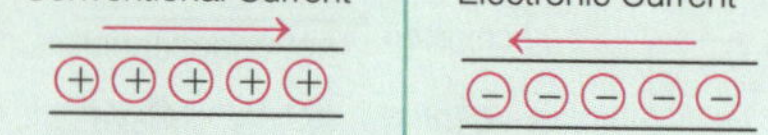

Direction of current The direction of motion of positive charge.

Direction of current The direction of motion of negative charge.

Electric Current

The rate of flow of charge through any cross-sectional area of a conductor.

$$I = \lim_{\Delta t \to 0} \frac{\Delta Q}{\Delta t} = \frac{dQ}{dt}$$

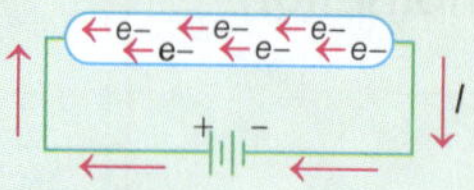

SI unit of Current ⟶ Ampere(A)

$$1\,\text{ampere} = \frac{1\,\text{coulomb}}{1\,\text{second}}$$

Current Density

Current flowing per unit area through any cross-section is called current density.

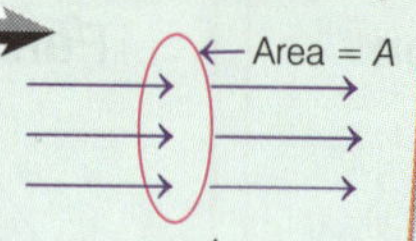

$$j = \frac{I}{A}$$

If the cross-section area A is not perpendicular to the current, then

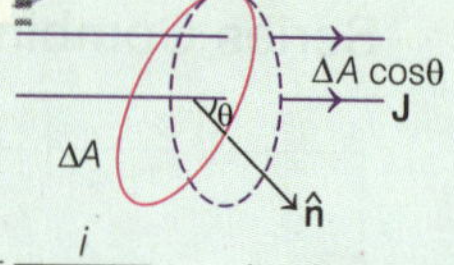

$$j = \frac{i}{\Delta A \cos\theta} \qquad i = \mathbf{J} \cdot \Delta \mathbf{A}$$

Relaxation Time (τ)

Average time taken by free electrons between two successive collisions.

Temperature increases ⟶ Relaxation time decreases

Mobility

$$\text{Mobility } (\mu) = \frac{\text{Drift velocity}}{\text{Electric field}} = \frac{v_d}{E}$$

$$\text{Unit of mobility} = \frac{m^2}{sV} = m^2s^{-1}V^{-1}$$

Drift Velocity

Average velocity with which the electrons get drifted towards high potential end of the conductor.

$$v_d = \frac{eE}{m}\tau$$

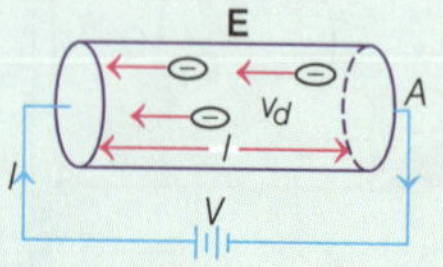

Electric current $(i) = neAv_d$

Current density $(j) = nev_d$

Drift velocity of electron $\approx 10^{-4}$ m/s

Ohm's Law

Potential difference ∝ Current

Condition - Temperature, mechanical strain etc. are kept constant.

$V \propto i \Rightarrow V = Ri \Rightarrow \frac{V}{i} = R =$ Constant $=$ Electrical resistance of the conductor

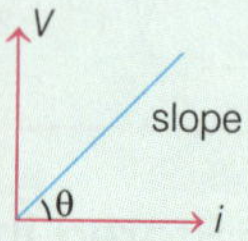

slope of line $= \tan\theta = \frac{V}{i} = R$

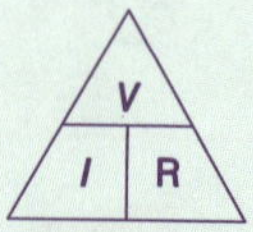

Ohm's law triangle

$V = i \times R$

$i = V/R$

$R = V/i$

Ohmic and Non-Ohmic Conductors

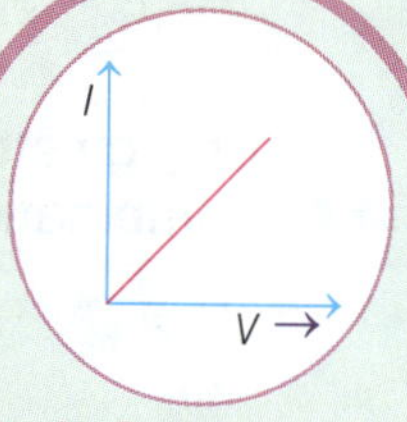

Ohmic Conductors

- Follow Ohm's law.
- Voltage and current varies linearly in ohmic conductors..

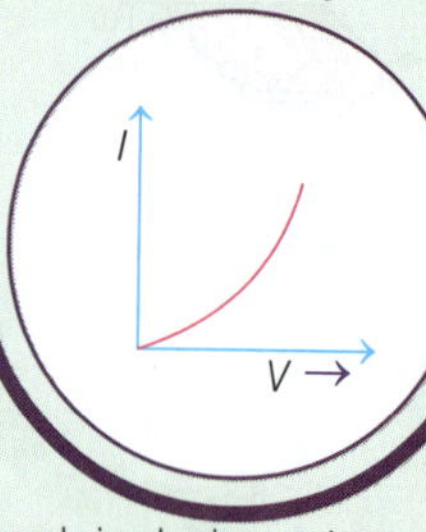

Non-Ohmic Conductor

- They do not follow ohm's law.
- Current depends on voltage but does not vary linearly.

POWER TIPS

Current follows scalar addition not vector addition

Current has both magnitude and direction but it does not follow vector addition rules, that's why it is scalar quantity.Direction of current is opposite direction to the flow of electrons

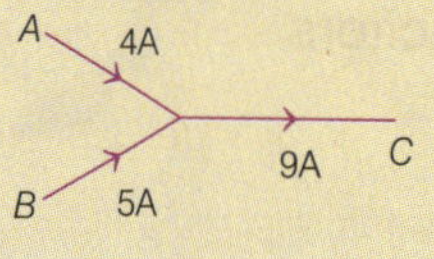

Vector form of Ohm's Law

The direction of current density = direction of electric field

$$\mathbf{E} = \rho\,\mathbf{J} \quad \text{or} \quad \mathbf{J} = \sigma\,\mathbf{E}$$

Resistance

The property of the conductor by which it opposes the flow of charges through it.

$R = \frac{V}{i}$ [The more the resistance, the less is the current]

SI unit = ohm (Ω)

$R \propto l$ [l = length of conductor]

$R \propto \frac{1}{A}$ [A = Area of cross-section of the conductor]

$$R = \rho\frac{l}{A}$$

ρ = Resistivity or specific resistance

Less resistance

More resistance

Resistivity

It depends only on the nature of the material.

$$\text{Resistivity } (\rho) = \frac{m}{ne^2\tau}$$

[Here, m = mass of electron; n = number density of free electron; τ = Relaxation time]

Conductance (G)

$$\text{Conductance} = \frac{1}{\text{Resistance}} \Rightarrow G = \frac{1}{R}$$

Conductivity (σ)

Reciprocal of resistivity

$$\text{Conductivity} = \frac{1}{\text{Resistivity}} \Rightarrow \sigma = \frac{1}{\rho} \Rightarrow \sigma = \frac{ne^2\tau}{m}$$

Symbols for resistors & meters

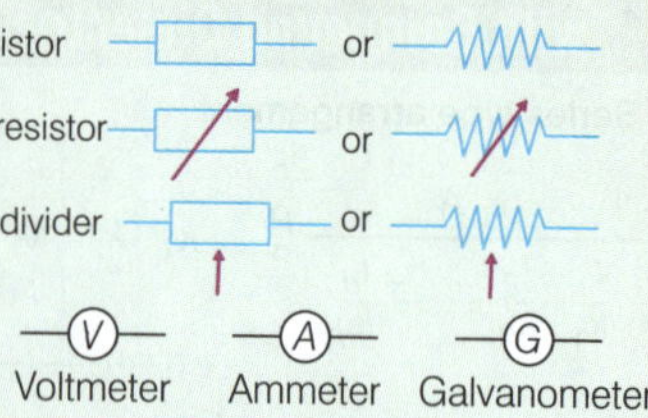

Variation of resistance of some electrical material with temperature

Material	Temperature coefficient of resistance	Effect of temperature rise on resistance
Metals	$\alpha > 0$	Increases
Solid non-metal	$\alpha = 0$	No effect
Semiconductors	$\alpha < 0$	Decreases
Electrolytes	$\alpha < 0$	Decreases
Alloys	$0 < \alpha < 1$	Nearly constant

Combination of Resistors

	Series Circuit	Parallel Circuit
Diagram	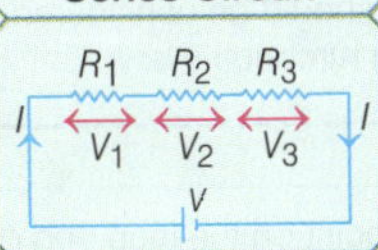	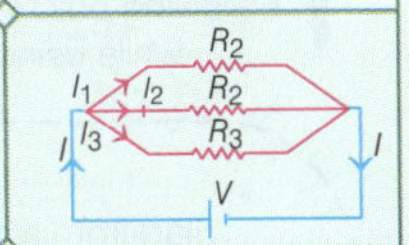
Resistance	$R_{eq} = R_1 + R_2 + R_3$	$\frac{1}{R_{eq}} = \frac{1}{R_1} + \frac{1}{R_2} + \frac{1}{R_3}$
Current	Same current (I) through each resistor	$I = I_1 + I_2 + I_3$
Voltage	$V = V_1 + V_2 + V_3$	Same Voltage (V) across each resistor

EMF

- EMF is the maximum potential difference between the two electrodes of the cell when no current is drawn from the cell.
- It is independent of the resistance of the circuit.

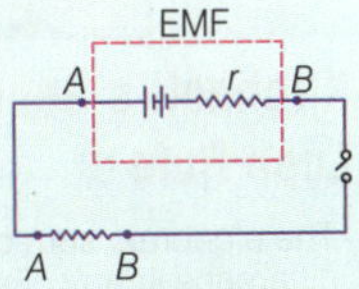

V/S

Potential Difference

- Potential difference is the difference of potential between any two points in a closed circuit.
- It is proportional to the resistance between the given points.

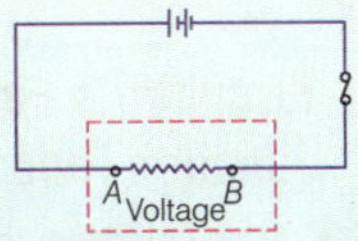

Electrical Cell

- It maintains a continuous flow of charge in a circuit by a chemical reaction.

Chemical Energy → Eletrical cell → Electrical Energy

- Electrical cell converts chemical energy to electrical energy.

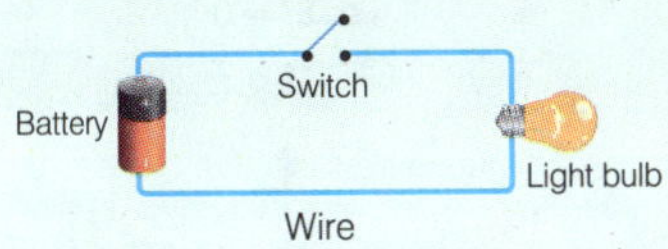

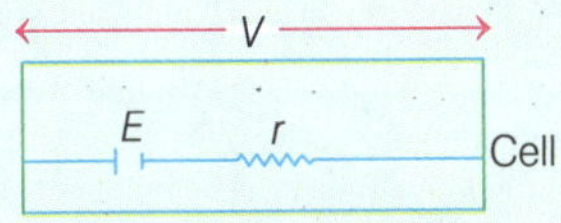

Electromotive Force (EMF)

It is maximum potential difference between its terminal when it is in the open circuit.

$V_A - V_B = E = \text{EMF}$

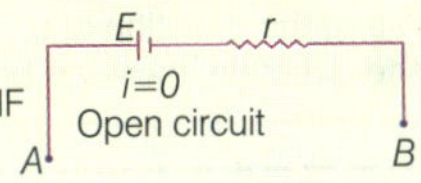

Internal Resistance (r)

The opposition of flow of current inside the cell. It depends on

- $r \propto$ Distance between electrodes — distance between electrodes increases → r increases
- $r \propto \frac{1}{\text{Temperature}}$ — Temperature increases → r decreases
- $r \propto \frac{1}{\text{(Area of electrode)}}$ — Area of electrode increases → r decreases
- $r \propto$ Concentration of electrolyte — Concentration of electrolyte increases → r increases

POWER TIPS

Relation between Internal Resistance, EMF and Terminal Potential Difference of a Cell.

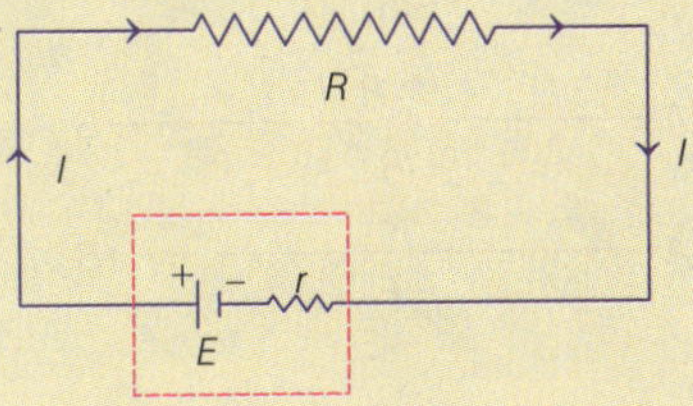

Terminal potential difference = emf – potential drop across the internal resistance

$$V = E - Ir \Rightarrow r = \frac{E-V}{I} = \frac{E-V}{V/R} = \left(\frac{E-V}{V}\right)R$$

Electrical Energy

Total work done W by the source of emf V in maintaining the electric current I in the circuit for a specified time t.

Electrical energy occurs due to the flow of electrons in a conductor.

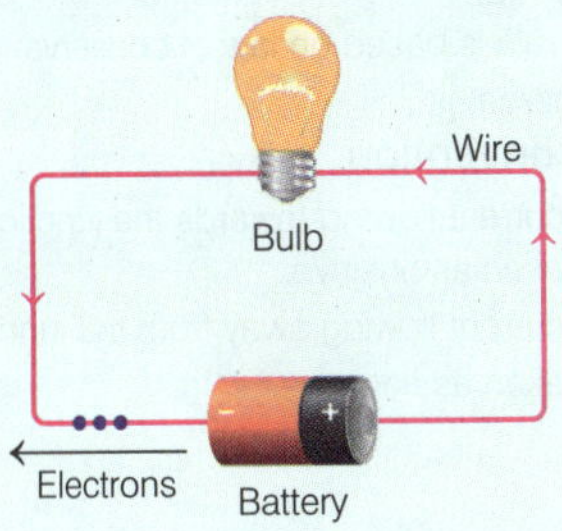

- Electrical energy, $W = Vit = i^2 Rt = \frac{V^2}{R}t$
- SI unit = Joule (J)
  1 Joule = 1 volt × 1 ampere x 1 second
  = 1watt × 1 second
  1 kilowatt hour (kWh) = 3.6×10^6 Joule

Electrical Power

It is the rate at which work is done by a source of emf in maintaining an electric current through a circuit.

$$P = \frac{W}{t} = VI = I^2R = \frac{V^2}{R}$$

- SI unit = watt (W)
  1Hp = 746 W

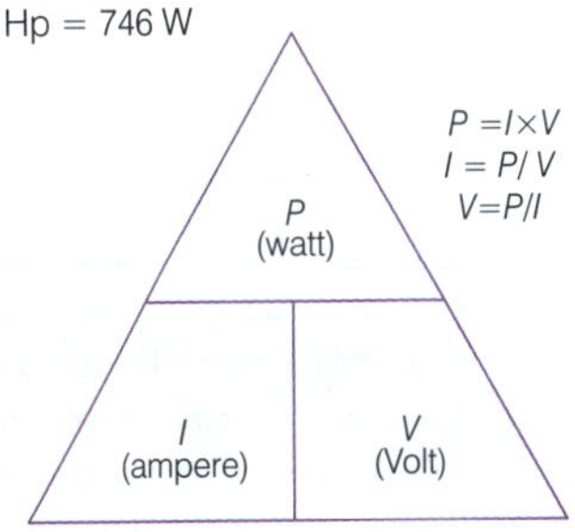

$P = I \times V$
$I = P/V$
$V = P/I$

	Cells in Series	Cells in Parallel	Mixed Grouping
Diagram	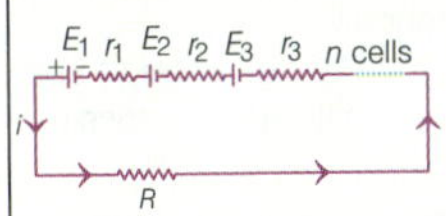	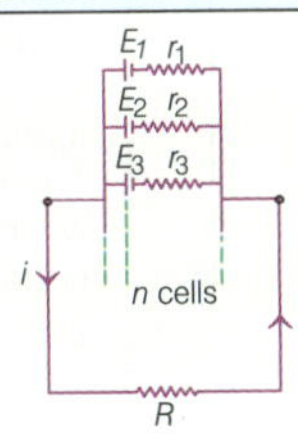	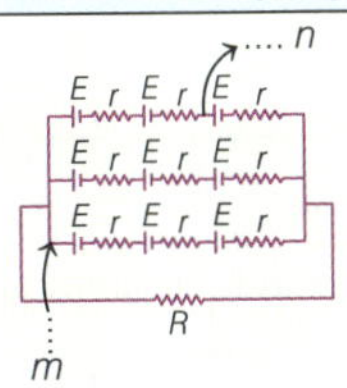 Row = n and Column = m
$E_{equivalent}$ $r_{equivalent}$	$E_1 + E_2 + E_3 + \ldots E_n$ $r_1 + r_2 + r_3 + \ldots r_n$	$E_{equivalent} = \frac{\frac{E_1}{r_1} + \frac{E_2}{r_2} + \frac{E_3}{r_3} + \ldots}{\frac{1}{r_1} + \frac{1}{r_2} + \frac{1}{r_3} + \ldots}$ $r_{equivalent} = \frac{1}{\frac{1}{r_1} + \frac{1}{r_2} + \frac{1}{r_3} + \ldots}$	$E_{equivalent} = nE$ $r_{equivalent} = \frac{nr}{m}$
Current	$i = \frac{\sum_{i=1}^{n} E_i}{\sum_{i=1}^{n} r_i + R}$ **Case** If $E_1 = E_2 = E_3 = \ldots E_n = E$ and $r_1 = r_2 = r_3 = \ldots r_n = r$ then $i = \frac{nE}{nr + R}$ (i) $nr >> R \Rightarrow i = E/r$ (ii) $nr << R \Rightarrow i = \frac{nE}{R}$	$i = \frac{E_{equivalent}}{r_{equivalent} + R}$ **Case** If $E_1 = E_2 = E_3 = \ldots E_n = E$ then $i = \frac{E}{\frac{r}{n} + R}$	$i = \frac{E_{equivalent}}{R + r_{equivalent}}$ $= \frac{nE}{R + \frac{nr}{m}}$

Kirchhoff's Law

Kirchhoff's First Law or Junction Rule

- At any junction, the sum of currents entering the junction = sum of currents leaving the junction,

i.e. $\Sigma I = 0$

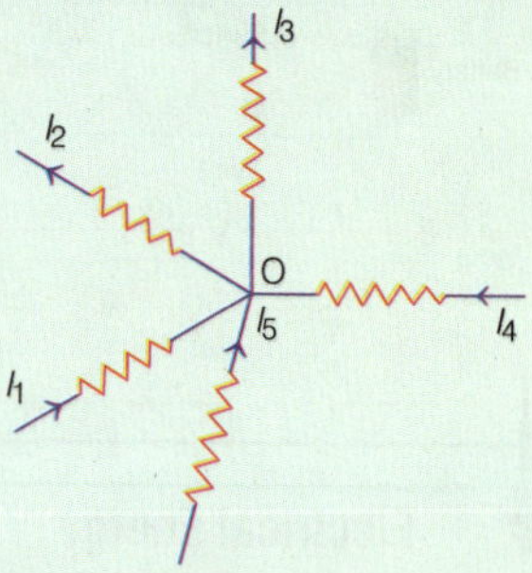

From the given figure,
$I_1 - I_2 - I_3 + I_4 + I_5 = 0$

- It is also known as Kirchhoff's current law (KCL).
- This rule is based on law of conservation of charge.

Sign convention

- The current flowing towards the junction are taken as positive.
- The current flowing away from the junction are taken as negative.

Kirchhoff's Second Law or Loop Rule

- The algebraic sum of the potential difference in any closed circuit is zero,

i.e. $\Sigma \Delta V = 0$ closed loop

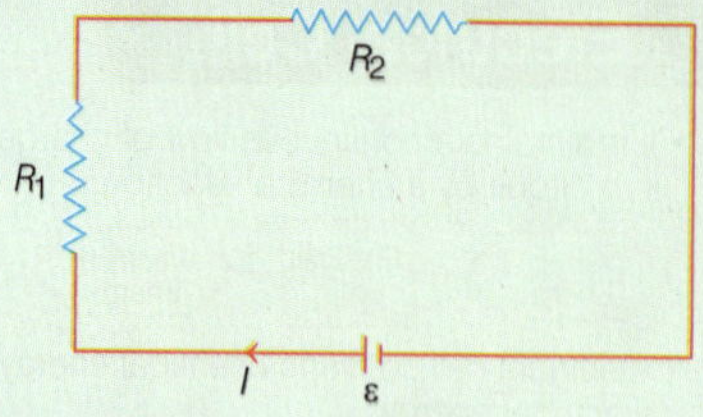

From the figure, $\varepsilon - IR_1 - IR_2 = 0$

- This rule is based on the law of conservation of energy.
- It is also known as Kirchhoff's voltage law (KVL).

Sign convention

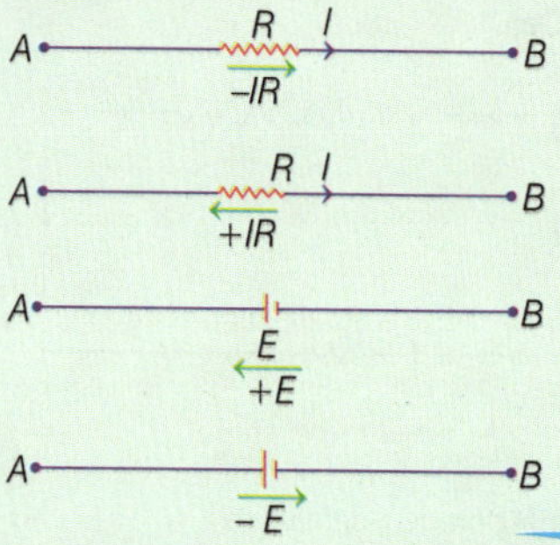

Application of Kirchhoff's Law

Following points should be considered while using Kirchhoff's law.

- Start from a point on the loop and go along the loop, either anti-clockwise or clockwise to reach the same point again.
- Balance current at junction as per KCL.
- There will be potential drop across a resistance if moving along the direction of current. If moving in opposite direction, there will be potential gain.
- The net sum of all these potential differences should be zero, using the KVL rule.

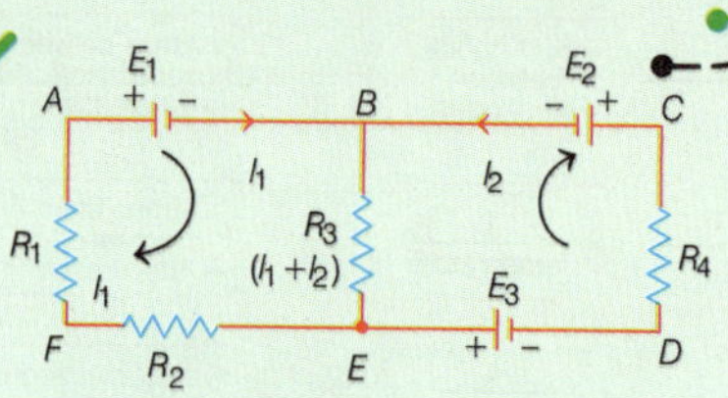

In closed loop $ABEFA$.
$-E_1 - (I_1 + I_2) R_3 - I_1 R_2 - I_1 R_1 = 0$

In closed loop $BCDEB$.
$E_2 + I_2 R_4 + E_3 + (I_1 + I_2) R_3 = 0$

Meter Bridge

It is the practical application of the Wheatstone bridge that is used to measure an unknown resistance.

For the balanced condition of the bridge

$$\frac{P}{Q} = \frac{R}{S} = \frac{\sigma L}{\sigma(100 - L)} = \frac{L}{(100 - L)}$$

σ = resistance per unit length

$$S = \frac{R(100 - L)}{L}$$

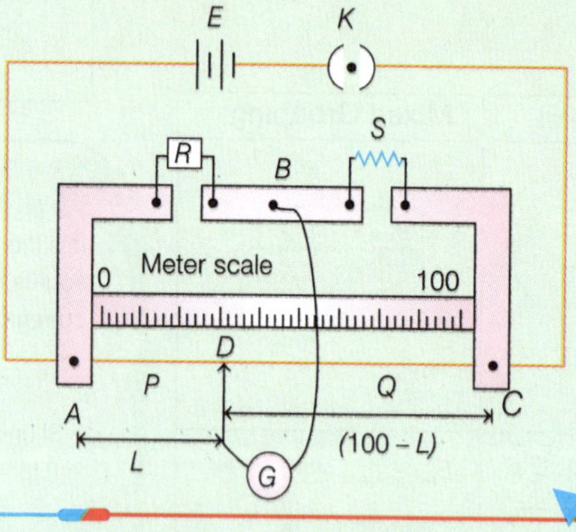

Wheatstone Bridge

Arrangement of four resistances used to determine one of these resistances in terms of the remaining three resistances.

The wheatstone bridge is said to be balanced when potential difference across the galvanometer is zero.

In the balanced condition of the Wheatstone bridge

$$\frac{P}{Q} = \frac{R}{S}$$

Unknown resistance, $S = \frac{Q}{P} R$

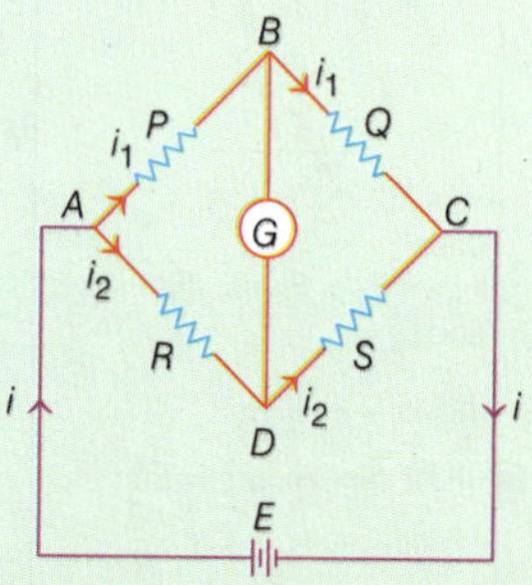

Sensitivity of a Wheatstone bridge

A wheatstone bridge shows a large deflection in the galvanometer for a small change of resistance in the resistance arm.

The sensitivity of the wheatstone bridge depends on two factors

1. Relative magnitude of the resistance in the four arm.
2. Relative positions of battery and galvanometer.

Chapter 18

Magnetic Effects of Current

Magnetic Field Due to Long Straight Conducting Wire

1 At point P, B is into the plane.

$$B=\frac{\mu_0 I}{4\pi r}(\sin\alpha+\sin\beta)$$

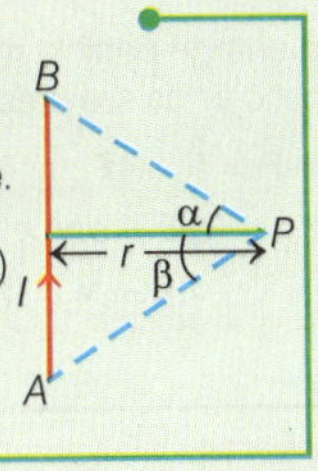

2 Wire of infinite length, $\alpha=90°$ and $\beta=90°$.

$$B=\frac{\mu_0 I}{4\pi r}(\sin 90°+\sin 90°)=\frac{\mu_0 I}{2\pi r}, \otimes$$

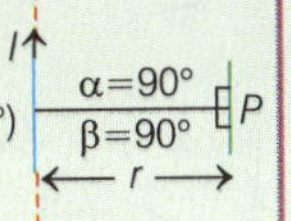

3 Wire of semi-infinite length.

$$B=\frac{\mu_0 I}{4\pi r}(\sin 90°+\sin 0°)=\frac{\mu_0 I}{4\pi r}$$

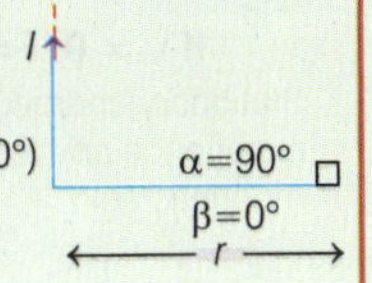

Biot-Savart Law

$$d\mathbf{B}=\frac{\mu_0}{4\pi}\frac{I\,d\mathbf{l}\times\mathbf{r}}{r^3} \quad \text{or} \quad dB=\frac{\mu_0}{4\pi}\frac{Idl\sin\theta}{r^2}$$

$\theta=0$, $\sin\theta=0$, $B=0$

$\theta=90°$, $\sin\theta=1$, So, dB is maximum.

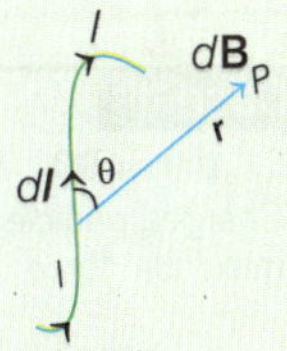

Magnetic Field For Different Configurations of the Circular Coil

Magnitude and direction of magnetic fields associated with different configurations of the circular coil.

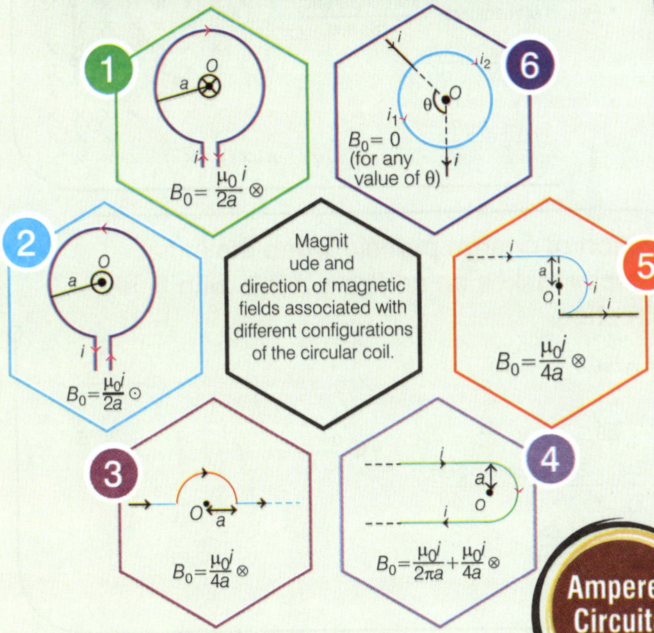

Magnetic Field on the Axis of Circular Loop

$$\mathbf{B}_p=\frac{\mu_0 IR^2}{2(R^2+x^2)^{3/2}}\hat{\mathbf{i}}$$

- For N number of turns

$$\mathbf{B}_p=\frac{\mu_0 NIR^2}{2(R^2+x^2)^{3/2}}\hat{\mathbf{i}}$$

- At centre, $x=0$

$$B_c=\frac{\mu_0 NI}{2R}=\frac{\mu_0 NIA}{2\pi R^3}$$

- At axial point lying away from coil, $R>>x$

$$B=\frac{\mu_0 NIR^2}{2x^3}=\frac{\mu_0 NIA}{2\pi x^3}$$

- Relation between field at centre and an axis

$$B_{axis}=\frac{B_C}{\left(1+\frac{x^2}{R^2}\right)^{3/2}}$$

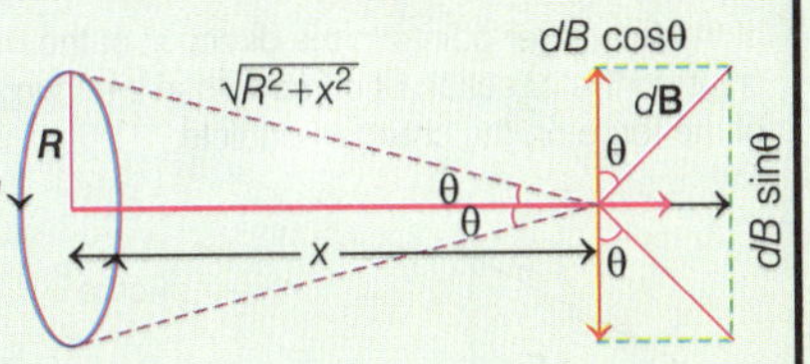

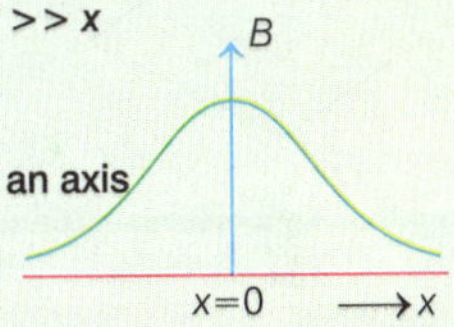

Ampere's Circuital Law

The line integral of the magnetic field $\mathbf{B}$ around any closed path is equal to μ_0 times the total current I.

$$\oint \mathbf{B}.d\mathbf{l}=\mu_0 I$$

Magnetic Field of Solenoid

- Magnetic field produced around and within the solenoid is as shown in the fig (a).

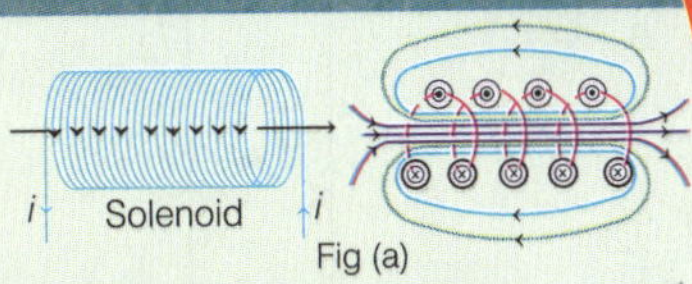

Fig (a)

- Magnetic field outside the ideal solenoid is zero. i.e $B=0$

(i) Finite length solenoid Magnetic field inside the long solenoid at any point is given by $B=\frac{\mu_0 ni}{2}[\cos\theta_1-\cos\theta_2]$

(ii) Infinite length solenoid If the solenoid is of infinite length and the point is well inside it i.e. $\alpha=\beta=(\pi/2)$, then $B_{in}=\mu_0 ni$

If the solenoid is of infinite length and the point is near one end, i.e. $\alpha=0$ and $\beta=(\pi/2)$, then $B_{in}=\frac{\mu_0 ni}{2}$

POWER TIPS

Net magnetic field due to two parallel current-carrying wires having infinite length.

$$B_p=B_1-B_2=\frac{\mu_0 I_1}{2\pi r_1}-\frac{\mu_0 I_2}{2\pi r_2}$$

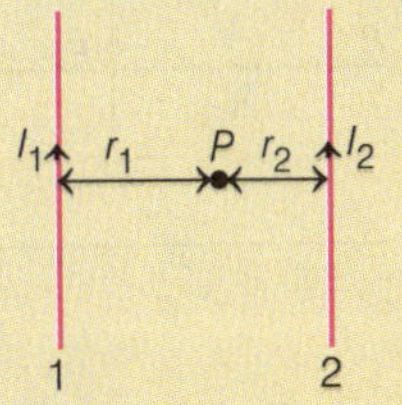

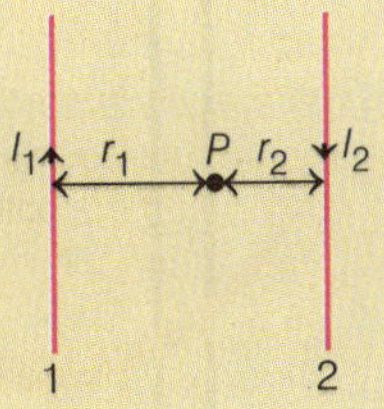

Net magnetic field due to two anti-parallel current-carrying wires having infinite length.

$$B_p=B_1+B_2=\frac{\mu_0 I_1}{2\pi r_1}+\frac{\mu_0 I_2}{2\pi r_2}$$

Magnetic Force on Moving Charge

Case I

If v = 0, F=0

Stationary charge does not experience any force in magnetic field.

Case II

If θ=0° or 180°, then F= 0

Charged particle moving parallel or anti-parallel to field does not experience any force.

Case III

If θ = 90°, F = qvB

Charged particle experience maximum force.

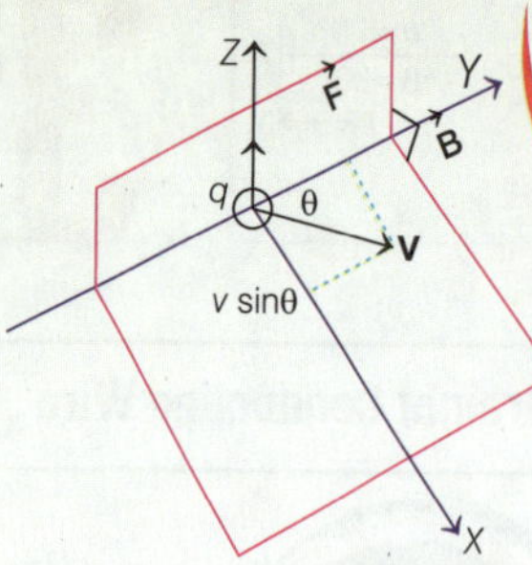

$$\mathbf{F} = q(\mathbf{v} \times \mathbf{B}) = qvB\sin\theta$$

LORENTZ FORCE

Force experienced by a charge particle moving in a region when both electric and magnetic fields are present.

$$\mathbf{F} = \mathbf{F}_e + \mathbf{F}_m = q\mathbf{E} + q(\mathbf{v} \times \mathbf{B}) = q(\mathbf{E} + \mathbf{v} \times \mathbf{B})$$

Motion of Charge Particle in Uniform Magnetic Field

- Particle will experience force
$$\mathbf{F} = q(\mathbf{v} \times \mathbf{B})$$
$$F = qvB\sin\theta$$
- When initial velocity is parallel to magnetic field, force will be zero.
- Radius of path, $R = \frac{mv}{qB}$
- Period of revolution $= \frac{\text{Circumference}}{\text{Speed}}$
$$T = \frac{2\pi R}{v} = \frac{2\pi m}{qB}$$
- Frequency of revolution
$$f = \frac{1}{T} = \frac{qB}{2\pi m}$$

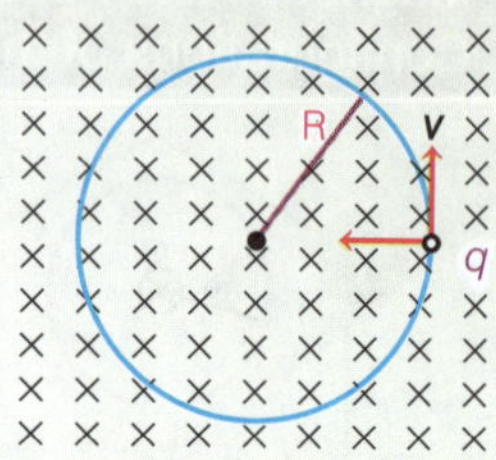

Fleming's Left Hand Rule

If the forefinger points in the direction of the magnetic field, central finger in the direction of current, then the thumb gives the direction of the force on the charged particle.

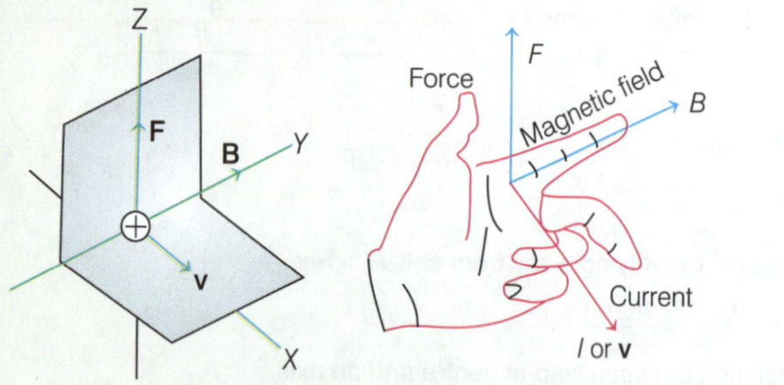

Motion of charge particle when the initial velocity makes an arbitrary angle with field direction

$$V_{\parallel} = v\cos\theta,\ v_{\perp} = v\sin\theta$$

$$r = \frac{mv_{\perp}}{qB}$$

$$T = \frac{2\pi r}{v_{\perp}} = \frac{2\pi}{v\sin\theta} \cdot \frac{mv\sin\theta}{qB} = \frac{2\pi m}{qB}$$

$$f = \frac{1}{T} = \frac{Bq}{2\pi m}$$

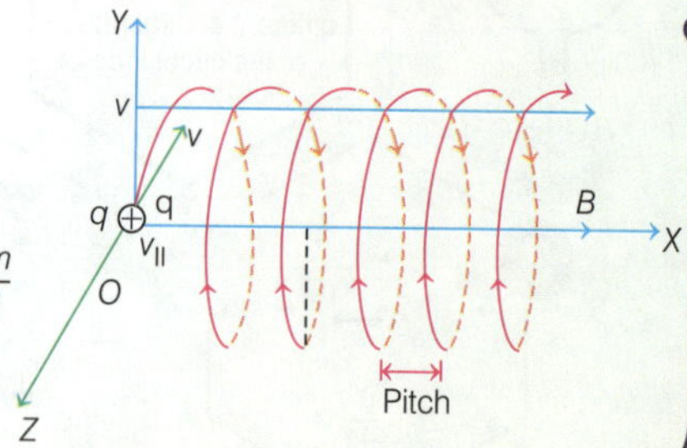

Force on a Current-Carrying Conductor

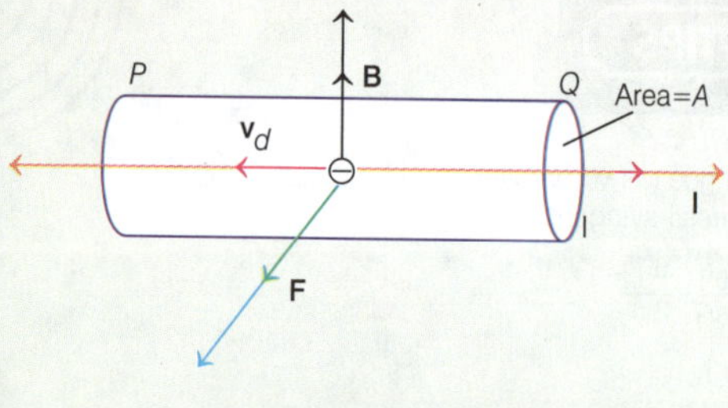

- $F = I(\mathbf{l} \times \mathbf{B}) = IlB\sin\theta$
- If $\theta = 0°, \theta = 180°$
$$F = 0$$
Particle does not experience any force.
- If $\theta = 90°$ $\quad F = IlB = F_{max}$
Particle will experience maximum force.
- Magnetic force on a closed loop is zero.

Force between Parallel Wires

$$B_1 = \frac{\mu_0 I_1}{2\pi r},\quad B_2 = \frac{\mu_0 I_2}{2\pi r}$$

$$F_2 = \frac{\mu_0 I_1 I_2}{2\pi r} \cdot l$$

$$F = \frac{F_2}{l} = \frac{\mu_0 I_1 I_2}{2\pi r}$$

$$\mathbf{F}_1 = -\mathbf{F}_2$$

- Parallel current attracts and anti-parallel repels.

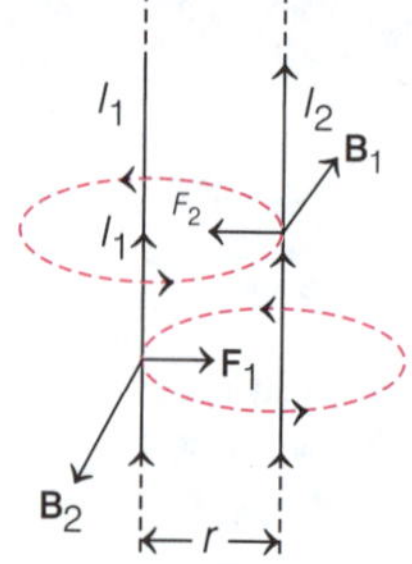

Parallel (Attract)

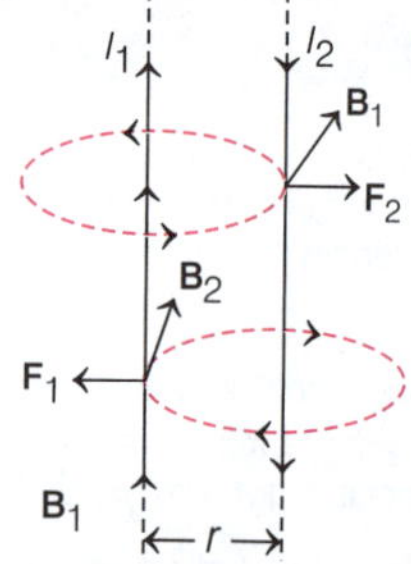

Anti-parallel (Repel)

Moving Coil Galvanometer

Torque Experienced by a Current Loop in Uniform Magnetic Field

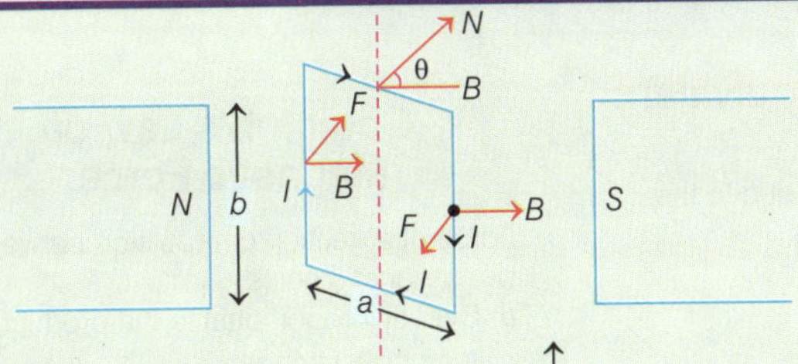

- **Torque experienced**
  $\tau = IBA \sin\theta$
- **For N turns**, $\tau = NIBA \sin\theta$
  $\tau = MB\sin\theta = \mathbf{M} \times \mathbf{B}$
- **Case I**, $\theta = 0°$, $\tau = 0$, torque is minimum
- **Case II**, $\theta = 90°$, $\tau = NIBA = \tau_{max}$, torque is maximum

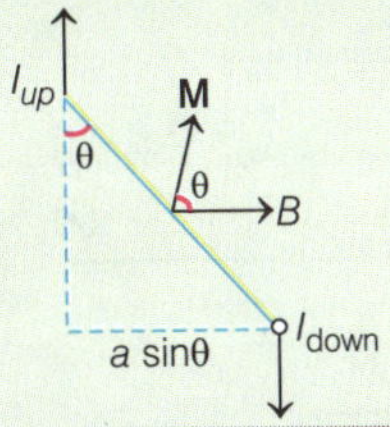

- An instrument used to measure small current.
- Operates on the principle that current carrying coil experiences a torque when placed in magnetic field.
- Deflection of coil is proportional to the current passing through it.
- Maximum torque experience is $\tau = NIBA$
- Restoring torque = Deflecting torque, $K\alpha = NIBA$

$$I = \frac{K}{NBA}\alpha = G\alpha$$

- **Figure of merit of a galvanometer** It is the current which produces a deflection of one scale division in galvanometer.

$$G = \frac{I}{\alpha} = \frac{K}{NBA}$$

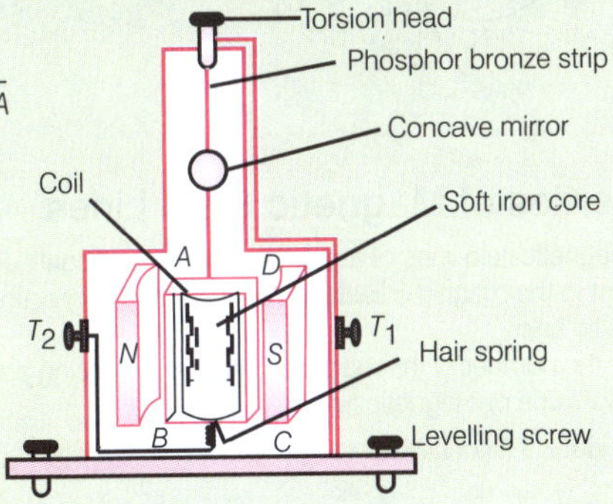

The linear relationship between I and α makes the moving coil galvanometer useful for current measurement and detection.

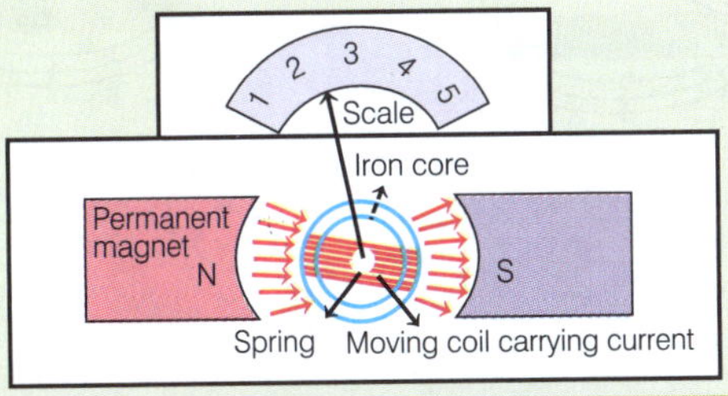

Sensitivity of Galvanometer

- It shows large scale deflection even when a small current is passed through it.

Current Sensitivity : The deflection produced in the galvanometer when a unit current flows through it.

$$I_s = \frac{\alpha}{I} = \frac{NBA}{K}$$

Voltage Sensitivity : The deflection produced in the galvanometer when a unit potential difference applied across its ends.

$$V_s = \frac{\alpha}{V} = \frac{\alpha}{IR} = \frac{NBA}{KR}$$

$$\text{Voltage sensitivity} = \frac{\text{Current sensitivity}}{R}$$

Factors affecting the sensitivity

- Number of turns N in its coil.
- Magnetic field.
- Area A of coil.
- Torsion constant k of the spring and suspension wire.

Factors which can increase the sensitivity

- By increasing the number of turns N of coil.
- By increasing the magnetic field.
- By increasing the area.
- By decreasing the value of torsion constant k.

Conversion of a Galvanometer

- **Into an Ammeter**

$$S = \frac{I_g}{I - I_g} \times G$$

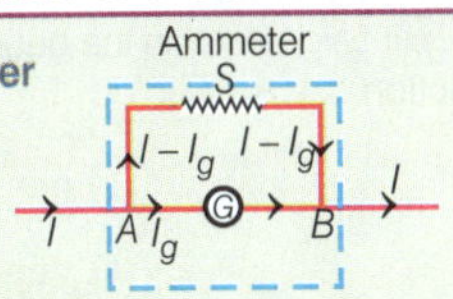

- An ammeter is a shunted or low resistance galvanometer. Its effective resistance is

$$R_A = \frac{GS}{G+S} < S$$

- **Into an Voltmeter**

$$R = \frac{V}{I_g} - G$$

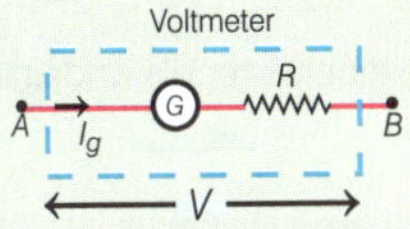

- Voltmeter is a high resistance galvanometer, its effective resistance is $R_V = R + G >> G$

Shunt Resistance

A low resistance which is connected in parallel with a galvanometer (or ammeter) to protect it from strong currents.

Uses

(I) To prevent a galvanometer from being damaged due to large current.
(ii) To convert a galvanometer into ammeter.
(iii) To increase the range of an ammeter.

Advantages and Disadvantages of Moving Coil Galvanometer

Advantages of Moving Coil Galvanometer

- **High Sensitivity** Detects very small currents.
- **Linear Scale** Deflection is directly proportional to current.
- **Good Accuracy** Provides precise readings.
- **Low Internal Resistance** Minimal effect on the circuit.
- **Smooth Operation** Stable deflection in a uniform magnetic field.
- **No Parallax Error** Clear and accurate readings.

Disadvantages of Moving Coil Galvanometer

- **Limited Range** Only suitable for low currents, requires modification for large currents.
- **Fragility**: Vulnerable to mechanical shock and vibration.
- **Not Ideal for AC** Primarily for DC measurements.
- **Limited Maximum Deflection** Cannot measure very high currents.
- **Temperature Sensitivity** Affected by temperature changes.
- **Needs Calibration** Regular maintenance to ensure accuracy.

Chapter 19

Magnetism and Matter

Bar Magnet

- Circular or rectangular cross-section.
- It is made up of iron, steel or any other ferromagnetic substance or ferromagnetic composite.
- It possess permanent magnetic properties.

Magnetism - A characteristic of magnet that causes attraction or repulsion.

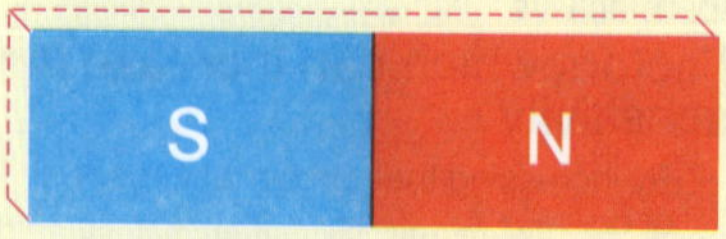

Solenoid as an Equivalent Bar Magnet

Magnetic field at point P due to the solenoid $= \frac{\mu_0}{4\pi}\frac{2M}{r^3}$

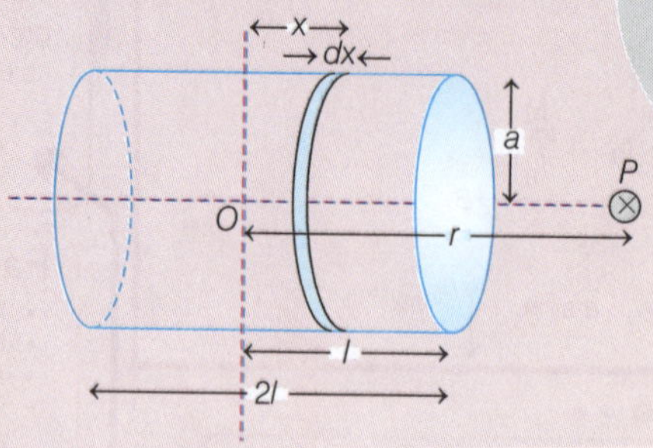

Coulomb's Law of Magnetic Force

Force of attraction or repulsion between two magnetic poles

(i) Directly proportional to the product of their pole strength.

(ii) Inversely proportional to the square of the distance between them.

$$F = \frac{\mu_0}{4\pi}\frac{q_{m1} q_{m2}}{r^2}$$

Properties of Magnet

(i) **Attractive Property** A magnet attracts small pieces of iron, cobalt, nickel etc.

(ii) **Directive Property** When a magnet is suspended freely, it allign itself in the geographical north-south direction.

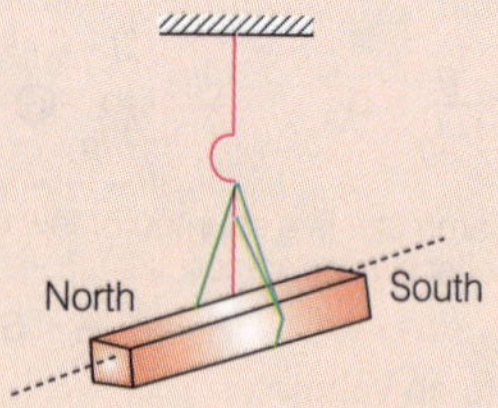

(iii) Like poles repels and unlike poles attracts each other.

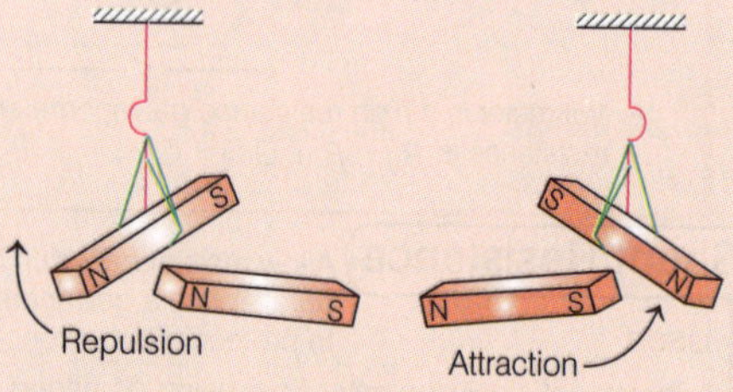

(iv) **Magnetic poles always exist in pair** Magnetic monopoles does not exist.

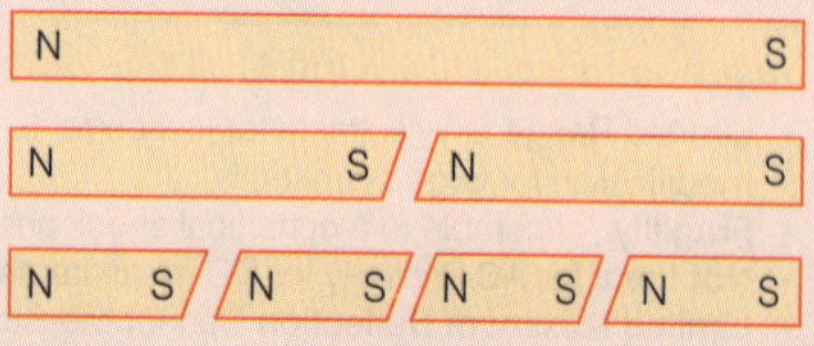

(v) **Magnetic Induction -** A magnet induces magnetism in a magnetic substance placed near it.

Magnetic Field Lines

The curve whose tangent at any point gives the direction of the magnetic field.

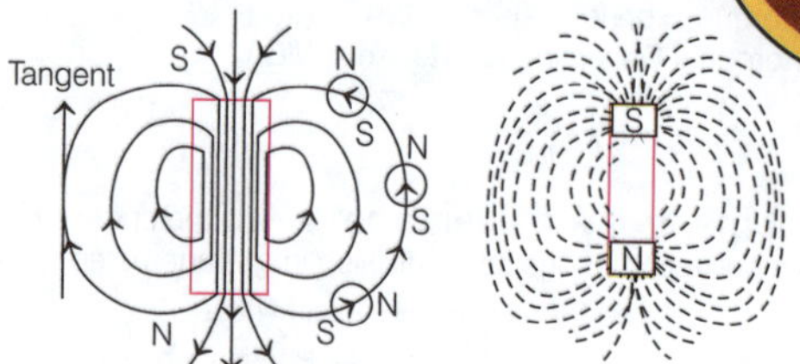

Properties of Magnetic Field Lines

- The magnetic field lines of a magnet form closed continuous loops.
- Tangent to the magnetic field lines represents the direction of net magnetic field.
- Larger the number of the magnetic field lines crossing per unit area, stronger the magnitude of magnetic field B.

Magnetic Field Lines

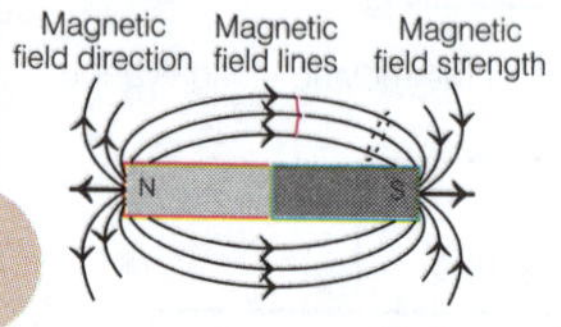

Bar Magnet Field Lines

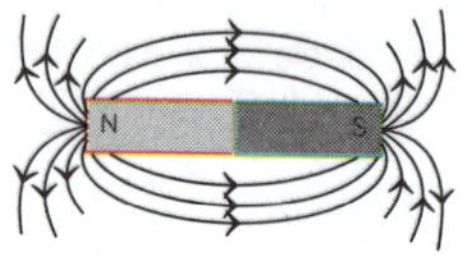

Between two bar magnets

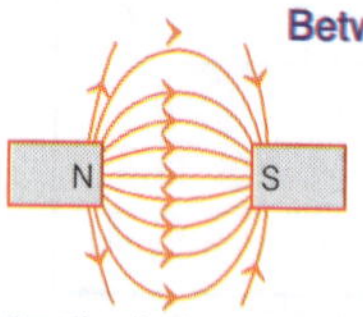

(a) Attraction between opposite poles

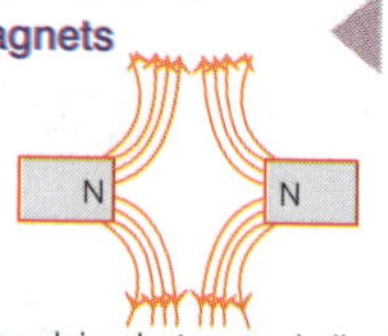

(b) Repulsion between similar poles

Magnetic field lines do not intersect each other.

Magnetic field in one direction

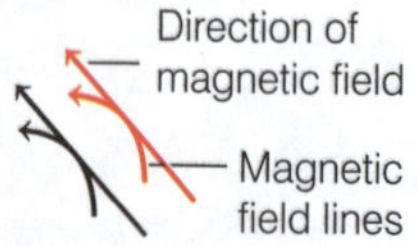

Magnetic field lines intersect

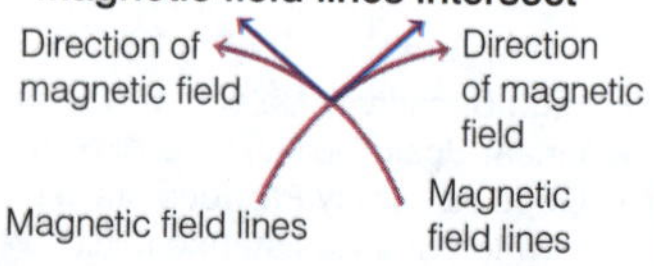

Two directions of magnetic field at a point is not possible.

Magnetic Dipole Moment

Torque on a Magnetic Dipole in a Uniform Magnetic Field

Torque = force × perpendicular distance between coupled forces

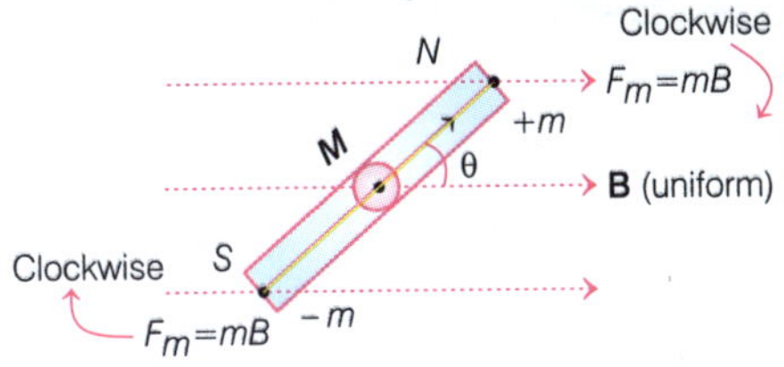

$\tau = \mathbf{m} \times \mathbf{B}$

$\tau = mB \sin\theta$

If $\theta = 90°$, then $\tau = mB \sin 90° \Rightarrow \tau_{max} = MB$

If $\theta = 0°$, then $\tau = mB \sin 0° \Rightarrow \tau_{min} = 0$

Time Period of a Magnetic Dipole

$$T = 2\pi\sqrt{\frac{I}{MB}}$$

I - Moment of Inertia of the body

M - Magnetic dipole moment

B - Magnetic field

Current Loop as a Magnetic Dipole

$M = IA$

If current carrying coil consists of N turns, then $M = NIA$

[Current loop as a magnetic dipole]

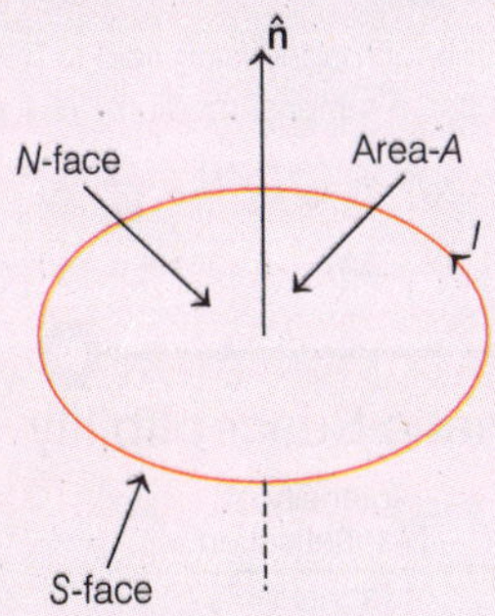

Magnetic Dipole Moment

$M = m \times 2l$

Vector quantity

Direction – South pole to North pole

Unit - Am^2

Unit of m = Am

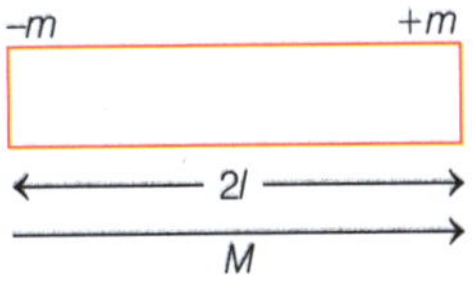

Magnetic field of a bar magnet at an axial point

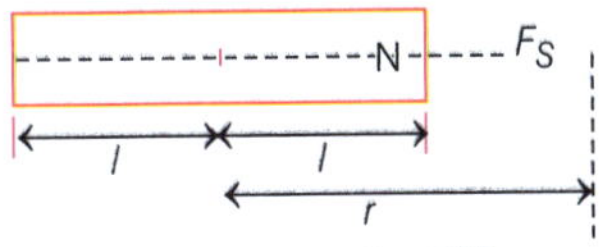

$$B_{axial} = \frac{\mu_0}{4\pi}\frac{2M}{r^3}$$

Magnetic field of bar magnet at an equatorial point

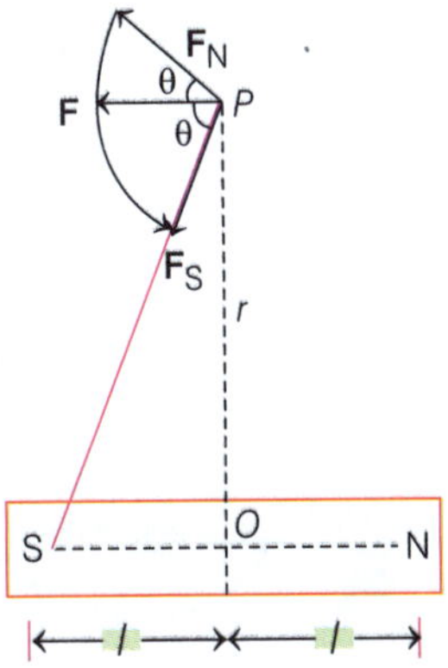

$$B_{equatorial} = \frac{\mu_0}{4\pi}\frac{M}{r^3}$$

Potential Energy of a Magnetic Dipole in a Uniform Magnetic Field

$U = -\mathbf{M}\cdot\mathbf{B} = -M.B\cos\theta$

When $\theta = 0°$, $U = -MB \rightarrow$ Stable equilibrium

$\theta = 180°$, $U = +MB \rightarrow$ Unstable equilibrium

Gauss's Law in Magnetism

Surface integral of a magnetic field over a closed surface is always zero.

$$\oint \mathbf{B}\cdot d\mathbf{S} = 0$$

Consequence of Gauss's Law

- Isolated magnetic poles (monopoles) do not exist.
- The magnetic poles always exists as unlike pairs of equal strengths.
- Number of magnetic lines of force entering a closed surface = number of magnetic lines of force leaving a closed surface.

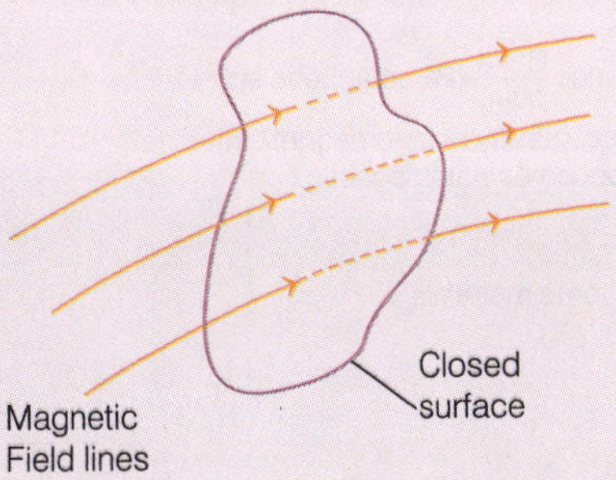

Magnetic Properties

Magnetic Induction

The total number of magnetic lines of force crossing per unit area normally through a material.
SI unit - tesla (T)

Magnetising Field

The magnetic field that exists in vacuum and induces magnetism is called magnetising field. If the solenoid has n turns per unit length, then magnetising field in the solenoid is

$$B_0 = \mu_0 n I$$

Magnetising Field Intensity

The ability of magnetising field to magnetise a material medium. $H = nI$

$$B_0 = \mu_0 n I = \mu_0 H \text{ or } H = \frac{B_0}{\mu_0}$$

SI unit - Am^{-1}

Intensity of Magnetisation

The magnetic moment developed per unit volume of a material.

$$I = \frac{M}{V} = \frac{\text{Induced Dipole Moment}}{\text{Volume}}$$

SI unit - $\frac{A}{m}$, $[I] = [L^{-1} A]$

Magnetic Permeability

It is the measure of the extent to which a material can be penetrated or permeated.

$$\mu = \frac{B}{H} = \frac{\text{Magnetic Induction}}{\text{Magnetic Intensity}}$$

SI unit - TmA^{-1}, $[\mu] = [MLT^{-2}A^{-2}]$

Relative Permeability

It is the ratio of the permeability of the medium to the permeability of the free space.

$$\mu_r = \frac{\mu}{\mu_0}$$

Relation between relative permeability and susceptibility

$$\mu_r = 1 + \chi_m$$

Magnetic Susceptibility

$$\chi_m = \frac{I}{H} = \frac{\text{Intensity of Magnetisation}}{\text{Magnetising Field Intensity}}$$

Classification of Magnetic Materials

Paramagnetic Substances

- Weakly attracted by a magnet. e.g. Al, Mn, Pt, Na, $CuCl_2$, O_2, etc. The magnetic lines of force prefer to pass through it than through the surrounding air.
- In non-uniform magnetic field, it moves from weaker to the stronger parts of the field.
- It aligns itself parallel to the magnetising field.
- The level of the paramagnetic liquid in the U-tube arm rises which is placed between the poles of strong magnet.
- μ_r is slightly greater than 1. Its susceptibility has small but positive value. Magnetic susceptibility $(\chi_m) \propto \frac{1}{T}$
- If magnetising field is removed, then paramagnetic substance looses its magnetism.

Diamagnetic Substances

01 It develop feeble magnetisation in the opposite direction of the magnetising field. e.g. Cu, Ag, Au, NaCl, H_2O, etc.

02 When a diamagnetic material is placed in a magnetic field, poles are induced in the opposite direction of the inducing field.

03 In a non-uniform magnetic field, a diamagnetic substance moves from stronger to the weaker parts of the field.

04 It aligns itself perpendicular to the magnetising field in a uniform magnetic field.

05 The level of the dielectric solution is depressed in the arm which is placed between the poles of strong magnet.

06 The magnetisation of a diamagnetic substance lasts so long as the magnetising field is applied.

Ferromagnetic Substances

- They are strongly magnetised in the direction of applied magnetic field. e.g. Fe, Ni, Co, Gd, Fe_2O_3, Alnico, etc.
- Highly concentrated lines of force in a ferromagnetic rod.
- It quickly aligns itself parallel to the magnetising field.
- It quickly aligns itself parallel to the magnetising field.
- Liquid rises to very high level in U-tube.
- μ_r of a ferromagnetic material is large positive value. μ_r for Iron = 1000
- χ_m of a ferromagnetic material is large positive value.
- It retains magnetism even after magnetising field is removed.

POWER TIPS

Curie Law

For paramagnetic substance,

$$\chi_m \propto \frac{1}{T}$$

At higher temperature

Ferromagnetic substance $\xrightarrow[\text{point}]{\text{Curie}}$ Paramagnetic substance.

At Curie point, the susceptibility of ferromagnetic material suddenly falls and it becomes paramagnetic.

$$\chi_m = \frac{C'}{T - T_C}$$

Curie temperature of some materials

Iron → 770°C

Nickel → 354°C

Cobalt → 1115°C

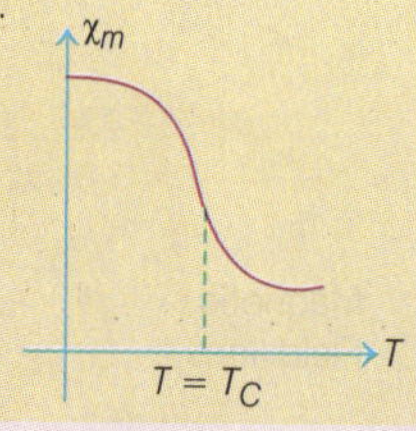

Chapter 20

Electromagnetic Induction

Magnetic Flux

- Number of field lines passing through any surface placed in a magnetic field.
- SI unit is weber (Wb).

$$\phi = \mathbf{B}\cdot\mathbf{A} = BA\cos\theta$$

- **In uniform magnetic field *B***

  If $\theta = 0°$ maximum flux, then $\phi = BA$.

  If $\theta = 90°$ minimum flux, then $\phi = 0$.

  If $\theta = 180°$ minimum flux, then $\phi = -BA$.

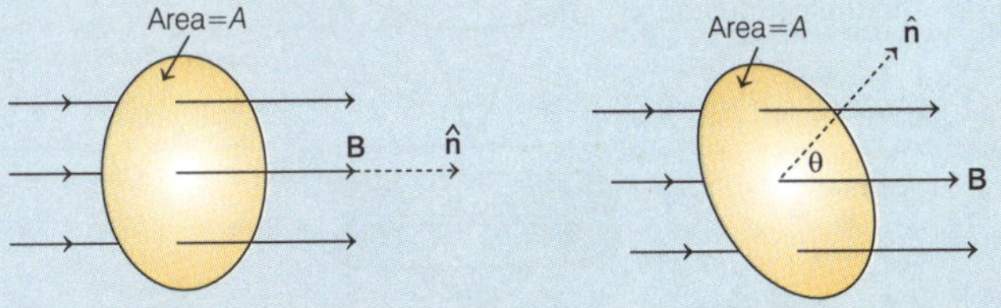

Process by which a changing magnetic field induces an electromagnetic force (EMF).

Principle of electromagnetic induction is used in devices like transformers, electric motors and generators

Electromagnetic Induction

Direction of Induced Current

- An Induced current always flows in a direction such that it opposes the change which produced it.

When the N pole of the magnet is moved towards the coil, end of coil become N pole.

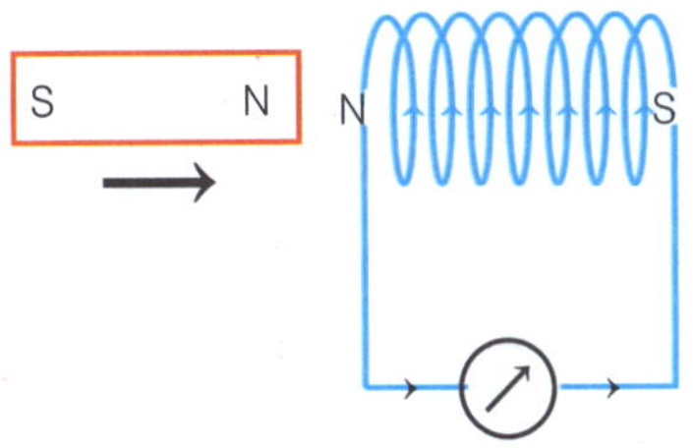

When the N pole of the magnet is moved away from the coil, end of coil becomes S pole.

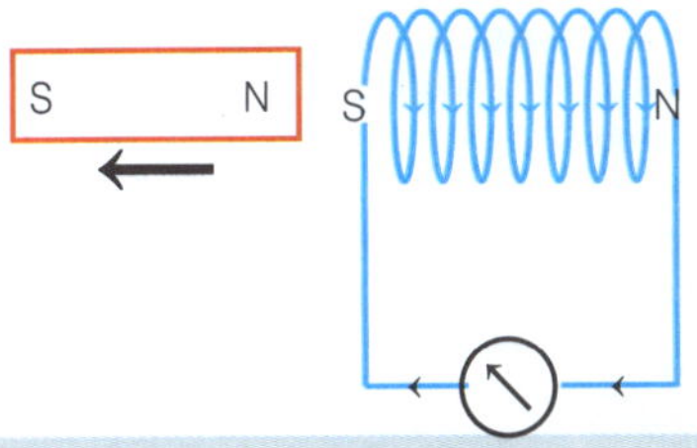

Faraday's Laws of Electromagnetic Induction

The induced EMF in a closed loop is directly proportional to the rate of change of magnetic flux through loop.

1 First Law — Whenever the magnetic flux changes in a closed circuit, an emf or current is induced.

2 Second Law — The magnitude of induced EMF linked with the closed circuit is equal to the rate of change of magnetic flux.

$$|\varepsilon| = \frac{d\phi}{dt}$$

• B changes	$\text{EMF} = -A\dfrac{dB}{dt}$	Avg. EMF $= \dfrac{A(B_2 - B_1)}{t}$
• A changes	$\text{EMF} = -B\dfrac{dA}{dt}$	Avg. EMF $= \dfrac{B(A_2 - A_1)}{t}$
• θ changes ($\theta = \omega t$)	$\text{EMF} = -NBA\omega\sin\omega t$	Avg. EMF $= \dfrac{NBA(\cos\theta_2 - \cos\theta_1)}{t}$

LENZ'S LAW

- The direction of the induced EMF and current opposes the change in magnetic flux that produced it.

01 The direction of current induced in the loop is such that it opposes the cause due to which it has produced.

02 It is in the accordance with law of conservation of energy.

03 Induced emf $= \dfrac{-d\phi}{dt}$

Negative is due to Lenz's law.

04 $\text{EMF} = \dfrac{-d\phi}{dt} = -\dfrac{d(\mathbf{B}\cdot\mathbf{A})}{dt}$

Motional EMF

The emf induced across the ends of a conductor due to its motion.

$\varepsilon = Blv$

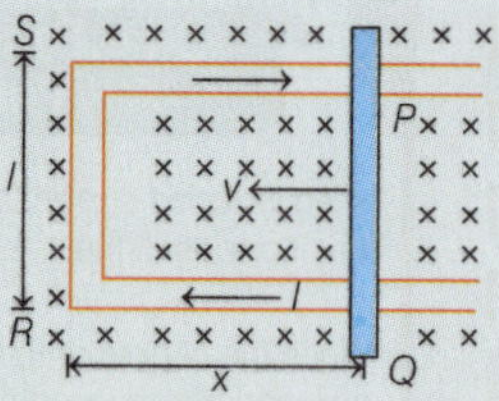

Motional EMF From Lorentz Force

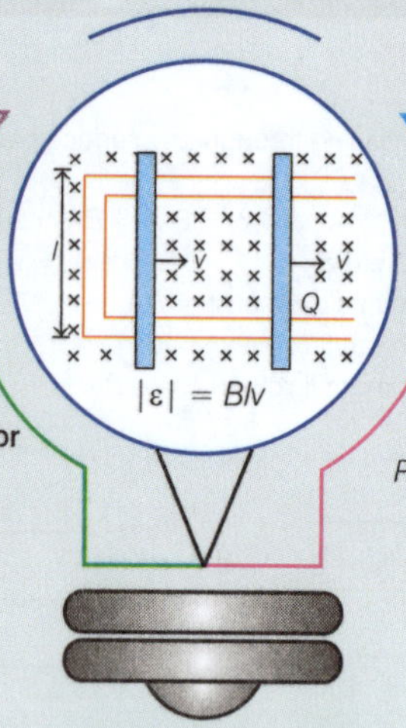

1 Induced Current

$i_{in} = \frac{e}{R} = \frac{Blv}{R}$

2 Magnetic force on the conductor

$F_m = \frac{B^2l^2v}{R}$

3 Power Dissipated

$P_{agent} = \frac{dW}{dt}$

$= F_{agent}\,v = \frac{B^2v^2l^2}{R}$

4 Electrical Power

$P_{thermel} = I^2R = \left(\frac{Bvl}{R}\right)^2 R$

$= \frac{B^2v^2l^2}{R}$

Fleming's Right Hand Rule

It is used to determine the direction of the induced current in a conductor moving through a magnetic field, or when a conductor is moving within a magnetic field.

It is commonly applied to generators and electromagnetic induction.

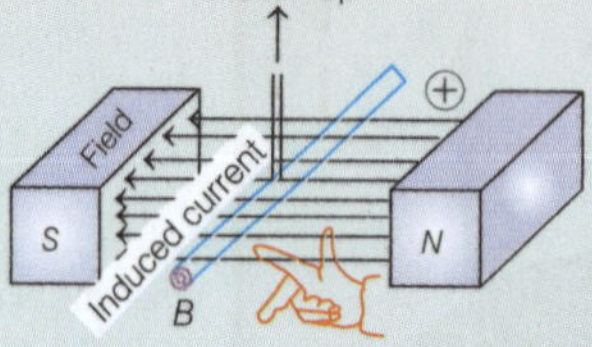

Right-Hand Rule

Thumb: Represents the motion of the conductor (or the direction of the moving wire).

Index Finger: Represents the magnetic field direction.

Middle Finger: Represents the direction of the induced current (in the conductor).

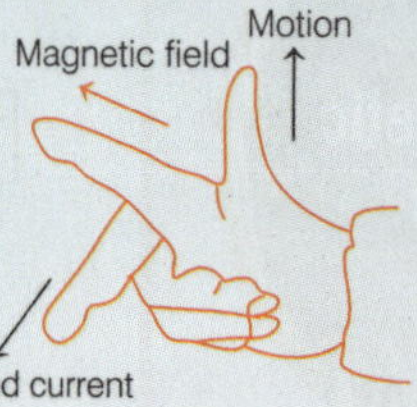

Motional Emf In Rotatory Motion

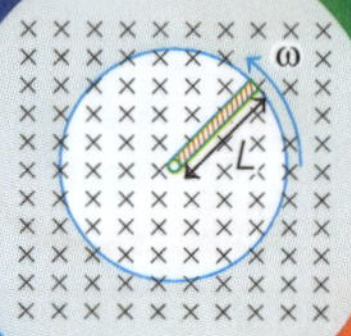

Induced emf

$\varepsilon = \frac{1}{2}B\omega L^2$

Induced current

$I = \frac{\varepsilon}{R} = \frac{1}{2}\frac{BL^2\omega}{R}$

Heat dissipated in time *t*

$Q = \frac{\varepsilon^2 t}{R} = \frac{1}{4}\frac{B^2L^4\omega^2 t}{R}$

POWER TIPS — MOTIONAL EMF OF VARIOUS SHAPES

- **Rotating Disc**

  Induced emf $\varepsilon = \frac{1}{2}B\omega L^2$

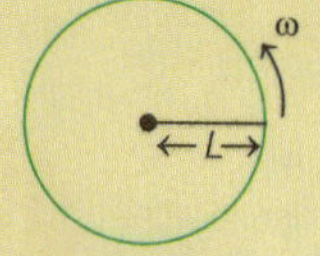

- **Circular coil**

  Induced emf $\varepsilon = Bv2L$

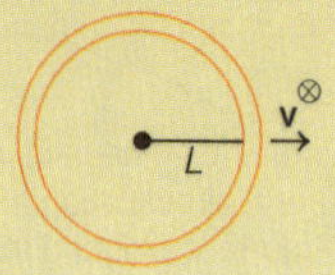

Method of Generating Induced EMF

Induced emf by changing relative orientation of the coil and magnetic field

$\phi = BA\cos\theta$

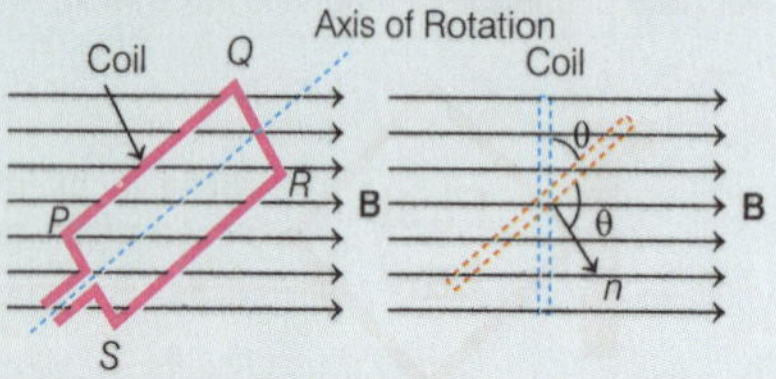

$\theta = \omega t$ ∴ $\phi = BA\cos\omega t$, An induced emf $\varepsilon = BA\omega\sin\omega t$

For number of turns

$\varepsilon = NBA\omega\sin\omega t$, $\varepsilon_{max} = NBA\omega = 2\pi\nu NBA$

$\varepsilon = \varepsilon_{max}\sin\omega t = \varepsilon_{max}\sin 2\pi\nu t$

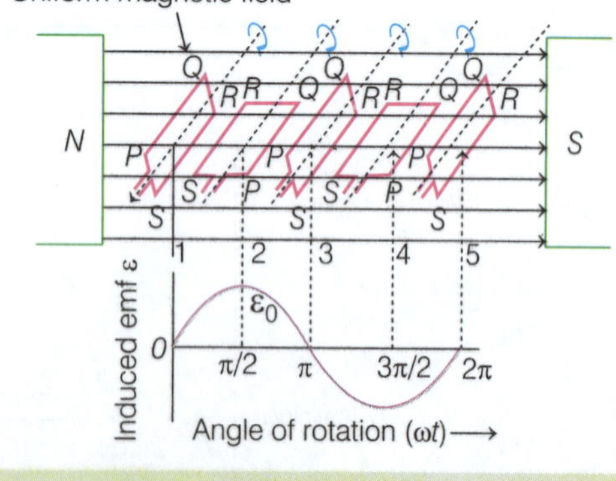

Eddy Currents

- Circulating current induced within a conductor when it is exposed to a changing magnetic field.
- It flows in closed loops within the conductor.

- Power loss due to eddy current,

$$P_{eddy} = \frac{B^2l^2v}{\rho}$$

- It causes unnecessary heating and wastage of power.
- It can be reduced by using laminated core.

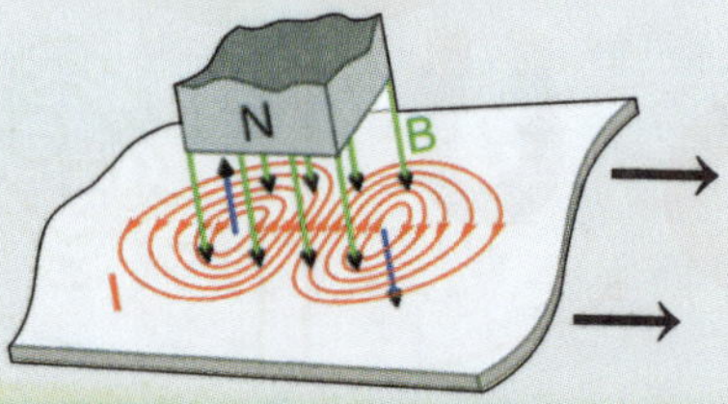

Inductance

Property of an electric conductor or circuit that causes an emf to be generated by a change in the current flowing through it.

The flux associated to a coil is directly proportional to the current flowing in same coil,

$$\frac{d\phi_B}{dt} \propto \frac{dI}{dt} \Rightarrow \frac{d\phi}{dt} = L\frac{dI}{dt}$$

Mutual-Inductance

- Phenomenon of production of induced EMF in one coil due to a change of current in the neighbouring coil.
- Coefficient of mutual induction, $\phi = MI$
- EMF induced $\varepsilon = -\frac{d\phi}{dt} = -M\frac{dI}{dt}$
- Mutual inductance of two coils is numerically equal to the magnetic flux linked with one coil when a unit current passes through the other coil. $\varepsilon = -M$

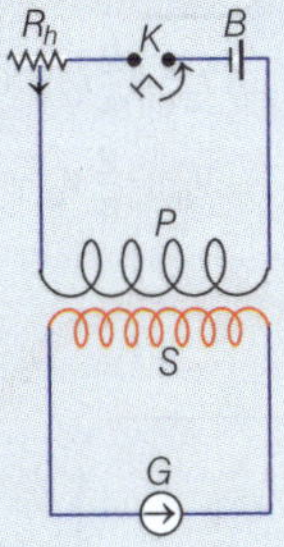

Mutual Inductance of two long Solenoids

Mutual Inductance

$$M = \frac{\mu_0 N_1 N_2 A}{l} = \mu_0 n_1 n_2 A l$$

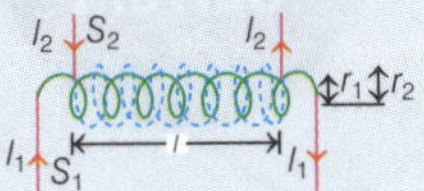

Factors Affecting Mutual Inductance

- **Number of turns** $M \propto N_1 N_2$
- **Common cross-sectional area** Larger the common cross-sectional area of two solenoids, larger will be their mutual inductance.
- **Relative separation** Larger the distance between two solenoids smaller will be magnetic flux, hence smaller will be the value of M.
- **Relative orientation of coils** M is maximum when the primary coil completely envelopes the secondary, M is minimum when primary coil is perpendicular to secondary coil.

Self-Inductance

- Phenomenon of production of induced emf in a coil when changing current passes through it.

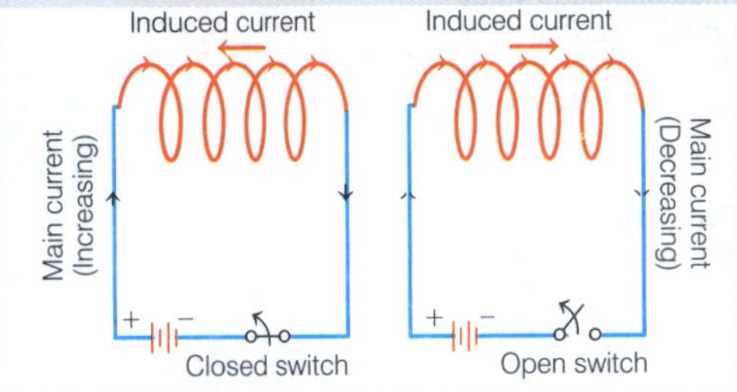

- Coefficient of self-induction $\phi = LI$
- Emf induced in the coil is $\varepsilon = \frac{-d\phi}{dt} = -L\frac{dI}{dt}$
- Self inductance is the induced emf set up in the coil due to a unit rate of change of current through it.
  $\therefore \quad \varepsilon = -L$

Self-Inductance of a Solenoid

- Self-inductance of a long solenoid is $L = \mu n^2 lA$
- For N number of total turns
  $L = \frac{\mu_0 N^2 A}{l}$ where $n = \frac{N}{l}$
- If coil is wound over a material with high relative magnetic permeability μ_r. $L = \mu_r \mu_0 \frac{N^2 A}{l}$

Factors affecting self-inductance

(i) **Number of turns** $L \propto N^2$

(ii) **Area of cross- section** $L \propto A$

(iii) **Permeability of core material** Self inductance of a solenoid increases μ_r times, if it is wound over an iron core of relative permeability μ_r.

Self-inductance of Coil

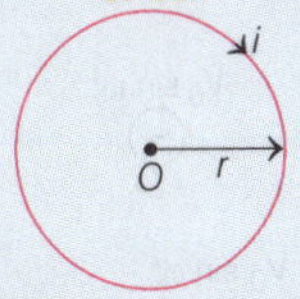

01 **Magnetic field due to coil** $B = \frac{\mu_0 N i}{2r}$

02 **Total flux for N turns** $\phi_B = NBA = \frac{\mu_0 \pi N^2 r i}{2}$

03 **Self-inductance** $L = \frac{\mu_0 \pi N^2 r}{2}$

Application of Eddy Currents

01 **Magnetic Braking**
Eddy current brakes use the opposing force generated by eddy currents in a conductor moving through a magnetic field to produce smooth, contactless braking.

02 **Induction Heating**
Eddy currents generate heat within conductive materials, used in **induction furnaces** or **metal hardening** processes to heat metals quickly and locally.

03 **Non-Destructive Testing (NDT)**
Eddy current testing is used for **crack detection** or **material defects** in metals by monitoring the variation in eddy currents caused by surface flaws.

04 **Electric Meters**
Eddy current meters are used in mechanical meters (like energy meters) where eddy currents generate torque to rotate a disk, measuring power consumption.

05 **Electromagnetic Shielding**
Eddy currents may be used for electromagnetic shielding.

Chapter 21

Alternating Current

Average Mean Value of AC

Instantaneous Value of AC Electric current flowing at any instant of time t in an AC circuit.

Peak value I_0 The value of AC becomes maximum (twice) in one cycle.

Average value Value of direct current which sends the same charge in a circuit in the same time as sent by the given alternating current in its half time period.

$$I_{av} = \frac{2}{\pi} I_0 = 0.637\, I_0$$

$$V_{av} = \frac{2}{\pi} V_0 = 0.637\, V_0$$

RMS Value of AC

01
- It is the square root of the average of the square of all instantaneous value of AC over one complete cycle.

02
- It represents the effective value of AC that produces the same heating effect as an equivalent DC circuit or voltage.

$$I_{rms} = \frac{1}{\sqrt{2}} I_0 = 0.707\, I_0,\ I_{rms} = 70.7\% \text{ of } I_0$$

$$V_{rms} = \frac{V_0}{\sqrt{2}} = 0.707 V_0,\ V_{rms} = 70.7\% \text{ of } V_0$$

Alternating Voltage

- Voltage which changes in magnitude and direction with respect to time.
- Produced by rotating a coil in a uniform magnetic field with uniform angular velocity.

Alternating Current

- Electric current, which keeps on changing in magnitude and direction periodically.
- Obeys Ohm's law and Joule's heating law.
- Produced using the principle of electromagnetic induction.

Phasor and Phasor Diagram

01 **Phasor** A rotating vector that represents a sinusoidally varying quantity.

02 **Phasor Diagram**

Diagram representing AC voltage or current as vectors with phase angle between them.

$I = I_0 \sin \omega t$

$V = V_0 \sin \omega t$

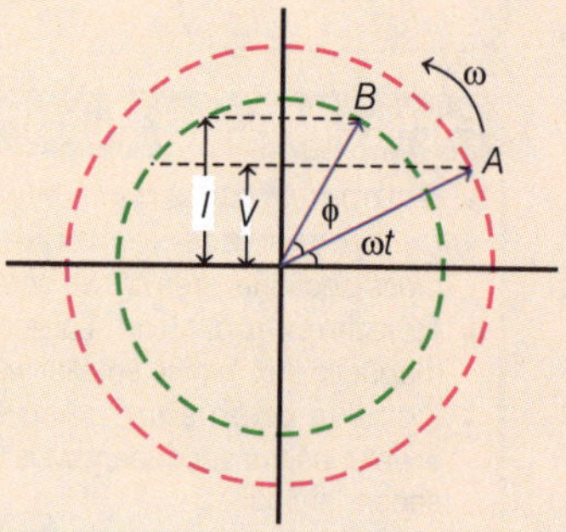

Single Component AC Circuits

01 AC Circuit With Resistor Only

- $V = V_0 \sin \omega t$
- $I = I_0 \sin \omega t$
- V and I are in same phase.

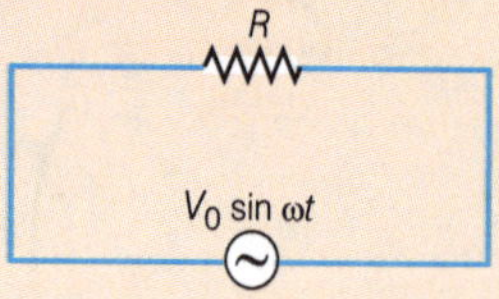

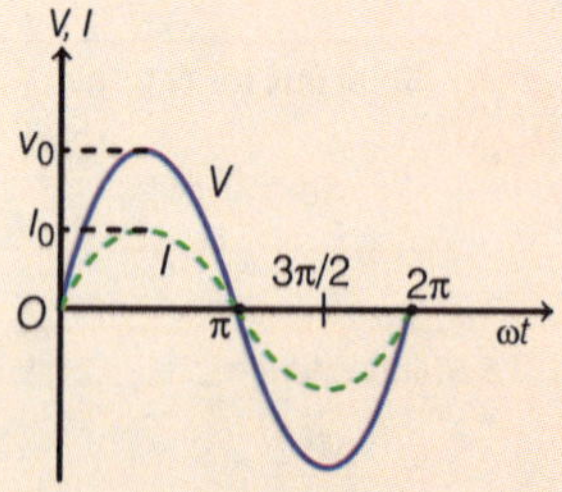

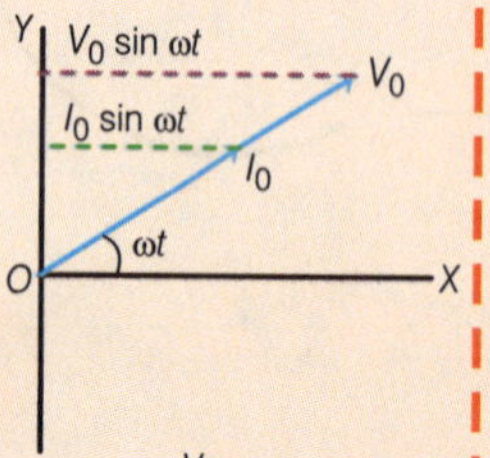

$I_0 = \frac{V_0}{R}$, $\quad I_{rms} = \frac{V_{rms}}{X_R}$

02 Ac Circuit With Capacitor Only

$V = V_0 \sin \omega t$

$I = I_0 \sin\left(\omega t + \frac{\pi}{2}\right)$

- Current leads the voltage by $\pi/2$.

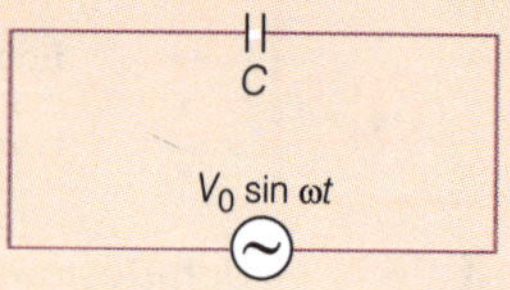

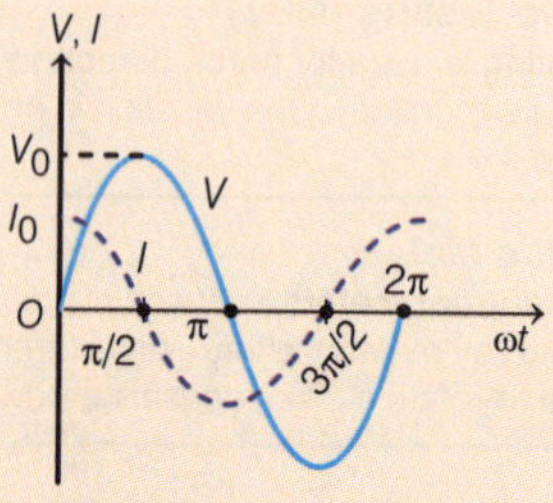

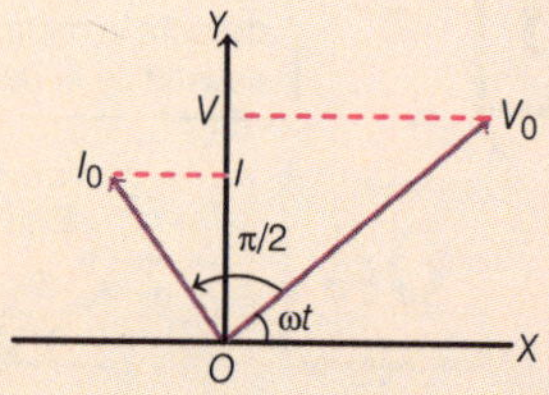

Capacitive rectance

$X_C = \frac{1}{C\omega} = \frac{1}{2\pi f C}$

$I_0 = \frac{V_0}{X_C}$, $\quad I_{rms} = \frac{V_{rms}}{X_C}$

Series AC Circuits

Series L-R Circuit

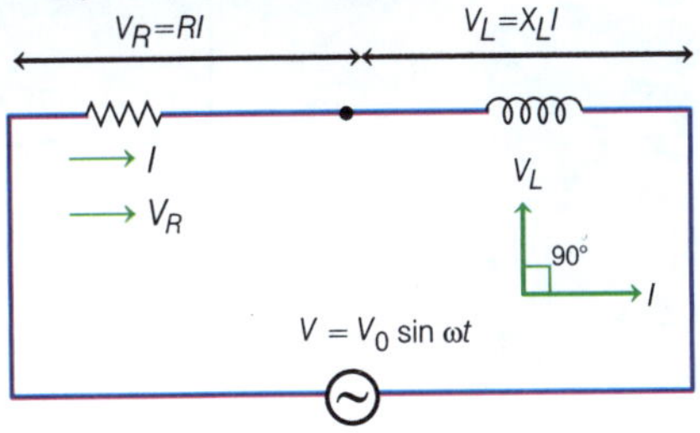

- $V = V_0 \sin \omega t$
- $I = I_0 \sin (\omega t - \pi/2)$
- $V_R = I_0 R$, $V_L = I_0 X_L$
- $V = \sqrt{V_R^2 + V_L^2}$
- $\tan \phi = \dfrac{V_L}{V_R}$
- Impedence,

$Z = \sqrt{R^2 + X_L^2}$

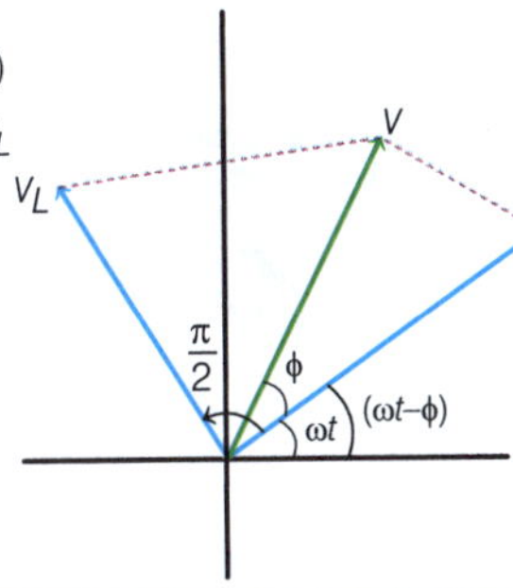

Series R-C Circuit

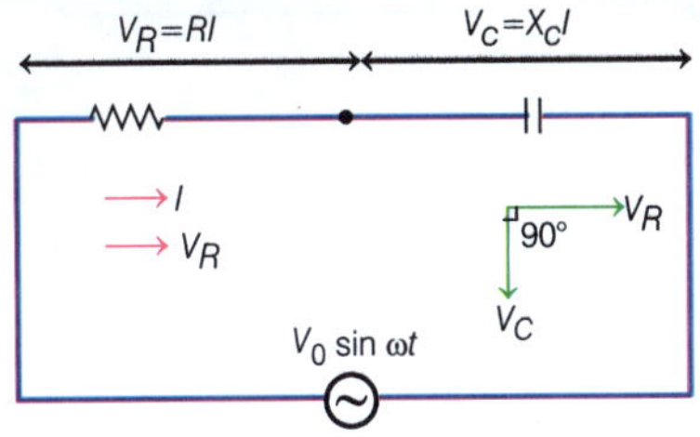

- $V = V_0 \sin \omega t$
- $I = I_0 \sin (\omega t + \pi/2)$
- $V = \sqrt{V_R^2 + V_C^2}$
- $\tan \phi = \dfrac{V_C}{V_R}$
- Impedence,

$Z = \sqrt{R^2 + X_C^2}$

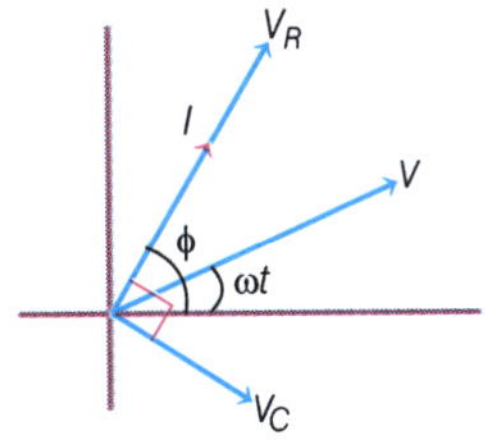

Series L-C-R Circuit

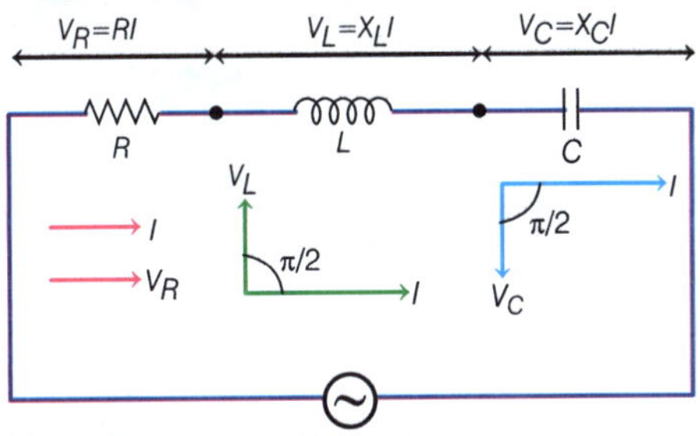

- $V = V_0 \sin \omega t$

- $I = I_0 \sin (\omega t - \phi)$

$V_R = I_0 R$, $V_L = I_0 X_L$, $V_C = I_0 X_C$

- $V = \sqrt{V_R^2 + (V_L - V_C)^2}$

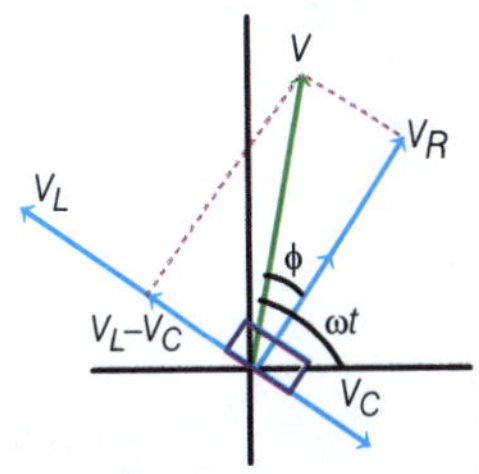

Phasor diagram (when, $V_L > V_C$)

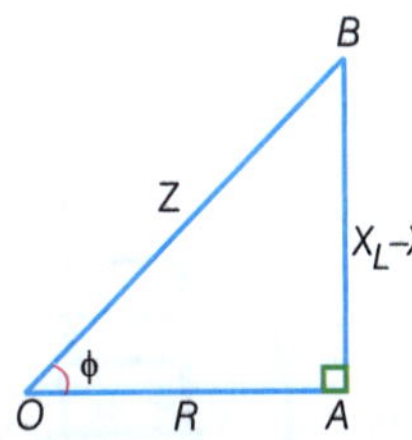

Impedence triangle (when, $X_L > X_C$)

- Resonance condition, $X_L = X_C$

$\omega_r = 2\pi f_r = \dfrac{1}{\sqrt{LC}}$, $f_r = \dfrac{1}{2\pi\sqrt{LC}}$

03 Ac Circuit With Inductor Only

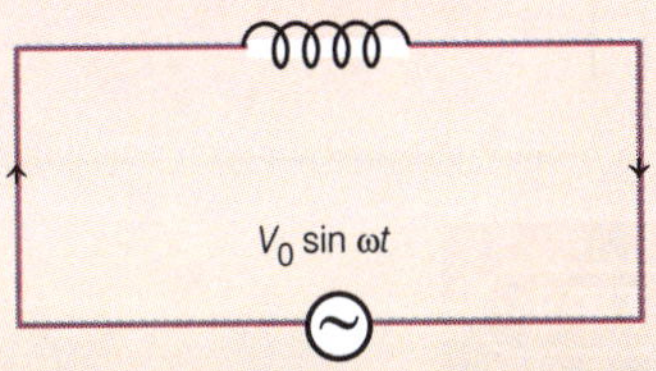

$I = I_0 \sin (\omega t - \pi/2)$ $\left(\text{where, } I_0 = \dfrac{V_0}{\omega L}\right)$

- Voltage leads the current by $\pi/2$.

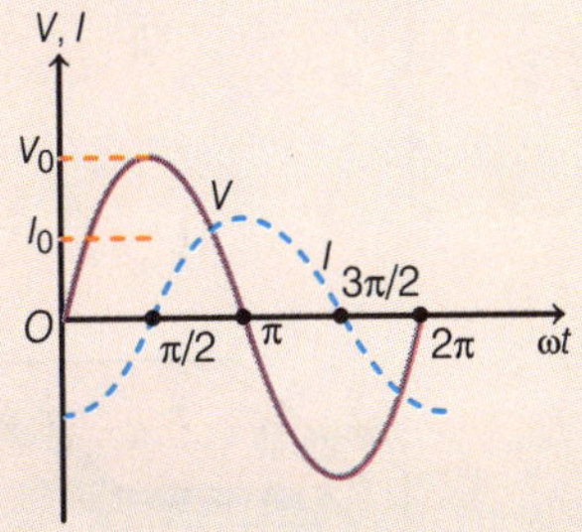

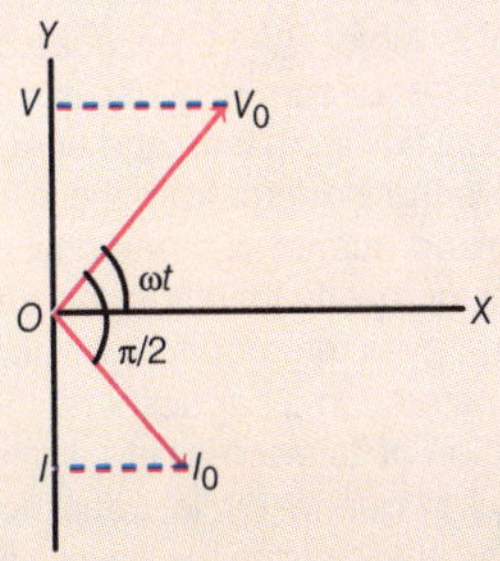

- Inductive reactance,

$X_L = \omega L = 2\pi f L$

$I_0 = \dfrac{V_0}{X_L}$ $\qquad I_{rms} = \dfrac{V_{rms}}{X_L}$

Power in AC circuit

The rate at which electric energy is consumed in an electric circuit.

01 Instantaneous power

$P = VI = V_0 I_0 \sin \omega t \sin(\omega t - \phi)$

$= \frac{V_0 I_0}{2}[\cos\phi - \cos(2\omega t - \phi)]$

02 Average power

$P_{av} = V_{rms} I_{rms} \cos\phi = V_{rms} I_{rms} \frac{R}{Z}$

- **Pure resistive circuit** $\phi = 0°$

  $P_{av} = I_{rms} \times V_{rms} \times 1$

  $= V_{rms} \times I_{rms}$

- **Pure inductive circuit** $\phi = \pi/2$

  Voltage leads the current in phase by $\pi/2$.

  $P_{av} = V_{rms} I_{rms} \cos\frac{\pi}{2} = 0$

- **Pure capacitive circuit**

  $\phi = -\frac{\pi}{2}$

  Voltage lags behind the current in phase by $\pi/2$

  $P_{av} = V_{rms} I_{rms} \cos\left(-\frac{\pi}{2}\right) = 0$

- **Series LCR circuit**

  $\tan\phi = \frac{X_L - X_C}{R} = \frac{\omega L - 1/\omega C}{R}$

  $P_{av} = V_{rms} I_{rms} \frac{R}{\sqrt{R^2 + \left(\omega L - \frac{1}{\omega C}\right)^2}}$

Power dissipated at resonance in *LCR* circuit
At resonance $X_L = X_C$ and $\phi = 0$,
$P_{av} = V_{rms} I_{rms}$

SPECIAL CASES

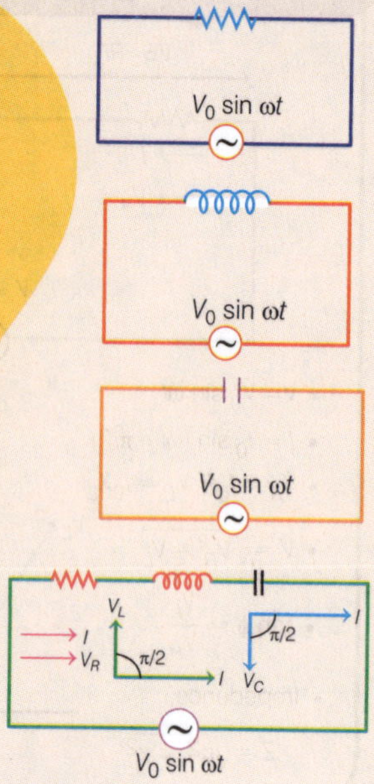

POWER FACTOR

Power Factor $= \frac{\text{True Power}}{\text{Apparent Power}}$

0 < Power Factor < 1

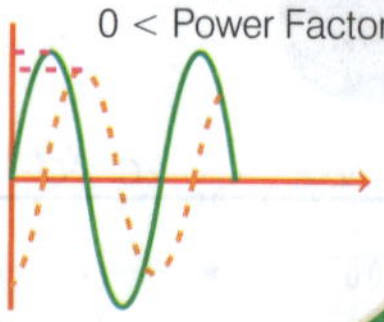

Power factor of a series *LCR* circuit

$\cos\phi = \frac{R}{Z} = \frac{R}{\sqrt{R^2 + \left(\omega L - \frac{1}{\omega C}\right)^2}}$

For a purely resistive or capacitive circuit, $\phi = 90°$
Power factor = cos90° = 0

For a purely resistive circuit, $\phi = 0°$
Power factor = cos 0° = 1

WATTLESS CURRENT

Wattless current $= I_{rms} \sin\phi$

- Wattless current does not consume any power in AC circuit.

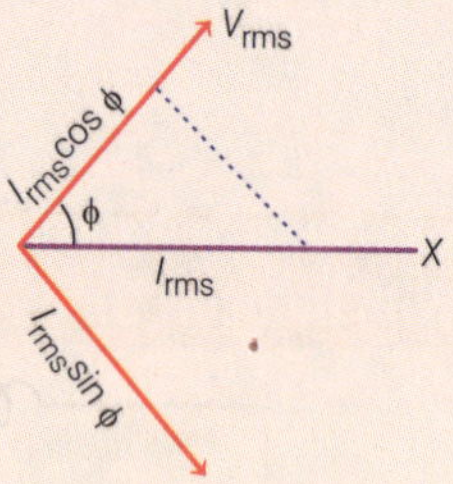

ENERGY IN INDUCTOR AND CAPACITOR

POINT 01

The work done is stored as the magnetic field energy in the inductor.

$U = \frac{1}{2}LI_0^2$

POINT 02

The work done is stored as the electrostatic energy in the capacitor

$U = \frac{1}{2}\frac{q^2}{C} = \frac{1}{2}CV^2$

POWER TIPS

- The energy stored in an inductor resides in the region of its magnetic field.
- For an inductor $P_{av} = 0$ because during first quarter of current cycle, as current increases flux increases and energy is stored in the inductor from the source.
- During 2nd quarter of current cycle, as current increases then flux decreases and energy is returned to the source.
- Energy stored in a capacitor resides in the region of its electric field.
- During first quarter cycle, capacitor absorbs energy from the source as it is charged and during next quarter cycle it returns energy to source as it is discharged.

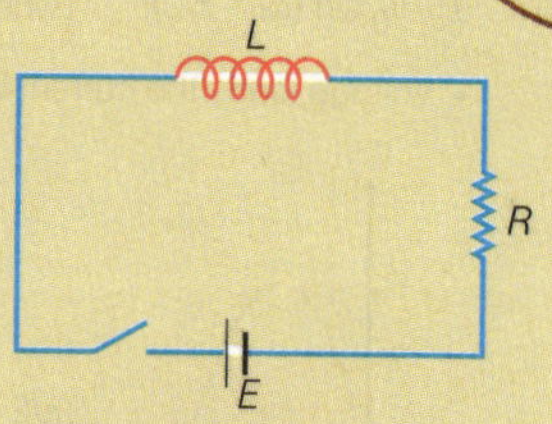

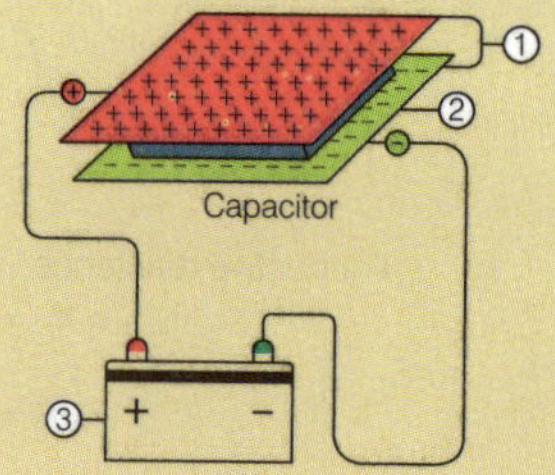

Transformer

The, device that transfers electric energy from one alternating current circuit to one or more other circuits, either increasing (stepping-up) or reducing (stepping-down) the voltage.

- It converts AC at low voltage to high voltage.
- It converts AC at high voltage to low voltage.
- **Principle** - Electromagnetic Induction.

1 Step-up transformer

Increases the input voltage

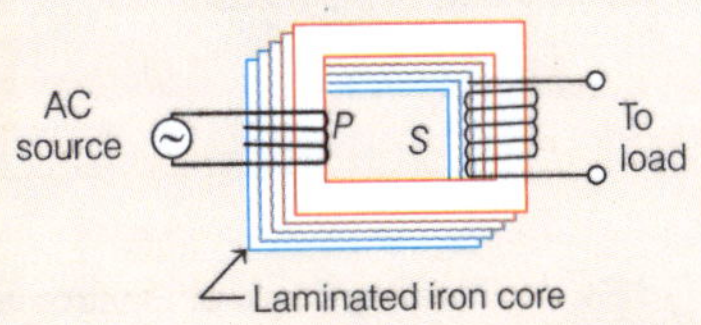

$$\frac{\varepsilon_2}{\varepsilon_1}=\frac{\text{output emf}}{\text{Input emf}}=\frac{N_2}{N_1}$$

$$=\frac{\text{Number of turns in the secondary coil}}{\text{Number of turns in the primary coil}}$$

For ideal transformer

There is no energy loss.

Input power = Output power

$$\varepsilon_1 I_1 = \varepsilon_2 I_2$$

$$\therefore \quad \frac{I_1}{I_2}=\frac{\varepsilon_2}{\varepsilon_1}=\frac{N_2}{N_1}$$

2 Step-down transformer

Decreases the input voltage

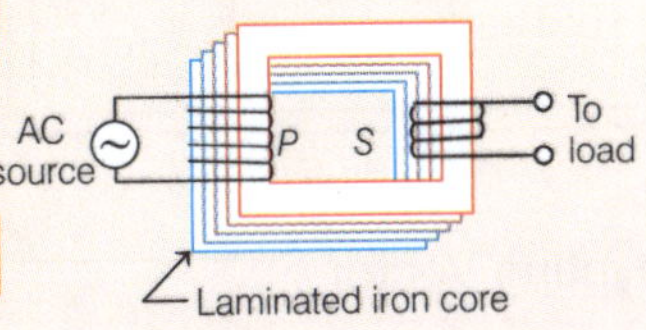

AC Devices

Types of arrangement for winding

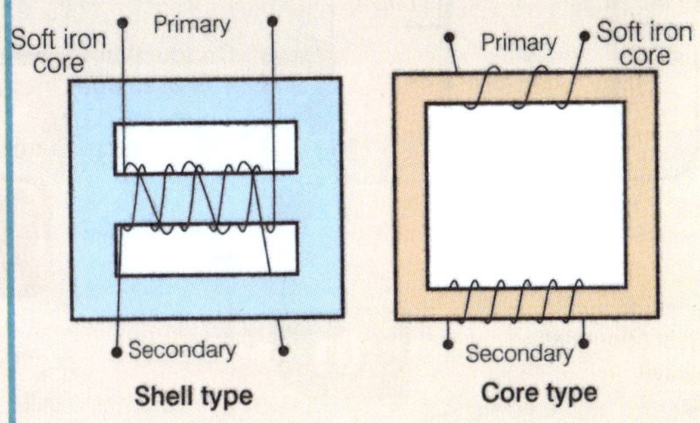

EFFICIENCY OF A TRANSFORMER

$$\eta=\frac{\text{Output power}}{\text{Input power}}=\frac{P_{out}}{P_{in}}=\frac{V_S I_S}{V_P I_P}$$

$\eta = 1$ [for ideal transformer]

The efficiency of real transformers ≈ (90 – 99%)

Energy Losses In Transformers

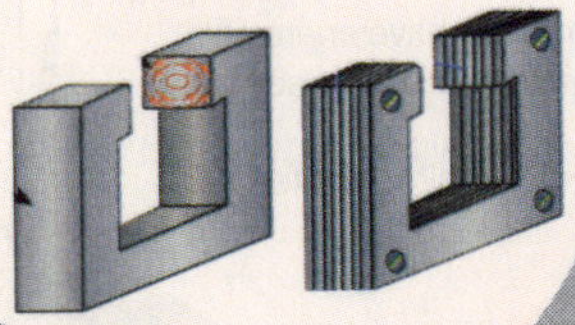

Copper loss → Due to heating of copper wires.
Power loss = I^2R

Eddy current loss The alternating magnetic flux induces eddy currents in the iron core which leads to some energy loss in the form of heat.

Hysteresis loss Due to cycles of magnetisation and demagnetisation.

Flux leakage Some of the flux may leak into air.

Humming loss Due to phenomenon of magnetostriction, humming sound produces. So, electrical energy is lost in the form of humming sound.

AC Generator

Principle Electromagnetic Induction

$$\varepsilon=-\frac{d\phi}{dt}=NBA\,\omega\sin\omega t=\varepsilon_0\sin\omega t$$

$$i=\frac{\varepsilon}{R}=I_0\sin\omega t$$

N = Number of turns in the coil
A = Face area of each turn
B = Magnitude of the magnetic field
θ = Angle between normal to the coil and magnetic field (**B**)

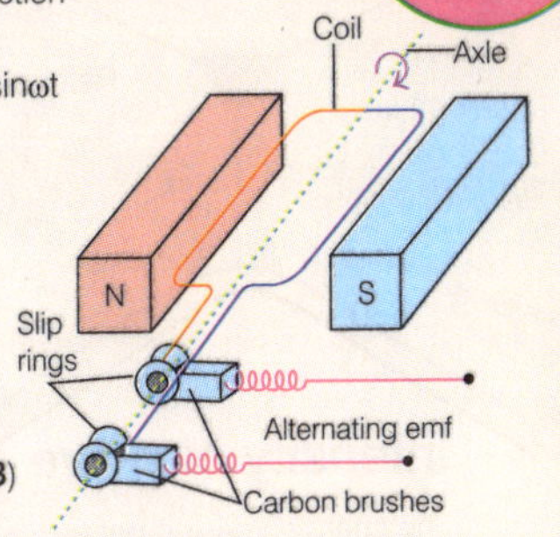

Working An alternating emf is generated by a loop of wire rotating in a magnetic field as shown in figure below.

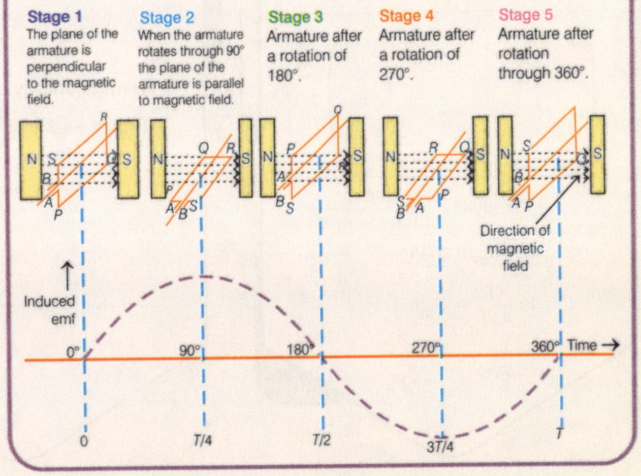

Chapter 22

Electromagnetic Waves

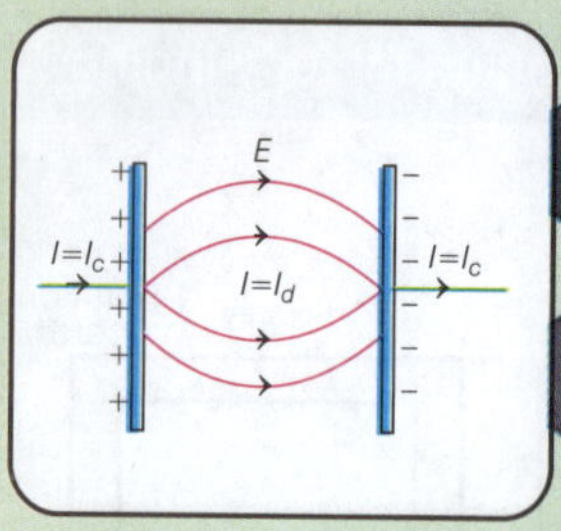

Displacement Current The current due to changing electric field between the plate of the capacitor.

$$I_d = \varepsilon_0 \frac{d\phi_E}{dt}$$

Conduction Current - The current due to the flow of charges in a conductor.
It is denoted by I_c.
Displacement Current = Conduction Current

Electromagnetic Wave

01 It is non-mechanical wave.

02 Transport energy, momentum and carries information.

03 Transverse in nature and hence can be polarised.

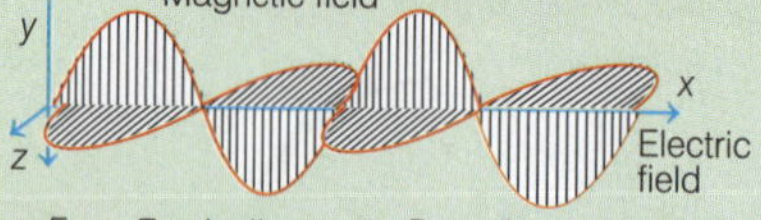

$E_y = E_0 \sin(kx - \omega t)$, $B_z = B_0 \sin(kx - \omega t)$

04 Oscillating electric and magnetic fields which oscillate in two mutually perpendicular planes and both are perpendicular to the direction of propagation of wave.

Maxwell's Equation

01 **Gauss's Law of Electrostatic**

$$\oint \mathbf{E} \cdot d\mathbf{S} = \frac{q}{\varepsilon_0}$$

02 **Gauss's Law of Magnetism**

$$\oint \mathbf{B} \cdot d\mathbf{S} = 0$$

03 **Faraday's Law of Electromagnetic Induction**

$$\text{Emf} = \oint \mathbf{E} \cdot d\mathbf{l} = \frac{-d\phi_B}{dt}$$

04 **Maxwell - Ampere's Circuital Law**

$$\oint \mathbf{B} \cdot d\mathbf{l} = \mu_0[I_c + I_d] = \mu_0\left[I_c + \varepsilon_0 \frac{d\phi_E}{dt}\right]$$

Properties of Electromagnetic Waves

- Both electric and magnetic field vary in phase with each other.
- Speed of EM wave (vacuum) is $c = \frac{1}{\sqrt{\mu_0 \varepsilon_0}} = 3 \times 10^8$ m/s
- Speed of EM wave (medium) is $v = \frac{1}{\sqrt{\mu_0 \mu_r \varepsilon_0 \varepsilon_r}} = \frac{1}{\sqrt{\mu_m \varepsilon_m}}$
- Refractive index, $\mu_m = \frac{c}{v} = \sqrt{\mu_r \varepsilon_r}$
- $c = \frac{E_0}{B_0} = \frac{\text{Amplitude of electric field}}{\text{Amplitude of magnetic field}}$

Poynting Vector

$$S = \frac{\mathbf{E} \times \mathbf{B}}{\mu_0} = \frac{\text{Power}}{\text{Area}}$$

Direction ⇒ Along the direction of wave propagation

SI unit $= \frac{W}{m^2}$

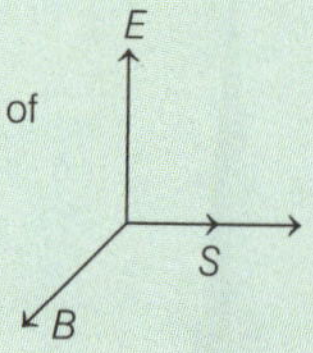

Intensity of Wave

The energy crossing per unit area per unit time perpendicular to the direction of wave

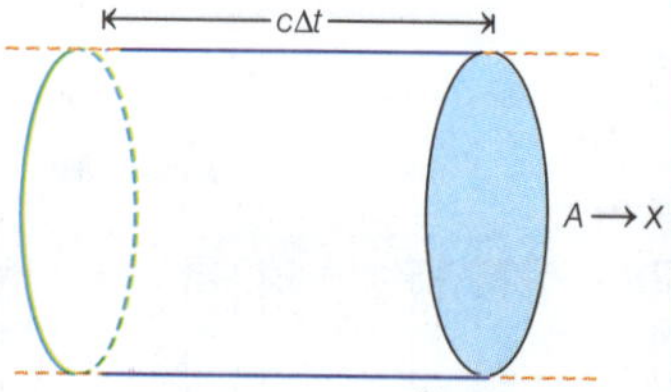

$$\text{Intensity } (I) = \frac{\text{Energy}}{\text{Time} \times \text{Area}}$$

$$U = U_{av}(c\Delta T)A$$

$$I = \frac{U}{A\Delta T} = U_{av}c$$

$$I = \frac{1}{2}\varepsilon_0 E^2 c = \frac{B_0^2 c}{2\mu_0}$$

Energy Density

$$U_E \text{ (Electric field)} = \frac{1}{2}\varepsilon_0 E^2$$

$$U_B \text{ (Magnetic field)} = \frac{1}{2\mu_0} B^2$$

Average energy density

$$(U_{av}) = \frac{1}{4}\varepsilon_0 E_0^2 + \frac{1}{4\mu_0} B_0^2$$

$$U_{av} = \frac{1}{2}\varepsilon_0 E_0^2 = \frac{1}{2\mu_0} B_0^2$$

Momentum of EM wave

- The linear momentum carried by the portion of wave have energy U.
- If the wave is completely absorbed $p = U/c$
- If the wave is totally reflected. $p = 2U/c$

POWER TIPS

Radiation Pressure

- For perfectly absorbing surface, $P = \frac{I}{c}$
- For perfectly reflecting surface, $P = \frac{2I}{c}$

Electromagnetic Waves

Electromagnetic Spectrum

Electromagnetic Spectrum

Orderly distribution of the electromagnetic waves in accordance with their wavelength or frequency.

1 Gamma Rays

Production
Nuclear reactions, emitted by radioactive nuclei.

Wavelength Range 10^{-14} m to 10^{-10} m

Application
They are used in medicine to destroy cancer cells.

2 X - Rays

Production
High energy electrons to bombard on metal.

Wavelength Range
10 nm to 10^{-4} nm

Application
- It is used as a diagnostic tool in medicine.
- Treatment for certain forms of cancer.

3 Ultraviolet rays

Production
It is produced by special lamps and very hot bodies.

Wavelength Range 400 nm to 0.6 nm

Application
LASIK eys surgery, kill germs in water purifiers.

4 Visible rays

It is the part of the spectrum that is detected by the human eye.

Frequency Range
4×10^{14} Hz to 7×10^{14} Hz

Wavelength Range 700 nm to 400 nm
- Our eyes are sensitive to this range of wavelength.

5 Infrared waves

Production They are produced by hot bodies and molecules.
Application Remote switches of household electronic system such as TV sets, video recorder and wifi systems.

6 Microwaves

Production It is produced by oscillating current in special vacuum tubes.
Frequency Gigahertz (GHz) range
Application Radar system, Microwave ovens etc.

7 Radiowaves

Production Accelerated motion of charges in conducting wires.
Frequency Range 500 kHz to 1000 MHz
Application It is used in radio and television communication system. e.g. Cellular phone etc.

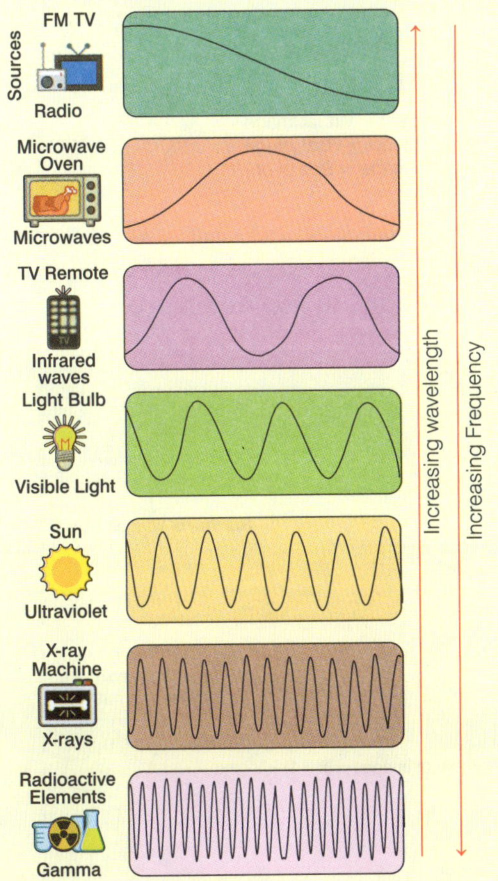

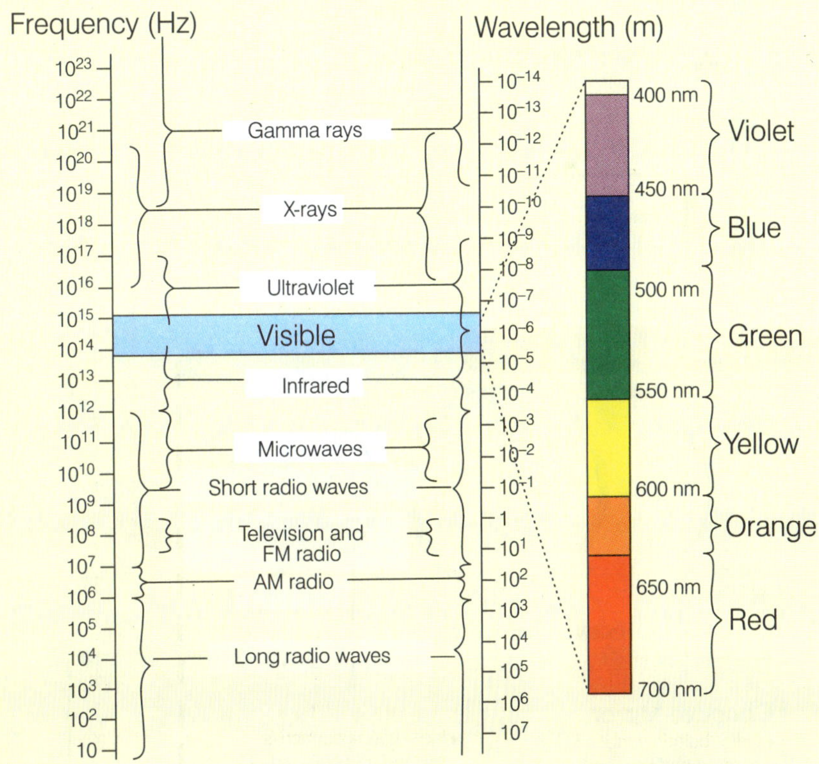

Chapter 23

Ray Optics

Behaviour of Light at the Interface of Two Media

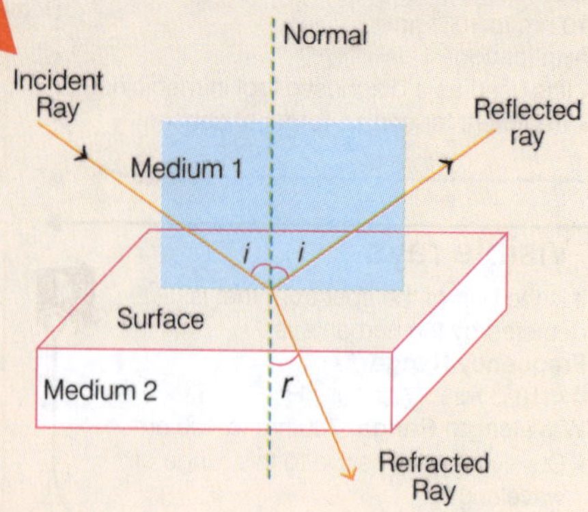

Absorption of Light

A part of the incident light is absorbed by the second medium.

Refraction of Light

A part of the incident light is transmitted into the second medium.

Reflection of Light

A part of the incident light is turned back into the first medium.

Plane Mirror

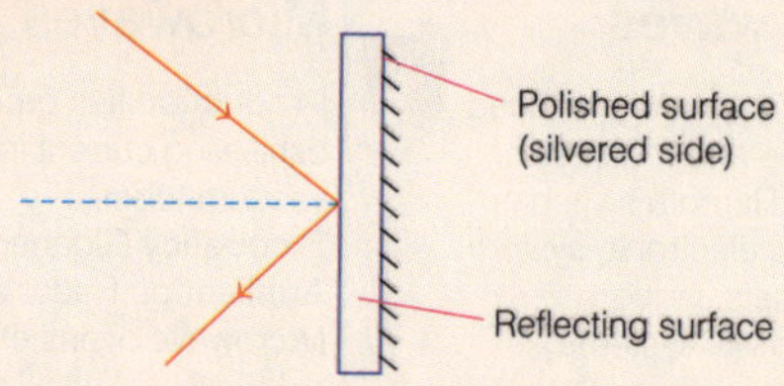

Characteristics Image Formed by Plane Mirror

- Real object = Virtual image
- Virtual object = Real image
- Size of Image = Size of object

Laws of Reflection

Angle of incidence (i) = Angle of reflection (r)

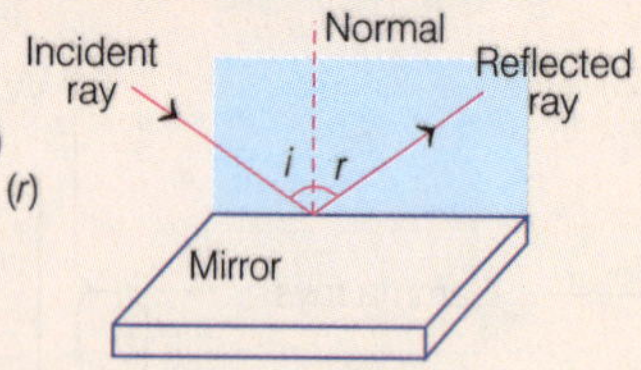

Incident ray, reflected ray and the normal at the point of incidence all lie in the same plane.

Spherical Mirrors

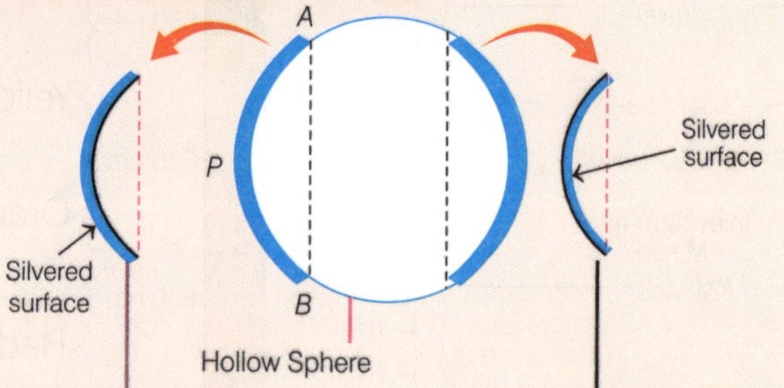

Concave Mirror

- Outer bulged surface is silvered and polished.
- Reflection of light takes place from the inner hollow surface.

Convex Mirror

- Inner hollow surface is silvered and polished.
- Reflection of light takes place from the outer bulged surface.

Number of Images In Inclined Mirror

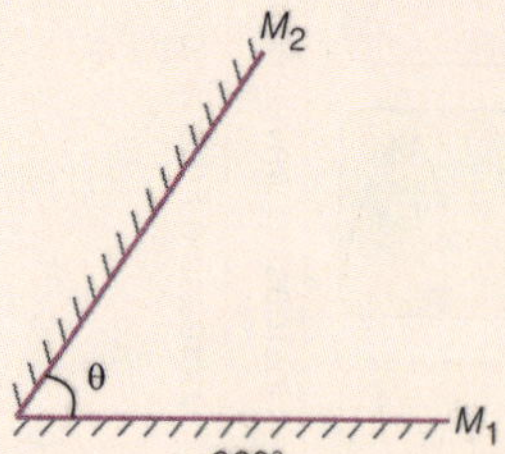

$$\frac{360°}{\theta} = n$$

- n = even → Number of images = $(n-1)$
- n = odd →
  - Object lying symmetrically between mirrors → Number of images = $(n-1)$
  - Object lying unsymmetrically between mirrors → Number of images = n

Fundamentals of Spherical Mirror

Terms Related to Spherical Mirror

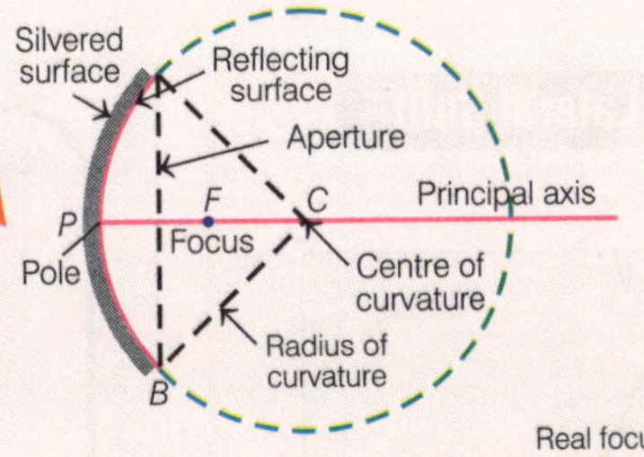

Radius of Curvature

Radius of the sphere of which the mirror forms a part.

$PC = R =$ Radius of curvature

Principal Focus

- Principal focus of a concave mirror→ Beam of light parallel to the principal axis converges to a point F in Fig(a).
- Principal focus of convex mirror→ Beam of light parallel to the principal axis appears to diverge from a point F in Fig(b)

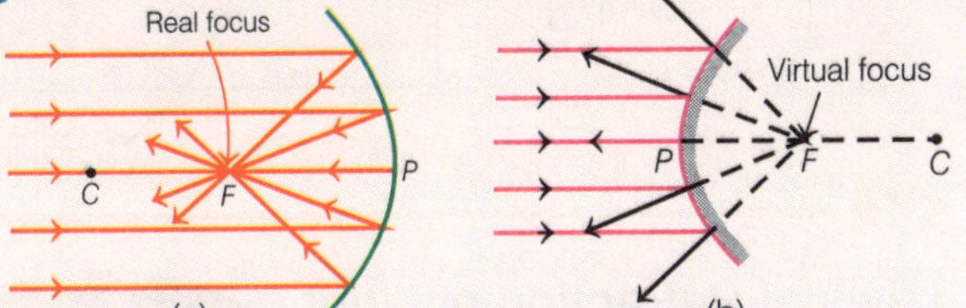

(a) (b)

Focal Length

It is the distance ($f = PF$) between the focus and pole of the mirror.

The Mirror Formula $\frac{1}{u} + \frac{1}{v} = \frac{1}{f}$

$f = x$ -coordinate of focus
$u = x$ -coordinate of object
$v = x$ -coordinate of image

Relation Between F and R

Focal length $= \frac{1}{2} \times$ Radius of curvature

$$f = \frac{R}{2}$$

Sign Convention for Spherical Mirror

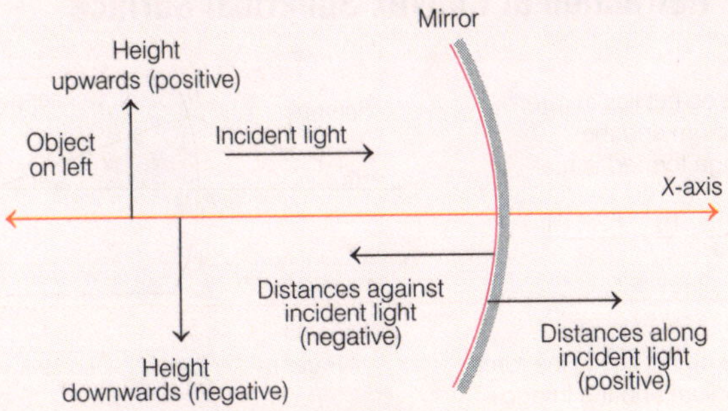

POWER TIPS

- **Newton's Formula**

$x_1 x_2 = f^2$ where, $x_1 \Rightarrow$ Object distance from focus
$x_2 \Rightarrow$ Image distance from focus

- **Longitudinal Magnification**

$$m_L = \frac{\text{Length of image}}{\text{Length of object}} = \frac{h_2}{h_1},$$

- **Transverse Magnification**

$$m_T = \frac{\text{Height of image}}{\text{Height of object}} = \frac{h_2}{h_1}$$

$$m_T = \frac{h_2}{h_1} = -\frac{v}{u}$$

where, $h_2 = y$ co-ordinate of image
$h_1 = y$ co-ordinate of object

For small objects, $m_L = -m_T^2$

Image Formation by Concave Mirrors

S.No.	Position of Object	Ray Diagram	Properties of Image
(i)	At infinity	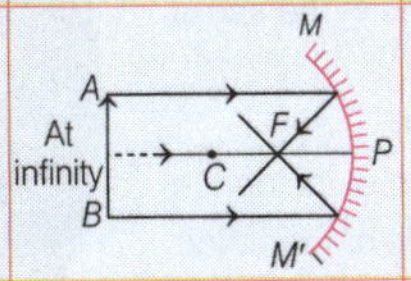	• Real • Inverted • At F • Very small
(ii)	Between infinity and C	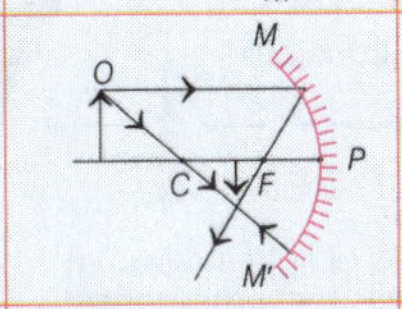	• Real • Inverted • Diminished • Between F and C
(iii)	At C	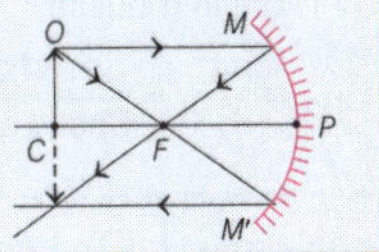	• Real • Inverted • Same size • At C
(iv)	Between F and C	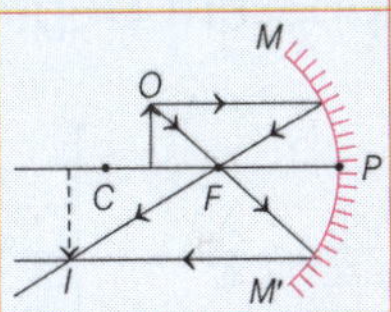	• Real • Inverted • Very large • Between C and infinity
(v)	At F	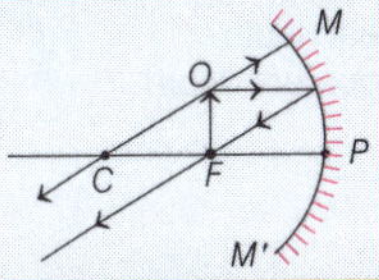	• Real • Inverted • Very large at infinity
(vi)	Between F and P	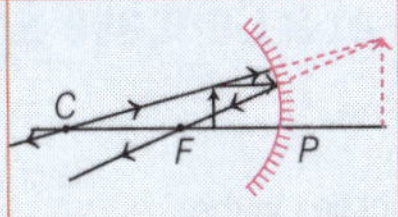	• Virtual • Erect • Large in size • Behind the mirror

Image Formation by Convex Mirrors

S.No.	Position of Object	Ray Diagram	Properties of Image
(i)	At infinity	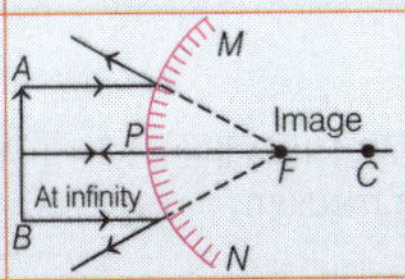	• Virtual • Erect • Very small in size • At F
(ii)	In front of mirror (at finite distance)	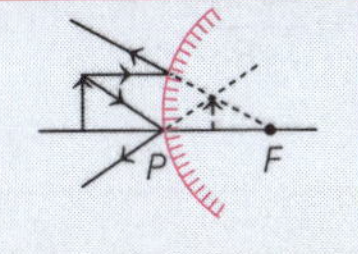	• Virtual • Erect • Diminished between P and F

Lateral Shift

Lateral shift = Perpendicular distance between the incident and emergent rays.

Lateral shift,

$$x = t\sin i\left[1 - \frac{\cos i}{(\mu^2 - \sin^2 i)^{1/2}}\right]$$

$$x_{max} = t\sin 90 = t$$

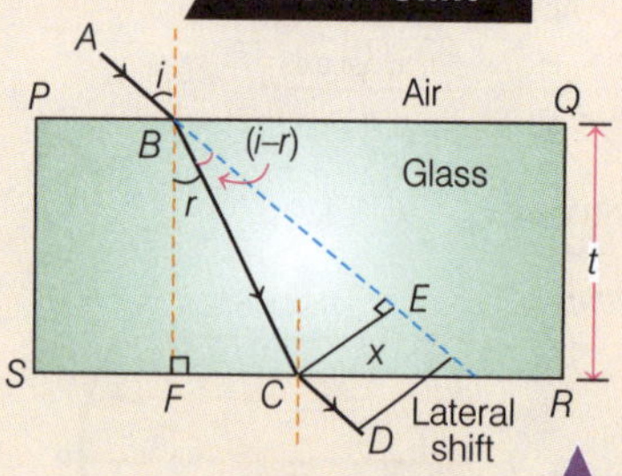

Laws of Refraction of Light

- **First Law**
  The incident ray, the refracted ray and the normal to the interface, all lies in the same plane.
- **Second Law**

$$\frac{\text{sine of the angle of incidence}}{\text{sine of the angle of refraction}} = \frac{\sin i}{\sin r} = {}^1\mu_2 = \text{constant}$$

Refraction of Light

Bending of light rays as they pass from one medium to

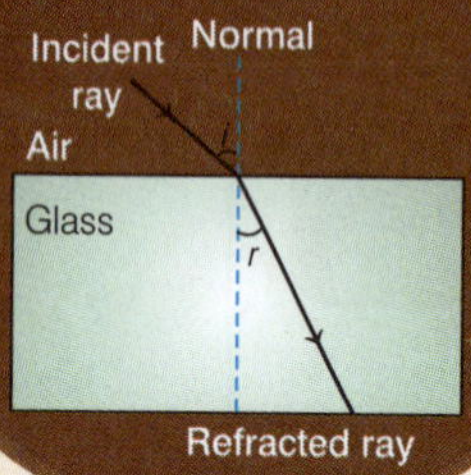

Refractive Index

$$\text{Refractive Index} = \frac{\text{Speed of light in vacuum}}{\text{Speed of light in medium}}$$

$$\mu = \frac{c}{v} = \frac{\lambda_{vacuum}}{\lambda_{medium}}, \quad {}^1\mu_2 = \frac{\mu_2}{\mu_1}, \quad = \frac{\text{Speed of light in medium1}}{\text{Speed of light in medium 2}} = \frac{v_1}{v_2}$$

Real and Apparent Depth

- Refractive index,

$$\mu = \frac{\text{Real depth}}{\text{Apparent depth}} = \frac{AO}{AI}$$

- Normal shift = Real depth – Apparent depth

$$d = t\left(1 - \frac{1}{\mu}\right)$$

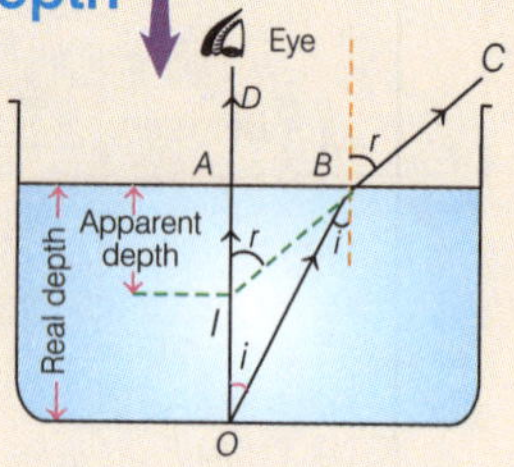

Critical Angle and Total Internal Reflection

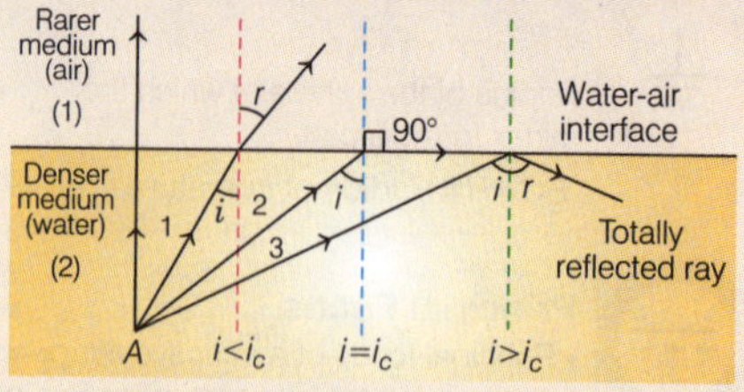

- **Critical Angle (i_c)**
  Angle of incidence in the denser medium for which angle of refraction in the rarer medium is 90° $\Rightarrow i = i_c$ for which $r = 90°$
- **Total Internal Reflection**
  Conditions of **TIR** angle of incidence > critical angle (i_c)
  Light travelling from denser to rarer medium,
  then, light totally reflected back into the denser medium.

Retraction of Light at Spherical Surface

Refraction at Convex Spherical Surface

(i) The object lies in rarer medium and the image formed is real.

$$\frac{\mu_2}{v} - \frac{\mu_1}{u} = \frac{\mu_2 - \mu_1}{R}$$

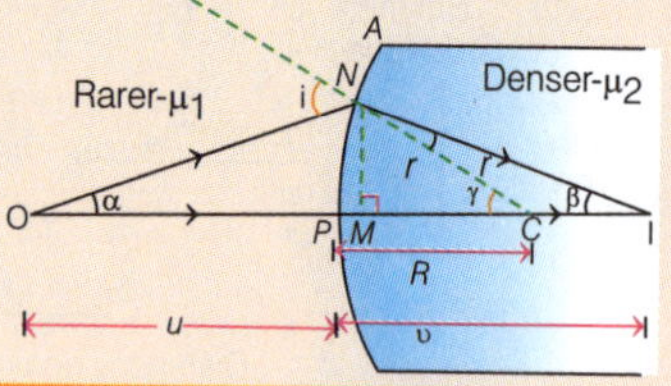

(ii) The object lies in the rarer medium and the image formed is virtual.

$$\frac{\mu_2}{v} - \frac{\mu_1}{u} = \frac{\mu_2 - \mu_1}{R}$$

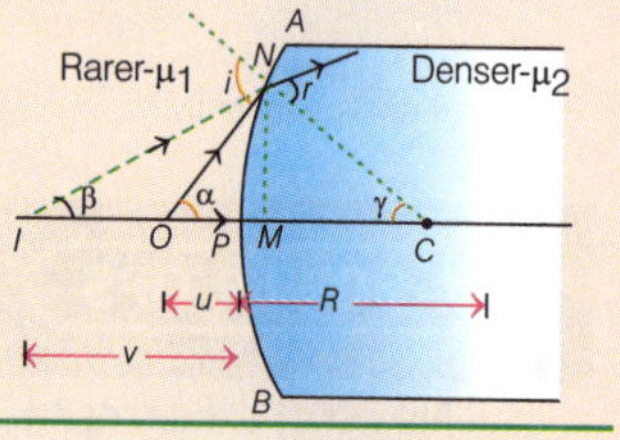

(iii) The object lies in the denser medium and the image formed is real.

$$\frac{\mu_1}{v} - \frac{\mu_2}{u} = \frac{\mu_1 - \mu_2}{R}$$

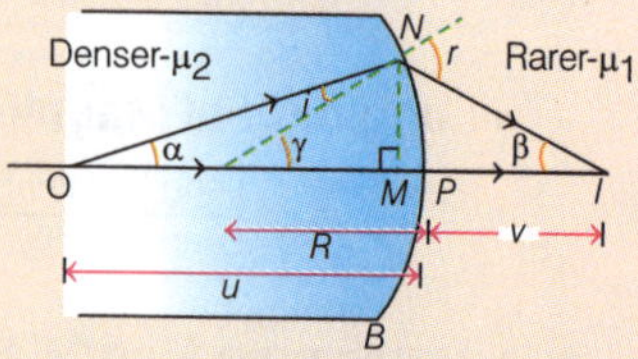

(iv) The object lies in the denser medium and the image formed is virtual.

$$\frac{\mu_1}{v} - \frac{\mu_2}{u} = \frac{\mu_1 - \mu_2}{R}$$

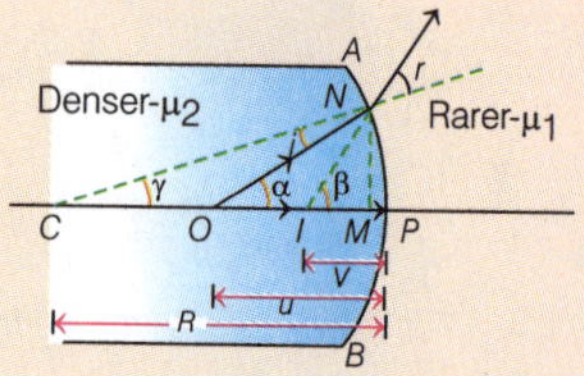

Refraction at a Concave Spherical Surface

(i) The object lies in the rarer medium.

$$\frac{\mu_2}{v} - \frac{\mu_1}{u} = \frac{\mu_2 - \mu_1}{R}$$

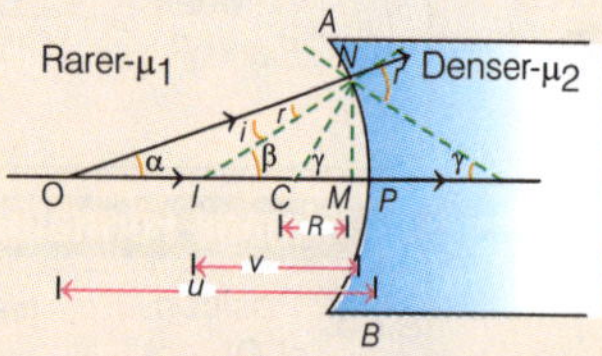

(ii) The object lie in the denser medium.

$$\frac{\mu_1}{v} - \frac{\mu_2}{u} = \frac{\mu_1 - \mu_2}{R}$$

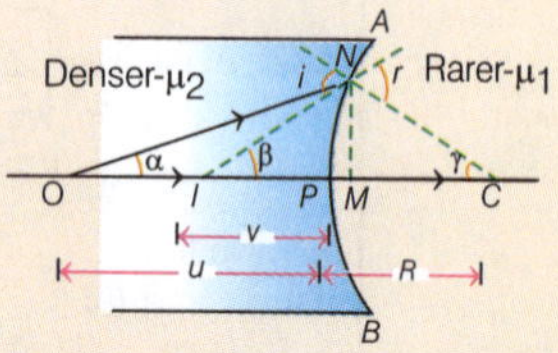

Lens Maker's Formula

$$\frac{1}{f}=\left[\frac{\mu_2-\mu_1}{\mu_1}\right]\left[\frac{1}{R_1}-\frac{1}{R_2}\right]$$

$$\frac{1}{f}=(\mu-1)\left[\frac{1}{R_1}-\frac{1}{R_2}\right]$$ if $\mu_1=1$, then $\mu_2=\mu$

- **Thin Lens Formula** $\Rightarrow \frac{1}{v}-\frac{1}{u}=\frac{1}{f}$
- **Linear Magnification**

$$m=\frac{\text{Size of image}}{\text{Size of object}}=\frac{h_2}{h_1}=\frac{v}{u}$$

Power of a Lens

$\tan\delta=\frac{h}{f}$

If $h=1$, then $\tan\delta=\frac{1}{f}$ or $P=\frac{1}{f}$

- Power → Reciprocal of focal length
- SI unit → Diopter

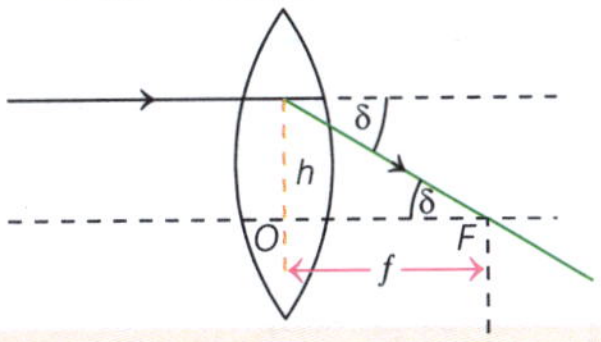

Combination of Thin Lenses

- Two lenses are in contact $\frac{1}{f}=\frac{1}{f_1}+\frac{1}{f_2}$

∴ Equivalent power $P=P_1+P_2$

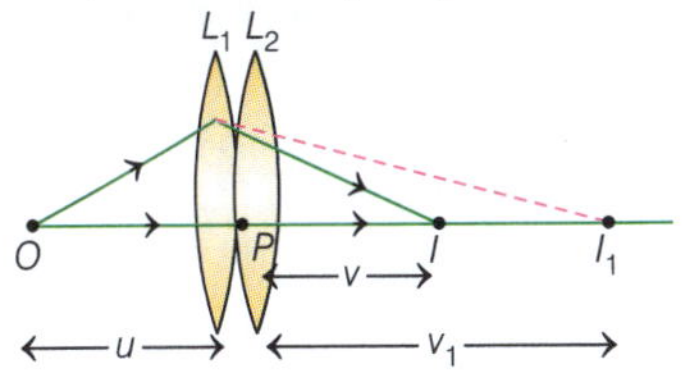

- Thin lenses separated by a small distance $\frac{1}{f}=\frac{1}{f_1}+\frac{1}{f_2}-\frac{d}{f_1f_2}$

∴ Equivalent power $P=P_1+P_2-dP_1P_2$

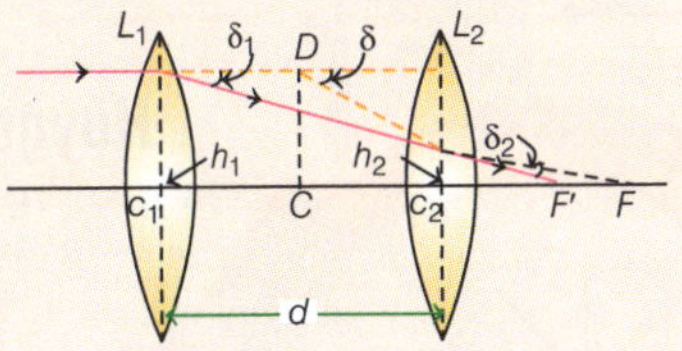

Refraction Through a Prism

- Angle of deviation $(\delta)=i+i'-A$
- Angle of incidence + Angle of emergence = Angle of prism + Angle of deviation

$$i+i'=A+\delta$$

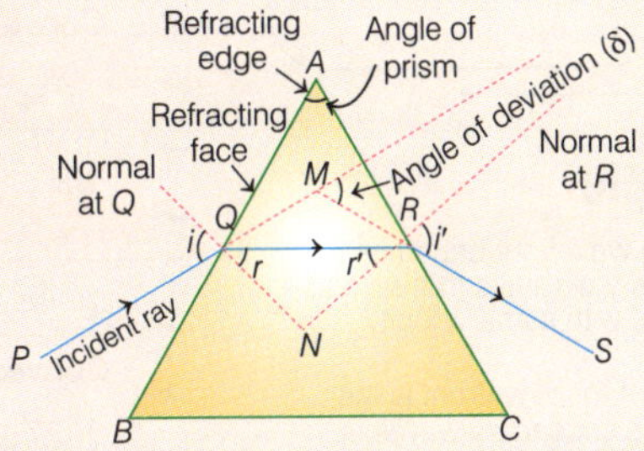

- Variation of angle of deviation with angle of incidence.

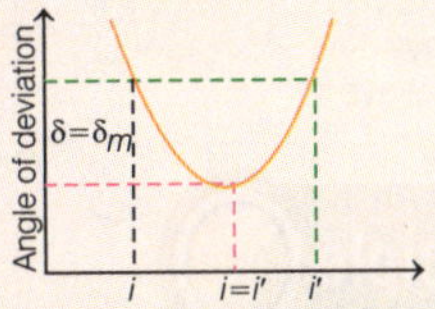

- Relation between refractive index and angle of minimum deviation

$$\mu=\frac{\sin\left(\frac{A+\delta_m}{2}\right)}{\sin\left(\frac{A}{2}\right)}$$

- Deviation produced by a prism of small angle $\delta=(\mu-1)A$

Optical Instruments

Simple Microscope

Convex lens of short focal length, held close to eye.

Case 1

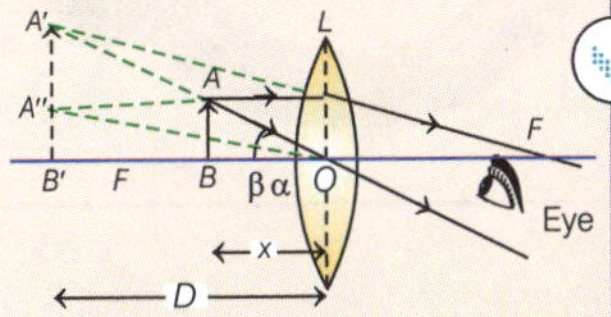

A simple microscope with the eye focused at the near point

$$\text{Magnifying power}=\frac{\text{Angle subtended by the image at the least distance of distinct vision}}{\text{Angle subtended by the object at the least distance of distinct vision}}$$

$$m=\frac{\beta}{\alpha}=1+\frac{D}{f}$$

Case 2 When the final image is formed at infinity

$$m=\frac{D}{f}$$

⇒ Magnification, when image is formed at near point = 1 + magnification when image is formed at infinity

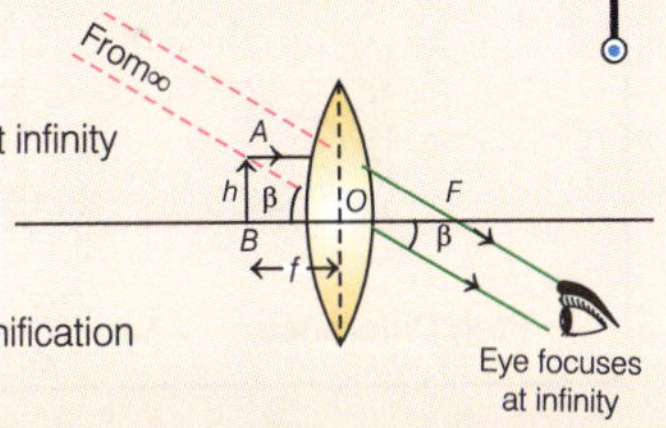

Astronomical Telescope

Optical device used to see heavenly bodies like stars, planets, satellites etc.

Case 1 When the final image is formed at the least distance of distinct vision

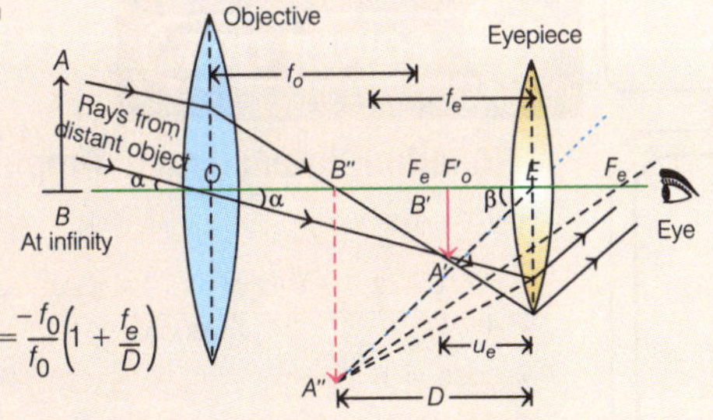

$$m=\frac{-f_o}{f_o}\left(1+\frac{f_e}{D}\right)$$

Case 2 When the final image is formed at infinity, Normal adjustment

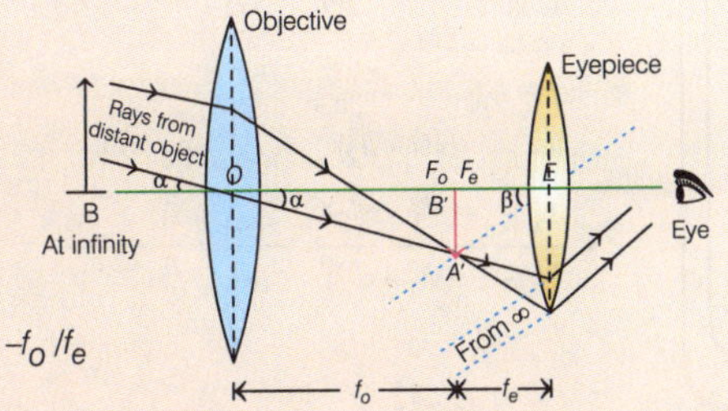

$$m=-f_o/f_e$$

Compound Microscope

It is an optical device used to see magnified image of small objects.

Case 1 When the final image is formed at the least distance of distinct vision.

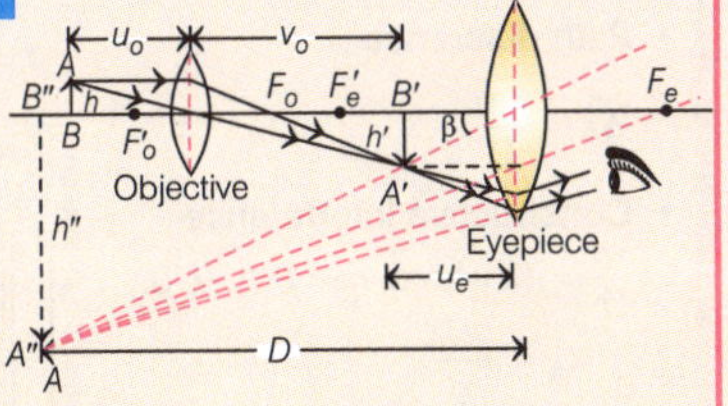

$$m=\frac{v_o}{u_o}\left(1+\frac{D}{f_e}\right)$$

$v_o=L=$ distance between the two lenses

$u_o=-f_o$

$$m=\frac{-L}{f_o}\left(1+\frac{D}{f_e}\right)$$

Case 2 When the final image is formed at infinity,

$$m=m_o\times m_e=\frac{-L}{f_o}\times\frac{D}{f_e}$$

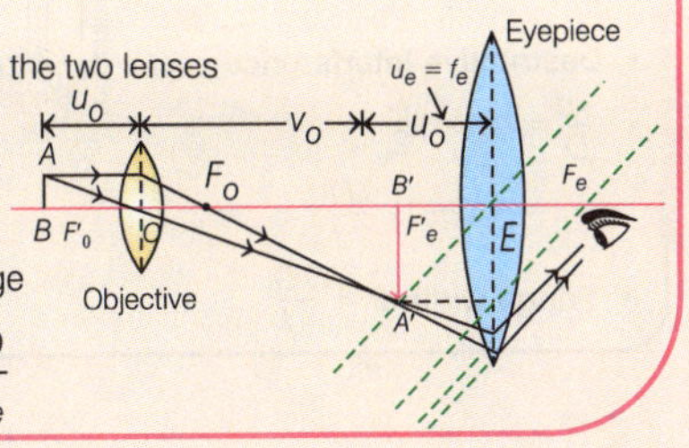

Chapter 24

Wave Optics

Wavefront

Continuous locus of all such particles of the medium which are vibrating in same phase at any instant.

Spherical Wavefronts

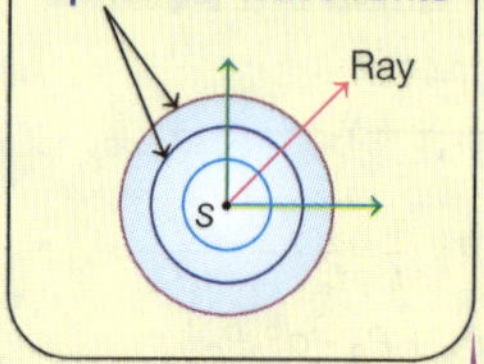

Cylindrical Wavefronts

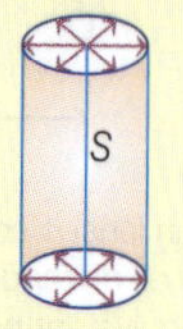

Plane Wavefront

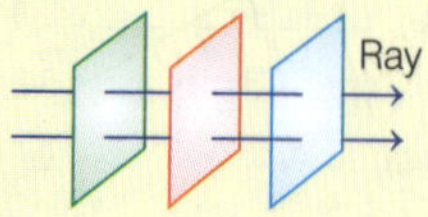

Huygens' Principle

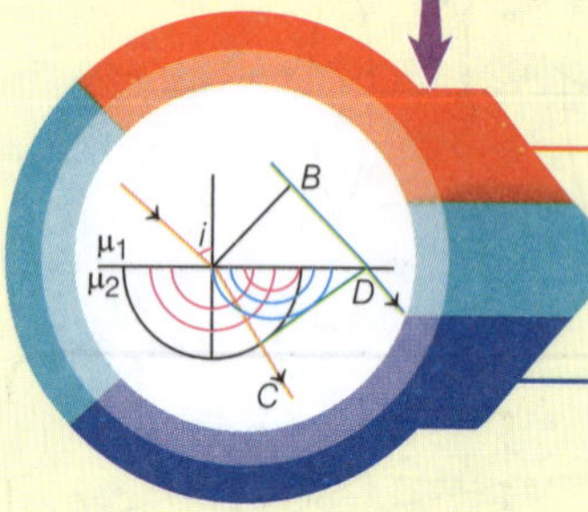

- Every point on the wavefront becomes a source of secondary wavelets that spread out in all directions with same velocity.
- The new position of the wavefront is the tangent to all these secondary wavelets.
- The wavefront in medium is always perpendicular to the direction of wave propagation .

Behaviour of Mirror, Lens and Prism

	Incident wavefront	Reflected wavefront
Concave Mirror 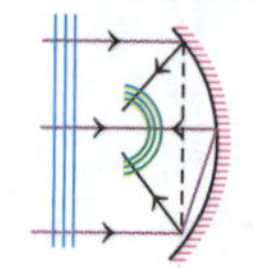	Plane wavefront	Spherical converging wavefront
Convex Mirror 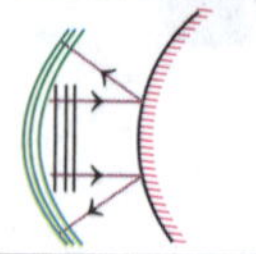	Plane wavefront	Spherical diverging wavefront
	Incident wavefront	**Refracted wavefront**
Convex Lens 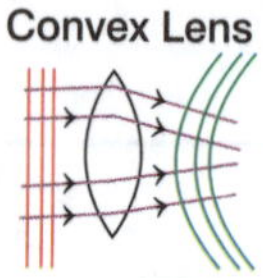	Plane wavefront	Spherical converging wavefront
Concave Lens 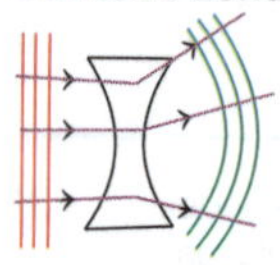	Plane wavefront	Spherical diverging wavefront
	Incident wavefront	**Refracted wavefront**
Prism 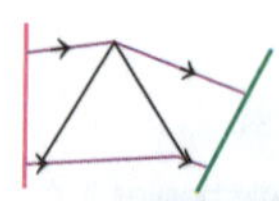	Plane wavefront	Plane wavefront

Superposition Principle

- When number of waves travelling through a medium superimpose, the resultant displacement of the wave is equal to the vector sum of the displacement of the individual waves.

$$y = y_1 + y_2 + y_3 + ... + y_n$$

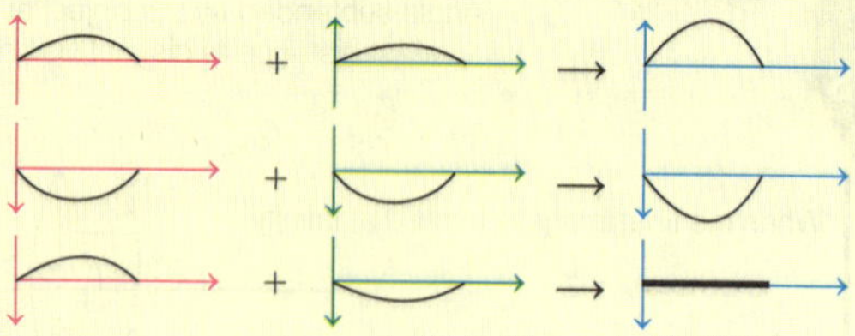

- **Path Difference** $\Delta\phi = \frac{2\pi}{\lambda}\Delta x$

Young's Double Slit Experiment

- **Path difference**

$$\Delta x = \frac{x.d}{D}$$

- **Constructive Interference**

$\frac{xd}{D} = n\lambda$ where, $n = 0, 1, 2, 3...$

$$x_n = \frac{nD\lambda}{d}$$

- **Destructive Interference**

$$\frac{xd}{D} = (2n-1)\frac{\lambda}{2}$$

$$x_n = (2n-1)\frac{\lambda D}{2d}$$

- **Fringe width** $\beta = \frac{\lambda D}{d}$

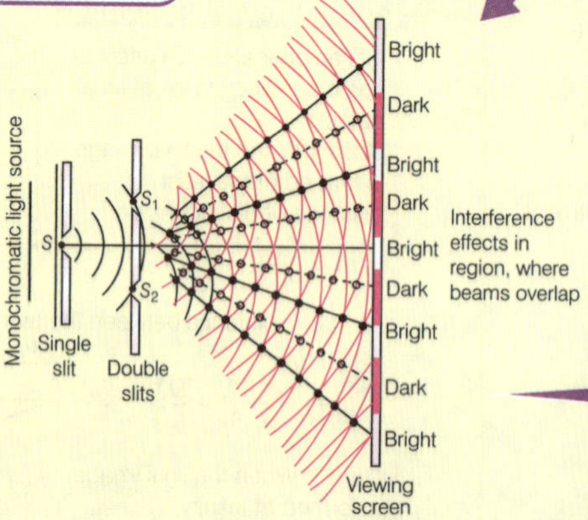

POWER TIPS

Resultant Intensity and Amplitude

- $y_1 = A_1\sin\omega t,\ y_2 = A_2\sin(\omega t + \phi)$

$$I = I_1 + I_2 + 2\sqrt{I_1 I_2}\cos\phi$$

- $A = \sqrt{A_1^2 + A_2^2 + 2A_1A_2\cos\phi}$
- $\cos\phi = 1$

$I = I_{max},\ A = A_{max}$

$I_{max} = (\sqrt{I_1} + \sqrt{I_2})^2,\ A_{max} = A_1 + A_2$

- $\cos\phi = -1$

$I = I_{min},\ A = A_{min}$

$I_{min} = (\sqrt{I_1} - \sqrt{I_2})^2,\ A_{min} = A_1 - A_2$

- $\frac{I_{max}}{I_{min}} = \frac{(\sqrt{I_1} + \sqrt{I_2})^2}{(\sqrt{I_1} - \sqrt{I_2})^2},\ \frac{A_{max}}{A_{min}} = \frac{A_1 + A_2}{A_1 - A_2}$
- $I_1 = I_2 = I_0$

$$I = 4I_0\cos^2\frac{\phi}{2}$$

Diffraction

- The bending of light around obstacles or the spreading of light when it passes through a narrow opening.
- It occurs because light behaves as a wave, and this wavefront interacts with edges or apertures.
- For diffraction obstacle must be of the order of the wavelength of wave. $\frac{a}{\lambda} \approx 1$

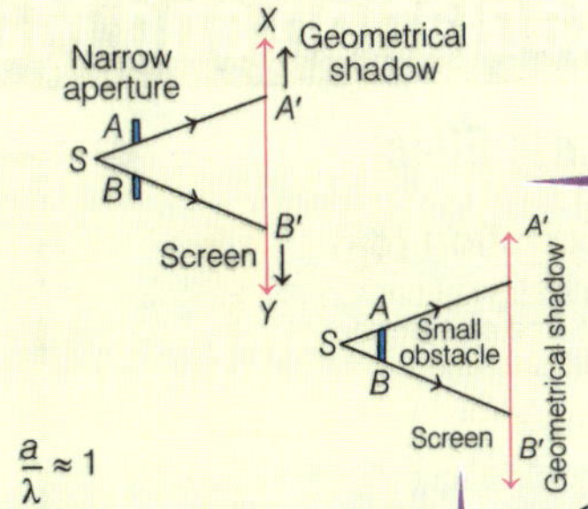

Diffraction Due to Single Slit

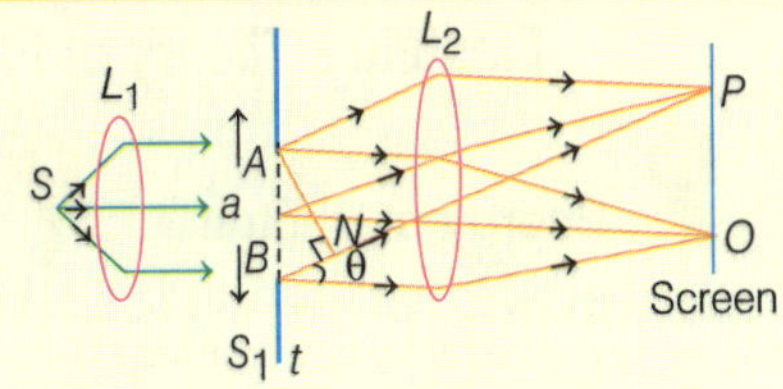

- **Condition for nth minima**
  $a\sin\theta = n\lambda$, $n = 1, 2, 3, ...$
- **Intensity**
  $$I = I_0\left(\frac{\sin\beta}{\beta}\right)^2, \quad \beta = \frac{\pi a\sin\theta}{\lambda}$$
  I_0 is central maximum intensity
- **Condition for nth secondary maxima**
  $a\sin\theta = (2n + 1)\frac{\lambda}{2}$, $n = 0, 1, 2, 3, ...$

Types of Diffraction

• Fresnel Diffraction	• Fraunhofer Diffraction
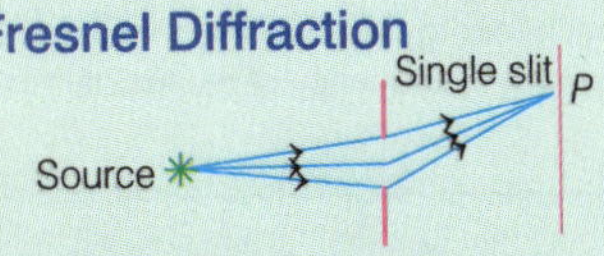	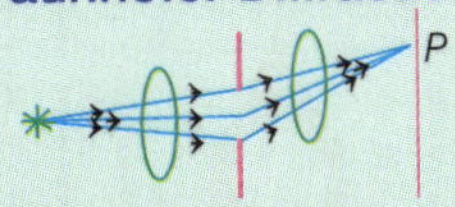
• The distance between source and obstacle and screen and obstacle is finite.	• The distance between source and obstacle and screen and obstacle is effectively infinite.
• No lenses are required to study Fresnel diffraction in laboratory.	• Two convex lenses are required to study Fraunhofer diffraction in laboratory.
• The wavefront incident on the aperture is either cylindrical or spherical.	• The wavefront incident on the aperture is plane.
• The diffracted wavefront is spherical or cylindrical.	• The diffracted wavefront is plane.
• The initial phase of secondary wavelets is different at different points in the plane of the aperture.	• The initial phase of secondary wavelets is same at all points in the plane of the aperture.

Intensity Distribution Curve

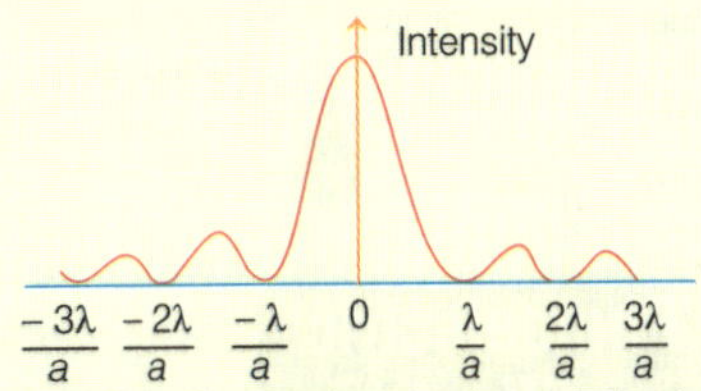

- Intensities of secondary maxima relating to the Intensity of central maxima are in ratio.
  $1 : \frac{1}{21} : \frac{1}{61} : \frac{1}{121} ...$
- Intensity of first secondary maxima is just 4% of that of central maxima.

Polarisation

- Phenomenon of restricting the oscillations of wave to just one direction in the transverse plane.
- Light can be polarised by reflection, transmission or scattering.

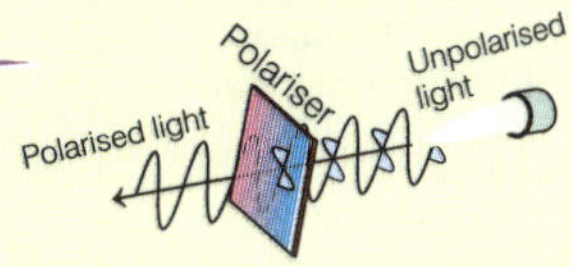

Malus Law

- Intensity of transmitted light passed through an analyser is
  $I = I_0 \cos^2\theta$
- For N polarisers,
  $I_N = I_0 \prod_{n=1}^{N} \cos^2\theta_n$
- If θ is same
  $I = I_0\cos^n\theta$, where $n = 2(N - 1)$

Polaroids

Polaroids are thin commercial sheets which make use of the property of selective absorption to produce an intense beam of plane polarised light.

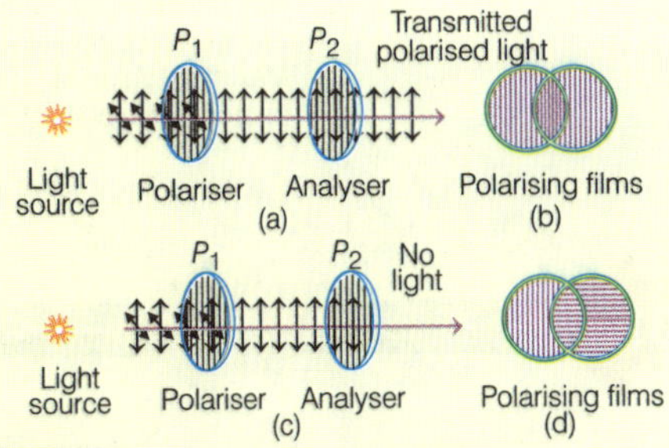

Uses of Polaroids

(i) Polaroids are used in goggles and cameras to avoid glare of light.
(ii) Polaroids are useful in three dimensional motion pictures, i.e. in holography.
(iii) They are used to eliminate the head light, glare in motor cars.
(iv) They are used to improve contrast in old oil paintings.
(v) They are used as window glasses to control the intensity of incoming light.

Brewster's Law : Polarisation by Reflection

- When angle of incidence is equal to polarising angle, the reflected and refracted rays will be perpendicular.
- The refractive index of a medium is equal to the tangent of polarising angle i_p.
  $\mu = \tan i_p$
- Polarising angle will be different for different wavelengths
- For complete polarisation, incident light should be monochromatic.

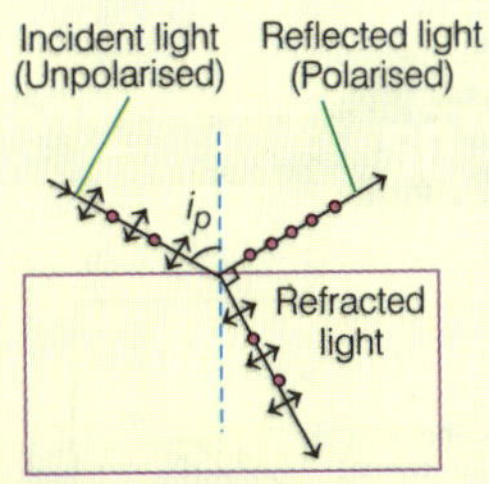

	Reflected ray	Refracted ray
• $i_p = \theta_p$	Completely polarised	Partially polarised
• $i_p < \theta_p$ or $i_p > \theta_p$	Partially polarised	Partially polarised

- For glass, $\theta_p = \tan^{-1}(1.5) \approx 57°$, water $\theta_p = \tan^{-1}(1.13) \approx 53°$

Chapter 25

Dual Nature of Radiation and Matter

Einstein's Theory of Photoelectric Effect

Energy of Photon

$E = h\nu$

ν = frequency of incident light

$\nu = \frac{c}{\lambda}$

Work Function (ϕ_0)

"Minimum energy of photon required to free an electron from a metal surface".

$\phi_0 = h\nu_0 = \frac{hc}{\lambda_0}$

ν_0 = Threshold frequency

λ_0 = Threshold wavelength

Work function only depends on nature of metal.

Threshold Frequency (ν_0)

The frequency below which photoelectric effect does not take place.

$\nu_0 = \frac{\phi_0}{h}$

Stopping Potential (V_0)

Minimum magnitude of anode potential which just stops the photocurrent.

$eV_0 = KE_{max}$

Einstein's Photoelectric Equation

Photon energy = KE_{max} of electron + work function

$h\nu = KE_{max} + \phi_0$

$h\nu \; eV_0 + \phi_0$

Hertz's Observation

When a *UV* light incidents on two metal electrodes with a voltage applied across them, the light develops a change in voltage at the point where the sparking occurs.

Lenard's Observation

The amount of energy released by the electrons increases with the frequency of the incident radiation.

Experimental Set-up of Photoelectric Effect

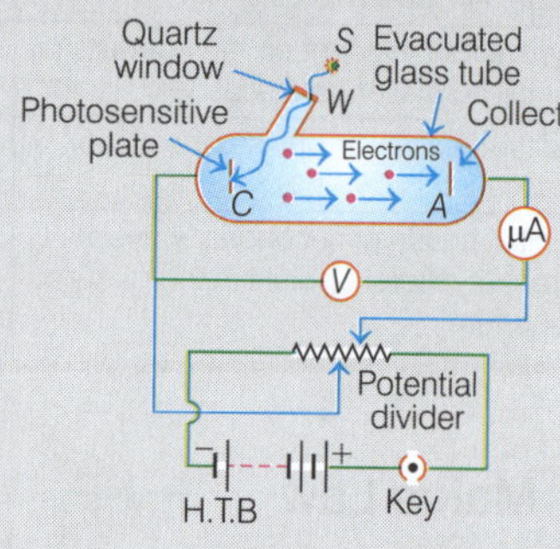

Photoelectric Effect

The emission of electrons from metallic surface when illuminated with light of certain minimum frequency.

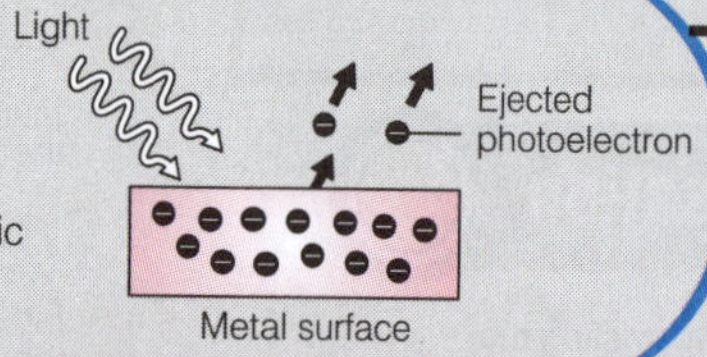

Graphs For Photoelectric Effect

Effect of Intensity of Light on Photocurrent

Photocurrent ∝ Intensity
[Frequency = constant
Potential = constant]

Effect of Potential on Photoelectric Current

Frequency = constant
Intensity = constant

- Photoelectric current increases with increase in accelerating potential.
- Saturation current = Maximum value of photoelectric current.

Effect of Frequency of Incident Radiation on Stopping Potential

Frequency increases

- Energy increases
- Maximum kinetic energy increases
- Stopping potential increases

Stopping Potential *versus* Frequency Graph

$\therefore eV_0 = h\nu - h\nu_0$

$V_0 = \frac{h\nu}{e} - \frac{\phi_0}{e}$

- Slope $= m = \tan\theta = \frac{h}{e}$ same for all metals

X-intercept $= \nu_0$

Y-intercept $= -\frac{\phi_0}{e}$

KE_{max} *versus* Frequency(ν) Graph

From graph

Work function of metal *B* > Work function of metal *A*

i.e. $|\phi_B| > |\phi_A|$

01

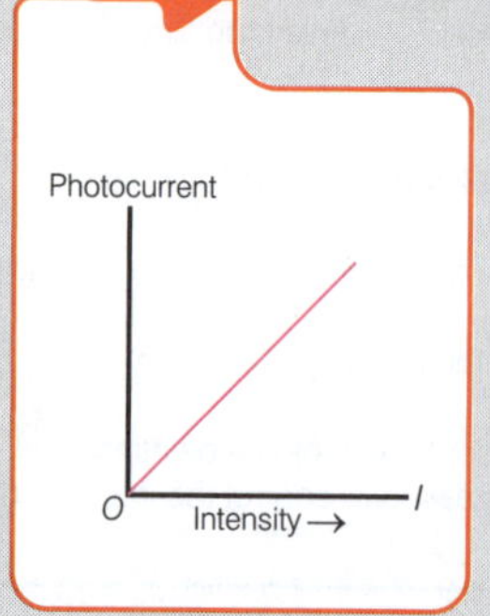

02

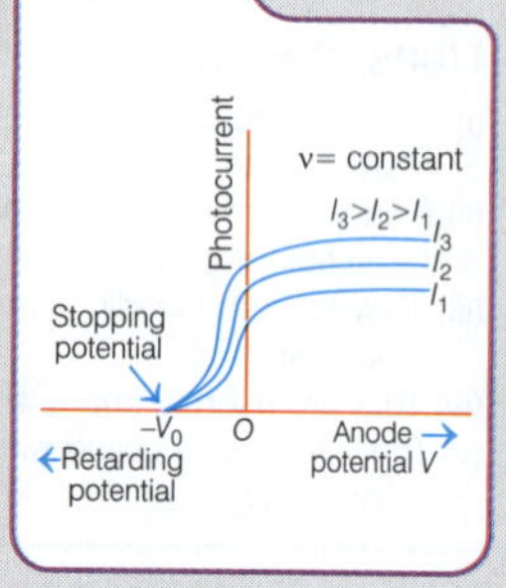

03

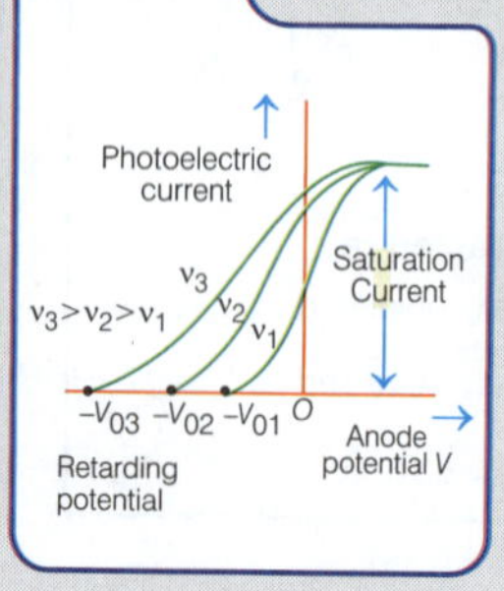

04

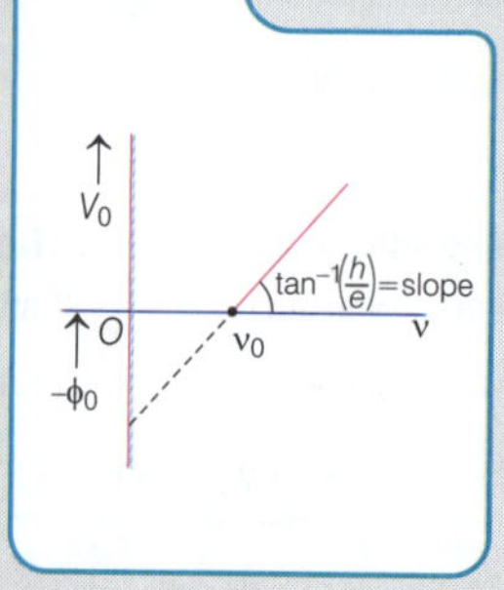

05

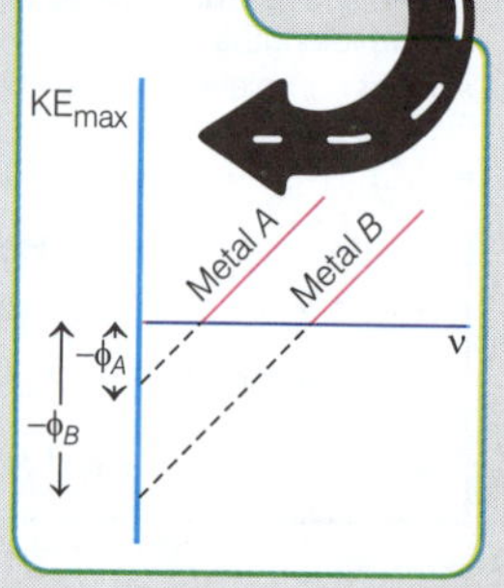

Particle Nature of Light : The Photon

01 Photon

Small packets of energy radiated from a source. Energy of photon ∝ Frequency of radiation.

$$E=\frac{hc}{\lambda}=\frac{12400}{\lambda(\text{Å})}\text{eV}$$

where, $h=6.62\times10^{-34}$ J-s

02 Linear Momentum of Photon

$$p=\frac{E}{c}=\frac{h}{\lambda}$$

03 Effective Mass of Photon

$$m=\frac{E}{c^2}=\frac{h}{c\lambda}$$

e.g. Mass of violet light photon > mass of red light photon

General Formula for Radiation Pressure

$$p=\frac{(1+\alpha)I}{c}$$

- $\alpha = 0$, for completely absorbing surface
- $\alpha = 1$, for completely effecting surface
- $0<\alpha<1$ (for any other surface)

Intensity of Photon

$$\text{Intensity}=\frac{\text{Energy}}{\text{Area}\times\text{Time}}$$

$$I=\frac{E}{At}=\frac{P}{A}=\frac{\text{Power of source}}{\text{Area}}$$

$$I=\frac{N(h\nu)}{At}=\frac{n(h\nu)}{A}$$

$n=\frac{N}{t}=$ Number of photon per second.

$$\frac{P}{A}=\frac{n(h\nu)}{A}\Rightarrow n=\frac{P}{(h\nu)}=\frac{P\lambda}{hc}$$

Force Exerted by Photon

Force exerted by photon on perfectly reflecting surface

Force on surface $F=n\left(\frac{2h}{\lambda}\right)$

$n=$ number of photons per second falling on surface

$$F=\frac{2P}{c}$$

- Pressure $=\frac{F}{A}=\frac{2I}{c}$

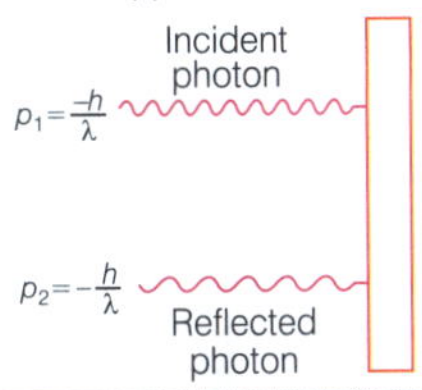

When a photon is incident at an angle θ on perfectly reflecting surface

$$F=\frac{2IA\cos^2\theta}{c}$$

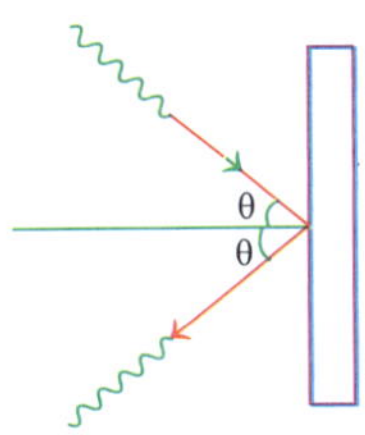

When a photon is incident at angle θ on perfectly absorbing surface

$$F=\frac{IA\cos^2\theta}{c}$$

Wave Nature of Matter

- Any particle in motion can act like a wave.
- **de-Broglie wavelength**

$$\lambda=\frac{h}{p}=\frac{h}{mv}=\frac{h}{\sqrt{2m(\text{KE})}}=\frac{h}{\sqrt{3mk_BT}}=\frac{h}{\sqrt{2mqV}}$$

KE $=qV$ [for charged particle],

where, $V=$ accelerating potential in volt

KE $=\frac{3}{2}K_BT$ (Thermal neutron)

where, $k_B=$ Boltzmann's constant and

$T=$ Temperature in kelvin

- For an electron revolving in nth orbit of Bohr's hydrogen atom

$$mvr=\frac{nh}{2\pi}\Rightarrow\lambda=\frac{h}{mv}=\frac{2\pi r}{n}$$

electron's momentum, $mv=\frac{h}{\lambda}$

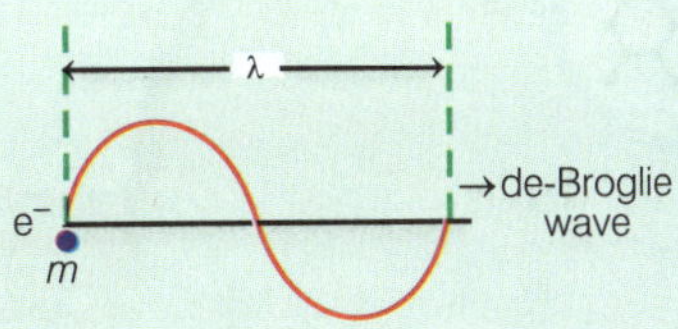

POWER TIPS

de-Broglie Wavelength Associated with the Particle

- Thermal neutron, $\lambda=\frac{30.83}{\sqrt{T}}$ Å
- Electron, $\lambda=\frac{12.27}{\sqrt{V}}$ Å
- Proton, $\lambda=\frac{0.286}{\sqrt{V}}$ Å
- Deutron, $\lambda=\frac{0.202}{\sqrt{V}}$ Å
- α-particle, $\lambda=\frac{0.101}{\sqrt{V}}$ Å

Chapter 26

Atoms

Rutherford's α-Particle Scattering Experiment

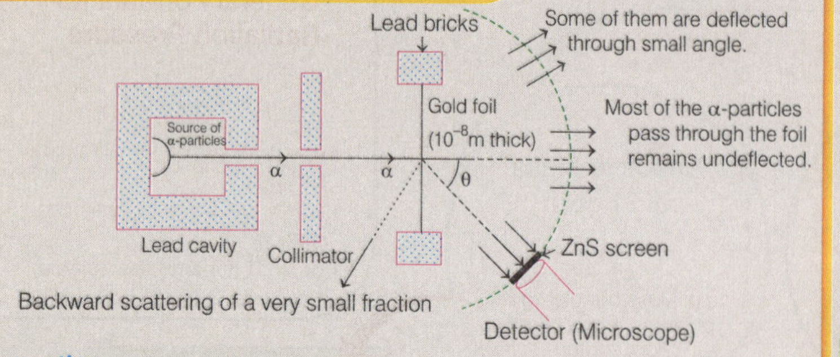

Observation

(i) A few α-particles, about 1 in 8000, get deflected through 90° or more.

(ii) A very few α-particles return back i.e. deflected by 180°.

$$N(\theta) \propto \frac{1}{\sin^4 (\theta/2)}$$

$N(\theta)$ = number of α–particles scattered per unit area

θ = scattering angle

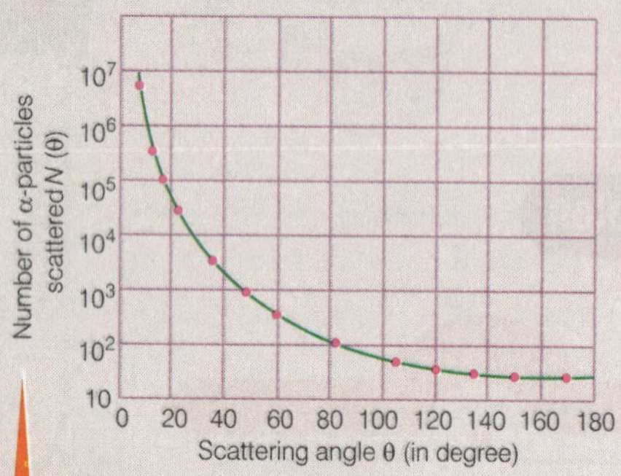

Distance of Closest Approach

Minimum distance from the nucleus up to which α-particle approaches is called distance of closest approach.

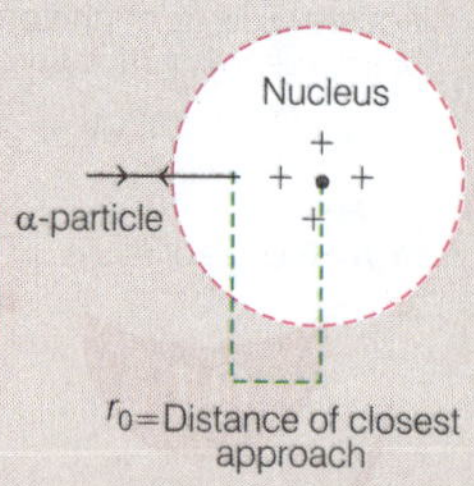

At distance of closest approach,

KE of α-particle = Electrostatic PE of α-particle

$$r_0 = \frac{4kZe^2}{mv^2}$$

Rutherford's Atomic Model

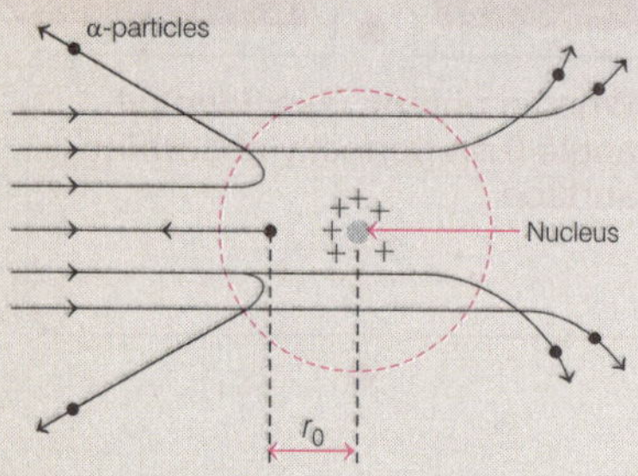

- Entire positive charge and most of the mass of the atom is concentrated in a small volume called nucleus.
- Size of nucleus $\rightarrow 10^{-15}$ m to 10^{-14} m.
- Size of an atom $\rightarrow 10^{-10}$ m
- Most of an atom has empty space.

- Electrons revolve around the nucleus as planets revolve around the sun.
- Electrons are so light that they does not effect the path of α-particle.

Impact Parameter

Perpendicular distance of the initial velocity vector of the α-particle from the centre of the nucleus.

$$b = \frac{1}{4\pi\varepsilon_0} \frac{Ze^2 \cot\theta/2}{\frac{1}{2}mv^2}$$

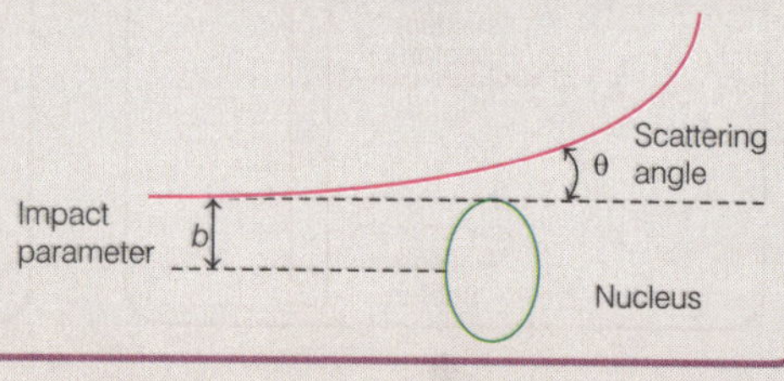

Limitations of Rutherford's Atomic Model

- An electron revolving around the nucleus in under continuous acceleration towards the centre.
- It should continuously lose energy and move in orbits of gradually decreasing radii.
- The electron should follow a spiral path and finally it should collapse into the nucleus.
- Thus, the Rutherford's model cannot explain the stability of an atom.

Bohr's Atomic Model

Centripetal force = Electrostatic attraction between the electrons and the nucleus.

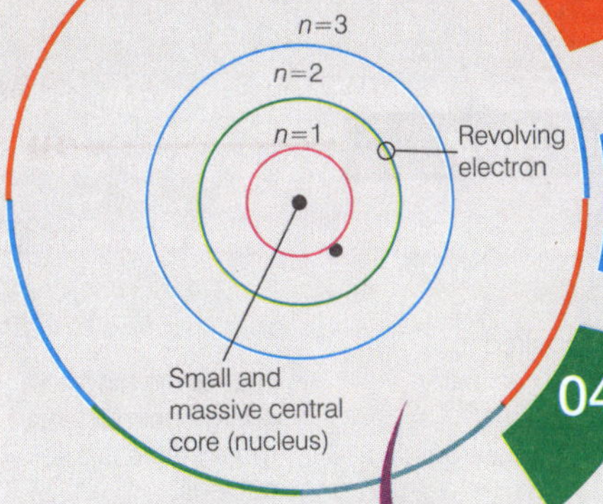

01

02 Quantum condition

For any permitted orbit,

$L = mvr = \frac{nh}{2\pi}$, where $n = 1, 2, 3....$

This is the famous Bohr's quantisation condition for angular momentum.

03 Stationary orbits

In the stationary orbits, an electron does not radiate energy.

04 Frequency condition

An electron jumps from a higher to a lower orbit → Emit radiation

An electron jumps from a lower to a higher orbit → Absorb radiation

$h\nu = E_2 - E_1$

Analysis of Bohr's Atomic Model

For hydrogen like atoms with atomic number Z.

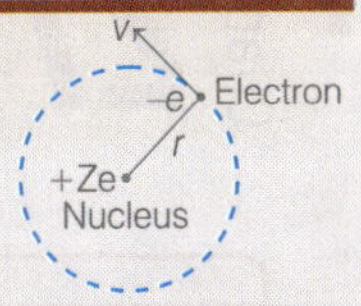

01 **Orbital radius** $r_n = \frac{\varepsilon_0 n^2 h^2}{\pi m e^2 Z}$

02 **Bohr's radius** $n = 1, Z = 1$

$r_1 = a_0 = \frac{h^2\varepsilon_0}{\pi m e^2} = 0.53 \text{ Å} \Rightarrow r_n = 0.53 \frac{n^2}{Z} \text{ Å}$

$r_n \propto n^2$

03 **Orbital Velocity** $v_n = \frac{Ze^2}{2\varepsilon_0 nh} = \alpha\left(\frac{cZ}{n}\right)$

$\alpha = \frac{e^2}{2h\varepsilon_0 c}$ = summer field's fine structure = constant

$v_n \propto 1/n$

04 **Velocity of electron** $n = 1, Z = 1$

$v_1 = \frac{e^2}{2h\varepsilon_0} = \frac{c}{137} \simeq 2.19 \times 10^6$ m/s

05 **Orbital frequency** $\nu_n = \frac{kZe^2}{nhr_n}$

As $r_n \propto \frac{n^2}{Z} \Rightarrow \nu_n \propto \frac{Z^2}{n^3}$, $T_n = \frac{nhr_n}{kZe^2}$, $T \propto \frac{n^3}{Z^2}$, $\omega_n \propto \frac{Z^2}{n^3}$

Energy Level Diagram For Hydrogen

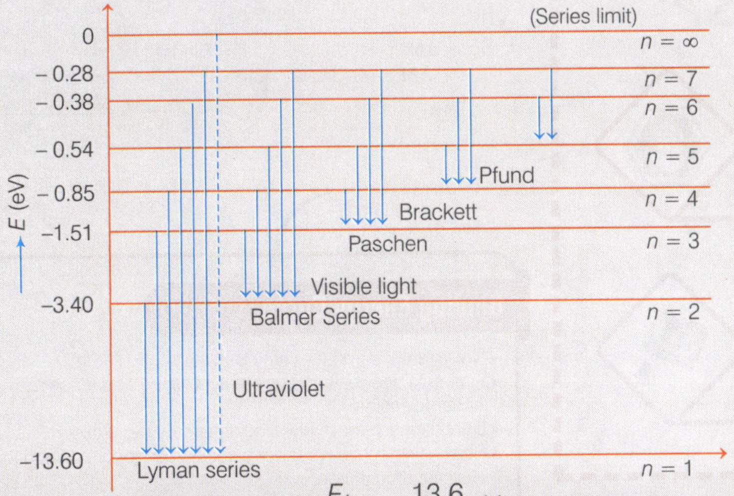

$\therefore E_n = \frac{E_1}{n^2} = -\frac{13.6}{n^2}$ eV

$E_n = -\frac{2\pi^2 mk^2 Z^2 e^4}{h^2} \cdot \frac{1}{n^2}$

For hydrogen $Z = 1$

$E_n = -\frac{2\pi^2 mk^2 e^4}{h^2} \cdot \frac{1}{n^2}$

Energy of the electron in the first orbit ($n=1$)

$E_1 = -13.6$ eV

$E_n = \frac{-13.6}{n^2}$ eV

$E_2 = \frac{-13.6}{2^2} = -3.4$ eV

$E_3 = \frac{-13.6}{3^2} = -1.51$ eV

$E_4 = \frac{-13.6}{4^2} = -0.85$ eV

$E_5 = \frac{-13.6}{5^2} = -0.54$ eV

Excitation and Ionisation Energy

- **Excitation Energy**

  The energy required by electron to jump from the ground state to any one of the excited state.

  First excitation energy of hydrogen,

  $E_2 - E_1 = -3.4 - (-13.6) = 10.2$ eV

- **Ionisation Energy**

  The energy required to knock an electron completely out of the atom.

  Ionisation energy of hydrogen

  $E_\infty - E_1 = 0 - (-13.6) = 13.6$ eV

POWER TIPS

ENERGY OF THE ELECTRON

- Kinetic energy $(K_n) = \frac{RhcZ^2}{n^2}$, $R = \frac{me^4}{8\varepsilon_0^2 ch^3}$ = Rydberg's constant $= 1.09 \times 10^7 \text{m}^{-1}$
- Potential energy $(U_n) = \frac{-2RhcZ^2}{n^2}$
- Total energy $(E_n) = \frac{-RhcZ^2}{n^2} = -\frac{13.6}{n^2}$ eV

  $|U_n| = 2|K_n|$, $E_n = -K_n$
- Rydberg formula

  wave number $(\bar{\nu}) = \frac{1}{\lambda} = \frac{\nu}{c} = R\left[\frac{1}{n_1^2} - \frac{1}{n_2^2}\right]$

Chapter 27 Nuclei

Nucleus

A dense, positively charged central core of an atom, composed of protons and neutrons.

It accounts for nearly all of the atoms mass.

Composition Of Nucleus

- Mass number = No. of protons + No. of neutrons
  $A = P + n$
  $M_p = 1.673 \times 10^{-27}$ Kg
  $M_n = 1.674 \times 10^{-27}$ Kg
- Atomic no. (Z) = No. of protons (p) = Number of neutron (n)

Nuclear Size

- $R = R_0 A^{1/3}$
- $R_0 = 1.2$ fm
- Radius of nucleus is in the order of 10^{-15} m.
- Size of an atom is in the order of 10^{-10} m.

Nuclear Density

- Independent of a mass number.
- Nucleus density $= \dfrac{\text{Nucleus mass}}{\text{Nucleus volume}}$
- It is of the order of 10^{17} kg m^{-3}. Average nuclear density is about 2.3×10^{17} kg m^{-3}.

Atomic Mass Unit

- It is 1/12th of the mass of $_6C^{12}$ atom
- 1amu $= 1.66 \times 10^{-27}$kg

Mass Defect

- Difference between total mass of nucleus and actual mass of the nucleus.
  $\Delta m = [Zm_p + (A-Z)m_n - M_{nucleus}]$

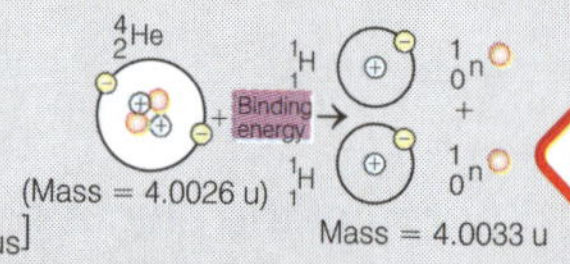

Packing Fraction

- Mass defect per nucleon.
- Packing fraction $= \dfrac{\Delta m}{A} = \dfrac{M-A}{A}$
- If packing fraction is positive, then the nucleus is unstable.
- If packing fraction is negative, then the nucleus is stable.
- Packing fraction is zero for $_6C^{12}$.

Nuclear Forces

- POINT 01: Strongest force in nature.
- POINT 02: Acts only in the range of fermi meters.
- POINT 03: Balances electrostatic force between protons in nucleus.
- POINT 04: Charge independent, non-central forces.

Binding Energy

- Energy required to break up a nucleus into its constituent protons and neutrons.
- Higher the binding energy per nucleon, more stable is the nucleus.
- BE = mass defect $\times c^2$
  $BE = \Delta Mc^2$
  $= \Delta M \times 931$ MeV
- Binding Energy per nucleon = Binding fraction
  $\dfrac{BE}{\text{Mass No.}} = \dfrac{\Delta M \times 931 \text{ MeV}}{A}$

Binding Energy Curve

- Nuclei around iron (Fe) are more stable.
- Elements heavier than iron are less stable and tends to undergo fission.
- Light elements have low binding energy per nucleon.
- Heavy elements have lower binding energy per nucleon than element around iron.
- Light elements fuse to heavier elements releasing energy as binding energy per nucleon increases.
- Heavy elements split into smaller nuclei, releasing energy as binding energy per nucleon increases in the product.

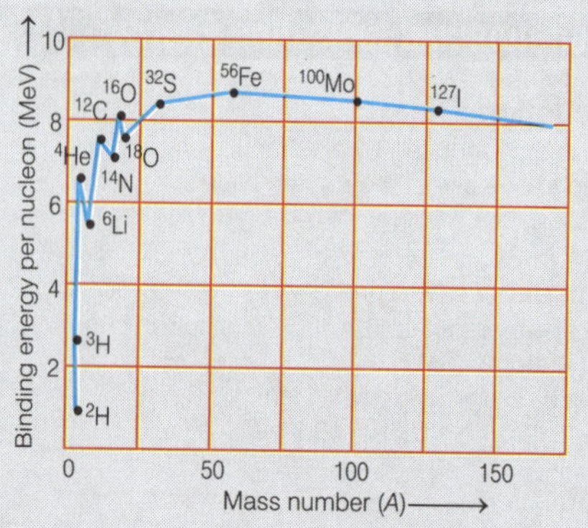

Nucleus Reactions

01 Involves a change in the composition of an atomic nucleus, typically through interaction of nucleons or other particles.

02 Releases large amount of energy.

03 $X + a \longrightarrow C \longrightarrow Y \longrightarrow b + Q$

Parent nucleus, Incident particle, Compound nucleus, Product nucleus, Daughter nucleus, Energy

Q-value

- Net energy released or absorbed during the nucleus reaction.
- It is the difference in the total mass-energy of the reactants and products.

Q=[Mass of reactants – Mass of products]c^2

Interpretation

- **Positive Q-value** Energy is released (exothermic reaction).
- **Negative Q-value** Energy is required for the reaction to occurs (endothermic reaction).

Conservation Laws

STEP 1 Mass number and electric charge is conserved.

$\Sigma Z_{\text{initial}} = \Sigma Z_{\text{final}}$

$\Sigma A_{\text{initial}} = \Sigma A_{\text{final}}$

STEP 2 Linear momentum and angular momentum are conserved.

STEP 3 Total energy of the reaction remains conserved.

Nuclear Fission

- A process in which heavy atomic nucleus (such as uranium - 235) splits into two smaller nuclei.
- It releases a huge amount of energy.
- Often produces radioactive waste.

$${}^{235}_{92}U + {}^{1}_{0}n \rightarrow {}^{236}_{92}U \rightarrow {}^{144}_{56}Ba + {}^{89}_{36}Kr + 3\,{}^{1}_{0}n + Q$$

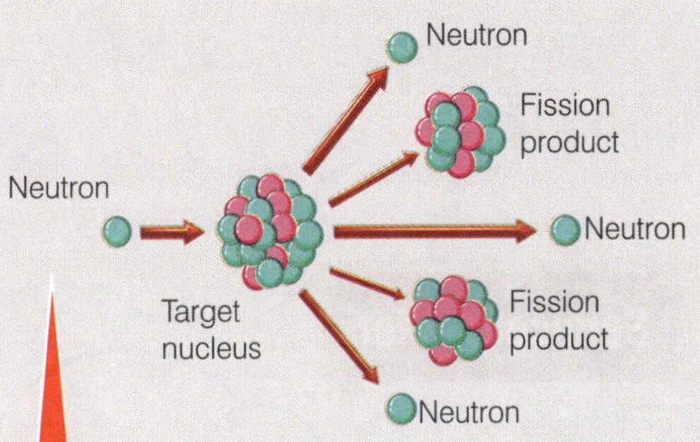

Nuclear Fusion

Process where two light nuclei combine to form a heavier nucleus and releasing energy.

Occurs at extremely high temperature and pressure.

Releases much more energy per unit mass than fission

$${}^{2}_{1}H + {}^{2}_{1}H \rightarrow {}^{3}_{2}He + {}^{1}_{0}n + 3.27\text{ MeV}$$

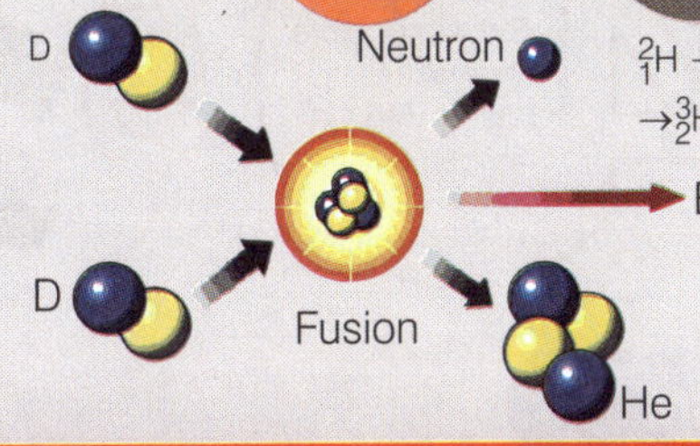

Chain Reaction

- A self sustaining series of nuclear fission reactions.
- The amount of fissile material must reach the minimum quantity needed to keep the reaction going.

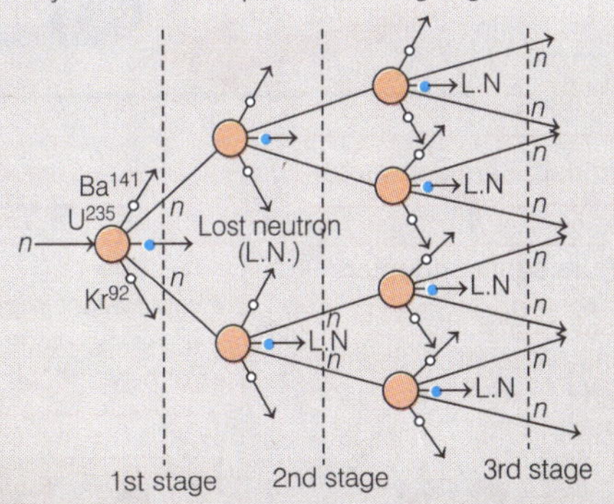

- **Multiplication Factor**

$$R = \frac{\text{Rate of production of neutron}}{\text{Rate of loss of neutron}}$$

$R = 1$, reaction is steady.

$R > 1$, reaction grows faster. Material size is supercritical.

$R < 1$, reaction comes to hault. Material size is subcritical.

Necessary Conditions for Nuclear Fission

01 The mass of the compound nucleus must be greater than the sum of masses of fission product.

02 The binding energy per mass number of compound must be less than that of the fission product.

03 Requires fissile nuclei that can sustain chain reaction.

03 The absorption of the neutron causes the nucleus to become unstable and splits into two smaller nuclei.

Chapter 28

Electronic Devices

Conductor, Insulator and Semiconductor

Properties	Conductor (Metal)	Insulator	Semiconductor
Resistivity	$10^{-8}-10^{-2}\ \Omega$-m	$10^{11}-10^{19}\ \Omega$-m	$10^{-5}-10^{6}\ \Omega$-m
Conductivity	$10^{2}-10^{8}$ mho/m	$10^{-19}-10^{-11}$ mho/m	$10^{-6}-10^{5}$ mho/m
Temperature coefficient of resistance 'α'	Positive	Negative	Negative
Current	Due to free electrons	No current	Due to electrons and holes
Energy band diagram	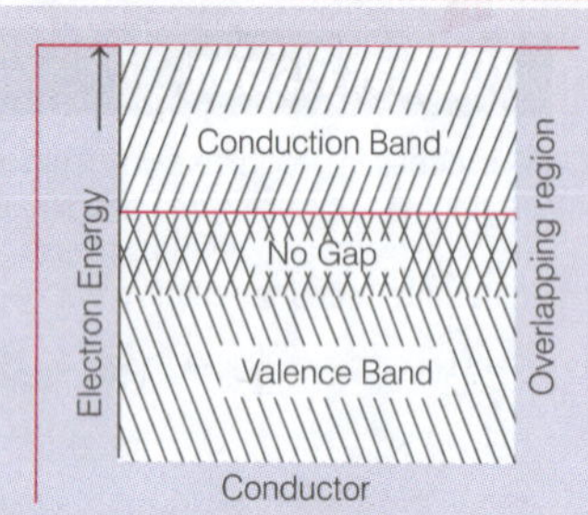	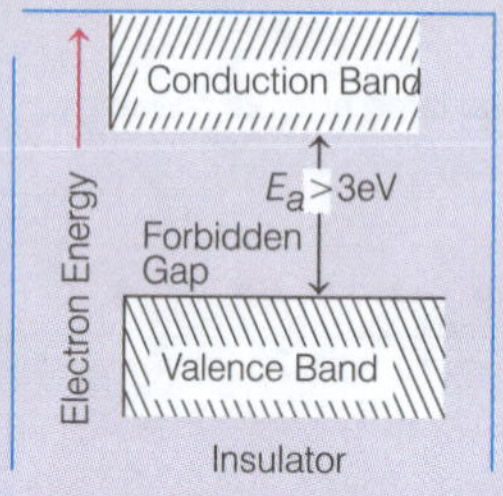	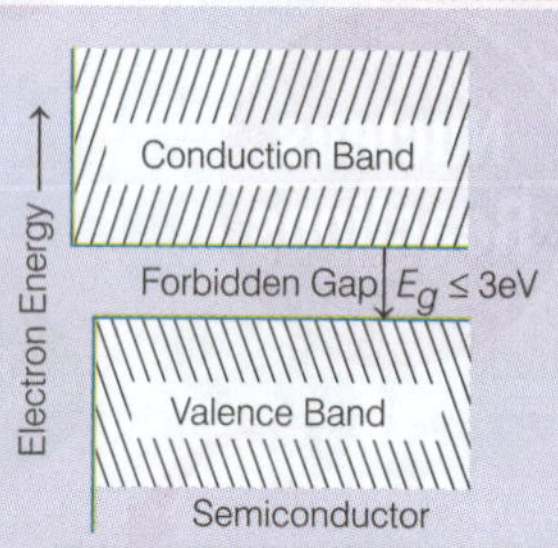
Forbidden energy gap	≈ 0 eV	> 3 eV	≤ 3 eV
Example	Al, Cu, Ag, Pt	Wood, Plastic, Diamond, Mica	Si, Ge, GaAs, GaF_2

Semiconductor

1. A solid substance that allows heat or electricity to pass through it.
2. It has much higher resistivity than metals.
3. Considerably lower number density of charge carriers than metals.
4. Resistivity of semiconductors decreases rapidly with temperature.
5. e.g. Si, Ge, GaAS, CdS etc.

Classification of Semiconductors

Intrinsic Semiconductor

Pure semiconductors
$n_e = n_h = n\ I = I_e + I_h$

Unbounded free electron (+5 valency atom)

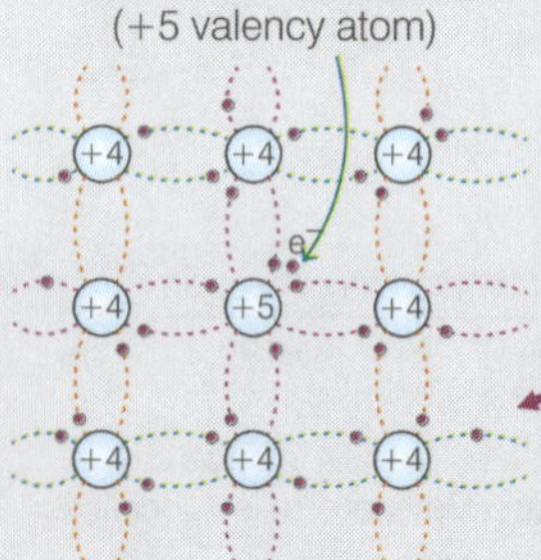

Extrinsic semiconductor (doped semiconductor)
$n_h n_e = n_i^2$

***n* - type**
- Pentavalent impurity (P, As, Sb etc.)
- For *n*-type $n_e >> n_h$

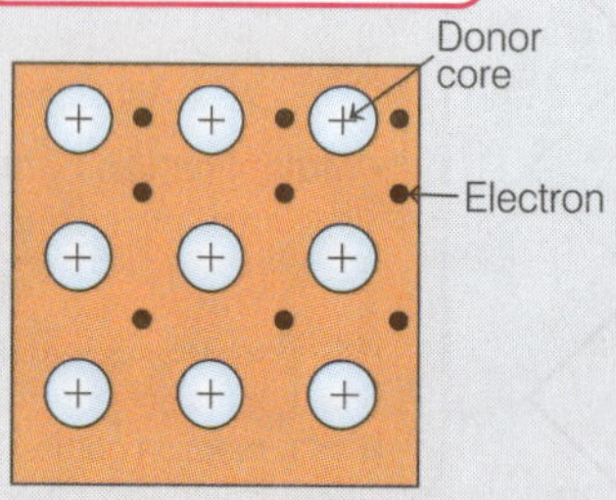

***p* - type**
- Trivalent impurity (Ga, B, In, Al)
- For *p*-type $n_h >> n_e$

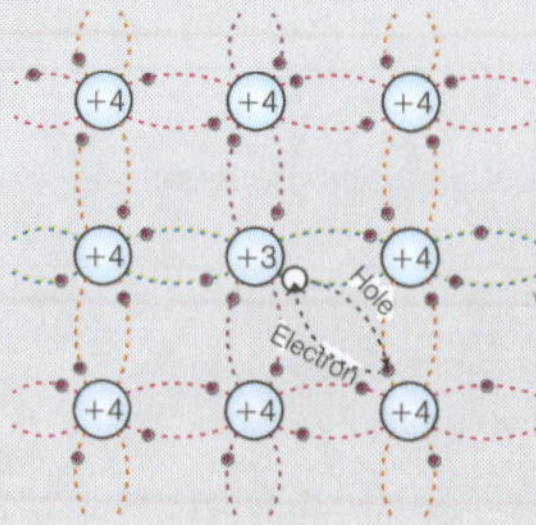

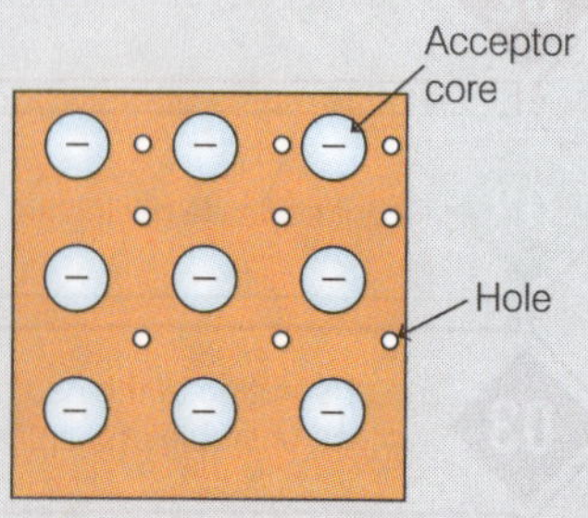

1 Energy band diagram of *n*-type semiconductor

The energy of the donor electron is slightly less than conduction band.

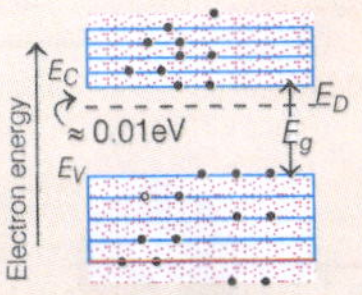

(a) $T > 0K$

2 Energy band diagram of *p*-type semiconductor

The acceptor energy level E_A lies slightly above the top of the valence band.

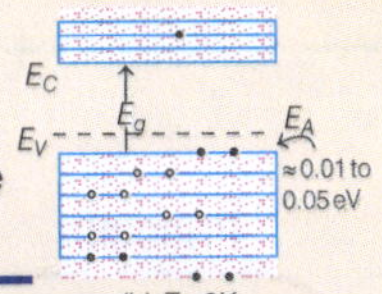

(b) $T > 0K$

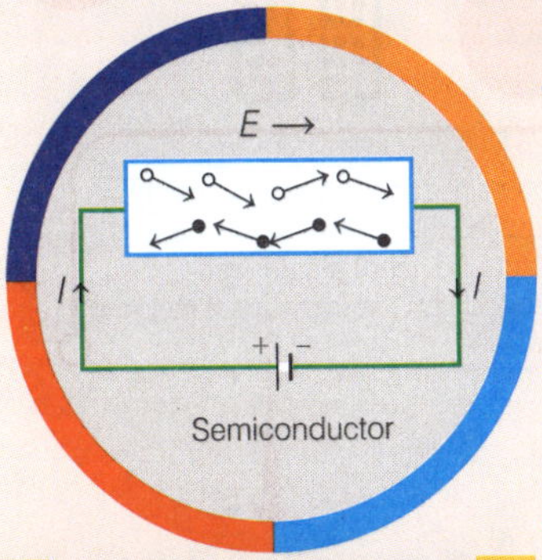

Holes: The absence of an electron in the bond of covalently bonded crystal.

Electrical Mobility: Drift velocity per unit electric field, $\mu_0 = -V/E$
The mobility of an electron in conduction band $> \mu_e > \mu_h$ mobility of a hole in the valence band.

Electrical Conductivity of a Semiconductor: Conductivity $(\sigma) = \frac{1}{\rho} = e(n_e\mu_e + n_h\mu_h)$ and Resistivity $(\rho) = \frac{1}{e(n_e\mu_e + n_h\mu_h)}$

Variation of Conductivity with Temperature: $\sigma = \sigma_0 e^{-Eg/2k_BT}$
Conductiviity of semiconductor increases with increase of temperature.

p-n Junction Diode

- Single crystal of Ge or Si doped.
- One half portion of it acts as *p*-type semiconductor.
- Other half as a *n*-type semiconductor.

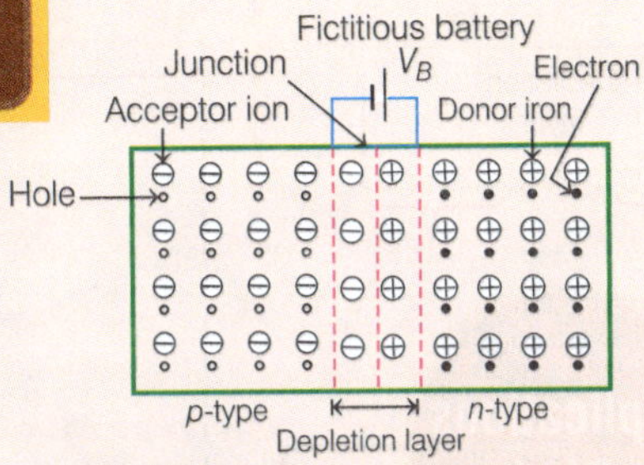

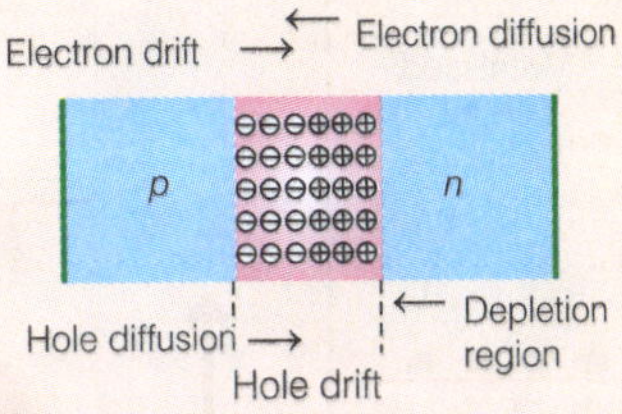

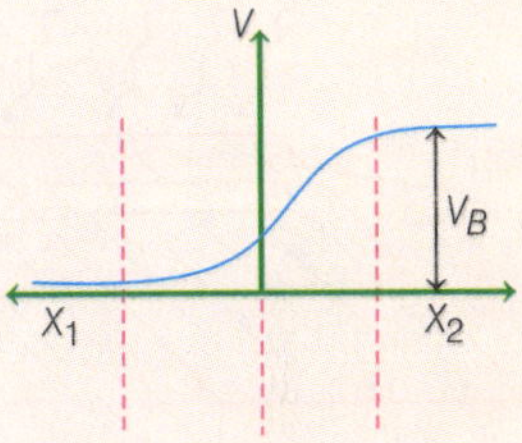

Depletion Region

- Small region in the vicinity of the junction.
- No free charge carriers.
- Only immobile ions.

Barrier Potential

- The accumulation of negative charges in the *n*-regions and positive charge in the *p*-regions sets up potential difference across the junction.
- This acts as a barrier called barrier potential. V_B for Ge= 0.3 V and for Si= 0.7 V.

Diffusion Current

- Due to the flow of majority charge carriers.
- Electric current from *p-n* side.

Drift Current

- Due to the flow of minority charge carriers.
- Electric current from *n-p* side.

Biasing

Forward Bias

- Positive terminal of a battery connected to *p*-side and the negative terminal of a battery connected to the *n*-side.
- Potential barrier reduces.
- Width of depletion layer decreases.
- Current flow mainly due to majority carriers.
- Forward resistance,

$$R_f = \frac{\Delta V_f}{\Delta I_f} \approx 100\ \Omega$$

- Cut-in voltage for Ge → 0.3 V, Si → 0.7 V

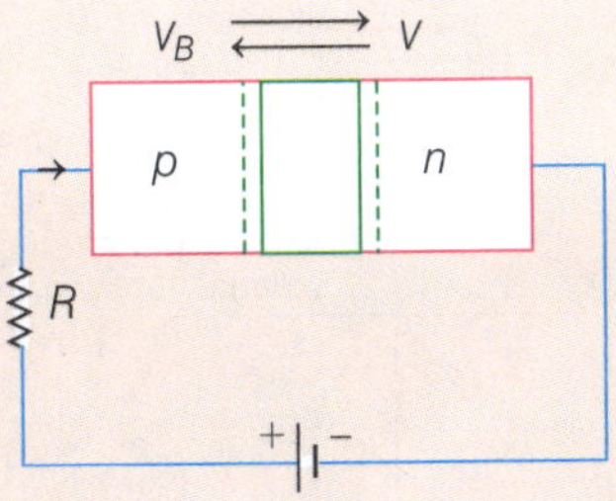

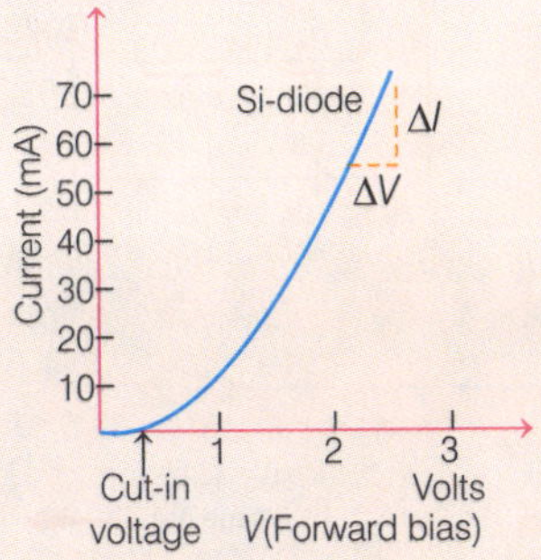

Forward characteristic curve

Reverse Bias

- Positive terminal of a battery is connected to the *n*-side and negative terminal of a battery connected to the *p*-side.
- Potential barrier increases.
- Width of depletion layer increases.
- Current flow mainly due to minority carriers.
- Reverse resistance,

$$R_r = \frac{\Delta V_r}{\Delta I_r} \approx 10^6\ \Omega$$

- Breakdown voltage → Ge=25V, Si=35V

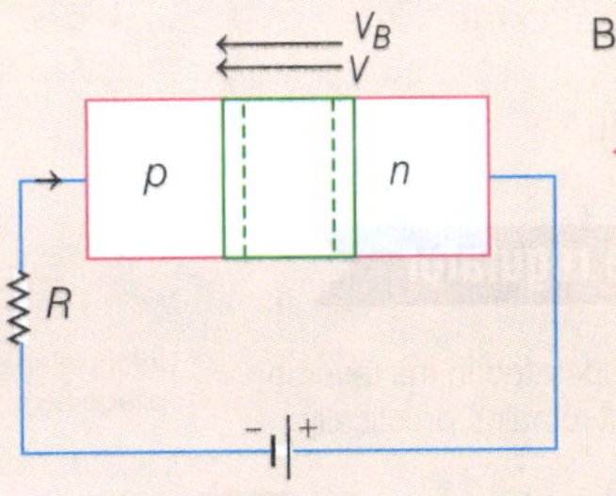

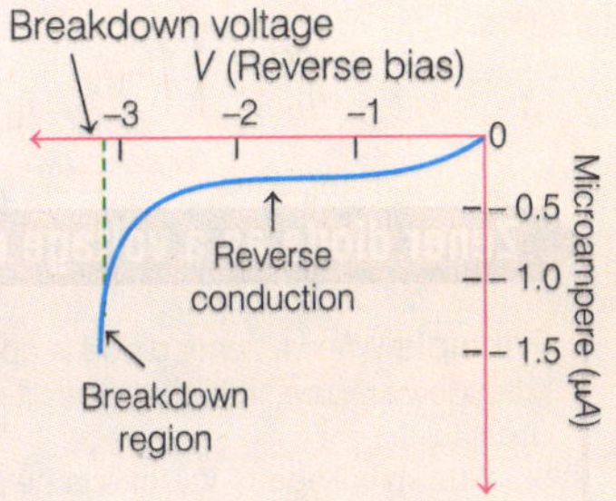

Reverse characteristic curve

Solar Cell

1 Principle

- It is a junction diode which converts solar energy into electrical energy.
- It is based on photovoltaic effect
- Diode is unbiased.

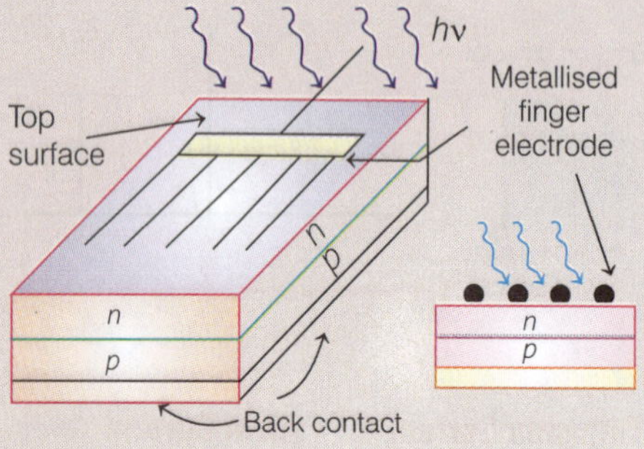

2 Working

p-side becomes positive and *n*-side becomes negative giving rise to photo voltage across the junction.

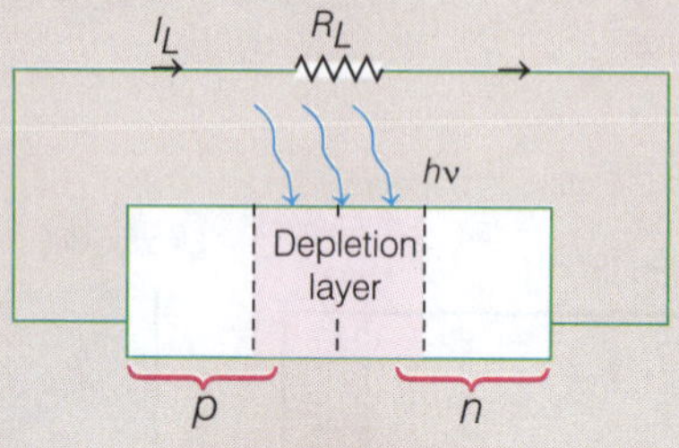

3 V-I Characteristic Curve For Solar Cell

- Solar cell does not draw current but supplies the current to the load.
- Output power of a solar cell depends on the intensity of incident sunlight.

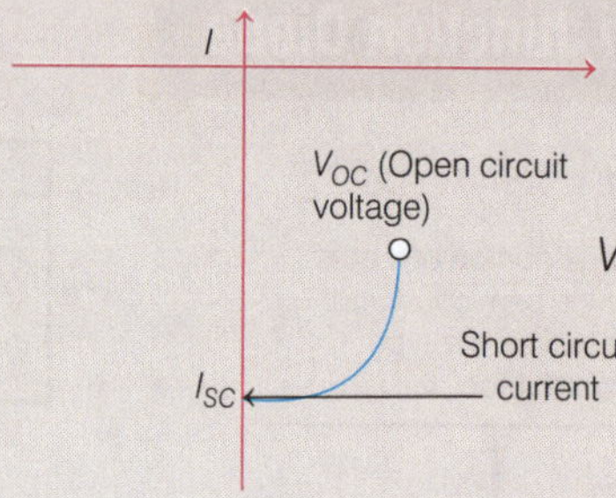

Applications of Diodes

Zener Diode

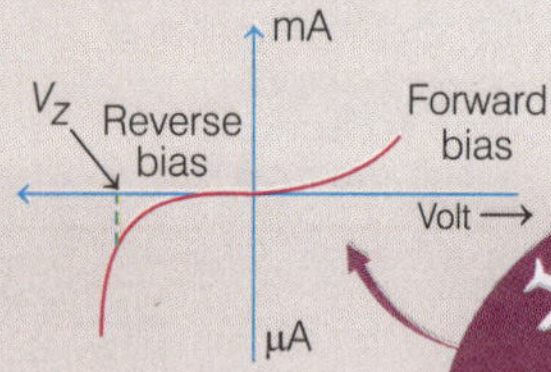

Releases large amount of energy.

It is specially designed to operate only in the reverse breakdown region continuously (without getting damaged)

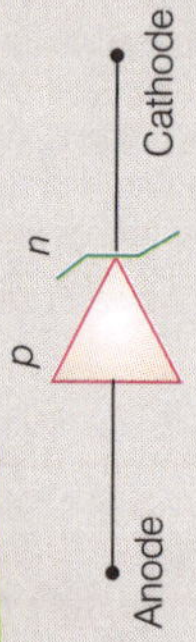

V-I characteristic curve for an avalanche diode

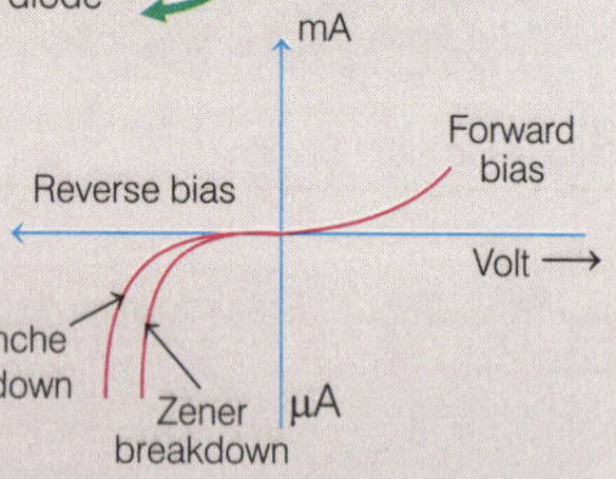

Photodiodes

- *p-n* junction fabricated from a photosensitive with a transparent window.
- Operated in reverse biased condition.

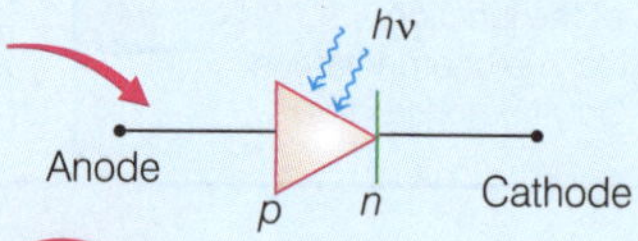

- Reverse biased photodiode illuminated with light

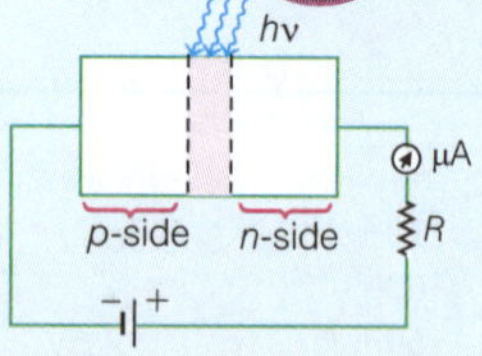

- Reverse saturation current increases with the increase in intensity of incident light.

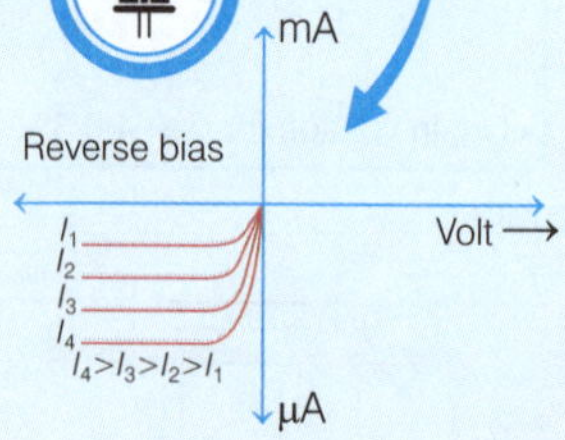

Zener diode as a voltage regulator

Principle When a zener diode is operated in the reverse breakdown region, voltage across it remains practically constant.
breakdown voltage = V_Z, for a large change in the reverse current

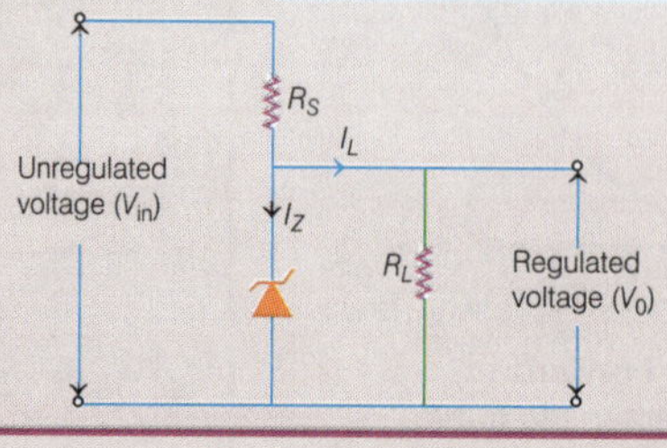

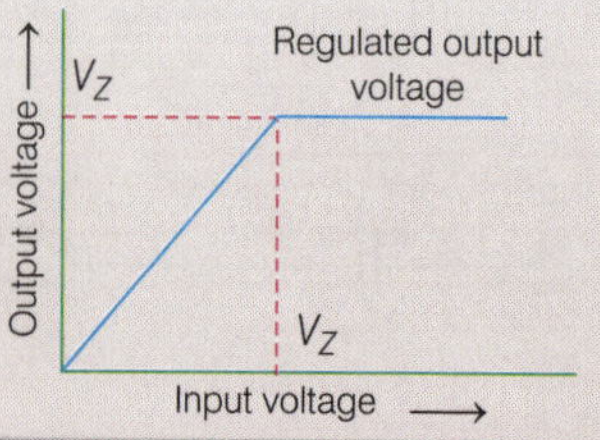

LED

- It is heavily doped
- Forward - biased p-n junction.
- Spontaneously converts the biasing electrical energy into optical energy, like infrared and visible light.

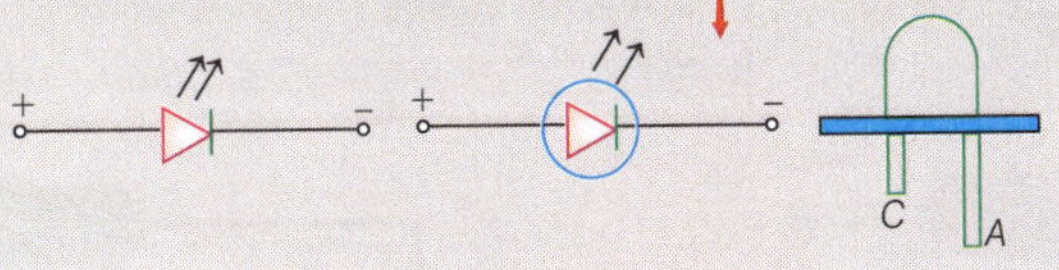

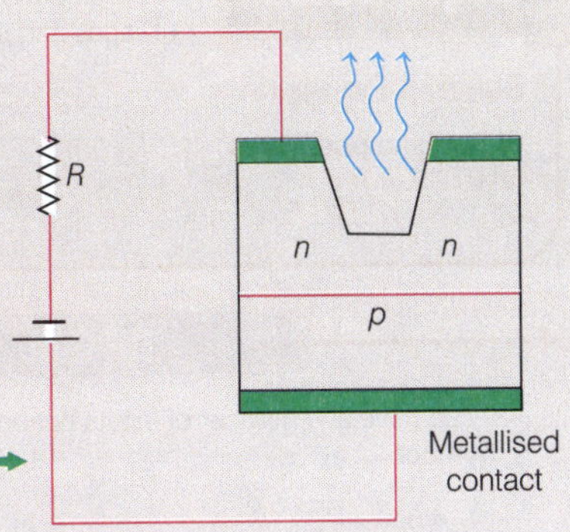

Forward Biased Led

A negative voltage is applied to n type and a positive voltage on the p side. When this occurs in LED , free electrons in the conduction band recombine with holes in the valence band. This leads to energy emission. Hence, the LED is forward biased.

V-I Characteristic Curve For Led

- Shape is similar to normal p-n junction diode.
- Barrier potentials are much higher and slightly different for each colour.

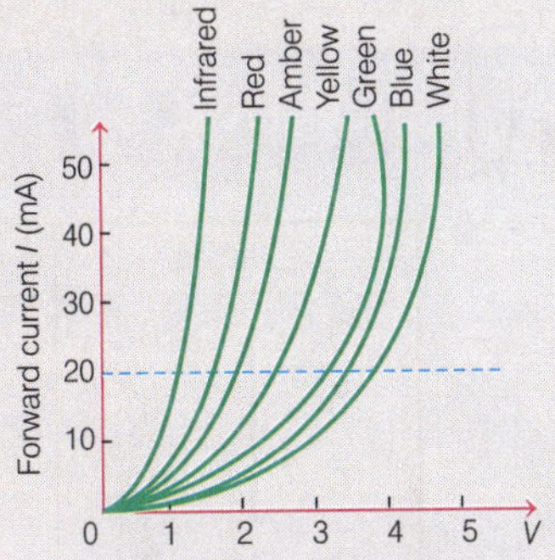

Diode as a Rectifier

Rectifier- The device used for converting AC to DC signal

Junction Diode as a Half-wave Rectifier

- **In positive half-cycle →** Diode is in forward biased- output signal is obtained.
- **In negative half-cycle -** Diode is in reverse biased → output signal is not obtained.

Rectifies Half of the AC Wave

- Average output per cycle $I_{DC} = \frac{I_0}{\pi}; V_{DC} = \frac{V_0}{\pi}$
- Ripple frequency = Frequency of AC input

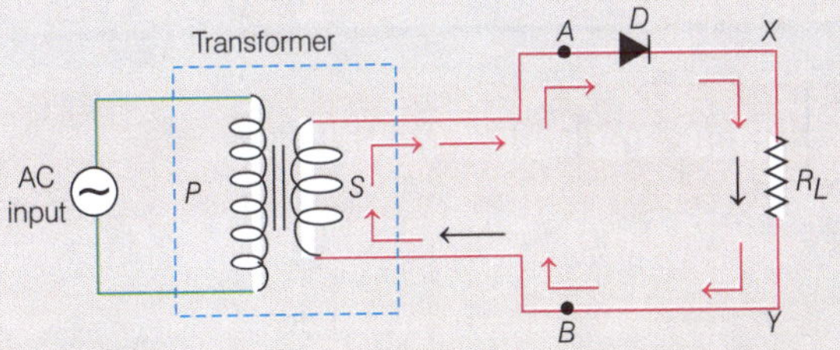

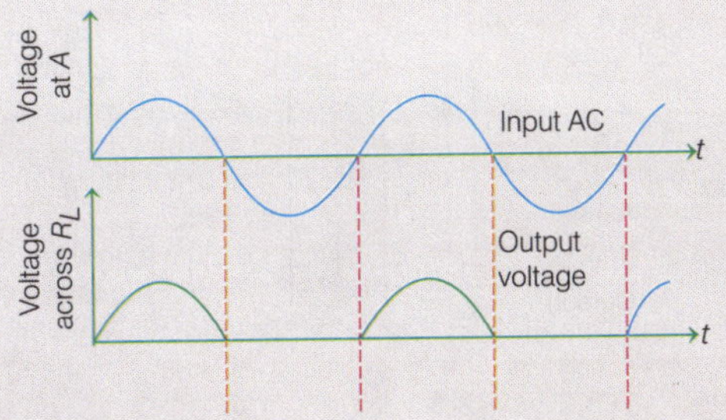

Junction Diode as a Full Wave Rectifier

- **Positive half-cycle diode** D_1- forward biased, D_2- Reverse biased
- **Negative half-cycle diode** D_1- reverse biased, D_2- forward biased

Rectifies Full AC Wave

- Average output per cycle, $I_{DC} = \frac{2I_0}{\pi}; V_{DC} = \frac{2V_0}{\pi}$
- Ripple frequency = 2×Frequency of AC input

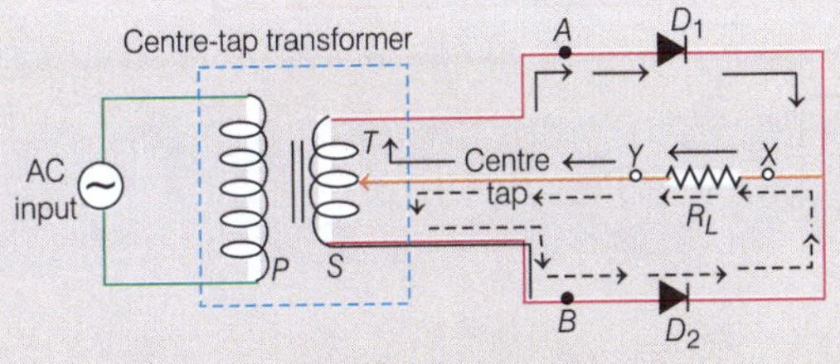

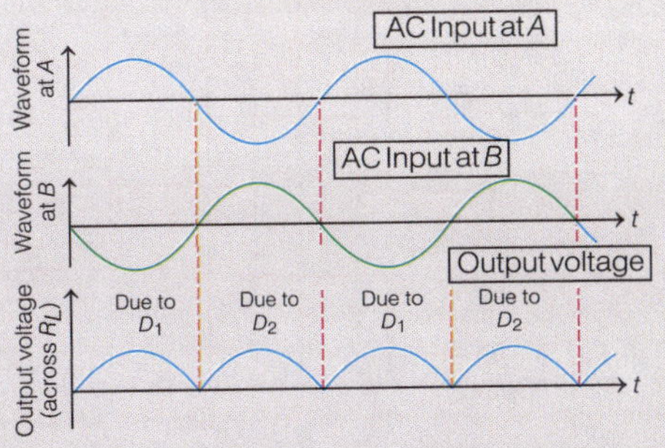

Logic Gates

- "Building block of the digital circuits",
- Diodes and transistors are used to perform switching functions.

Boolean Expression

(i) Boolean postulates

(a) $0 + A = A$ (b) $1 + A = 1$ (c) $0.A = 0$

(d) $1.A = A$ (e) $A + \overline{A} = 1$ (f) $A.\overline{A} = 0$

(ii) Identity law

(a) $A + A = A$

(b) $A.A = A$

(iii) Negation law $\overline{\overline{A}} = A$

(iv) De-Morgan's theorem

$\overline{A + B} = \overline{A}.\overline{B}$

$\overline{A.B} = \overline{A} + \overline{B}$

OR Gate

It can have any number of inputs but only one output.

Symbol

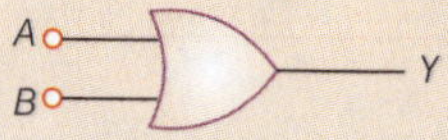

Boolean expression $A + B = Y$

1 Truth Table

Inputs		Output
A	B	$Y=A+B$
0	0	0
0	1	1
1	0	1
1	1	1

2 Electrical Analogue

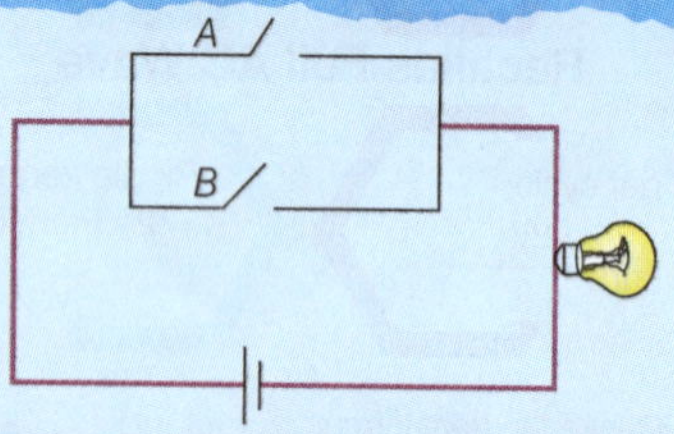

3 Input and Output Waveforms

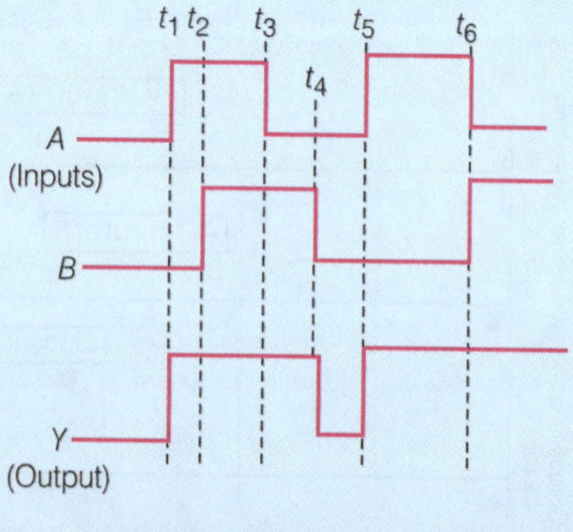

AND Gate

It can have any number of inputs but only one output.

Symbol

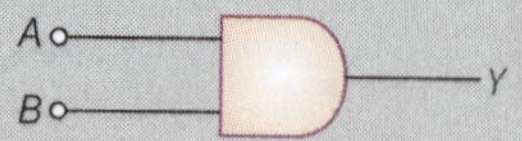

Boolean expression $A \cdot B = Y$

1 Truth Table

Inputs		Output
A	B	$Y=A \cdot B$
0	0	0
0	1	0
1	0	0
1	1	1

2 Electrical Analogue

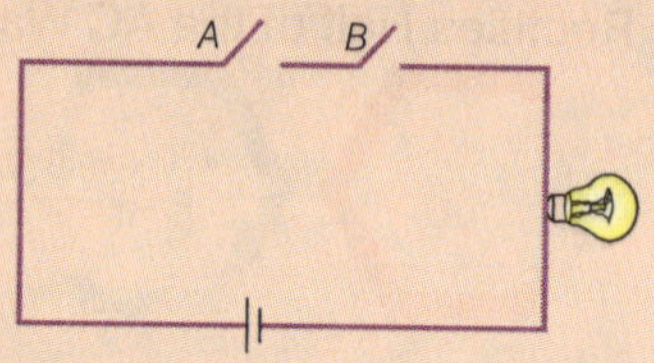

3 Input and Output Waveforms

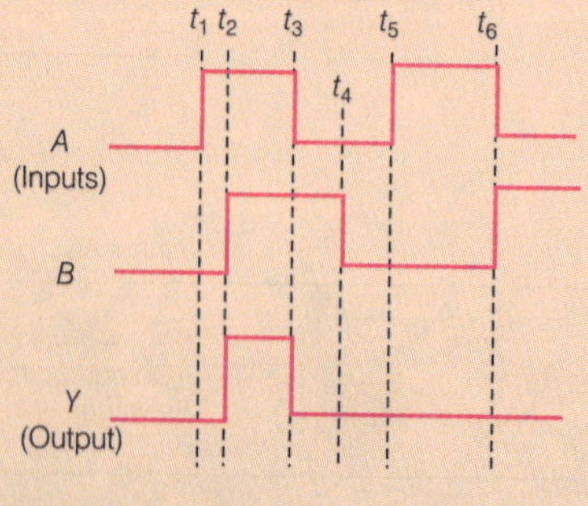

NOT Gate

- It is the simplest gate with one input and one output.
- Whatever the input, the NOT gate inverts it.

Symbol-

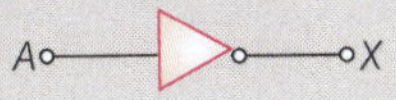

Boolean expression $\overline{A} = Y$

① Truth Table

Inputs	Output
A	Y
0	1
1	0

② Electrical Analogue

③ NOT Gate by NAND Gate

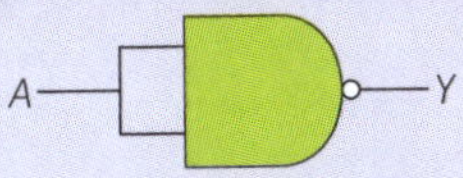

NOT Gate by NOR Gate

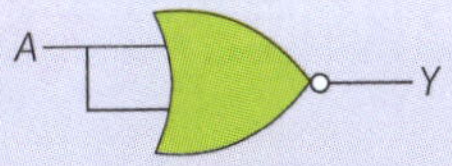

④ Input & Output Waveforms

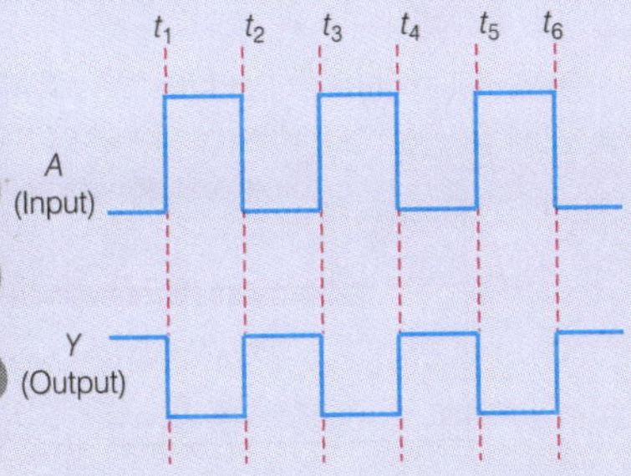

NAND Gate

- It is combination of an AND and a NOT gate [AND+NOT]

Symbol-

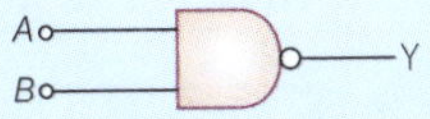

Boolean expression $\overline{A \cdot B} = Y$

① Truth Table

Inputs		Output
A	B	$Y = A \cdot B$
0	0	1
0	1	1
1	0	1
1	1	0

② Electrical Analogue

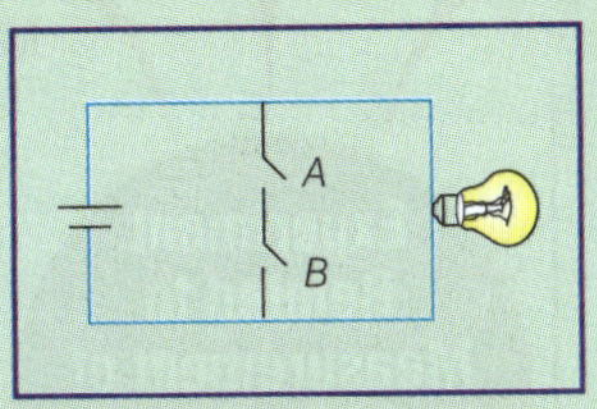

③ NAND Gate using NOR Gate

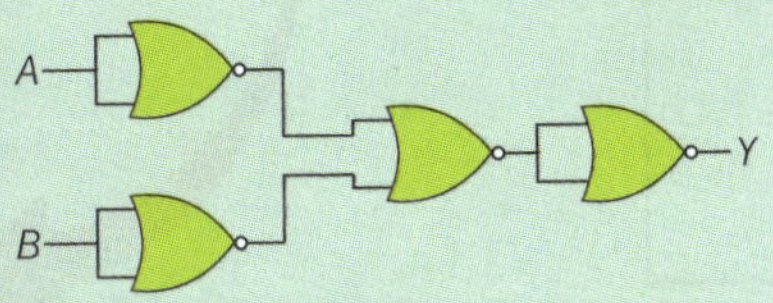

④ Input & Output Waveforms

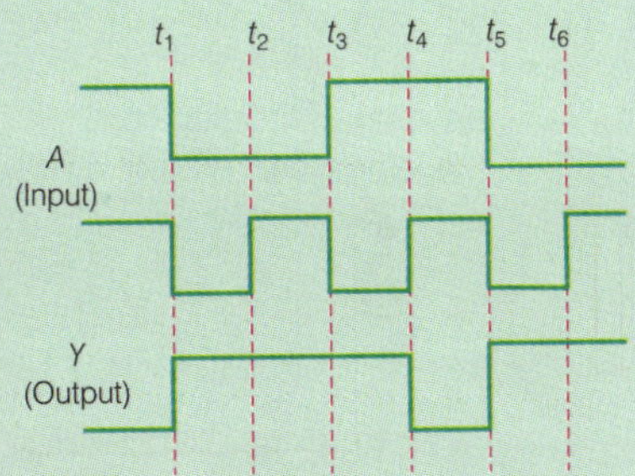

NOR Gate

- It is combination of an OR and a NOT gate

Symbol-

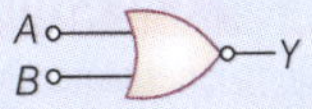

Boolean expression $\overline{A + B} = Y$

① Truth Table

Inputs		Output
A	B	Y
0	0	1
0	1	0
1	0	0
1	1	0

② Electrical Analogue

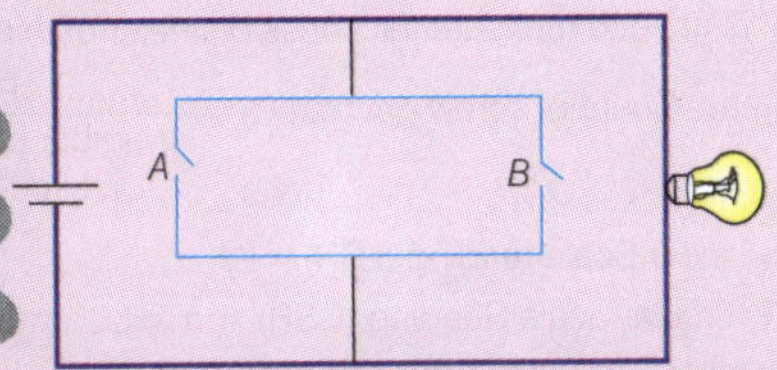

③ NOR Gate using NAND Gate

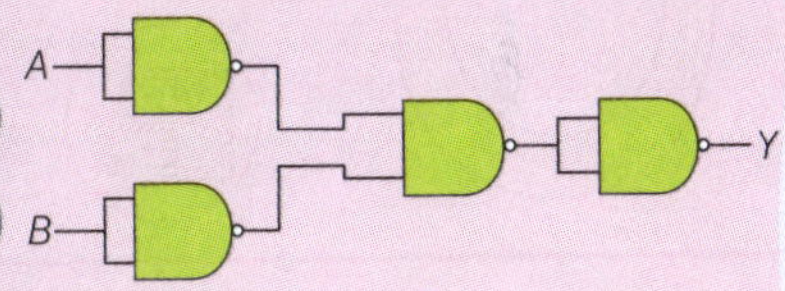

④ Input & Output Waveforms

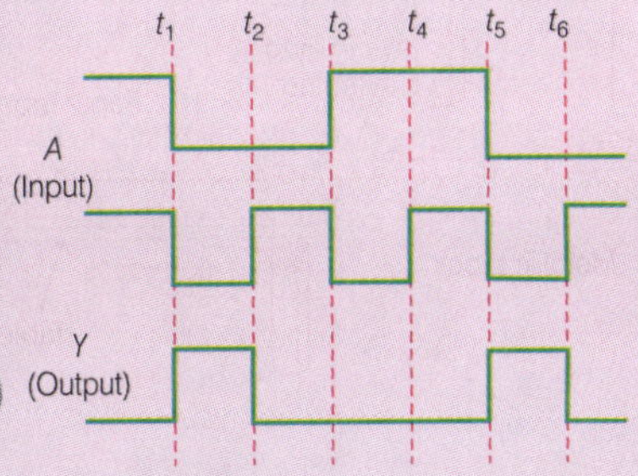

Chapter 29 Experimental Skills

Experiment Related to Measurement of Physical Quantity and Damped Oscillation

01 EXPERIMENT

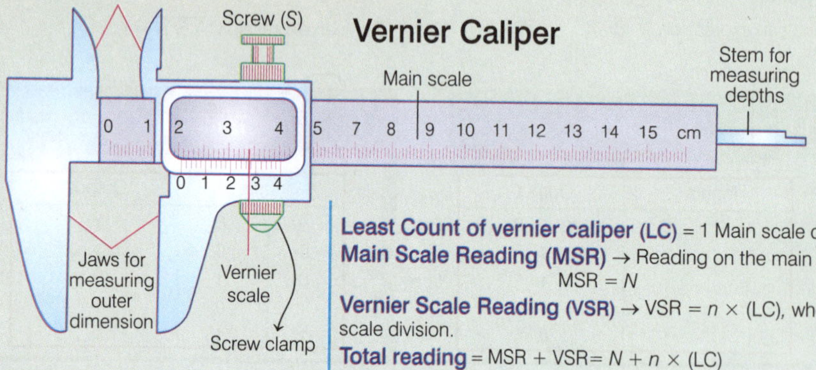

Vernier Caliper

It is used to measure internal and external diameter and depth of a vessel.

Least Count of vernier caliper (LC) = 1 Main scale division / Number of division in vernier scale

Main Scale Reading (MSR) $\rightarrow$ Reading on the main scale to the left of the zero mark on the vernier.

$$MSR = N$$

Vernier Scale Reading (VSR) $\rightarrow$ VSR $= n \times$ (LC), where n is nth division of vernier scale coincides with main scale division.

Total reading = MSR + VSR $= N + n \times$ (LC)

02 EXPERIMENT

Screw Gauge

It is used to measure thickness/diameter of thin sheet/wire.

$$\text{Least Count of screw gauge(LC)} = \frac{\text{Pitch}}{\text{Number of divisions on circular scale}}$$

- Linear Scale reading (LSR) $= N$
- Circular Scale Reading (CSR) $= n \times$ LC
  where, n is nth division of circular scale lies over reference line
- Total Reading (TR) = LSR + CSR $= N + n \times$ LC

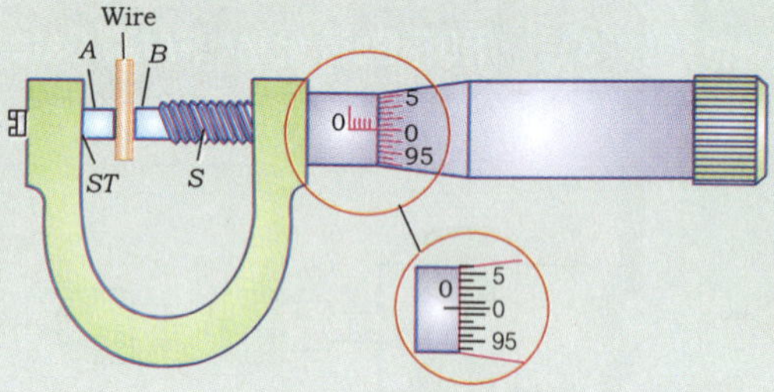

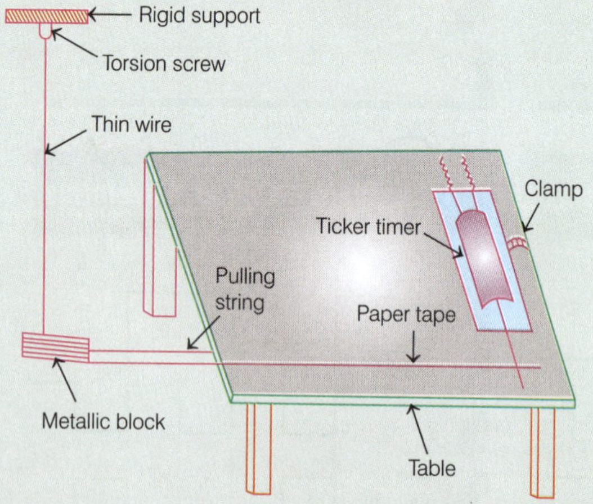

04 EXPERIMENT

Meter Scale

The mass of a given object by the principle of moments.

$$mg \times OA = Mg \times OB,\ OA = l_1 \text{ and } OB = l_2$$

$$mg \times l_1 = Mg \times l_2 \quad m = M\left(\frac{l_2}{l_1}\right)$$

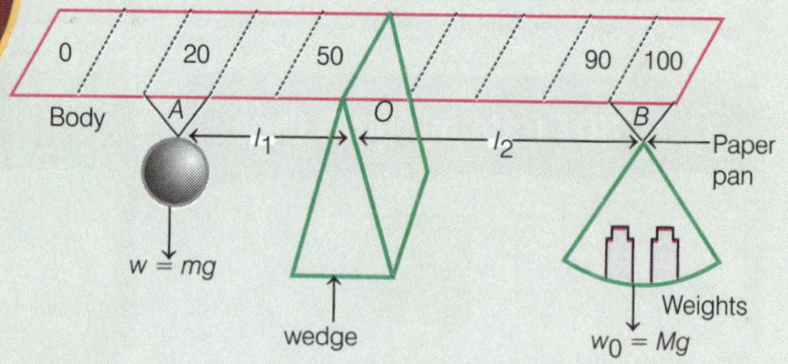

EXPERIMENT 03

Simple Pendulum

Dissipation of energy by plotting a graph between the square of amplitude and time.

Equation of damped motion, $\frac{md^2x}{dt^2} + \frac{bdx}{dt} + kx = 0 \Rightarrow x = A_0 e^{-bt/2m} \cos(\omega t + \phi)$

- *x versus t* graph

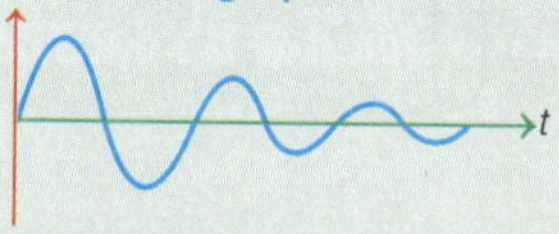

- Damped Oscillation

(i) (Amplitude)^2, $A^2 = A_0^2\, e^{-bt/m}$

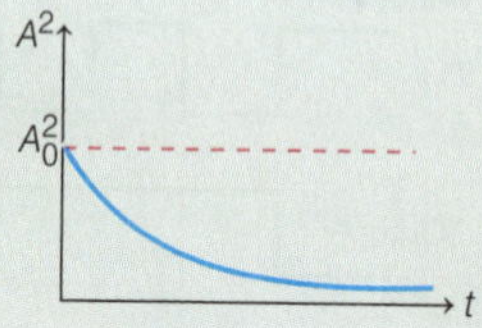

(ii) Total energy, $E = \frac{1}{2}kA^2 = \frac{1}{2}k\left[A_0 e^{-\frac{bt}{2m}}\right]^2$

$$E = \left(\frac{1}{2}kA_0^2\right)e^{-bt/m} = E_0 e^{-bt/m} = E_0 e^{-\lambda t}$$

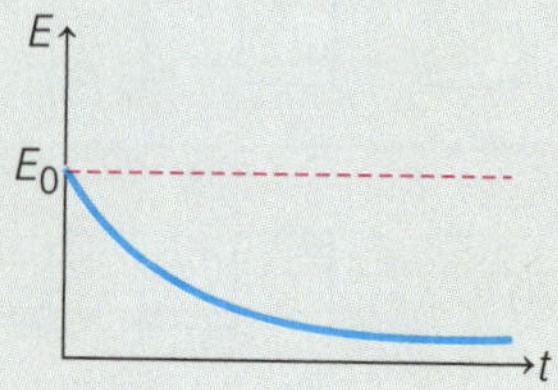

Experiment related to properties of solids liquids and speed of sound

05 EXPERIMENT

Young's Modulus

To determine Young's modulus of elasticity of the material of a metallic wire.

Young's modulus, $Y = \frac{FL}{Al} = \frac{mgL}{\pi r^2 l}$

where, l = extension of the wire under load mg
r = radius of the wire
L = length of the wire

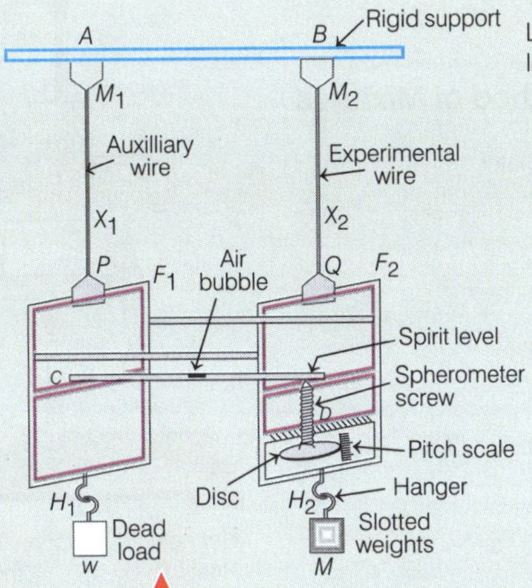

Load - extension graph is a straight line, it verifies the Hooke's law

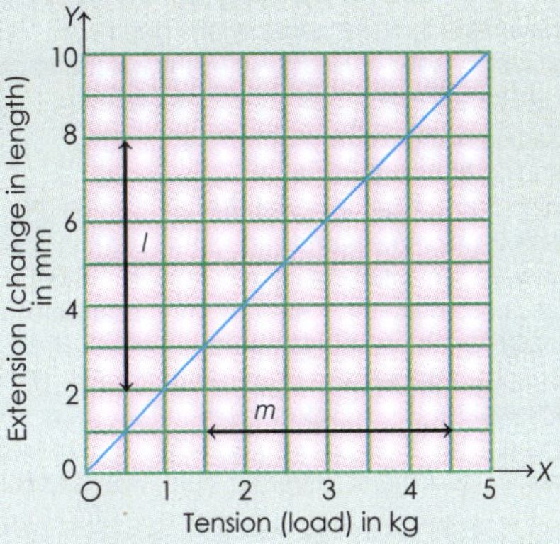

EXPERIMENT 06

Surface Tension of Water

To determine the surface tension of water by capillary rise method and effect of detergents

$$T = \frac{r\left(h + \frac{r}{3}\right)\rho g}{2}$$

where, r = radius of capillary
ρ = liquid density
h = height (capillary rise)
T = surface tension

- Adding detergent to water lowers the surface tension of water.

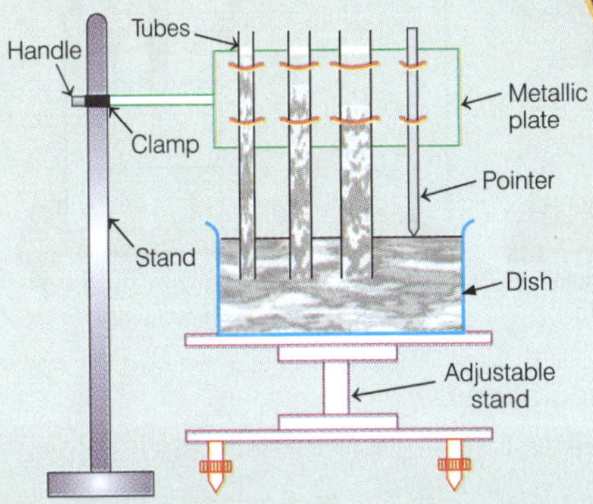

07 EXPERIMENT

Coefficient of Viscosity

To determine the coefficient of viscosity of a given viscous liquid by measuring terminal velocity of a given spherical body.

Resistive force due to viscosity of the liquid,

$$F_D = 6\pi r\eta v$$

where, r = radius of spherical body
η = coefficient of viscosity of fluid
v = velocity

Terminal velocity $(v_T) = \frac{2r^2(\rho - \sigma)g}{9\eta}$

$$\eta = \frac{2}{9}\frac{r^2(\rho - \sigma)g}{v_T}$$

where,
ρ = density of sphere
σ = density of liquid

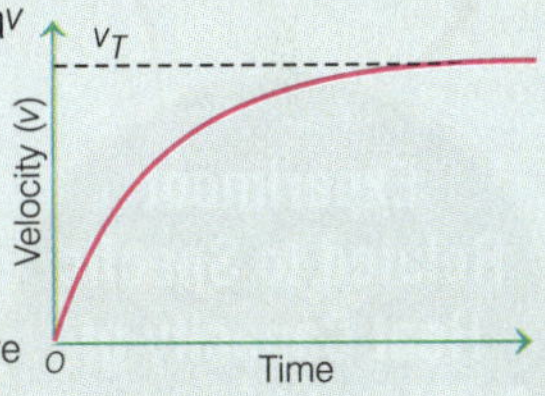

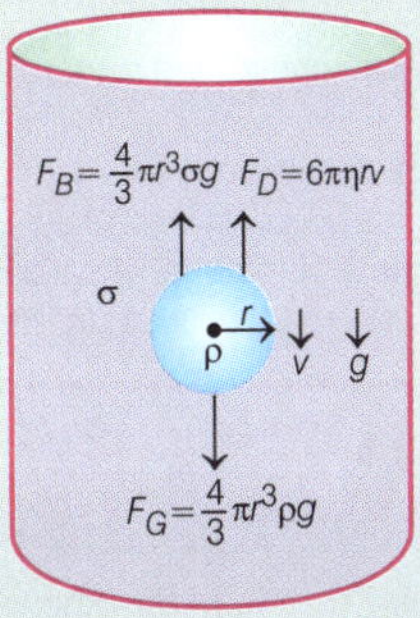

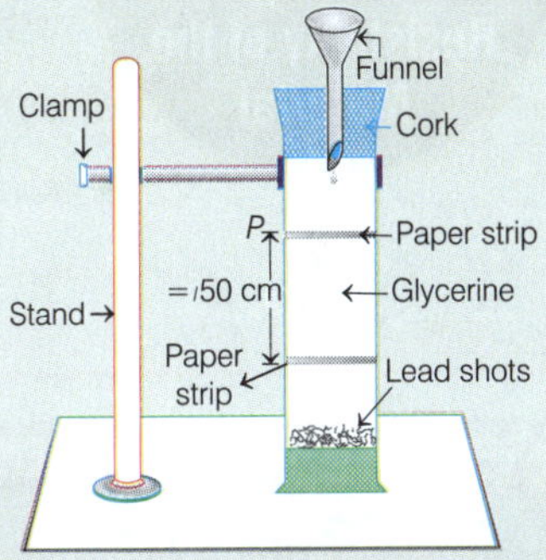

EXPERIMENT 08

Speed of Sound in Air

To determine the speed of sound in air at room temperature using a resonance tube.

Speed of sound in air, $v = 2\nu\,(l_2 - l_1)$

ν = frequency of tuning fork
l_1 = length of the air column at first resonance
l_2 = length of the air column in second resonance with tuning fork

(i) For tuning fork of 480 Hz

$$v_1 = 2 \times 480 \times (l_2 - l_1) = ... \text{ ms}^{-1}$$

(ii) For tuning fork of 512 Hz

$$v_2 = 2 \times 512 \times (l_2' - l_1') = ... \text{ ms}^{-1}$$

Mean value of velocity of sound in air $= \frac{v_1 + v_2}{2} = ... \text{ ms}^{-1}$

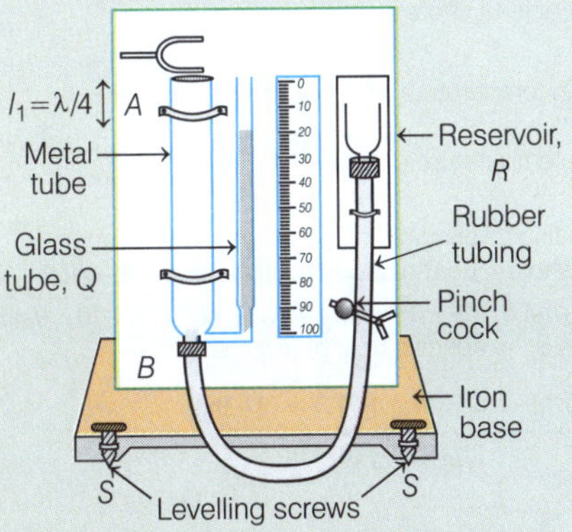

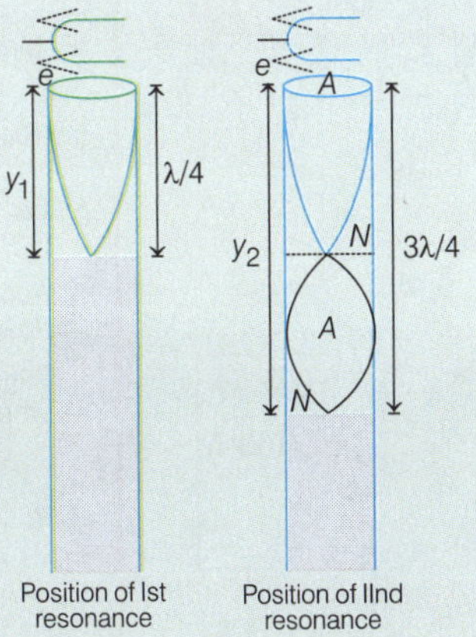

9(A) EXPERIMENT

Specific Heat Capacity of Solid by Method of Mixtures

To determine the heat capacity of a given solid.

Heat lost by solid = Heat gain by the water and calorimeter

Observations

- Reading of thermometer $A = T_A = ... ^\circ C$
- Reading of thermometer, $B = T_B = ... ^\circ C$
- Correction applied in B w.r.t. A $(T_A - T_B) = ... ^\circ C$
- Mass of calorimeter and stirrer, $m = ... g$
- Water equivalent of calorimeter, $w = m \times 0.095 = ... g$
- Mass of calorimeter + stirrer + lid + cold water $= m_2 = ... g$
- Steady temperature of hot solid $= T_S = ... ^\circ C$
- Corrected temperature of hot solid, $T = T_S - (T_A - T_B) = ... ^\circ C$
- Temperature of cold water $= t = ... ^\circ C$
- Temperature of mixture $= \theta = ... ^\circ C$
- Mass of calorimeter, stirrer, lid, cold water and solid $= m_3 = ... g$

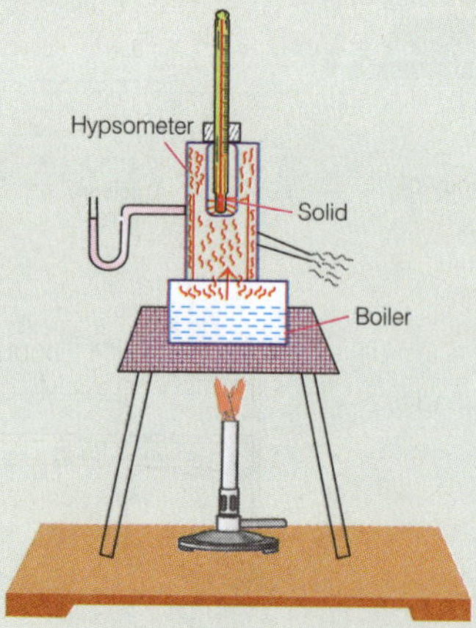

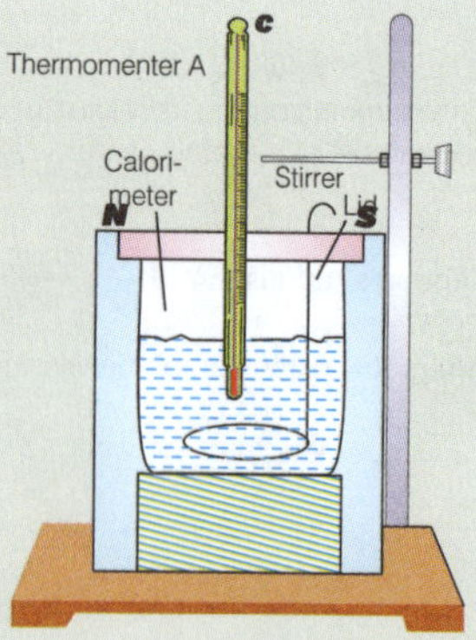

Calculations

- Mass of cold water $= m_2 - m_1 = ... g$
- Mass of hot solid $= m_3 - m_2 = ... g$
- Rise of temperature of cold water and calorimeter $= \theta - t = ... ^\circ C$
- Fall in temperature of solid $= T - \theta = ... ^\circ C$

- Heat gain by calorimeter, cold water and stirrer $= [\omega + (m_2 - m_1)(\theta - t)]$
- Heat lost by solid $= (m_3 - m_2) \times C \times (T - \theta)$
- Here, C is the specific heat of solid to be calculated.
- According to principle of calorimeter, heat lost = heat gained

$$(m_3 - m_2) \times C \times (T - \theta) = [W + (m_2 - m_1)(\theta - t)]$$

$$C = \frac{W + (m_2 - m_1)(\theta - t)}{(m_3 - m_2)(T - \theta)}$$

Experiment Related to Specfic Heat Capacity of Solid and Liquid and Resistivity of the Material

EXPERIMENT 9(B)

Specific Heat Capacity of Liquid by Method of Mixtures Liquid

Observations

(I) Mass of empty calorimeter + stirrer,
$m_1 = ... g$

(ii) Mass of calorimeter + water + stirrer,
$m_2 = ... g$

(iii) Mass of calorimeter + water + stirrer + lead shots,
$m_3 = ... g$

(iv) Initial temperature of water in calorimeter,
$\theta_0 = ... ^\circ C$

(v) Steady temperature of lead shots in hypsometer
$\theta_l = ... ^\circ C$

(vi) Final temperature of lead mixture,
$\theta = ... ^\circ C$

(vii) Specific heat of water,
$S_1 = 4.2\ Jg^{-1}{}^\circ C^{-1}$

(viii) Specific heat of material of calorimeter,
$S_2 = ...\ Jg^{-1}{}^\circ C^{-1}$

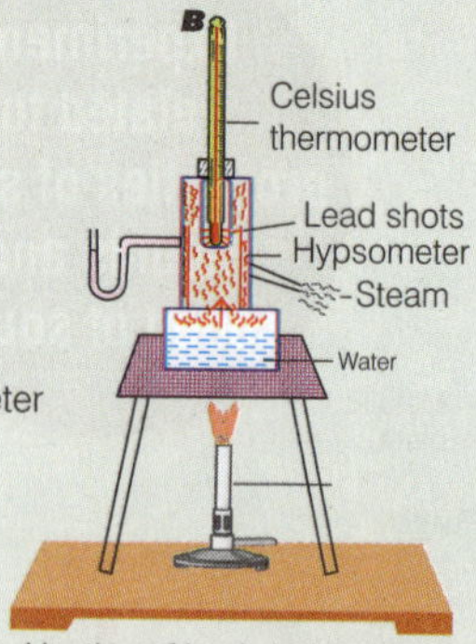

Heating of lead shot in steam using hypsometer

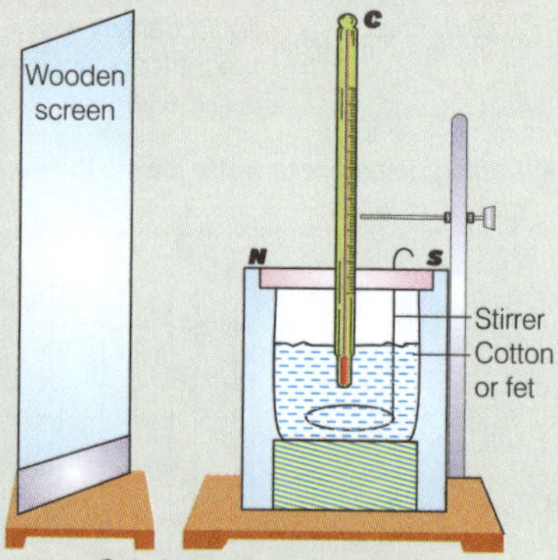

Calorimeter in jacket containing insulating material

Calculations

(i) Water equivalent of (calorimeter + stirrer),

$$w_1 = \frac{m_1 S_2}{S_1} = ... g$$

(ii) Mass of water in calorimeter
$= (m_2 - m_1) = ... g$

(iii) Mass of lead shots
$= (m_3 - m_2) = ... g$

(iv) Rise in temperature of water and calorimeter
$= (\theta - \theta_0) = ... ^\circ C$

(v) Fall in temperature of lead shots
$= (\theta_l - \theta) = ... ^\circ C$

According to principle of calorimeter, Heat lost by lead shots = heat gained by calorimeter and water

$(m_3 - m_2) S_L (\theta_l - \theta) = (m_2 - m_1 + w_1) \times 4.2 (\theta - \theta_0)$
where, S_L = specific heat of given solid.

$$S_L = \frac{(m_2 - m_1 + w_1) \times 4.2 \times (\theta - \theta_0)}{(m_3 - m_2)(\theta_l - \theta)} = ...\ Jg^{-1}{}^\circ C^{-1}$$

10 EXPERIMENT

Resistivity of the Material

To determine the resistivity of the material of a given wire using a meter bridge.

Meter bridge is based on wheatstone bridge.

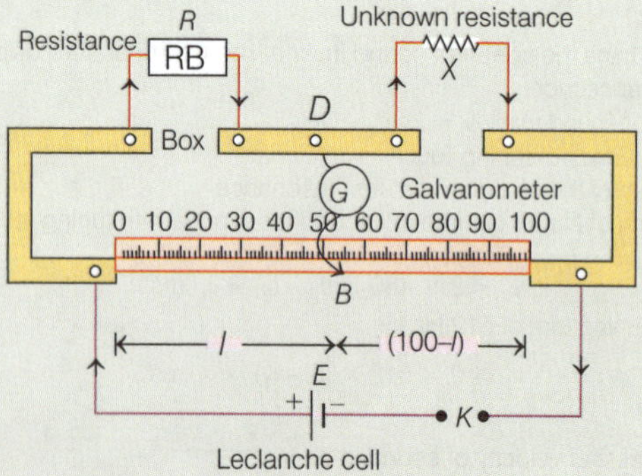

R = known resistance
X = unknown resistance
l = balancing length
A = area of cross section of wires.

$$\frac{R}{X} = \frac{\lambda l}{\lambda(100 - l)} \Rightarrow X = \frac{R}{l}(100 - l)$$

$$\text{Resistivity} = \frac{XA}{l}$$

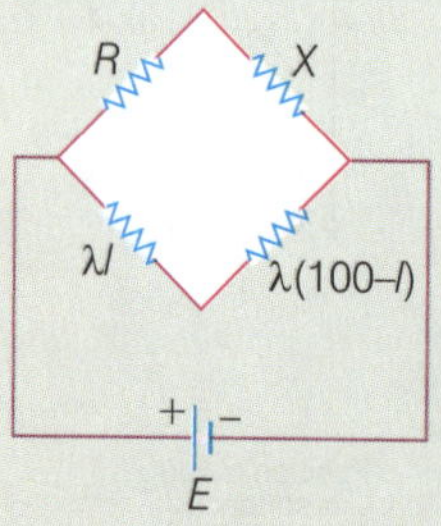

11 EXPERIMENT

Ohm's law

To determine the resistance of given wire using Ohm's law. According to Ohm's law,

$V \propto I$

$V = RI$

$\frac{V}{I} = R$

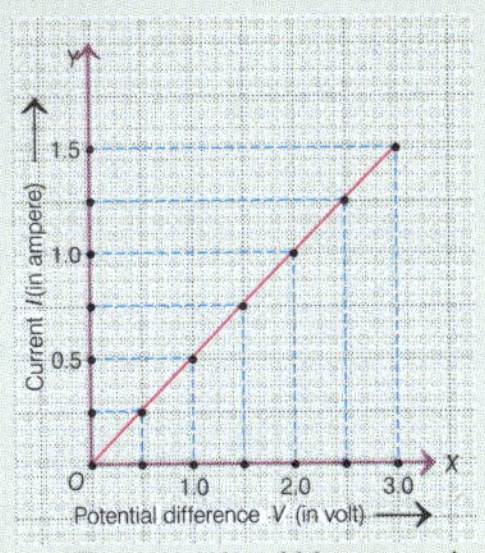

The graph of *V versus I*

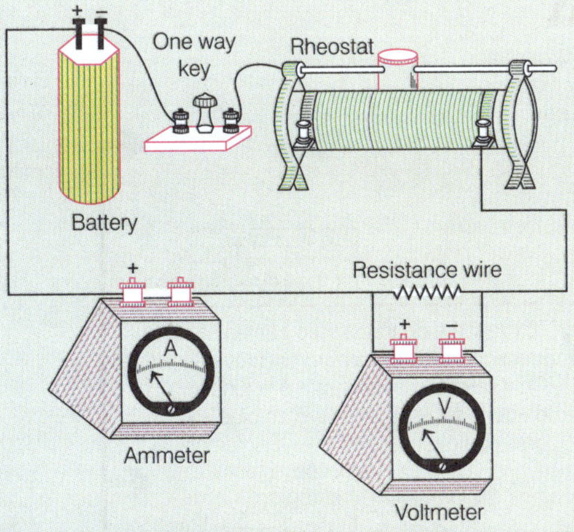

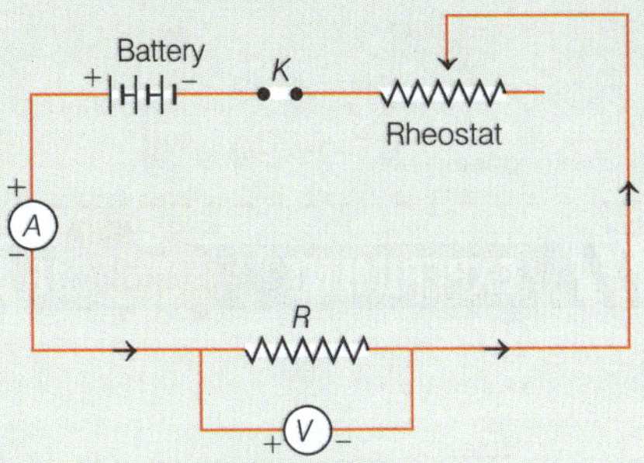

Experiments Related to Current Electricity, Magnetic Effect of Current, Spherical Mirror and Concave Lens

12 EXPERIMENT

To determine the resistance and figure of merit of a galvanometer by half deflection method.

(a) To determine the resistance of galvanometer

$$G = \frac{RS}{R - S}$$

where, G = resistance of the galvanometer

R = resistance of the resistance box

S = shunt resistance

(b) To determine the figure of merit

S = shunt resistance

$$K = I/\theta$$

$$K = \frac{E}{(R + G)\theta}$$

where, I = current in the circuit

K = figure of merit

θ = deflection

E = EMF of the cell

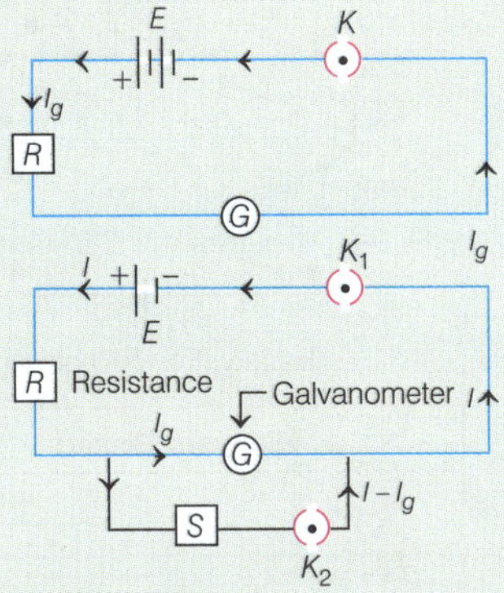

13 EXPERIMENT

To determine the focal length of

(i) concave mirror

(ii) convex mirrors and

(iii) convex lens, using the parallax method

(i) Focal length of concave mirror

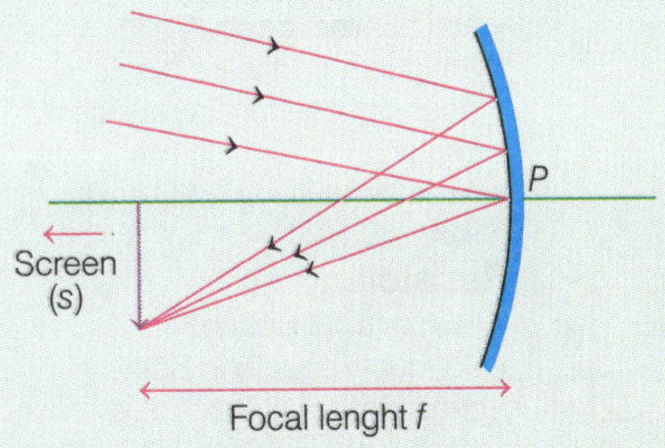

Observation Table

S.No	Position of concave mirror	Position of screen	Focal length
1			f_1
2			f_2
3			f_3

$$f_{mean} = \frac{f_1 + f_2 + f_3}{3}$$

(ii) Focal length of convex mirror

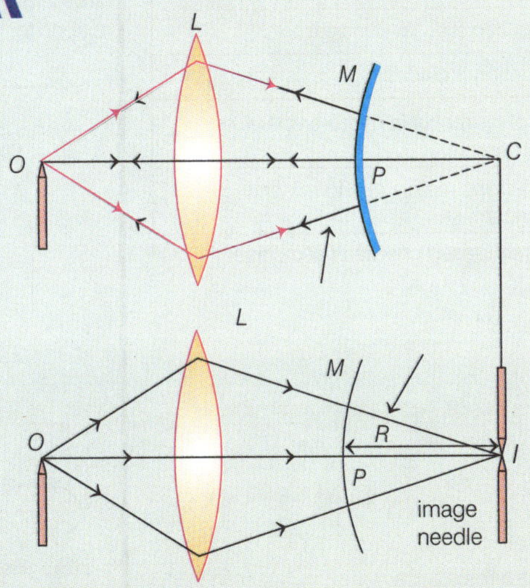

Observation Table

S.No	Object pin O (cm)	Covex lens L (cm)	Convex mirror P (cm)	R=PC (cm)	Focal length f
1					
2					
3					

$f = \frac{R}{2} = ...$ cm

(iii) Focal length of convex lens

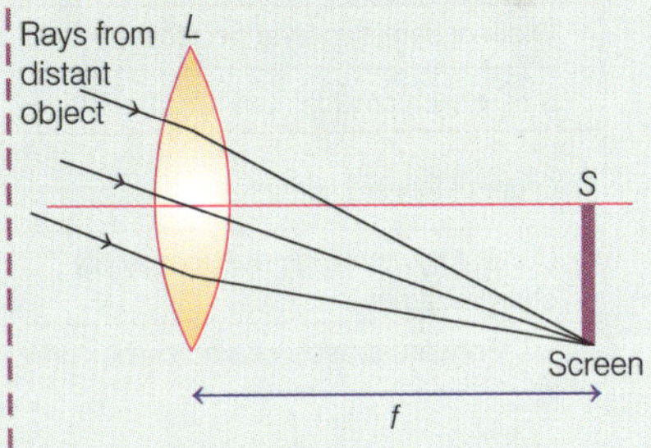

Observation Table

S.No	Position of convex lens	Position of screen	Focal length
1			f_1
2			f_2
3			f_3

$$f_{mean} = \frac{f_1 + f_2 + f_3}{3}$$

Experiments Related to Prism, Refractive index of glass slab and Semiconductors

14 EXPERIMENT

Plot the angle of deviation *versus* angle of incidence for a triangular prism

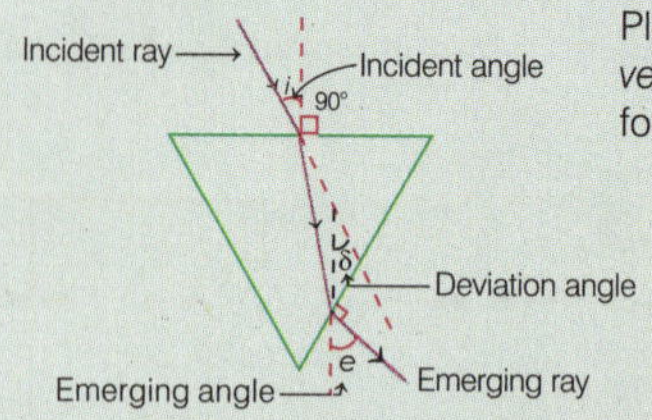

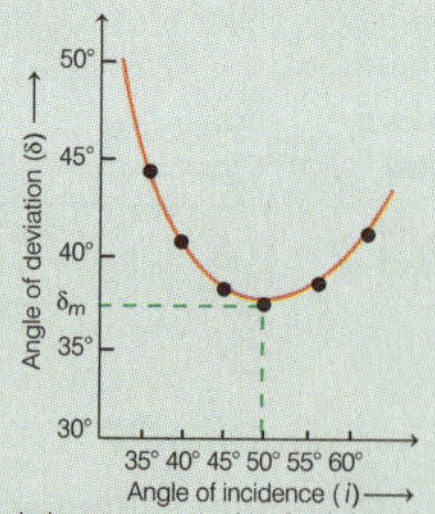

Here, δ_m is known as angle of minimum deviation.

EXPERIMENT 15

To determine the refractive index of glass slab using a travelling microscope.

Refractive index of a glass slab using a travelling microscope is given below.

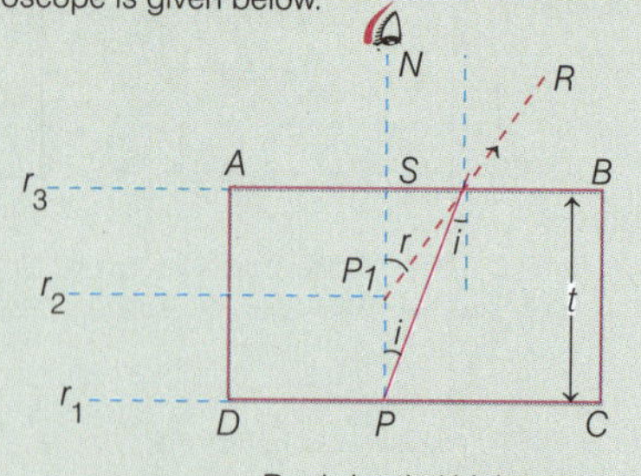

Formula $\mu = \dfrac{\text{Real depth (thickness)}}{\text{Apparent depth (thickness)}}$

Refractive index (in this case), $\mu = \dfrac{r_3 - r_1}{r_2 - r_1}$

EXPERIMENT 16

To draw the characteristic curves of a *p-n* junction diode in forward and reverse bias

Characteristic curves of a *p-n* junction diode in forward and reverse bias are given below.

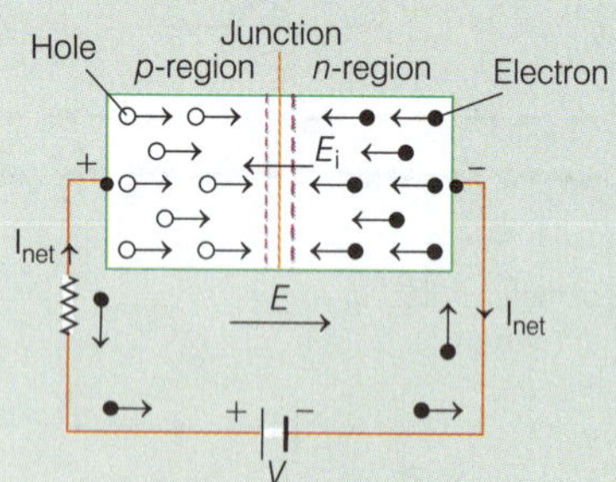

Battery (Forward biased)

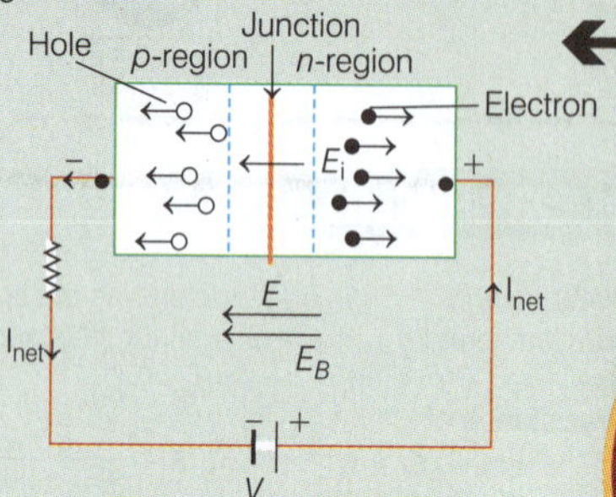

Battery (Reverse biased)

Forward Biased	Reverse Biased
$p \to$ positive, $n \to$ negative 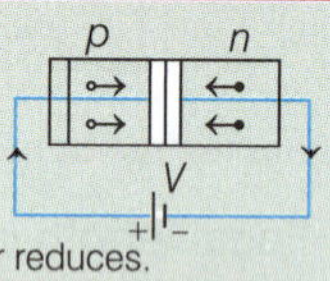 Potential barrier reduces.	$p \to$ negative, $n \to$ positive 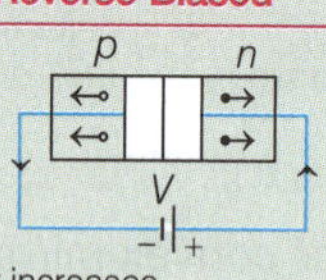 Potential barrier increases.
Width of depletion layer decreases.	Width of depletion layer increases.
p-n junction provides very small resistance.	*p-n* junction provides high resistance.
Order of forward current is in milliampere.	Order of current is in micro-ampere or nanoampere.
Current flows mainly due to majority charge carrier.	Current flows mainly due to minority charge carrier.

Forward biased characteristic curve

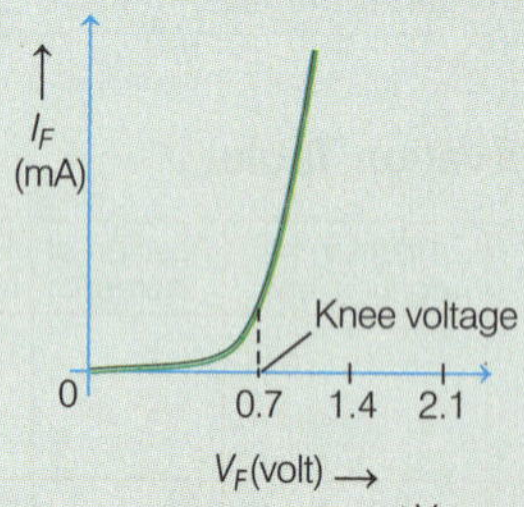

Reverse biased characteristic curve

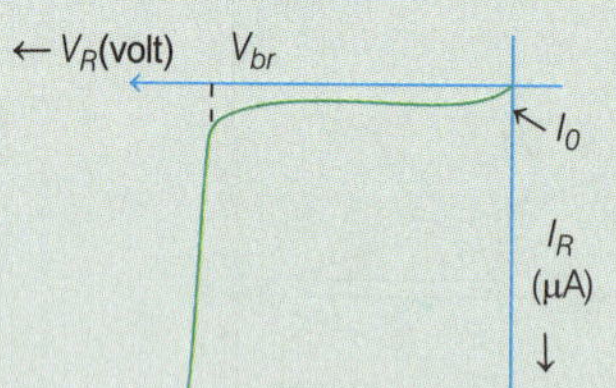

Forward resistance, $R_f = \dfrac{\Delta V_f}{\Delta I_f} \approx 100\,\Omega$

Reverse resistance, $R_R = \dfrac{\Delta V_R}{\Delta I_R} \approx 10^6\,\Omega$

17 EXPERIMENT

To draw the characteristic curve of a zener diode and finding reverse break down voltage.

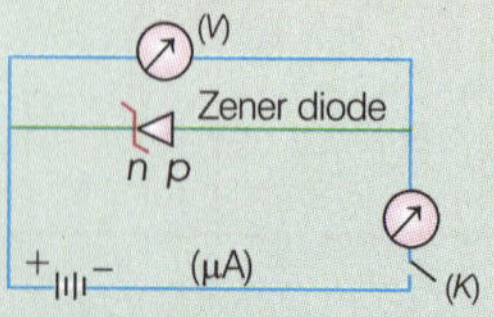

Circuit parameters in the circuit as shown in the figure above.

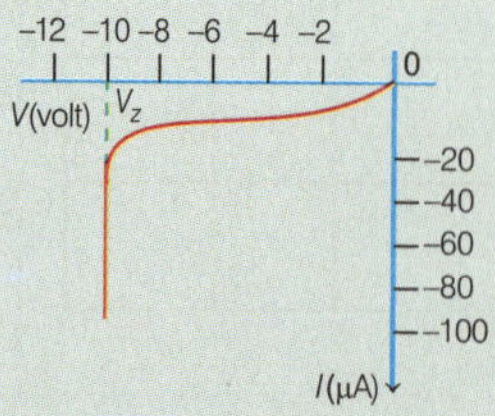

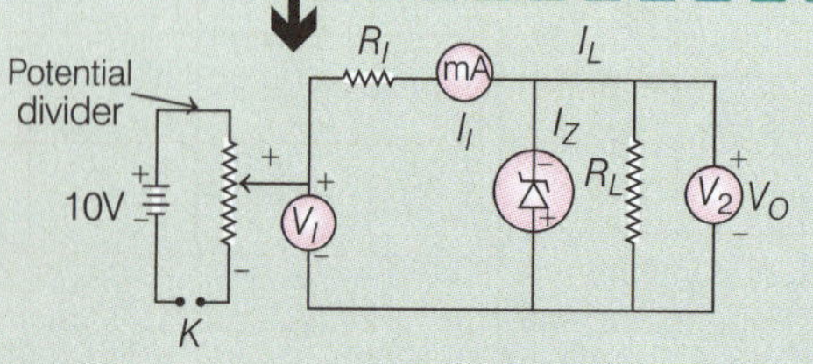

Relations

$I_L = I_I - I_Z$

$V_O = V_I - R_I I_I$

$V_O = I_L R_L$

18 EXPERIMENT

Identification of diode, LED, resistor, capacitor from a mixed collection of such items.

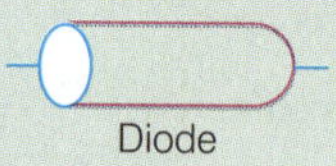

Diode

Diode

- Two terminal device
- Conducts in forward bias and does not conduct in reverse bias

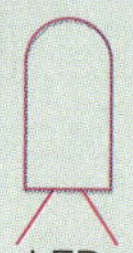

LED

LED

- Light emitting diode
- Two terminal device
- Conducts in forward bias and does not conduct in reverse biased
- While conducting, LED emits light

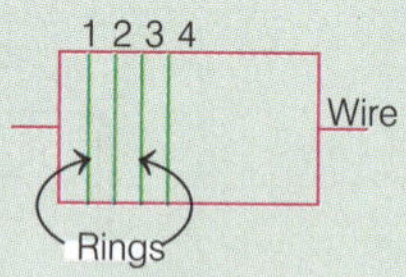

Resistor

Resistor

- Two terminal device
- Conducts equally in both directions
- It conducts in AC and DC voltage

Capacitor

Capacitor

- It store electric charge
- It blocks the passage of DC while it allows AC to pass through it.